International Organizations

Fifth Edition

KELLY-KATE S. PEASE

Webster University

Longman
Boston   Columbus   Indianapolis   New York   San Francisco   Upper Saddle River
Amsterdam   Cape Town   Dubai   London   Madrid   Milan   Munich   Paris   Montreal   Toronto
Delhi   Mexico City   Sao Paulo   Sydney   Hong Kong   Seoul   Singapore   Taipei   Tokyo

Senior Acquisitions Editor: Vikram Mukhija
Editorial Assistant: Beverly Fong
Senior Marketing Manager: Lindsey Prudhomme
Production Manager: Fran Russello
Project Coordination, Text Design, and Electronic
    Page Makeup: Moganambigai Sundaramurthy / Integra Software Services Pvt. Ltd
Cover Design Manager: Jayne Conte
Cover Designer: Suzanne Behnke
Cover Illustration/Photo: © Massimo Percossi/epa/Corbis
Printer and Binder: Courier Compaines, Inc.

Credits and acknowledgments borrowed from other sources and reproduced, with permission, in this textbook appear on appropriate page within text.

Library of Congress Cataloging-in-Publication Data

Pease, Kelly-Kate S.,
    International organizations : perspective on governance in the twenty-first century/Kelly-Kate Pease.—5th ed.
        p. cm.
    Includes bibliographical references and index.
    ISBN-13: 978-0-205-07587-4 (alk. paper)
    ISBN-10: 0-205-07587-8 (alk. paper)
    1. International agencies.   2. International organization.   3. Regionalism (International organization)   I. Title.
JZ4839.P43 2012
341.2—dc22

                                                2010047262

1 2 3 4 5 6 7 8 9 10—CRS —14 13 12 11

Longman
is an imprint of

www.pearsonhighered.com

ISBN-13: 978-0-205-07587-4
ISBN-10:   0-205-07587-8

BRIEF CONTENTS

DETAILED CONTENTS

PREFACE

I wrote this book out of passion and frustration. International organizations are fascinating objects of study. They are almost organic entities—evolving, changing, adapting, and even dying. However, many texts on international organizations tend to view the lives of international organizations through liberal lenses. Liberal lenses are not exactly rose-colored, but they are colored by the implicit assumption that international organizations are inherently "good" and that their "good" efforts are often thwarted by organizational weaknesses, world politics, or self-interested governments. Liberalism has contributed much to our understanding of global politics, but it has its blind spots. Examining international organizations solely from a liberal vantage does a disservice to the study of international organizations and to its development as a discipline. It unnecessarily narrows analysis; worse, it suggests that just one view of the world exists. This text brings other theoretical perspectives to bear on the study of international organizations. It integrates international organizations with international relations theory by showing how international organizations matter in the worlds of the realist, the Marxist, the feminist, and the constructivist, as well as the liberal.

International organizations are in a period of transition. Since the publication of the fourth edition of this book, the global economy has experienced an unprecedented financial crisis that almost led to the total collapse of the world's financial system. The ensuing "great recession" has generated a great deal of conflict in international relations and has called into question the extent to which international relations are governable. International organizations responded to the crisis and the resulting instability by attempting to coordinate the responses of governments and offering economic and political prescriptions. Yet, the United Nations (UN) remains marginalized by the United States even after the United States ended combat operations in Iraq. Political discord still thwarts reform efforts to strengthen the UN's role in human rights and humanitarian affairs as states are more focused on domestic needs rather than on the needs of others. The World Trade Organization still has not held a successful round of trade negotiations, and the currency of the European Union almost collapsed because of the sovereign debt of several members. The global financial meltdown has tightened the purse strings of nongovernmental organizations as they struggle to respond to the catastrophic earthquake that decimated Haiti in 2009 and the unprecedented flooding in Pakistan which displaced as many as 14 million people. Multinational corporations are weathering the global economic recession; however, global economic growth remains stagnant. Hence, the optimism that permeated analyses of international organizations in the 1990s has given way to more cautious explanations of their roles and contributions to contemporary world politics. The fifth edition of this book accounts for the political and structural changes occurring in world politics and international organizations.

NEW TO THIS EDITION

In addition to the usual updating and correction of errors that accompany any new edition, this fifth edition also contains several new and useful features to students of international organizations.

- The **nexus between international law and international organizations** is explored to show how they complement and influence each other. Each issue chapter highlights the relevant treaties, norms, and customs, and interprets the impact of international law on the politics of the issue.
- Not only does this book cover international and human security concerns but it now looks at the growing danger posed by the **proliferation of weapons of mass destruction**, with special emphasis on the spread of nuclear weapon technology.
- A new in-depth case study on **Iran** explores Iran's quest for nuclear technology against the backdrop of its legal duties and obligations under **Nuclear NonProliferation Treaty (NPT)**. The case also examines the role of the **International Atomic Energy Agency (IAEA)** in managing the use of nuclear technology and energy.
- An updated analysis of **global climate change** is provided to explain the political outcomes of the **2009 Copenhagen Conference**.
- An exploration of **international criminal law** with special reference to the International Criminal Tribunal for the Former Yugoslavia (ICTY) and the International Criminal Court (ICC).
- Every chapter includes the **most recent political events, scholarship, and data**, especially as it relates to the impact of the global financial crisis on trade and development.

FEATURES

The fifth edition also retains its basic organization in that, in addition to the nuts-and-bolts descriptions of international organizations, it applies international relations theory to specific case studies to analyze and explain their behavior. This particular feature allows students to understand international organizations from different worldviews and allows professors to highlight organizations and activities they deem worthy of study. Professors can also assign other case studies for students to research. Each chapter ends with the sections "Key Terms" and "Suggested Readings" to help students organize and retain the material, as well as find where they can look for more information.

SUPPLEMENTS

Longman is pleased to offer several resources to qualified adopters of *International Organizations* and their students that will make teaching and learning from this book even more effective and enjoyable.

Passport for International Relations

With Passport, choose the resources you want from MyPoliSciKit and put links to them into your course management system. If there is assessment associated with those resources, it also can be uploaded, allowing the results to feed directly into your course management system's gradebook. With over 150 MyPoliSciKit assets like video case studies, mapping exercises, comparative exercises, simulations, podcasts, *Financial Times* newsfeeds, current events quizzes, politics blog, and much more, Passport is available for any Pearson introductory or upper-level political science book. Use ISBN 0-205-07409-X to order Passport with this book. To learn more, please contact your Pearson representative.

MySearchLab

Need help with a paper? MySearchLab saves time and improves results by offering start-to-finish guidance on the research/writing process and full-text access to academic journals and periodicals. Use ISBN 0-205-07400-6 to order MySearchLab with this book. To learn more, please visit www.mysearchlab. com or contact your Pearson representative.

The Economist

Every week, the *Economist* analyzes the important happenings around the globe. From business to politics, to the arts and science, its coverage connects seemingly unrelated events in unexpected ways. Use ISBN 0-205-00260-9 to order a 15-week subscription with this book for a small additional charge. To learn more, please contact your Pearson representative.

The Financial Times

Featuring international news and analysis from journalists in more than fifty countries, the *Financial Times* provides insights and perspectives on political and economic developments around the world. Use ISBN 0-205-07395-6 to order a 15-week subscription with this book for a small additional charge. To learn more, please contact your Pearson representative.

Longman Atlas of World Issues (0-205-78020-2)

From population and political systems to energy use and women's rights, the *Longman Atlas of World Issues* features full-color thematic maps that examine the forces shaping the world. Featuring maps from the latest edition of *The Penguin State of the World Atlas*, this excerpt includes critical thinking exercises to promote a deeper understanding of how geography affects many global issues. Available at no additional charge when packaged with this book.

Goode's World Atlas (0-321-65200-2)

First published by Rand McNally in 1923, *Goode's World Atlas* has set the standard for college reference atlases. It features hundreds of physical, political, and thematic maps as well as graphs, tables, and a pronouncing index. Available at a discount when packaged with this book.

The Penguin Dictionary of International Relations (0-140-51397-3)

This indispensable reference by Graham Evans and Jeffrey Newnham includes hundreds of cross-referenced entries on the enduring and emerging theories, concepts, and events that are shaping the academic discipline of international relations and today's world politics. Available at a discount when packaged with this book.

Research and Writing in International Relations (0-205-06065-X)

With current and detailed coverage on how to start research in the discipline's major subfields, this brief and affordable guide offers the step-by-step guidance and the essential resources needed to compose political science papers that go beyond description and into systematic and sophisticated inquiry. This text focuses on areas where students often need help—finding a topic, developing a question, reviewing the literature, designing research, and last, writing the paper. Available at a discount when packaged with this book.

ACKNOWLEDGMENTS

Several people have contributed to the development of the fifth edition of this book. First, I thank the anonymous reviewers of the fourth edition who provided valuable insights and criticism. I would also like to thank the following reviewers for their helpful suggestions: W. Meredith Bacon of the University of Nebraska at Omaha, William M. Batkay of Montclair State University, Adriana Crocker of the University of Illinois at Springfield, Darren Hawkins of Brigham Young University, Houman A. Sadri of the University of Central Florida, and Howard Tolley of the University of Cincinnati. I would also like to acknowledge Webster University, which provided some financial assistance through its Faculty Research Grant Program. Finally, I would like to thank David P. Forsythe, my mentor and friend, for guiding me as a graduate student, for advising me as I wrote my dissertation, and for providing sage and sound advice as I rose through the professorial ranks. I would like to dedicate this fifth edition to him to congratulate him on his promotion to Professor Emeritus at the University of Nebraska-Lincoln.

KELLY-KATE PEASE

Introduction

International organizations (IO) are in an extraordinary period of transition. Organizations like the United Nations (UN), the World Trade Organization (WTO), and the International Monetary Fund (IMF) play important and often controversial roles in the governance of the international and domestic affairs of many societies. Scholars, politicians, and citizens worldwide ask questions that address the nature and behavior of international organizations: Who created international organizations and why? Whose interests do these organizations serve? How do their activities affect individuals, groups, and societies? How do we make international organizations more effective? What is the future of international organizations? In this textbook, we examine the theory and practice of international organizations, recognizing that international organizations are part of a complex web of relations that can have subnational, national, international, and transnational ties. To trace the patterns of this complex web, we employ five theoretical frameworks—realism, liberalism, Marxism, feminism, and constructivism—as a means of approaching the subject. Technically speaking, a theory is a set of generalized principles that have descriptive, explanatory, and predictive value (Bennett 1995, 15). We can think of international relations theory as a way of systematizing and understanding world politics.

Theoretical frameworks are based on organizing assumptions that simplify the world and guide analysis. In many respects, theoretical frameworks are quite similar to worldviews (sets of widely held beliefs): both serve as mental maps, providing guides as to how the world works. However, worldviews are more informal. They are shaped by values, norms, and culture. Theoretical frameworks build upon worldviews, yet are more rigorous in that they become mechanisms for methodically generating hypotheses, explanations, and predictions about world politics.

Another way to think about theoretical frameworks is to envision them as a pair of glasses whose different lenses allow us to view the distinct political,

1

economic, and social characteristics and processes that shape world politics. These lenses act as filters, directing attention toward (and away from) certain kinds of actors and focusing discussion on certain kinds of questions. Through these theoretical lenses, we see different reflections, different explanations regarding which units of analysis—states, individuals, class, or gender—should figure most prominently in our understanding of international relations and organizations. In addition, these lenses guide our analysis, allowing us to examine particular kinds of international dynamics—anarchy, interdependence, capitalism, and patriarchy. Our theoretical lenses reveal different patterns and provide divergent interpretations regarding the nature and roles of international organizations in international politics. They also prescribe different strategies for addressing global problems. But, let us start with the basics.

WHAT IS AN INTERNATIONAL ORGANIZATION?

The history of international organizations as a field of study suggests no clear answer to the question of what an international organization is. The analytical shifts from "formal institutions" to "institutional processes" to "organizational roles" to "international regimes" have expanded the concept of international organization to include almost any type of patterned, repetitive behavior (Kratochwil and Ruggie 1986, 753–775; Rochester 1986, 777–813). Traditionally, international organizations have been conceived as formal institutions whose members are states. Such organizations are called **intergovernmental organizations (IGOs)** because the governments of nation-states voluntarily join, contribute financing, and make decisions within the organization. Their purpose, structures, and decision-making procedures are clearly spelled out in a charter or treaty. Examples of IGOs include the UN, the North Atlantic Treaty Organization (NATO), the European Union (EU), and the League of Arab States (the Arab League).

All IGOs have governments as their formal members and can be further categorized by rules of membership. IGOs may have universal membership whereby all states are allowed to join. For example, all states may become members of the UN, at least in principle. Chapter II, Article 4 (1), states that UN membership is open to all peace-loving states "which accept the obligations contained in the present Charter, and, in the judgment of the Organization, are able and willing to carry out these obligations." States seeking UN membership must petition the UN Security Council, which then makes a recommendation to the General Assembly. The General Assembly then makes the final decision. While membership decisions can be quite political, the UN has, for the most part, practiced an open-door policy.

IGOs may also have limited membership in that participation is restricted by some objective criteria. The Arab League, for example, is a voluntary association of states whose people mainly speak Arabic. This association seeks to strengthen Arab ties and promote common political and economic goals.

NATO, a security alliance, limits its membership by restricting it to a combination of specific political, geographic, and military considerations.

IGOs are also categorized by their purpose. IGOs can be multi- or general-purpose organizations, meaning they can take up any international issue. General-purpose IGOs, such as the UN, consider a variety of international issues that affect their members. IGOs can also have narrow mandates and thus may focus on specific economic or social issues. The International Labor Organization (ILO), for example, is charged with setting international labor standards, and the World Health Organization (WHO) is responsible for addressing health issues ranging from child immunization to cholera outbreaks and AIDS. These specialized IGOs provide focused and expert analysis to very specific international issues.

The Legal Context of IGOs   IGOs have a special legal status under international law in that they have **international legal personality**. International legal personality means IGOs have the capacity to act under international law. In order to attain legal personality, the organization must be a permanent association of states that possesses some power that is distinct from that of its member states, with that power being exercised at the international level (Slomanson 1990, 65). The legal personality of IGOs enables them to act in a manner that is similar to how states act. IGOs can reach international agreements with other international organizations and states. IGOs have many of the same privileges of states, such as legal immunity or the right to sue in national courts. The international legal personality of an IGO is usually established through a **constitutive treaty**, which is the charter of the IGO. For example, Chapter II, Article 3, of the Charter of the Association of Southeast Asian Nations (ASEAN) confers legal personality upon ASEAN.

When a charter or treaty does not explicitly confer international legal personality, it can be conferred by case law. The legal personality of the UN was established in the famous **Reparation for Injuries Suffered in the Service of the United Nations** (1949) case, through an advisory opinion issued by the International Court of Justice (ICJ). The legal issue at hand centered on whether the UN had the legal personality to sue for harm done to UN employees. The ICJ, citing several treaties and UN Charter provisions, opined that the legal personality of the UN can be inferred from the Charter even though it is not explicitly stated. The UN's legal personality was subsequently recognized by national courts in the United States and in Europe.

Traditional studies of international organizations tended to focus solely on the institutional framework and norms of IGOs in order to explain their roles and behavior in international relations. This legalistic and descriptive approach to IGOs has proved inadequate for understanding the behavior and function of international organizations. It fails to explain, for example, why the activities of IGOs do not usually square with their stated missions. Charters may detail goals, objectives, and procedures; yet, the practices of international organizations can be quite different. For instance, the UN Charter charges the UN Security Council with maintaining international peace and security and countering aggressive war. But during the Cold War, the UN Security Council did little to fulfill that mission. In the 1960s, scholarly research shifted to trying to understand the institutional processes and the organizational roles of IGOs. Scholars sought to understand how the interests of states enhanced or interfered with the purposes of international organizations. Faced with the incongruence between the written purposes of international organizations and their practices, scholars were compelled to address the "politics" and the "economics" of international organizations.

At the same time, scholars also sought to explain why some international organizations seemed to function well in nonpoliticized issue areas. These **functionalist analyses** showed that cooperation in the nonpolitical (economic and social) spheres could "spill over" into highly politicized areas such as security. Spillover is thought to foster the integration of societies into a single economic and political community (Haas 1958, 1964; Mitrany 1948, 1966). The focus on institutional processes and organizational roles showed the duality between the interests of states and the idea that IGOs could also become important actors in their own right, even though states were the principal members.

In the 1980s, the study of international organizations saw an explosion in analyses of **international regimes.** The study of international regimes concentrates on other types of international interactions that occur either in conjunction with or independent of IGOs. An international regime is defined as "sets of implicit or explicit principles, norms, rules and decision-making procedures around which actors' expectations converge in a given issue area" (Krasner 1983, 2). Regime analysis extends analysis to include other actors beyond states and IGOs.

One such actor is another kind of international organization, the **nongovernmental organization (NGO)** NGOs are essentially nonprofit, private organizations that engage in a variety of international activities. They can be oriented toward a single issue or can have a multipurpose agenda. NGOs participate in international politics by defining goals, providing information, and giving expert advice. They also pressure governments and IGOs through direct and indirect lobbying techniques. NGOs such as Amnesty International, Greenpeace, and the International Committee for the Red Cross are instrumental in setting international norms and executing international policy. While most NGOs receive some funding from governments, their activities can be autonomous and are often coordinated with IGOs.

Another important kind of international organization is the **multinational corporation (MNC).** MNCs are for-profit firms that have subsidiaries in two or more countries and engage in transnational production activities involving the movement of goods and services across national boundaries. IGOs, NGOs, and MNCs are the kinds of international organizations that are examined extensively in regime analysis. Regime analysis delves into the tangible principles and rules that are codified in charters, treaties, and other forms of international law. Informal principles, rules, norms, and decision-making procedures are also examined (presuming that they are identifiable) even though they are not spelled out in any formal sense. Regime analysis seeks to explain and model the complicated nature of international relations in which multiple actors engage in a variety of international and transnational activities. It seeks to understand the very complex web of international relations that invariably develops through any kind of international organization.

Hence, the term "international organization" may refer to many different entities. IGOs (e.g., the UN), NGOs (e.g., Greenpeace), and MNCs (e.g., General Electric) are types of international organization. International organization also refers to the institutions, processes, norms, laws, and regimes that are part and parcel of **global governance**. Global governance focuses on how state and nonstate actors (such as the international organizations discussed earlier) define and address global problems absent a world government. Global problems include war, terrorism, the arms proliferation, economic instability, poverty, disease, environmental degradation, and human rights abuses. Global problems represent serious challenges for the international community because managing them is beyond the reach of even the most powerful states. Global governance also involves making and sustaining the rules and the norms of world order (Held 1999, 50).

Here is where the interrelationship between **international law** and IOs comes into play. When we speak of making and sustaining international rules or codifying international norms or values, we are talking about creating international law. International law refers to the formal rules and principles that govern the relations of states and international organizations. Since there is no world government or global legislature, international law must be created by states formally through treaties or informally through custom. International law must also be enforced by states and IOs, and although enforcement in some issue areas is difficult (like the laws during war), international law works reasonably well most of the time. The nexus of international law and international organizations has several dimensions. The legal personality of IGOs comes from a constitutive treaty agreed upon by states. IGOs also play a central role in helping states implement international agreements and following through on states' international obligations (Joachim, Reinalda, and Verbeek 2008). NGOs and MNCs are objects of international law in that their activities are affected by international legal regulation. At the same time, IGOs, NGOs, and MNCs shape international law by promoting values and norms and pressuring the governments of states. International law ranging from war to climate change, to human rights, and to landmines has been influenced directly or indirectly by nonstate actors. Oil MNCs lobbied strenuously against the Kyoto Protocol (a treaty to combat climate change) and an NGO, the International Campaign to Ban Landmines, was central to the development of a treaty designed to eliminate antipersonnel landmines (Scott 2010, 63–71). Global governance involves this interplay of international law and organizations, but the "nature" of global governance remains contested. Who really makes the rules and whose values should be privileged in the world order? How are the rules made and the norms institutionalized? Who benefits and who loses in the process of global governance? How is change affected? Theory helps us answer these very important questions.

ORGANIZATION OF THE TEXT

The central purpose of this text is to explore the nature, role, and behavior of international organizations in world politics, while paying considerable attention to the nexus between international organizations and international law. In order to achieve this purpose, international organizations are analyzed using five theoretical perspectives: realism, liberalism, Marxism, feminism, and constructivism. No attempt is made to rank these theories in terms of importance. Students must determine for themselves the utility of a particular explanation, while recognizing that one theoretical approach may be useful for analyzing one kind of organization or situation, but not another. Students are also cautioned against dismissing descriptions, explanations, and insights generated by a theoretical approach that is incongruent with their own worldviews.

Chapter 2 provides a nuts-and-bolts overview of three kinds of international organization: the IGO, the NGO, and the MNC. The structure and the principles of several specific IGOs are detailed and NGOs are examined generally in terms of their roles and functions. MNCs are analyzed in the context of their activities and goals. The purpose of Chapter 2 is mainly to be informative, designed to give the student an idea of the basic composition of certain IGOs and functions of NGOs and MNCs. International relations theories are used in subsequent chapters to interpret the activities of international organizations in world politics.

International organizations do not exist in a vacuum. They are part and parcel of the world's political landscape—a landscape in which scholars and observers disagree about the relative importance of certain actors and dynamics. As Wolff and Resnick (1987, 10) have argued, the differences between theories are not minor. Theoretical differences amount to profound disagreements as to how the world works and what ought to be changed. Differences about policy are differences about theory. The priorities and actions of international organizations cannot be adequately understood unless considerable attention is paid to the theories that provide meaning to their activities. Unfortunately, the development of theory is not a tidy process. Scholars and practitioners do not always fit neatly into one framework, nor are the lines between theories clear and distinct. The lines are easily blurred, and this, in turn, increases complexity and contributes to conceptual confusion. But despite their shortcomings, theoretical frameworks are both necessary and useful for helping us understand the intricacies and diversity of today's international organizations.

In this text, realism, liberalism, Marxism, feminism, and constructivism are used as mental maps that help make sense of contemporary international relations and international organizations. Then we apply these theoretical approaches to substantive issue areas addressed by international organizations—security, trade, development, the environment, and human rights. Each uses different units of analysis and centers on different international dynamics. Each theory employs different conceptions of states and of international organizations. Each has very different things to say about the nature of global governance in the twenty-first century.

Realism

Chapter 3 discusses realist theory, which, as a worldview, conceives of world politics as essentially conflictual. World politics center on sovereign states seeking power and exercising power against each other. States exist in a hostile and dangerous world that forces them to be prepared for war and other forms of violent conflict. For realists, the state is the principal unit of analysis. While realists recognize that nonstate actors exist, nonstate actors are not as important because, ultimately, they are responsible to the state or, at least, are vulnerable to state action. Relations between states are "international relations" for realists. They also assume that the state is a unitary rational actor, meaning that it behaves as if it were a single entity capable of engaging in a cost–benefit analysis when selecting courses of action or policy. The state seeks to survive and maximize its national interest in an uncertain and dangerous world. The darker side of human nature, resource scarcity, and the constant threat of a violent attack guarantee that international relations between will be contentious.

The concept of anarchy is critical to an understanding of the realist view of international relations. Anarchy is defined as the absence of a higher authority or world government. The international system is organized around sovereign states, meaning that the state, or its representatives (the government), has the final say within its territorial jurisdiction. The absence of a higher authority requires states to engage in "self-help" in order to guarantee their security and other national interests. International relations are essentially conflictual because states, each pursuing their self-interest, often collide with each other. This collision can very easily, and often does, result in violence. With no world government, no referee exists to settle disputes or prevent war. States, therefore, must seek power because it is through power that states can maximize their interests and guarantee their security under the condition of anarchy.

The realists' emphasis on anarchy does not mean that they see the international system as chaotic. On the contrary, they point to the distribution of capabilities, or the balance of power, as a source of order in the international system. While there is no higher authority in international relations other than the state, there is a hierarchy of power. Through this hierarchy of power, realists explain the creation of international organizations and their role in maintaining international order and cooperation. According to proponents of hegemonic stability theory, world order is established by a single, dominant power that creates and administers international organizations. These organizations serve the interests of the hegemon and legitimize its dominant position. The hegemon will maintain and support international organizations as long as the gains outweigh the costs. Other states join these organizations even though they serve the interests of the hegemon because the hegemon, through its power, is able to provide positive incentives and inducements. The hegemon also bears the costs of maintaining international organizations. International organizations, therefore, are created by and serve the interests of the dominant states. States will belong to and use international organizations if it is in their interest to do so. However, they will also ignore or even undermine them if that is in their self-interest.

Order and stability in international relations are based on a hegemon's power. As that power declines, so do the world order and the international organizations that provide the foundation. Hence, most realists are very pessimistic about the independent role of international organizations in fostering cooperation among sovereign states. Rather, it is the hegemon's power reflected in international organizations that facilitates international cooperation. Realists tend to view international organizations as extensions of the great powers or as great-power directorates. The interests and behavior of international organizations must be understood in the context of the interests of dominant states. Conceptually, international organizations are IGOs, which are no more than the sum of their member states. For realists, global governance is a great-power concert facilitated by international organizations.

Liberalism

Chapter 3 also examines the liberal theoretical approach to international relations and international organizations. As a worldview, liberalism maintains a strong belief in the value of the individual, the idea of limited government, the market, and the rule of law. The liberal tradition in international relations, which grew out of a critique of realism, draws heavily upon the economic theory of Adam Smith and the political theory of John Locke. Liberals tend to be more optimistic about the prospects for cooperative relations between societies. They point out that much of international relations is based on the peaceful exchange of goods, services, and ideas among societies. While war is a major problem, it does not define international relations. International relations are also shaped by important economic and social transactions.

Liberals argue that nonstate actors, such as MNCs and IGOs, are also important actors in international relations. This is not to say that states are unimportant, only that other actors can and do influence world politics. Some liberals see the state as a more fluid entity, an aggregation of competing individuals and interests within a society. Many of these interests have transnational ties that extend beyond a state's borders. The governments of states can also be composed of executive, legislative, judicial, and bureaucratic agents that have personal and sectoral interests. These domestic factors can influence the decision-making process as much as international considerations. Understanding the individuals and types of groups that compete for control of the government is necessary in order to understand how a state behaves in international relations. Rationality cannot necessarily be assumed, given that the different influences on the government can lead to suboptimal decisions.

Liberals see international relations as a combination of cooperation and conflict. Human beings are self-interested, but they are also cooperative, economic creatures. The instincts of humans to "truck, barter, and trade" draw them together in a market. The market that generates wealth and prosperity also creates complex interdependence. The expanding global market brings societies together, connecting them through international trade and finance. Societies come to rely on each other for security and economic well-being, and that reliance provides incentives for actors to cooperate with each other. Even when conflict arises, complex interdependence reduces the likelihood of that conflict turning violent. Complex interdependence promotes more peaceful relations between societies.

Liberals see international organizations in one of two ways. Some see international organizations as the early institutions—precursors—of world government. That is, they are the foundations of a nascent "new world order." International organizations are evolving into supranational organizations that exercise authority and jurisdiction over nation-states. Others see international organizations as mechanisms that assist governments in overcoming collective-action problems and help them to settle conflicts and problems peacefully. International organizations are important in their own right, cooperating with governments and also acting independently. For liberals, global governance is based on the interaction of several kinds of actors—individuals, interest groups, government agencies, IGOs, NGOs, and MNCs—competing and working together to define and promote the "international collective good" and to address global problems.

Marxism

Chapter 4 is devoted to critical theories and approaches to international relations and international organizations. Critical theories challenge the "conventional wisdom" and provide alternative frameworks for understanding the world. The first critical theory examined in Chapter 4 is Marxism. The Marxist perspective is distinguished by its attention to modes of production (the manner in which goods and services are produced) and economic forces that shape international life. It emphasizes economic and political inequality in international relations, an inequality that leads to superior–subordinate relationships. Such relationships result in both violent and nonviolent international conflict.

For Marxists, capitalism is the defining feature of the international system. Capitalism is a way of producing goods that is based on four attributes—private property, profit motive, wage labor, and a free market. Capitalists seek to maximize profits in a competitive global market. Such competition creates winners and losers and determines the position and behavior of actors in international affairs. The capitalist accumulation process and the exigencies of the market affect individuals and societies in ways that are not always positive.

Marxists focus on economic class as the principal unit of analysis. Class is defined as a person's relationship to the means of production. Actors in international relations are distinguished by their role in the production of goods and services worldwide. Capitalism spawns two primary, yet unequal, classes: the bourgeoisie (owners of the means of production) and the proletariat (salaried and wage-earning workers). Class analysis includes these economic classes as well as economic classes of nation-states. Core states (advanced industrialized countries) provide capital and finance. Periphery states (Third World countries) provide cheap raw materials and unskilled labor. Semiperiphery states (newly industrializing countries) provide offshore sourcing and inexpensive skilled labor. The economic interaction of core, periphery, and semiperiphery results in the production of goods and services for global markets, yet the distribution of benefits and costs is inherently unequal.

International relations for Marxists are conflictual because capitalism is based on exploitation. Capitalists seek to exploit resources, markets, and labor in order to maximize profits. In other words, capitalism exploits people and breeds social, political, and economic inequality. The nature of economic relations is essentially a zero-sum game in which one player (class or class of states) wins, while someone else loses. The core exploits the periphery and the semiperiphery, benefiting at their expense. Hence, international relations are conflictual, divided between rich and poor. The division between rich and poor exists both between nations and within societies. In a global context, the experience of most of the world's population with capitalism is one of violence and poverty.

Marxists posit that economic factors are most important for understanding both domestic and international politics. Governments are reflections of the dominant economic class, and this dominant class formalizes its interests as the interests of society as a whole. Wars and other forms of violent conflict are rooted in class exploitation, and issues that seem to be geostrategic are really economic in nature. If you want to understand the nature of contemporary international conflict, you have to understand the nature of contemporary capitalism.

For Marxists, the nature of international organizations is determined by the underlying economic order. Contemporary international organizations reflect, legitimize, and promote global capitalism. International financial institutions, such as the World Bank and the IMF, are mechanisms of capitalist domination. They pry open markets, forcing privatization and encouraging foreign investment. MNCs entangle societies in a malignant web of dependency that causes underdevelopment and a gross maldistribution of wealth within and between societies. International organizations and law further the interests of capitalists, particularly regarding capital that is transnational rather than national in nature. Capitalism expands under the guise of promoting global economic and social welfare.

Feminism

Chapter 4 also presents the feminist theoretical framework. This framework examines international relations and international organizations through the lens of gender. It challenges conventional understandings by examining world politics in terms of how it affects women and how gender biases influence contemporary international relations theory. Feminists seek to understand what it means to be "feminine," in both theory and practice of international organizations. That is, the feminist approach examines the status, roles, and contributions of women in international organizations and seeks to understand how the actions and policies of international organizations affect women. Feminist analyses also highlight the gender bias of the realist, liberal, and Marxist perspectives.

The feminist theoretical approach is organized around several assumptions. First, gender matters. Conventional scholarship regarding international relations and organizations either minimizes gender or assumes universality. Feminists argue that contemporary explanations are inadequate because the experiences of women in war, politics, markets, and class are not always addressed. With gender as the principal unit of analysis, new insights into world politics become possible. Gender is not simply the sex of an individual. Gender is associated with social expectations about what it means to be masculine and feminine.

Second, international relations are conflictual. Conflict results from the superior–subordinate nature of gender relationships. Biology may account for many differences between men and women, but whether "masculine" and "feminine" differences are considered superior or inferior is socially constructed. This assumption extends the analysis of international conflict to women in order to understand how their experiences differ from that of men. It also allows scholars to examine exploitation that extends beyond the market or economic class.

Third, patriarchy is the main feature of the international system. Patriarchy means "male dominance." Most of the edifices of international relations (e.g., states, international organizations, and firms) are either masculinist in nature or dominated by men. Feminists argue that ignoring this feature narrows analysis to principally masculine issues that are the domain of men. Also, scholars implicitly assume universality when they ignore gender, thereby making masculine issues, traits, and behavior universal.

Fourth, the hierarchy of contemporary international issues is ordered on the basis of masculine preferences, marginalizing many "feminine" issues. The priorities of governments, heads of states, decision makers, ambassadors, and senior-level bureaucrats of organizations such as the UN and WTO are masculine not because they are evil men but because they conceptualize and understand the world in a masculine way. Those who attempt to address feminine issues or consider feminine approaches are faced with the unfortunate reality that feminine attributes and issues are of a lower status and are even the subject of ridicule.

These interrelated assumptions provide an alternative framework for systematically criticizing realism, liberalism, and Marxism and offer an alternative lens for viewing international relations and international organizations. The feminist theoretical approach brings the issue of gender to the study of international organizations by highlighting and evaluating the role of women in international organizations. This kind of gendered analysis examines the employment practices of international organizations to see what kinds of positions women occupy and to assess the status of those positions. Feminist scholarship emphasizes the exclusion of women from important decision-making positions and also seeks to value the contributions of women in their traditional gender roles as caregivers, nurturers, and supporters. The disparate impact of the policies and activities of international organizations on each gender is also a focus of inquiry.

The feminist approach also explores NGOs in considerable detail because they are, arguably, more "feminine" in nature and empower women to take more control over their lives. NGOs tend to be more horizontally structured, and they often work with IGOs to provide aid and relief to the "victims of world politics." NGOs challenge traditional (masculine) approaches to international problems by focusing on grassroots- and community-level efforts to ameliorate poverty and check human rights violations. Realism, liberalism, Marxism, and feminism provide different ways of understanding international organizations in terms of their nature and the role they play in world politics. Table 1.1 summarizes the different approaches in terms of their key theoretical features. These theories are "grand" theories of international relations that describe, explain, analyze, and predict how the world works. However, grand theories are not the only way to understand international organizations. **Constructivism** has gained considerable currency among scholars seeking to explain the activities and behavior of international organizations.

Constructivism

Constructivism centers on the role of ideas, beliefs, and interests in shaping the interactions and understandings of actors in world politics. It involves the "processes by which leaders, groups and states alter their preferences, shape their identities and learn new behavior" (Genest 2003, 259). Constructivists seek to identify the social norms and shared identities that are developed and disseminated by international organizations (see, e.g., Finnemore 2004).

Goldstein and Pevehouse (2006, 119) point out that constructivism is more an "approach" than an overarching theory of international relations. As such, constructivism does not rest on a framework of assumptions or propositions that say anything about world politics, per se. Nor does it rely on any specific level of analysis. Rather it rests on the notion that reality or "interest" is **socially constructed**. Values and ideas are created by human beings who are shaped by their social ties and identities. Moreover, those values and ideas change over time as human beings learn more information. Constructivists, therefore, do not seek to explain the world how it is but how the world is what we make it.

Constructivism, as applied to international organizations, explores how rules and norms are created and disseminated throughout the international system. These norms are developed by a variety of actors, from a variety of cultures, with a variety of interests. International organizations socialize individuals and states as to how to behave in international relations and how

TABLE 1.1

Comparison of Theoretical Approaches

	Realism	Liberalism	Marxism	Feminism
Unit(s) of analysis	States	Individuals, groups, and states	Economic class or economic classes of states	Gender
Nature of international relations	Conflict	Cooperation and conflict	Conflict	Cooperation and conflict
Principal feature(s) of international system	Anarchy and balance of power	Complex interdependence	World capitalism	Patriarchy
Nature of international organizations	Principally IGOs; extensions of great-power interests	Regimes; mechanism for collective action and international problem-solving	IGOs, MNCs, reflections of the underlying economic order	Varied: IGOs are patriarchal; NGOs are more horizontally structured
Behavior of international organizations	Nonautonomous; determined by great-power interests and the underlying distribution of capabilities	Foster cooperative relations among states and nonstate actors; autonomous	Promote and reinforce capitalist production; tools of capitalist domination	Varied; reinforce and challenge patriarchy

to view international problems. The nature of global governance, thus, is fluid in that it is constructed by individuals and groups (and therefore states) differently at different times.

The Issues

This text also examines international organizations in practice. Chapters 5 through 9 are organized around three sections. The first section introduces the issue area and provides a brief overview of some of the relevant international organizations in terms of their charters, operations, and mandates. It also highlights the international law and politics surrounding the issue. The second part outlines the relevant facts of two case studies. The third section then examines case studies using the different theoretical approaches. Borrowing from Graham Allison's (1971) classic case study of the Cuban Missile Crisis, *The Essence of Decision*, international events are examined using the different theoretical perspectives to guide the analysis. This technique provides the student with multiple and often competing interpretations of the same event. This method yields improved explanations regarding the nature, behavior, and role of international organizations in world politics.

Specifically, we examine the issues of security, trade, development, environmental protection, and human rights by combining international relations theory with the study of international organizations, which in turn provides a more comprehensive explanation of the nature of global governance. Currently, more than 192 nation-states and self-governing territories exist on the planet. The human population is approximately 6.1 billion people. The complexity of contemporary world problems and their elusive solutions are the result, at least in part, of competing worldviews about how the world operates. The first step in addressing this dilemma is to understand and explore worldviews other than one's own. Looking at an issue from a different perspective or worldview creates an expanded knowledge base and can assist in resolving disputes or fashioning strategies in a way that is acceptable to the parties involved.

KEY TERMS

theory 1
worldviews 1
intergovernmental
  organizations
  (IGOs) 2
international legal
  personality 3
constitutive treaty 3
Reparation for Injuries
  Suffered in the Service
  of the UN (1949) 3

functionalist
  analyses 4
international
  regimes 4
nongovernmental
  organization
  (NGO) 4
multinational
  corporation
  (MNC) 4
global governance 5

international law 5
realism 7
liberalism 8
Marxism 9
feminism 10
constructivism 12
socially constructed 12

SUGGESTED READINGS

Krasner, Stephen. 1983. *International Regimes.* Ithaca, NY: Cornell University Press.

Mingst, Karen A., and Margaret P. Karns. 2006. *The United Nations in the Twenty First Century.* Boulder, CO: Westview Press.

Slomanson, William R. 1990. *Fundamental Perspectives on International Law.* New York: West Publishing.

Weiss, Thomas G., David P. Forsythe, Roger Coate, and Kelly-Kate Pease. 2007. *The United Nations and Changing World Politics.* 5th ed. Boulder, CO: Westview Press.

Whitworth, Sandra. 1994. *Feminism and International Relations: Toward a Political Economy of Gender in Interstate and Nongovernmental Institutions.* Basingstoke, UK: Macmillan Press.

International Organizations: Nuts and bolts

A variety of different international organizations actively participate in world politics. This chapter details several major intergovernmental organizations (IGOs) in terms of their structures and functions. These IGOs were selected on the basis of their significance to world and regional politics and their geopolitical orientation. Although other IGOs are discussed in later chapters, the purpose here is to provide an abbreviated overview of some of the IGOs central to international relations.

This chapter also examines nongovernmental organizations (NGOs) and multinational corporations (MNCs) in terms of their broad, general characteristics. Since these kinds of international organizations number in the tens of thousands, an extended classification scheme is presented in order to sort them out in a meaningful fashion. While international organizations do not exist in a political vacuum, sometimes "the devil is in the details." The structures and procedures of international organizations can, and often do, affect political outcomes.

GLOBAL INTERGOVERNMENTAL ORGANIZATIONS

Historical Antecedents

The idea of international organization has probably been around since the advent of the first governments. From the writings of ancient Greek philosophers we learn of military alliances and international trading agreements. And we know that the early Greek city-states of Athens, Sparta, and Macedonia once employed a common currency, which required a high degree of international cooperation. Most contemporary scholars, however, point to the Congress of Vienna (1815–1822) as the earliest modern precedent to today's IGO. The Congress of Vienna, a multipurpose IGO, was created by the European great powers to reestablish order and stability on the continent after the Napoleonic Wars. It was a forum for international collaboration on European security and commerce. It also strengthened the Rhine River Commission (1804), a bilateral IGO between France and the German confederation. This Commission established navigation rules for the Rhine River and an adjudication board to prosecute individuals accused of violating those rules. Similar river commissions were subsequently created for the Danube and Elbe rivers in Central and Eastern Europe.

League of Nations

The first global IGO with universal membership was the **League of Nations** (1919–1939). The League was created after World War I and was organized around three bodies: the Council, the Assembly, and the Secretariat. The Council was the chief executive organ of the League. It consisted of the victors of World War I, together with any four lesser powers that they chose to invite. The Council was mainly responsible for addressing issues relating to international war and threats to international peace. In addition, according to the League's Charter, the Council could "deal at its meetings with any matter within the sphere of action of the League" (Article 4, Section 4). The Assembly functioned as a quasi-legislative body; it, too, was entitled to address any matter within the purview of the League. All members of the League of Nations belonged to the Assembly, and each member could have up to three representatives. The Secretariat served as the League's bureaucracy, responsible for carrying out the League's policies and mandates.

In addition to the League's three principal organs, several autonomous and semiautonomous organizations were established under the League's Charter. The Permanent Court of International Justice (PCIJ) and the International Labor Organization (ILO) were created to help member states meet their obligations under the League's Charter. Article 13 committed members to submit any matter unsolved by diplomacy to international arbitration or judicial settlement. The PCIJ considered disputes that arose regarding treaty interpretation or breaches of international obligations assumed under international law. The ILO was created, in part, to help member states meet their social responsibilities to workers. Article 23(a) stated that members of the League "will endeavor to secure and maintain fair and humane conditions of labor for men, women and children, both in their own countries and in all countries to which their commercial and industrial relations extend, and for that purpose will establish and maintain the necessary international organizations." The ILO, one of the few surviving League institutions, remains the central IGO responsible for setting and preserving international labor standards. It also has the potential to be an important vehicle for recognizing workers' rights as human rights (McIntyre 2008).

The League of Nations was based on three important principles that have since been incorporated by its successor, the United Nations (UN). First, the League of Nations embraced the idea of collective security where international security is directly tied to the security of member states. Second, the League established as a norm the peaceful settlement of disputes through such nonviolent measures as mediation, negotiation, arbitration, and adjudication. Third, the League was founded to foster international cooperation in the economic and social realms. The ideals of the League were innovative. They were heavily influenced by American values, as one of the principal architects of the League was President Woodrow Wilson. Ultimately, however, the U.S. government chose not to join the organization—a decision that is widely considered to have compromised the League's effectiveness during the interwar period. The League was politically challenged by the Japan–China conflict in Manchuria (1931) and the Italy–Ethiopia conflict (1935). The outbreak of World War II spelled the demise of the League as a viable international organization. However, its legacy lives on.

The United Nations

The UN system was created in 1945 at the end of World War II. The founders of the UN, meeting in San Francisco, sought to strengthen the idea of the multipurpose, universal IGO first envisioned by the League of Nations. The UN was designed to be the center of multilateral diplomacy in postwar world politics. Its central purposes are: to maintain international peace and security; to develop friendly relations among nations; to address economic, social, cultural, and humanitarian problems; and to promote respect for universal human rights. The UN retains the age-old principle of the sovereign equality of all states; however, it also commits members to the nonuse of force and the peaceful settlement of disputes.

The UN is a comprehensive IGO to which, effectively, any state can belong. The UN system is structured around six principal organs—the General Assembly, the Security Council, the International Court of Justice (ICJ), the Economic and Social Council (ECOSOC), the Secretariat, and the Trusteeship Council. These organs serve as an umbrella to other UN agencies and autonomous bodies (Figure 2.1). The six principal organs of the UN, together with its several agencies and autonomous organizations, comprise the UN family of IGOs; collectively, they address just about every conceivable global issue, including war, civil disorder, arms control, trade, development, the environment, and human rights.

The General Assembly The UN General Assembly serves as a quasi-legislative, deliberative body. Its principal, *de jure* (legal) functions are assigned by the UN Charter (Chapter IV) and are fivefold. First, the General Assembly may deliberate and consider any issue or questions that may arise under the Charter. While its resolutions are nonbinding, the General Assembly may address issues that relate to international peace, security, and disarmament, and it may bring to the attention of the Security Council any matter that may cause a breach of the peace. Second, it is responsible for initiating studies and making recommendations for promoting political cooperation and the progressive development of international law. Third, it is responsible for promoting international cooperation in the

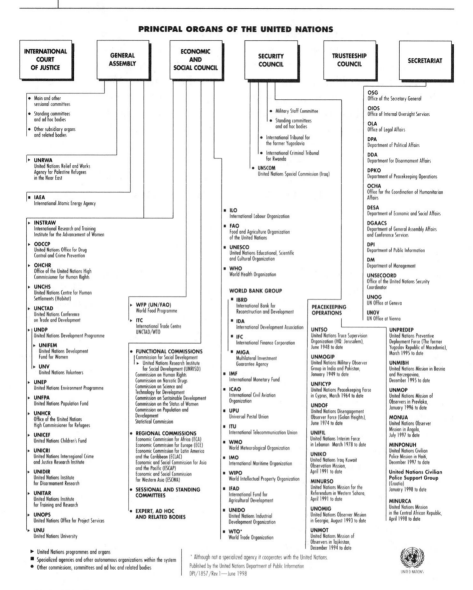

FIGURE 2.1

The United Nations System.

Source: Courtesy of the UN Publications Office.

economic, social, cultural, educational, and health care fields. Fourth, it is charged with drafting and approving the UN budget. And fifth, it oversees the UN bureaucracy.

The General Assembly is based on the liberal democratic principles of political equality and majority rule. It is a plenary body, meaning that all member states may attend and fully participate in General Assembly meetings. Originally, the General Assembly consisted of 51 nation-states. Today, 192 states are represented. Decisions are made on a one-state/one-vote basis, with a simple majority deciding most issues. A qualified majority of two-thirds is required for important questions, such as recommendations made with respect to the maintenance of international peace and security or the election of the nonpermanent members of the Security Council. The General Assembly operates much like a congress or parliament, although it does not produce binding law. Rather, its resolutions function as an expression of general legal principles, often forming the basis of the "hard" international law, which is created through treaties. The General Assembly, through its activities and its resolutions, best approximates the priorities and sentiments of the "international community."

The Security Council The UN Security Council (discussed in more detail in Chapter 5) is the organ whose primary responsibility is maintaining international peace and security. This task is quite complicated because it involves identifying threats to international peace and security, crafting an appropriate international response, building international consensus, and carrying out collective security actions. Unlike General Assembly resolutions, Security Council decisions are binding on member states, and members are obligated to abide by and help carry out these decisions. Not all Security Council resolutions are binding, only those in which a formal "decision" under Chapter VII is issued.

The Security Council has limited membership. It is composed of both permanent and nonpermanent, elective members and is headed by a president, an office that rotates among all the members. The permanent members include the five great-power victors of World War II, while the ten elected members are selected from and by the General Assembly. Each of the Security Council's permanent members possesses an absolute veto over substantive Security Council decisions. This veto allows one member to kill Security Council actions (excluding procedural questions), and it cannot be overridden. Absent a veto, Security Council resolutions are passed by an affirmative vote of nine members.

The International Court of Justice The ICJ is also known as the World Court and was created to be the principal judicial organ of the UN. Incorporating much of the statute of the League's Permanent Court of International Justice, the ICJ has semiautonomous status within the UN family. Chapter XIV of the UN Charter authorizes the ICJ to adjudicate disputes arising under the Charter and international law. The ICJ statute mandates that the court consist of fifteen justices, no two of whom may be nationals from the same state. The justices of the Court are elected for nine-year, staggered terms by the General Assembly and the Security Council through a complicated nomination and selection process. These justices hear cases submitted to the Court by member states, and decisions are reached through a majority vote. A quorum of nine justices is required for the Court to hear a case; however, the Court does not have compulsory jurisdiction over all cases. Article 36 of the ICJ statute, often referred to as the "Optional Clause," allows parties to decide whether they want to give the Court jurisdiction over their current and future international legal disputes. Very few states have given the Court this kind of jurisdiction; thus, states usually consent to the court's jurisdiction on a case-by-case basis. Access to the ICJ is also limited to states. That is, only states may be parties in cases before the court. Private individuals are barred from bringing cases to the ICJ, and the court has refused to consider private petitions and requests. All the states involved in a legal dispute must be willing to have the ICJ hear the case before the Court will consider the merits. As a result, the ICJ hears only one or two cases a year, and it is generally considered an ineffective mechanism of international adjudication. The ICJ remains "marginal to most of the structural issues of international relations" (Forsythe 1998, 385).

The ICJ can, however, influence world politics as it is also responsible for providing advisory opinions on legal questions for the Security Council or the General Assembly, upon their request. Other agencies of the UN, when authorized by the General Assembly, may also request advisory opinions on any legal question that may arise in the scope or course of their activities. The ICJ has issued advisory decisions for a variety of UN agencies ranging from the ILO to the International Monetary Fund (IMF) to the World Meteorological Organization (WMO). In 2003, the General Assembly requested an advisory opinion on the legality of the separation barrier being built by Israel in occupied Palestinian territories. The opinion, issued in 2004, held that the construction of the wall violated international law and the human rights of Palestinians living in the occupied territories. This opinion generated considerable controversy as it called into question a key element of Israeli security strategy and complicated the "roadmap" to peace. Its effect also gave the legal and moral high ground to opponents of the barrier and strengthened the Palestinians' bargaining position in any future peace negotiations. In 2008, the General Assembly requested an ICJ advisory opinion as to whether Kosovo's unilateral declaration of independence from Serbia is in accordance with international law. In the much anticipated 2010 opinion, the ICJ found that the declaration of independence did not violate general international law. This opinion will likely frame the legal arguments for separatist movements and status quo states for decades to come. It also shows how the ICJ can shape the legal dimensions of international relations.

The Economic and Social Council The ECOSOC was established under the UN Charter (Chapter X) to promote economic and social cooperation among member states. It is actively involved in the substantive issue areas of economic development, human rights, and social welfare. The ECOSOC consists of fifty-four members elected by the General Assembly for three-year, staggered terms. Each member has one vote, and decisions are based on majority rule. Retiring members are eligible for immediate reelection.

The ECOSOC has several important functions and powers. First, it "may make or initiate studies and reports with respect to international economic, social, cultural, educational, and health and related matters and may make recommendations with respect to any such matters to the General Assembly, to the Members of the United Nations, and to the specialized agencies concerned" (Article 62, Section 1). Second, the ECOSOC may make recommendations for promoting and protecting human rights. Third, it may prepare draft conventions relating to economic and social issues. Finally, it may call international conferences on matters falling within its competence.

The ECOSOC is a collaborative body with authority to create commissions to promote human rights and economic and social cooperation. It invites all UN members and representatives of the specialized agencies and certain NGOs to participate in its activities. While these non-ECOSOC members do not have a vote in ECOSOC decisions, they provide perspective and expertise to ECOSOC proceedings.

The Trusteeship Council   The Trusteeship Council was created to oversee the transition of colonies into self-governing territories. Its mandate is to ensure that the interests of the inhabitants of these non–self-governing territories are placed at the forefront of the decolonization process. Among the members of the Trusteeship Council are UN member states that administer trust territories. These members take an oath to respect the cultures of the people involved and to respect their political, economic, and social development. The Trusteeship Council also includes permanent members of the Security Council that are not administering trust territories. In addition, the Trusteeship Council is balanced; it must consist of "as many other members elected for three-year terms by the General Assembly as may be necessary to ensure that the total number of the Trusteeship Council is equally divided between those Members of the United Nations which administer trust territories and those which do not" (Article 86, Section 1c). Decision making is based on a one-member/one-vote, majority-rule arrangement.

The Trusteeship Council, while pivotal in the 1960s, is largely obsolete today. All the original UN trusts have become autonomous or self-governing, and there is little left for the Trusteeship Council to do. Its historical legacy is its oversight of the volatile decolonization process, a process for which there have been as many critics as champions. The Trusteeship Council's role in this process has been to debate and deliberate different strategies for decolonization, as well as to monitor the effects of the process on trust populations. It has also supervised the process by issuing binding decisions on member states that were not permanent members of the Security Council and making recommendations to those that were. At the 2005 UN World Summit, the heads of member states agreed to wind up the business of the Trusteeship Council, reflecting the completion of the role of the Trusteeship Council and the UN in decolonization.

The Secretariat   The Secretariat serves as the UN bureaucracy. It consists of the Secretary-General and the bureaucratic staff necessary to carry out the UN's complex tasks and functions. The Secretary-General (discussed in more detail in Chapter 5) is the chief diplomat, whose task is to represent the UN to member states. The staff of the Secretariat is supposed to be recruited on the basis of efficiency, competence, integrity, and geographic diversity, although political patronage is not unknown. The bureaucratic agencies of the Secretariat are created by the General Assembly; however, both the ECOSOC and the Trusteeship Council are explicitly assigned their own staff. The size, expense, and priorities of the UN bureaucracy are widely criticized today; yet, most agree that some kind of bureaucracy is necessary to carry out the large, complex tasks that characterize today's global issues.

Management reform has been a high priority for the UN and its largest contributor, the United States. Member states have agreed in principle to strengthen the UN's oversight capacity, especially in relation to the Office of Internal Oversight Services and the new Ethics Office. They have also agreed to overhaul policies relating to budgets, finance, and staff to streamline UN activities. The United States has demanded that the UN change the way it does business, and the scandals involving corruption relating to the "Oil-For-Food" program and the procurement office accentuated the need for reform. The specifics of these reforms are currently being fleshed out and remain contentious at the UN.

The Principles of the United Nations

The UN is based on several complementary principles. First, the UN is founded on the principle of the sovereign equality of all members. This means that each state, at least in legal theory, retains the right to determine its own internal and external affairs. Second, UN members voluntarily accept responsibility to carry out certain international obligations upon joining the UN, one of which is to abide by Security Council decisions. The third founding principle of the UN is the **peaceful settlement of disputes.** Fourth, member states agree not to threaten or use force in their international relations. Fifth, the UN is enjoined from intervening in the domestic jurisdiction of member states. The principles of sovereign equality, the peaceful settlement of disputes, **nonuse of force**, and **nonintervention** are companion principles critical to the maintenance of international peace and security.

The UN Charter attempts to strengthen international peace and security by permitting regional arrangements. Chapter VIII recognizes that regional and local solutions to regional and local problems are often preferable to UN action as regional organizations are more familiar with the actors, issues, and dynamics. The UN Charter does require that the UN be kept informed of regional activities and events that may threaten international peace and security. Furthermore, the Charter restricts regional enforcement activities by stating that "no enforcement action shall be taken under regional arrangements or by regional agencies without the authorization of the Security Council" (Article 53). The architects of the Charter wanted to balance the benefits of regionalism with the need for universal approaches to international problems. The post–World War II era has witnessed an explosion of regional organizations. Two of these organizations, both multipurpose, are the European Union (EU) and the Organization of Islamic Conference (OIC), and are discussed later in this chapter.

UN Ambitions and Challenges

The UN continues to have a role in preventive diplomacy, peacekeeping, peacemaking, conflict resolution, and economic and social development. However, several challenges threaten to derail or restrict UN activities in these areas. First, the UN suffers from resource difficulties. The United States, which is the UN's largest contributor, is also its largest debtor. The United States and the UN have been at odds for years over financing for a variety of political reasons. In 1999, a deal was struck between the UN and the United States that broke the impasse that might have led to the loss of the U.S. vote in the General Assembly (Schmitt 1999, A18). This impasse was between the UN and the United States over exactly how much is owed (the United States rejects numerous UN assessments) and between the then Clinton administration and the Republican-controlled Senate over the financing of international organizations that provide abortions or promote abortion rights. The United States agreed to release $1 billion in UN payments in exchange for the implementation of a ban on using that money to fund abortion rights groups. The Bush administration continued the ban; however, the then Republican-controlled House of Representatives continued to withhold payments to the UN until September 2001 and released them only after the World Trade Center and Pentagon attacks. Release of the funds was a goodwill gesture in an effort to enlist UN help in the U.S. "war on terror." However, the conduct of this war, especially the U.S. invasion of Iraq, as well as allegations of UN corruption and mismanagement relating to the UN-administered "Oil-for-Food" program for Iraq, once again led to additional tensions between the UN and its largest contributor. The U.S. arrears account for approximately 84 percent of what is owed to the UN; however, the Obama administration has begun making payments on the arrears and legislation is pending in the U.S. Congress to pay in full.

Second, the UN has had enormous difficulties in protecting its personnel. Since the 1990s, UN workers have been assaulted, kidnapped, and killed in record numbers in hot spots such as Lebanon, Mozambique, Afghanistan, Angola, Sudan, Cambodia, Somalia, Rwanda, Haiti, the Congo, and Iraq. Given the crisis of resources and the reluctance of member states to commit militarily, UN personnel remain at risk while attempting to deliver humanitarian and development assistance. The UN suffered a particularly devastating blow in 2003 when its headquarters in Iraq was the target of suicide bombings. The attacks killed dozens of UN personnel, including Special Envoy Sergio Vieira De Mello. Referred to as the UN's 9/11, the attack further exacerbated tensions between the organization and its most powerful member. The United States as the occupying power had the responsibility for security, yet, at the same time, the UN itself bore some responsibility. It did not take adequate security precautions and sent its people into Iraq under a fuzzy and underfunded mandate (Wolffe 2003, 32).

The security of UN personnel in conflict areas remains a priority and a pressing problem for the UN. In December 2007, UN offices and personnel were attacked by a suicide car bomb in Algeria, killing 17 people and injuring many more. In early 2008, UN peacekeepers and aid workers were assaulted in the Darfur region of Sudan, and in 2009, the UN lost 28 people worldwide. The inability of the UN to carry out its protective and relief activities means vulnerable populations in the world's hot spots remain at grave risk.

Third, the UN has suffered from a lack of state leadership. The United States, under the Bush administration, demonstrated its preference for unilateral approaches by withdrawing from the Kyoto Protocol and the International Criminal Court (discussed in Chapters 8 and 9, respectively). The attacks on the United States in September 2001 further complicated the political landscape and raised questions about the appropriate role of the UN in the "war on terrorism." The then Secretary-General Kofi Annan argued that only the UN could give "global legitimacy" to the war on terrorism (Schmemann 2001, B3); however, the United States considered the UN a minor partner to this threat to international peace and security. The U.S. invasion of Iraq in 2003 without UN authorization damaged UN–U.S. relations. The specifics of this tension are discussed in detail in Chapter 5; however, the war in Iraq and the subsequent marginalization of the UN by the United States raised serious questions about the future efficacy of the UN role in international security. The election of Barack Obama and his desire to reengage the UN has signaled the possibility of a renewed UN role, especially as it relates to nuclear nonproliferation and disarmament.

UN Reform

In September 2005, the world's leaders held the World Summit to celebrate the sixtieth anniversary of the UN and to formally address the issue of UN reform. The actual action items that emerged from the Summit are discussed in the following chapters, but the politics of the meeting warrants review here. The Summit was beset with contentiousness, reflecting the tension between the United States and other powerful members, the conflict between advanced industrialized and developing countries (the North–South conflict), and the general disagreement regarding the future direction of the UN. What was hoped to be a San Francisco II—namely, a grand conference aimed at remaking the UN to meet the challenges of the twenty-first century—resulted in very modest outcomes. Almost every major initiative was watered down, postponed, or deliberately left vague. While some noteworthy reforms were agreed to, such as the creation of a new Peacebuilding Commission and Human Rights Council (discussed in Chapters 5 and 9, respectively), the significance of the reforms seems marginal absent specifics and appropriate financing. The more substantial reforms, such as changing the composition of the Security Council, defining terrorism, and establishing clear guidelines for the use of force, generated such intense debate and disagreement that they were not formally considered at the Summit. The proposals were either superficially treated or not formally considered at all. Perhaps, the only issue that did not generate significant discord was the proposal to revise and update the UN

Charter by closing down the obsolete Trusteeship Council. The politics of the World Summit were illustrative of the complexities and competing visions as to the causes and consequences of today's most pressing global problems. The theories described in the next two chapters will help explain the behavior of the major actors regarding UN reform and the role of the UN in contemporary global governance.

REGIONAL INTERGOVERNMENTAL ORGANIZATIONS

The European Union

The EU is a comprehensive, multipurpose regional organization that has been under construction since the end of World War II. The original goals of the EU revolved around the economic and political integration of fifteen European states—France, Great Britain, Germany, Italy, Belgium, the Netherlands, Luxembourg, Denmark, Greece, Spain, Portugal, Ireland, Austria, Sweden, and Finland. In 2004, ten new members joined the EU: Poland, Hungary, the Czech Republic, Slovakia, Estonia, Latvia, Lithuania, Malta, Slovenia, and Cyprus. In 2007, both Bulgaria and Romania joined the EU, making a grand total of 27 members. The EU demonstrates how a series of IGOs can be tied together to create a supranational organization, albeit one in its nascent stages, which combines the interests of diverse nation-states. The EU perhaps represents the highest degree of economic, political, and social integration found in a contemporary international organization.

The construction of a united Europe has been a long and arduous process, and it continues today, as fifteen of the twenty-seven EU members are implementing a common currency, the "euro." The process began with the Paris Treaty (1951), in which Germany and France agreed to merge their steel and coal industries. Then, in 1952, the European Coal and Steel Community (ECSC) was created as Italy and the Benelux countries (Belgium, the Netherlands, and Luxembourg) joined with France and Germany to coordinate their steel and coal policies. Later, the Treaty of Rome (1957) extended ECSC cooperation to atomic energy with the creation of the European Atomic Energy Community (EURATOM). The Treaty of Rome also established the European Economic Community (EEC), which was committed to formation of a common market. The three communities—ECSC, EURATOM, and the EEC—had separate commissions and councils but shared the European Parliament and Court of Justice in common (Noel 1994, 5). In 1979, the three communities evolved into a single organization, called the European Community, and then the EU, in 1992.

EU membership expanded gradually: Great Britain, Ireland, and Denmark joined in 1973; Greece in 1981; Spain and Portugal in 1986; Germany in 1990; and Sweden, Austria, and Denmark in 1994. In 2004, the 10 states noted above became new members. And, as EU membership expanded, its institutions became more powerful and formalized through a series of multilateral treaties. In the following sections, we look at the five institutions of the EU and outline the treaties designed to integrate the nation-states of Europe.

The European Council   The European Council, which consists of the heads of state/government of EU members, represents the political leadership of the EU. The European Council was formally established by the Single European Act of 1985 and was strengthened by the Maastricht Treaty of 1992; however, the Council has existed informally since 1974. The Council meets twice a year with representatives from other EU institutions in order to coordinate EU policy with national policies and interests. It is playing an increasingly influential role in EU affairs but most political and military (and some monetary) decisions are still made at the national level. With the 2009 Lisbon Treaty, the European Council formally became the institution responsible of setting the priorities and direction of the EU. The Lisbon Treaty also conferred legal personality to the EU.

The Council of Ministers   The Council of Ministers, which is made up of the relevant ministers from the governments of EU members, is the chief decision-making body. According to Noel (1994, 6), each national government sends one of its ministers to the Council—which minister usually depends on the subject matter of the Council meeting. The Foreign Minister is usually considered the principal representative to the Council, but a variety of ministers, ranging from the Minister of Agriculture to the Minister of Transportation, regularly attend Council meetings. Formally, decisions in the Council are made through a weighted voting system with a qualified majority rule. Informally, most important policy decisions are made on the basis of unanimity (Noel 1994, 28–29). The Council of Ministers is a fluid body whose composition changes depending on the issue area. Members of the Council represent their national governments to the EU; consequently, the Council is an inherently political institution, often influenced by individual national interests.

The European Commission   The Council of Ministers is only part of the EU decision-making process. Most EU proposals and initiatives emanate from the European Commission, the bureaucratic arm of the EU. While the European Commission formally reports to the Council of Ministers, it exercises a great deal of autonomy. The Commission consists of twenty-seven members who are appointed for four-year terms and maintain a staff of approximately 5,000 people. Commission members are expected to further the interests of the EU as a whole as opposed to the interests of their own countries—hence Commission members and staff are often referred to as "Eurocrats" because of their priorities and allegiances. Commission members tend to be highly trained technocrats/bureaucrats who are skilled, complex-problem solvers. They are often technical experts and adept administrators in the areas of energy, trade, transportation, finance, and agriculture, rather than politicians with national constituencies.

The Commission has several important powers that help it develop common policies for the EU. It has the power to initiate policy proposals. While proposals are often initiated by the Council of Ministers or the European Parliament, the Commission has the authority to investigate strategies for addressing the problems it identifies. The Commission also has the power to execute EU policies. The European Parliament and the Council of Ministers generally approve broad policy goals, leaving it up to the Commission to create the specific rules, regulations, and procedures for reaching those goals. Coupled with the authority to set budgeting priorities, the execution of EU policies gives the Commission a great deal of influence over those policies. The European Commission has also emerged as the "Guardian of the Treaties." It is given the responsibility for implementing the multilateral treaties creating the EU and for building confidence among EU members.

The European Parliament   The European Parliament is mainly responsible for overseeing the Commission, although its legislative powers are limited. The Parliament can advise both Council and Commission on proposals, and it must approve the Commission's overall budget. It does not have the right of line-item approval. Even so, the Parliament is an important part of the co-decision process by virtue of its input in EU policy development. The co-decision procedure is a complex one, involving two readings and seven steps. First, the Commission develops a proposal. Second, the Parliament advises the Commission on other considerations and suggests revisions. Third, the Council of Ministers brings national concerns to the table, presenting their positions on the proposal. Fourth, the Parliament votes yes or no. Fifth, the Commission issues a second opinion of the now-revised proposal. Sixth, the Council issues its secondary opinion. Seventh, the European Parliament either accepts or rejects the final proposal. If a proposal reaches the seventh stage, it is almost always approved by the Parliament.

The co-decision process perhaps overemphasizes the legislative role of the Parliament. The Commission and the Council exercise the most influence over the formulation of common EU policy. The Parliament's influence remains largely deliberative and symbolic. The European Parliament consists of 736 members, each of whom is directly elected by voters in Europe. And, as with national legislatures, political parties feature prominently in European Parliament elections and operations. Europe's political parties reflect a broad political spectrum; they include, but are not limited to, the European Socialists, the Christian Democrats, the Greens, and the Democratic Alliance. Seating within the Parliament is based on political party sections; however, the members of the parties sit alphabetically in order to reduce any nationalist sentiments that may arise among the party members. The complicated composition of the Parliament is a surprising, yet effective, formula for projecting an image of European unity.

The European Court of Justice   The European Court of Justice was created in 1958 to adjudicate any legal disputes arising under the Treaty of Rome involving ECSC, EEC, and EURATOM activities. Over time, the jurisdiction of the Court has expanded to include disputes arising under later treaties such as the Single European Act (1986), the Maastricht Treaty (1992), and the Lisbon Treaty (2009). The Court is composed of 27 justices who are appointed by their national governments for renewable 6-year terms. The justices are assisted by advocates-general to handle the Court's expanding caseload. The Court functions much like the U.S. Supreme Court in that it interprets whether EU policies and national laws are congruent with EU treaties. But unlike the U.S. Supreme Court, the European Court is permitted to issue preliminary or advisory opinions that are referred to it by national courts.

The European Court of Justice is different from other international courts in that it may be used by individuals as well as governments. Traditionally, only states are subjects of international law, which means that only states may make claims in international courts. Individuals, though, are traditionally objects of international law, which means they must have their governments make claims on their behalf. The European Court of Justice is unique because individuals have standing to bring some cases before the Court. The Court has heard EU employment cases, for example, addressing such issues as job discrimination and equal pay for equal work.

EU Ambitions and Challenges

The impressive institutional structures of the EU indicate its ambitious goals. EU goals have been outlined in the **Single European Act, the Maastricht Treaty**, and **the Lisbon Treaty**. The Single European Act called for the final elimination of all internal barriers to trade in goods and services by 1992. This was a critical step to ensuring the free movement of goods, services, persons, and capital within the EU. The Maastricht Treaty is even more ambitious, calling for the final step of economic integration—the implementation of a common currency, known as the euro. The euro has been the European currency for international transactions since 1999, and it replaced the domestic currencies of 12 EU member states in January 2001. The transition to the euro was rocky. When put to a popular vote via a referendum in Denmark, citizens voted against the euro by a significant majority (Kuchment and Beith 2000, 5). The United Kingdom and Sweden remain outside of the eurozone. For those states that have adopted the euro, public opinion polls initially suggested that their citizens were at best indifferent to the euro and at worst would reject it if the decision were put to a public vote (*European Report* 2001, 102). Concerns also abounded about the initial value of the euro relative to the U.S. dollar, the security of the euro from theft and counterfeiting, and the loss of millions of dollars worth of undeclared income from Europe's underground economy. Both Germany and France repeatedly exceeded the permissible budget deficits, raising concerns that government deficits would undermine confidence in the euro. In spite of these challenges, the implementation of the euro was largely successful. In 2008, the euro was one of the strongest currencies in the world, posting record strength against the U.S. dollar, the British pound, and the Japanese yen.

In 2010, a sovereign debt crisis in Greece and to a lesser extent in Portugal, Ireland, and Spain created a crisis of confidence in the euro. Euro-skeptics have long warned that a common currency without a common political system implementing a common fiscal policy would enable governments to spend beyond their means and limit the ability of governments to respond to economic crises. After months of indecision, the EU along with the IMF and the United States finally took action with a bailout package of approximately 750 billion euro. The bailout stabilized the euro in the short term; however, against the backdrop of the global financial crisis, the future of the euro and the ability of indebted EU governments to pay their bills remain very serious concerns.

The Maastricht Treaty also calls for serious steps toward political and military integration. The Maastricht Treaty obligates EU members to begin the process of formulating a common foreign policy and providing for a common European defense. Both ambitious and controversial, the Maastricht Treaty has been slow in achieving ratification. Great Britain and Denmark have ratified the treaty but retain severe reservations that allow them to opt out of monetary and political union. Currently, no member is taking serious steps toward political and military integration. The integration of the ten new members into the euro-zone will be a gradual process conditioned on economic and fiscal considerations. The EU suffered a serious blow in 2005 when both France and the Netherlands, key members of the organization, rejected the proposed EU constitution in popular referenda. The main features of the constitution were to change most decision-making rules and to establish a single foreign minister for Europe. After the French and Dutch rejections, the EU conceived of the Lisbon Treaty as an alternative constitution. Because of different national procedures, the Lisbon Treaty only needed the approval of the governments of most member states, rather than approval through a popular vote. The only member that required a national referendum was Ireland and it rejected the treaty in 2008. After some minor changes to the treaty, Ireland revoted and the Lisbon Treaty came into force in December 2009.

The future direction of the EU is uncertain, and whether further economic and political integration will take place depends on the continued success of the euro and developments in the wars in Iraq and Afghanistan. Observers still question whether European monetary stability will take precedence over immediate national interests. Excessive government deficits, coupled with economic instability, raise the possibility that national interests may trump monetary stability. Furthermore, the wars in Afghanistan and Iraq have further divided EU members many of whom are also members of the North Atlantic Treaty Organization (NATO), the principal security organization. Great Britain, Spain, Italy, and Poland contributed forces to the U.S. "coalition of the willing," which invaded Iraq causing tension with Germany and France. Both Poland and Romania were suspected of hosting secret CIA prisons, angering antiwar EU members. The United States–led war in Iraq in 2003 tested alliance commitments (Terriff 2004). French and German skepticism and opposition to the United States at the UN Security Council spilled over into NATO politics as well. Then secretary of defense Donald Rumsfeld referred to these allies as "Old" Europe and intimated that the future lay with the "New" Europe—the newest members of the NATO alliance (Roter and Sabic 2004, 517–542).

Many of the new members of NATO joined the "coalition of the willing," with Poland contributing the largest force.

NATO's role in Afghanistan has become more important. Initially, the United States had to engage in serious arm-twisting to get NATO members to contribute more troops to the International Security Assistance Force (ISAF), the NATO peacekeeping mission in Afghanistan. In 2006, NATO and ISAF took responsibility for security in Afghanistan, working in tandem with the Afghan government. The mission has been plagued by increasing levels of violence and increasing NATO casualties, making the allies reluctant to commit more troops. For those troops already there, their governments prevented some from being deployed in combat zones. U.S. defense secretary Robert Gates warned that NATO could become a two-tiered alliance, where some allies are willing to fight and die while others are not (Myers and Shanker 2008). At the June 2008 ministerial summit, Secretary Gates asked NATO allies to share a greater burden by providing more combat troops and pooling resources; however, allies made only modest promises (Shanker 2008, 3).

For many, Afghanistan represents an existential crisis for NATO (Kay 2005, 82; see comments by key public figures in Myers and Shanker 2008). Failure in Afghanistan could shatter the alliance, which would also shatter the 60-year-old security architecture for the EU. The continued existence of NATO seems likely but in what capacity is in dispute. If NATO were to become moribund, a mere "alliance on paper" and a shell of its former self, then the prospects of a Europe with a single foreign policy become a great deal more complicated. Regardless, the EU remains a most remarkable international organization because of its success in uniting the diverse cultures and politics in Europe, creating a single European identity and one of the strongest economies and currencies in the world.

The Organization of Islamic Conference

The OIC was created in 1969 by 24 Islamic states to safeguard the well-being of their peoples and of Muslims in general. According to Article II of the OIC Charter, the OIC seeks to strengthen Islamic solidarity; consolidate cooperation among member states in the economic, social, cultural, and scientific fields; safeguard the Holy Places; support the struggle of the Palestinian people; and eliminate racial discrimination and all forms of colonialism. Currently, it is a 57-member IGO that is based on the following principles:

1. the full equality of member states;
2. the observation of the rights to self-determination and noninterference in the internal affairs of member states;
3. the observation of the sovereignty, independence, and territorial integrity of each state;
4. the settlement of any dispute that may arise among member states by peaceful means;

5. a pledge to refrain, in relations among member states, from resorting
to force or threatening to resort to force against the unity and territorial
integrity or the political independence of any one member state.

The OIC principles are similar to most post–World War II IGOs in that they
recognize the sovereign equality of members, nonintervention, and the peaceful
settlement of disputes. Its membership is open to all Islamic states that seek to
uphold the principles of OIC. States wishing to join may submit an application to
the OIC and membership is decided on the basis of a two-thirds vote of the member states. The OIC is not as comprehensive or institutionalized as the EU;
however, it does seek to organize a very diverse group of states that govern well
over 1 billion Muslims. Its goals are the promotion and protection of Islam as a
religion as well as Islamic cultural values. The OIC is financed by member states,
and each member state's assessment is based proportionally on its national income.

The birth of the OIC was turbulent. Its creation in 1969 was a unified
Muslim response to the Israeli policies after the 1967 Arab–Israeli War, includ-
ing the occupation and annexation of Jerusalem. Known as Al-Quds to the
Muslim world, Jerusalem is home to one of Islam's most holy sites, the Aqsa
Mosque. The Aqsa Mosque sustained extensive arson damage while under
Israeli control, and the subsequent Arab and Muslim outrage prompted the
formation of the OIC (Ahsan 1988, 23). The OIC was created to safeguard
Muslim holy sites and to be a voice for the Palestinian people.

The OIC is structured around four major components. At the top is the
Conference of the Kings and Heads of State and Government, which is also
known as the Islamic Summit Conference. According to Article IV, the Conference
of Kings and Heads of State and Government is the supreme authority of the OIC
and, with an amendment to the Charter in 1981, it meets once every three years
or when the vital interests of the Muslim nations warrant. Next in the hierarchy
is the Conference of Foreign Ministers, which meets once a year or when the need
arises. According to Article V, the Conference of Foreign Ministers shall be held
for the following purposes:

1. to consider the means of implementing the general policy of
the Conference;
2. to review the progress in the implementations of resolutions adopted
at previous sessions;
3. to adopt resolutions on matters of common interest in accordance with
the aims and objectives of the Conference set forth in the Charter;
4. to discuss the report of the Financial Committee and approve the budget
of the Secretariat-General;
5. to appoint the Secretary-General and the four assistants to the
Secretary-General on recommendation of the Secretary-General;
6. to fix the date and venue of the coming Conference of Foreign Ministers;
7. to consider any issue affecting one or more of the member states
whenever a request to that effect is made with a view to taking
appropriate measures in that respect.

Meetings at the foreign ministerial level require a quorum of two-thirds of the member states, and resolutions and recommendations are adopted on the basis of a two-thirds majority. Voting is based on a one-state, one-vote basis; however, the norm is that members proceed on the basis of consensus (Ahsan 1988, 26). Decisions and resolutions adopted with a two-thirds majority are not binding on members that either abstained or voted against (Moinuddin 1987, 106). In addition to the annual meeting of the Conference of Foreign Ministers, which is held in the member states by rotation, regular sessions are held in New York during UN General Assembly sessions since 1980.

The OIC political leadership is supported by an elaborate bureaucracy called the Secretariat-General. The Secretariat-General is headed by the Secretary-General, who is appointed for a nonrenewable four-year term. The Secretary-General is the chief bureaucrat and represents the OIC to member states and other states and international organizations. Article VI commits the Secretary-General to political neutrality in that "in the performance of their duties, the Secretary General, his assistants, or the staff of the General Secretariat, shall not seek to receive instructions from any government or authority other than the Conference. Member states undertake to respect this equality and the nature of their responsibilities, and shall not seek to influence them in any way in the discharge of their responsibilities." The Secretary-General, with the assistance of his staff, is responsible for executing OIC decisions and resolutions, as well as monitoring and drafting reports on existing operations and programs.

OIC Ambitions and Challenges

The OIC is the principal forum for Islamic cooperation; however, cooperation has been difficult to achieve. The OIC is not a regional organization in that the geographic location of member states extends from Africa to Southeast Asia. OIC also includes observer states that have large Muslim populations, like Bosnia-Herzegovina, Central African Republic, and Thailand. The OIC represents not only geographic diversity but also political diversity. Members are Islamic republics, monarchies, military dictatorships, national democracies, and democratic socialist republics (Ahsan 1988, 19). National income among IOC members is also unevenly dispersed. Some states are among the wealthiest in the world, like Oman and Saudi Arabia, while others are among the poorest, like Mali and Afghanistan. Cooperation is further complicated by the fact that while all members share a colonial past, not all have shed the colonial yoke. "The alien structures implanted in the member states of the OIC during the colonial period have failed to cater to the needs of the majority of the people; the colonial system of education and administration which introduced alien values and outlook has estranged the majority of the masses from their rulers" (Moinuddin 1987, 69). As a result, dissension within the OIC was evident during the Lebanese Civil War, the Iran–Iraq War, the Persian Gulf War, and the current U.S. wars in Afghanistan and Iraq.

In spite of all the differences between OIC members, its single unifying force is Islam. This religious commitment also involves protection of the Holy Sites and fostering the self-determination of Muslim people, including Muslims living in non-Muslim countries. This has placed the OIC squarely in the middle of some of the most explosive conflicts in contemporary world politics: the Palestinian–Israeli crisis, the Arab–Israeli crisis, the Bosnian crisis, and the crises in Kashmir, Iraq, and Afghanistan. In addition, the OIC has sought to protect Islamic culture from Western secular materialism. The heads of state of the OIC have declared that "strict adherence to Islam and to Islamic principles and values as a way of life constitutes the highest protection for Muslims against the dangers that confront them. Islam is the only path that can lead them to strength, dignity, prosperity, and a better future. Islam is the pledge and guarantee of the authenticity of the *ummah* safeguarding it from the tyrannical onrush of materialism" (Ahsan 1988, 19).

The OIC represents a challenge to the West's liberal world order in that it articulates a different view of the relationship of religion to politics, private property, and human rights. In 2006, the OIC took a unified stand against offensive cartoons depicting Prophet Mohammed that were solicited and published by a Danish newspaper and republished around the world. Muslim anger at the cartoons slowly grew and eventually erupted into widespread violent protests. According to Fattah (2006, A1), the rage of the Muslim world crystallized at an OIC summit meeting in Mecca. According to one political observer, "It was no big deal until the Islamic conference when the OIC took a stance against it" (Fattah 2006, A1). The OIC played a pivotal role by authoritatively speaking against the cartoons, and its member states had a hand in organizing the demonstrations that left scores dead and Danish embassies in flames. Perhaps this is why some view even the OIC as a subversive transnational religious actor undermining state sovereignty in order to further the goal of creating a pan-Islamic religious community (Haynes 2001).

Currently, the greatest challenge for the OIC is how to respond to Islamic terror. The Taliban, when they governed Afghanistan, only had observer status in the OIC because only three states (Pakistan, Saudi Arabia, and the United Arab Emirates) recognized them. On October 9, 2001, the then secretary-general of the UN, Kofi Annan, called upon the OIC to take a central role in devising a strategy to combat terrorism (SG/SM/7989). The OIC condemned the 2001 attacks on the United States, but Iran, Iraq, and Syria also condemned the U.S. military response in Afghanistan. Other OIC members wanted to see the evidence against Osama bin Laden and the Al Qaeda network. A communiqué issued on October 10, 2001, stated that "the conference also expressed its concern that confronting terrorism could lead to casualties among innocent civilians in Afghanistan and asserted the importance of assuring the territorial integrity of Afghanistan and its Islamic character" (http://www.oic-oci.org/english/conf/fm/All%20Download/frmex9.htm). The OIC also warned against the targeting of other Muslim states. The U.S. invasion and continued occupation of Iraq further exacerbated tensions. The OIC is in the difficult position of trying to balance a desire to have a cooperative working relationship with the West and the UN with anti-U.S., anti-Western sentiments among large sections of the Muslim population.

The African Union

The African Union (AU) is a 53-member regional organization created in 2002 to replace the Organization of African Unity (OAU). Like most multipurpose IGOs, whether regional or global, the AU is serviced by organs that deal with peace and security (The Peace and Security Council); quasi-legislative functions (The Pan-African Parliament); bureaucratic administration/secretariat (The African Commission); legal matters (the African Court of Justice), and economic and social matters (The Economic, Social and Cultural Council). The intent behind the AU was to correct the shortcomings of the OAU, which suffered from a lack of resources and little political unity and was often derided as a "dictators club." African states wished the AU to approximate the relative success of the EU in promoting stability and economic growth.

The geopolitical makeup of the AU and the relative poverty of member states suggest that the AU has a long way to go. Dictatorships still abound, and the democratic models of South Africa and Kenya have recently experienced troubling internal instability. The AU continues to be publically critical of the International Criminal Court's (ICC) indictment of President Bashir of Sudan on charges of crimes against humanity, war crimes, and genocide. Bashir is still able to travel to AU meetings and many AU functions without fear of arrest or extradition. The AU and the OIC sent representatives to Bashir's 2010 inauguration after he won a tainted election in Sudan. Still, it is noteworthy that the fledgling organization's first foray into international peacekeeping was in Sudan. The AU was the first organization to deploy peacekeeping troops to the Darfur region and while the original number of AU peacekeeping troops was insufficient for stabilizing the region, they were the first IGO to tangibly commit to trying to manage the problems in Darfur.

The Association of Southeast Asian States

The Association of Southeast Asian States (ASEAN) was formed in 1967 and is currently a ten-member body that is committed to promoting international peace and stability among members and fostering economic integration. It is similarly structured to the other IGOs discussed earlier. In 2007, ASEAN member states held a widely anticipated summit meeting for the purpose of furthering the institutionalization of the organization. The Charter was changed to explicitly provide ASEAN with international legal personality and include a plan for creating an economic bloc similar to the EU. At the same time, ASEAN retained the notion of the sovereign equality of states and the principle of nonintervention.

The principal goal of the 2007 ASEAN summit was to create a free trade zone by 2015. Unlike the EU, however, ASEAN was unable to agree as to whether to put conditions on members for joining, such as improved human rights protection or democratization. One member, Myanmar (formerly known as Burma), figured prominently in the discussion as it is governed by a military dictatorship with one of the worst human rights records in the world. The government has incarcerated pro-democracy advocate Aung San Suu Kyi (albeit on house arrest), which has made her a symbol of democracy in South East Asia. Prior to the summit, Buddhist monks staged anti-government protests to call attention to the deteriorating economic and social conditions in the country. The government responded by killing dozens and beating and detaining hundreds of others. ASEAN as an organization did little to respond to the crisis, instead deferring to the government, choosing to view the matter as an internal affair.

In 2008, Cyclone Nargis hit Myanmar killing tens of thousands. The Myanmar government refused to allow international assistance even though the international media, as well as numerous NGOs, reported that millions of people were at risk. ASEAN once again refused to put pressure on the government, deferring to Myanmar's sovereign right to accept or reject aid. Prominent ASEAN members, such as Thailand, Indonesia, and Malaysia, have and continue to experience their own internal difficulties regarding democracy and human rights. They are reluctant to set a precedent that would allow outsiders to interfere in what they consider a domestic affair. This does not bode well for the creation of an ASEAN customs union or for a common currency as these initiatives required states to yield many of sovereign prerogatives to international organizations.

NONGOVERNMENTAL ORGANIZATIONS

NGOs are, for the most part, private, nonprofit organizations that have transnational as well as subnational ties. When the first NGO was founded is a matter of considerable debate. Some observers date the first NGO back to 1674 when the Rosicurian Order, an educational fraternal order, was founded (Jacobson 1984, 10). Others date the first NGO back to 1846 with the formation of the World Evangelical Alliance (Feld et al. 1994, 25). Still others think bigger, arguing that the Catholic Church, with its associated orders, represents the first NGO. Whatever the founding date, classifying NGOs is exceptionally difficult by virtue of their multiple origins, purposes, and resources. Some NGOs might be social welfare organizations, such as World Vision and Doctors Without Borders; or they might be professional organizations, such as the International Studies Association and International Chamber of Commerce. NGOs can serve specific purposes, such as the International Olympic Committee and Amnesty International, or they can be multipurpose organizations, such as the Catholic Church. NGOs, whose membership can be either compulsory or voluntary, currently number more than 100,000. Their financing comes from private sources, including membership dues, income from investment earnings, and charitable contributions from individuals and businesses. NGOs may also receive financing from public sources, such as government agencies, and IGOs, which usually comes in the form of contracts and/or grants. Some NGOs, such as Doctors Without Borders or World Vision, command budgets in excess of $200 million (Donini 1996, 91).

NGOs interact with a variety of international actors, ranging from states to IGOs and MNCs. NGOs attempt to influence the activities and the decision making of these actors with a view to getting their help in achieving some or all of the goals of NGOs. This means that NGOs may employ both direct and indirect lobbying techniques. Direct lobbying techniques involve contacting officials (and their staffs) in order to persuade them to adopt appropriate initiatives or policies. Such contacts can also involve attempting to educate officials and staff. This entails addressing the IGO, state, or corporate agency directly or submitting relevant documentation. Indirect lobbying techniques involve multinational advertising campaigns aimed at shaping or mobilizing public opinion. These techniques also include executing grassroots campaigns that take place at the international and national levels. Such campaigns consist of encouraging members and others to write letters or otherwise contact national and international public officials (e.g., Graubart 2008). NGOs even use national courts to achieve their aims. They may bring cases directly, file briefs, or provide legal representation to individuals or groups. NGOs utilize both human and capital resources to further their respective aims. Success tends to depend on NGO objectives and resources. NGOs with more resources and narrower goals tend to be more effective than those having fewer resources or those seeking to change policy in some broad or fundamental way. Those that lack resources or seek substantial change may even employ alternative participation strategies such as civil disobedience, which involves peaceful but illegal behavior, and violence.

NGOs play three interrelated roles in world politics. The first revolves around information-related activities and issue advocacy. Many NGOs are actively engaged in gathering information, as they have people on the ground who are directly involved with an issue or a problem. In addition, NGOs share information with states, IGOs, MNCs, and each other. Fact-finding is crucial for identifying and managing problems. Another aspect of NGO information activity is providing expert analysis. NGOs often employ highly qualified individuals who are widely recognized experts in their respective fields. They bring their education and experience to bear on defining and addressing global issues. This involves publishing studies and articles and issuing documentation. NGOs are even responsible for establishing standards, guidelines, and regulations. Environmental NGOs are especially noted for moving state actors toward stronger domestic environmental regulations and more cooperative international efforts to combat environmental problems (Betsill and Corell 2008).

A second role of NGOs in world politics involves carrying out the policies of states and IGOs. Implementing policy is largely the domain of social-welfare NGOs, which are, in effect, "subcontractors." Working in conjunction with states and IGOs, many social-welfare NGOs serve as vehicles for delivering immediate humanitarian assistance to persons displaced by natural disaster, civil disorder, violent conflict, or war. In addition to responding to crises and emergencies, these NGOs work on a continuous basis with populations mired in poverty and afflicted by disease and starvation. They distribute medicines and medical care. Some NGOs are specifically involved with women's health issues. They provide information on birth control methods, dispense contraceptives, and deliver pre- and postnatal care. Many NGOs are also involved with elementary and secondary education as well as providing technical and skills training. In many respects, the web of social-welfare NGOs and IGOs provides the only safety net that many people have. The work of NGOs is so important that many have formal consultative status with the UN.

The nongovernmental delivery of social-welfare services encounters numerous obstacles, which can emanate both from governments and from nongovernmental, domestic groups. For example, NGO relief activities in war zones can run afoul of government wishes, and NGO access to populations at risk can be restricted (Duffield 1998, 139–147). NGOs are, for the most part, respectful of sovereign prerogatives, but problems can arise when a government does not control all the territory within a state. NGOs that deliver humanitarian assistance to populations in rebel-held territory can easily be seen as subversive, in effect "giving aid and comfort" to the enemy. Negotiating NGO access to war-torn areas is an arduous and tedious process—one that involves strategic and military calculations as well as humanitarian concerns.

Religious groups in both developed and developing countries may oppose NGO activities relating to reproductive rights. They may see NGOs' activities in this area as sinful or disruptive of traditional family values. NGOs that monitor human rights compliance are seen as threatening the sovereignty of states and undermining governmental stability. As with all international issues and problems, disagreements about definition and implementation exist. NGOs seeking to deliver social-welfare services may actually be exacerbating or creating problems rather than solving them.

A third role that NGOs play in world politics revolves around private interactions. International relations is no longer solely the domain of states. NGOs are involved in a variety of private international transactions that bring together groups and individuals. This includes student and faculty exchanges and study-abroad programs. NGOs often host conferences that facilitate the exchange of ideas. In many cases, such conferences are held jointly with conferences sponsored by IGOs. Some NGOs, such as the Ford or Rockefeller Foundations or the Pew Charitable Trusts, award huge grants for the research and development of projects that promote international cooperation. Many observers see the dramatic increase in private NGO interaction as critical to the formation of a global civil society (Pishchikova 2006; Yamamoto 1996). This civil society is based on shared ideas and values that can be quite removed from governments and IGOs. NGOs are seen as "the conscience of the world," influencing the moral development of states and IGOs, as well as civil society (Willetts 1996).

While NGOs can play constructive roles in world politics, their activities, like the activities of other international organizations, can generate controversy. NGOs often represent particular interests that can conflict with other powerful interests. NGO antiglobalization efforts in Seattle, Prague, Davos, Genoa, and Washington and their willingness to challenge status quo politics have made them targets of criticism by businesses, governments, and IGO officials (McFeely 2000, 14). NGOs can also complicate the policy- and decision-making processes of governments and IGOs. NGOs have long sought transparency in, and access to, UN agencies. However, when granted access to agencies and conferences, problem identifying and problem solving often become intractable. For example, when the World Trade Organization (WTO) invited NGOs to comment on a trade dispute between Canada and France (regarding a French ban on a type of asbestos), the dispute settlement process of the WTO was reduced to a muddled mess (*The Economist* Dec. 9, 2000, 6). Apparently many developing states claimed that the WTO had overstepped its authority and demanded that it must rescind its invitation, which the WTO did, based on an obscure technicality. The result was a lack of confidence in the WTO on the part of NGOs and developing nations.

Are NGOs "friends or foes"? The answer to the question depends on your worldview. Some complain about "pretender NGOs" (see Fowler 1991, cited in *Foreign Policy* 2001, 18). One such type is a **CONGO**, a commercial NGO, which is "set up by businesses in order to participate in bids, help win contracts, and reduce taxation" (*Foreign Policy* 2001, 18). Businesses then claim that they are participating in cooperative partnerships and are being good global and local citizens. Another type of "pretender NGO" is called a **MANGO**: a mafia NGO that provides services "of the money laundering, enforcement, and protection variety; prevalent in Eastern Europe" (*Foreign Policy* 2001, 18). Still another type is the **PANGO**, or party NGO, which is an "aspiring, defeated or panned political party or politician dressed as an NGO; a species of Central Asia and Indo-China" (*Foreign Policy* 2001, 18). Many businesses, government officials, and social conservatives complain that many of the NGOs accredited by the UN are either radical, leftist, feminist, pro-abortion, pro-environment, or pro-homosexual, whose politics are disruptive and unrepresentative of the mainstream. In other words, the so-called civil society can be decidedly uncivil.

Regardless of the divergent views, NGOs are becoming more prominent as international actors and as objects of study (see, e.g., Heins 2008; Ohanyan 2009; Vedder 2007; Weiss and Gordenker 1996). These private, nonprofit international organizations serve as information gatherers and providers; they help carry out the policies of states and IGOs; and they serve as the building blocks of global civil society. NGOs offer vehicles for individuals and groups to participate in international politics outside of their respective nation-states. In other words, NGOs enable a broader range of participation beyond the usual foreign policy elites. NGOs allow the average individual the opportunity to shape and influence the international political landscape, albeit in small, incremental, and often controversial ways.

MULTINATIONAL CORPORATIONS

[MNCs are private, for-profit organizations that have commercial operations and subsidiaries in two or more countries.] As Gilpin (1987, 231) so aptly states,

> [N]o aspect of the political economy has generated more controversy than the global expansion of multinational corporations. Some consider these powerful corporations to be a boon to mankind, superseding the nation-state, diffusing technology and economic growth to developing countries, and interlocking national economies into an expanding and beneficial interdependence. Others view them as imperialistic predators, exploiting all for the sake of the corporate few while creating a web of political dependence and economic underdevelopment.

These views of MNCs, while contradictory, indicate the significance of MNCs to world politics. These international organizations command huge resources and can influence entire national economies. In subsequent chapters of this text, we explore why these divergent views of MNCs exist. But for our purposes here, we define MNCs and look briefly at their historical evolution.

The origins of the first MNC are difficult to pinpoint in part because of the confusion attending their definition. Many companies engage in international activities. They may import goods or buy raw materials from foreign sources. They may export products and engage in a variety of trading activities abroad. MNCs are different from companies that engage in international transactions in that ownership, management, and sales activities of MNCs extend beyond several national boundaries. They are usually headquartered in one country with subsidiaries in secondary countries. The expansion of MNCs into other national jurisdictions is called foreign direct investment (FDI). FDI is distinguished from other types of investments because MNCs retain ownership and managerial control over subsidiaries. The principal economic objective of MNCs is to produce goods and services for world markets at the least possible cost (Gilpin 1987, 232). MNCs, at least in economic theory, seek to maximize their profits and their shareholders' returns. MNCs may also engage in portfolio investments in which they purchase shares in national companies and other MNCs.

One of the earliest MNCs was the **East India Company**, which was founded in the late seventeenth century. Involved with the production and distribution of tea, spices, jewels, and textiles on a global basis, the East India Company was headquartered in London, with offices and operations in the Netherlands, the Americas, China, Southeast Asia, and India. It was a private, joint stock company that was chartered by the British Crown (Ralph et al. 1991, 628). In fact, the Company helped the British government administer much of India when it was a colony during the nineteenth and early twentieth centuries. The Company's trading posts evolved into political administrative units used by Great Britain to govern India (and to protect Company interests).

Today, more than 35,000 MNCs exist. This proliferation of MNCs has changed the nature of international trade and international relations in general. MNCs fall into five broad categories. The first category includes MNCs involved in agriculture and extractive industries. Multinational agribusinesses, like Archer Daniels Midland (ADM) and Dole, produce and process a wide variety of agricultural products for stores and supermarkets around the world. MNCs engaged in extractive industries control and process natural and raw materials used for manufacturing. This extractive category also includes powerful petroleum MNCs such as BP (formerly British Petroleum), Royal Dutch Shell, Exxon, and Amoco. These MNCs control not only the means of access to the vast majority of the world's oil supply, but the processing and refining of crude oil as well.

A second category of MNCs centers on the provision of financial services. Financial MNCs include multinational banks, brokers, and insurance companies. Multinational banks provide hundreds of billions of dollars in venture capital and loans to businesses and governments. They engage in international currency exchange and trade. International brokers buy and sell securities in most of the world's stock markets. Global insurance companies insure everything from the legs of international supermodels to loans made by multinational banks. International financial services are the grease on the axles of the global economy.

A third category of MNCs is industrial corporations. These MNCs are involved in the manufacture of durable and other kinds of goods. The most famous of the industrial MNCs include General Electric, Motorola, Sony, and IBM. Included in this category are the global automobile manufacturers such as Ford, Volkswagen, General Motors, Toyota, Honda, and Daimler-Chrysler. Industrial corporations have workforces that number in the hundreds of thousands, and they own production facilities and sales activities that extend all over the world. A subcategory is retail corporations such as the Coca-Cola Company, the GAP, TieRack, and Eddie Bauer.

A fourth broad category of MNCs is general service companies. These companies sell everything from fast food to telephone and Internet services. The golden arches of McDonalds are symbols of the global expansion of MNCs. Burger King, Pizza Hut, and Starbucks are common in urban areas everywhere. AT&T, Sprint, and MCI are global telecommunication giants, providing local, cellular, and long-distance telephone services to individuals around the world, however remote their locations. America Online, CompuServe, and Prodigy provide Internet access to both individuals and firms. Information and technology firms link the world with instantaneous communication capabilities.

Finally, the last category is the retail MNC, also known as the "big boxes." These MNCs include Walmart, Tesco, Carrefour, and Target, and they are unique because market share allows them to offer the products and services of the other multinationals, all under one roof. This gives them an enormous amount of leverage over other firms because they can demand that they meet their price point in exchange for important shelf-space.

The proliferation of MNCs has been accompanied by a "trimming down" of certain kinds of operations and the "megamergers" among others. In addition, MNCs have entered into intercorporate alliances with other firms in order to spread risk and gain access to national markets (Gilpin 1987, 255). Most MNCs are headquartered in developed countries, and their national origins tend to be American, European, or Japanese. Their owners are shareholders from all over the world, although the vast majority are from the advanced industrialized countries. They are one of the many different kinds of international organizations that participate in and are affected by world politics.

CONCLUSION

Today's international organizations are diverse and complex. IGOs are organizations for states. Some IGOs, like the UN or the OIC, promote cooperation among sovereign nation-states. Others, like the EU, foster the economic, political, and social integration of diverse societies. But world politics involves more than just the affairs of states. The activities of NGOs and MNCs show the interconnectedness of private and public international relations. The activities of IGOs, NGOs, and MNCs overlap, complementing and challenging one another. Their activities influence the lives of billions of people.

International organizations do not exist in a vacuum. They are part of a complex political world that is shaped by a variety of actors, processes, and events. Scholars and observers of international politics disagree about which actors, processes, and events are important for understanding the world. Consequently, they disagree about the nature, the roles, and relative importance of international organizations. These differences are the result of divergent worldviews, which condition their knowledge of the world. In Chapter 3, we examine the mainstream theoretical approaches to international relations—realism and liberalism. These approaches approximate widely held worldviews about the central influences of international politics and the role of international organizations within those politics.

KEY TERMS

Congress of Vienna 15
the League of
  Nations 16
the United Nations 17
the General Assembly 17
the Security
  Council 19
the International Court
  of Justice 19

the Economic and Social
  Council 20
the Trusteeship
  Council 21
the Secretariat 21
sovereign equality 22
peaceful settlement of
  disputes 22
nonuse of force 22

nonintervention 22
the European
  Union 25
the European
  Commission 26
the European
  Parliament 27
the European Court of
  Justice 27

SUGGESTED READINGS

Ahsan, Abdullan. 1988. *The Organization of Islamic Conference.* Herndon, VA: The International Institute of Islamic Thought.

Betsill, Michelle, and Elisabeth Corell, eds. 2008 *NGO Diplomacy.* Boston, MA: MIT Press.

Caporaso, James A. 2000. *The European Union: The Dilemmas of Regional Integration.* Boulder, CO: Westview Press.

Heins, Volker. 2008. *Nongovernmental Organization in International Society: Struggles Over Recognition.* New York, NY: Palgrave Macmillan.

Jensen, Nathan M. 2008. *Nation-States and the Multinational Corporation: The Political Economy of Foreign Direct Investment.* Princeton, NJ: Princeton University Press.

Kennedy, Paul. 2006. *The Parliament of Man: The Past Present and Future of the United Nations.* New York, NY: Random House.

Makinda, Samuel M., and Wafula Okumu F. 2008. *The African Union: Challenges of Globalization, Security and Governance.* London: Routledge.

Nugent, Neill. 2003. *The Government and Politics of the European Union.* 5th ed. Durham, NC: Duke University Press.

Solidum, Estrella D. 2003. *The Politics of ASEAN: An Introduction to Southeast Asian Regionalism.* Singapore: Eastern University Press.

Mainstream Theories

Realism and liberalism represent mainstream theories to international relations and international organizations. Often thought of as the "conventional wisdom" in global governance, realism and liberalism approximate widely held worldviews about how the world operates and the role of international organizations within the broader context of world politics. Both theories are rooted in rich intellectual traditions, and each describes different actors and dynamics in international politics. In this chapter, we systematically examine their philosophical roots and organizing assumptions. Then we apply those theoretical frameworks to explain the creation and maintenance of international organizations. We also look at the role international organizations play in the governance of world affairs.

REALISM

Realism is one of the oldest theories to international relations and is widely held as a worldview. Often referred to as power politics or realpolitik, realism's central focus is the acquisition, maintenance, and exercise of power by states. Power can be "hard" in that it is identified in terms of tangible military capabilities such as tanks, planes, troops, and missiles; or power can be "soft," meaning that it stems from the influence that results from ideas, wealth, or political/economic innovation. The realist lens focuses on nation-states and directs analysis toward particular sets of international issues—security, war, and other forms of violent conflict. Realism also asks certain kinds of questions. What accounts for order and stability in international relations? How does order deteriorate, and why does order break down? Realism analyzes the perennial issue in international relations—the use of violence.

Generally speaking, realism as a worldview and as a theoretical framework has grown out of European historical experience and scholarship. Why the preoccupation with security and war? The European continent has witnessed some of the world's more destructive and brutal conflicts, from the Thirty Years War (1618–1648) to the Napoleonic Wars (1803–1815) and from World War I (1914–1918) to World War II (1939–1945). European states have also engaged in the violent endeavor of imperialism, which is the quest for colonies and empires. Beginning in the fifteenth century, European expansion brought violence to every region of the world. The United Kingdom (Great Britain) once controlled so much territory that "the sun never set on the British Empire."

The European experience of war and imperialism has shaped the realist framework for understanding international relations. Outside Europe, many have embraced this framework and its worldview because the framework generates valuable insights and lessons regarding world politics. Realists are generally pessimistic about the independent role of international organizations, arguing that international organizations can neither constrain state behavior nor prevent war. After all, many of the aforementioned wars ended with the creation of international organizations—organizations that were supposed to keep the peace. For example, when the Napoleonic Wars ended, the Congress of Vienna and the Concert of Europe were created. But the Concert of Europe could not prevent World War I. And in the ashes of that war, the League of Nations was formed. Then, when the League of Nations failed miserably in its task of promoting international peace, the world again slid into global conflict. After World War II, the United Nations was established, yet another organization charged with maintaining international peace and security. Yet, war is still with us and violent conflicts abound. Why?

Many realists see war as the inevitable result of uneven power distributions among states, in which case international organizations can do little in the face of state power. International organizations are, for all intents and purposes, tools that powerful states use to control weaker states. And if international organizations are largely extensions of the great powers, they respond only to great-power interests and direction. That is, international organizations are important only as reflections of great-power values and norms regarding appropriate state behavior in international relations. Hence, global governance boils down to a **great-power concert**, which is thinly veiled by international organizations. When the security interests of the great powers conflict, international organizations are either discarded, ignored, or marginalized by the states that created them.

How did realists come to such conclusions regarding the role of international organizations? In the following section, we detail the philosophic underpinnings of realist theory in order to gain historical insight into contemporary realist thought.

Philosophic Roots of Realism

The philosophical tradition of realism is a rich one, dating back before Plato and Aristotle. Contemporary realists owe a particular intellectual debt to the great historian of Athens, Thucydides (ca. 460–401 B.C.). **Thucydides**, a general in the Peloponnesian War, analyzed the exercise of power by the city-states

Melos, Athens, and Lacedaemonia (Sparta) in his *The Peloponnesian War*, covering the period of conflict from 431 to 411 B.C. In this tome, Thucydides offered many insights regarding the role of fear, power, and alliances among competing city-states.

In one of his most dramatic and influential passages, "The Melian Dialog," Thucydides shows that power is the final arbiter of disputes in international relations. In this passage, we see the politics of power in action after Athens has militarily surrounded Melos and demanded the Melians' surrender. The Melians argue, assuring the Athenians that they pose no threat to the security or well-being of Athens. They plead that they are neutral in the conflicts between Athens and the surrounding city-states, so that attacking them would be immoral and unjust. The Athenians respond by insisting on the total surrender of Melos. Failure to do so would result in their destruction. According to the Athenian representatives, "You must act with realism on the basis of what we both think, for we both alike know that in human reckoning the question of justice only enters where there is equal power to enforce it and the powerful exact what they can and the weak grant what they must" (Thucydides 1963, 181).

The first realist lesson is clear: **Might makes right.** What is just and moral is relative and usually defined by the powerful. It is, after all, the victors who write the history books, and they are not going to portray themselves as brutal, violent oppressors. The victors in any war are always just and righteous liberators.

The second realist lesson is equally clear: [The strong do what they have the power to do and the weak accept what they have to accept.] This statement is self-evident, yet has implications: "Good" does not always triumph over "evil," hence the only way to escape the fate of the weak is to join the ranks of the strong. Unfortunately, the road to the ranks of the strong is paved with murder, cheating, stealing, and lying. Those who wish to be strong must put aside their moral or religious beliefs and be prepared to engage in the same kind of behavior. The acquisition and maintenance of power must be of overriding importance to the state, given the consequences of being weak. Not only is the very survival of the state at stake but also the right to establish international rules, values, and norms.

Thucydides also questions the usefulness of alliances, a type of international organization. A security alliance is predicated on the notion that an attack on one member of an alliance is an attack on all members of the alliance. By joining together in an alliance, members seek to deter potential aggressors (usually a common enemy) from attacking any member of an alliance. This also enables members to divert resources away from security—that is, maintaining a large standing military—to other pursuits such as economic or social welfare.

In Thucydides' account, the Melians had an alliance with the Lacedaemonians; thus the Melians cautioned the Athenians that an attack on Melos would provoke a response by Lacedaemonia. The Athenians responded, "When you imagine that out of very shame they [Lacedaemonians] will assist you, we congratulate you on your blissful ignorance, but we do not admire your folly. . . . The path of expediency is safe, whereas justice and honor involve action and danger, which none are more generally averse to facing than the

Lacedaemonians" (Thucydides 1963, 184). Thucydides shows that alliances can lull states into a false sense of security. In spite of its advantages, an alliance is valuable only if it is credible that the allies will stick together. The Melians banked on their alliance with Lacedaemonia, rendering themselves vulnerable. Their only hope was for Lacedaemonian intervention, an intervention that was not to come. Since the Melians could not defend themselves, they really had just two choices: surrender or be destroyed. The end of the story is not pleasant. The Melians chose not to surrender, and the Athenians attacked. The adult males were massacred and the women and children were enslaved.

The lesson of the Melian story is that states must guarantee their own survival through their own military power. What is perceived to be right, just, or moral will not guarantee survival. An alliance will not necessarily deter an aggressor nor does it necessarily mean an ally will help. Power is the only thing adversaries will understand. On a side note, Thucydides wrote *The Peloponnesian War* in part as a scathing critique of Athenian and Greek foreign policy in general. Today, however, Athens is remembered for neither its violence nor its crimes against its neighbors, but as the birthplace of democracy. And the Greek civilization is known more for its brilliant philosophers, stately architecture, and breathtaking sculpture than for its wars. In effect, the Greeks won.

Niccolo Machiavelli (A.D. 1469–1527) was another early realist. His *The Prince is* a classic analysis of statesmanship and power, well known as a guide for acquiring and maintaining political power—in a word, Machiavellianism. While Machiavellianism has assumed negative connotations owing to the cruel tactics advocated in *The Prince*, Machiavelli is very clear in showing how the accumulation and judicious use of power are necessary for political survival and for attaining social and political goals. Issues of justice, right, and wrong are negligible to the prince (ruler) and to the survival of the state. Rather, the prince must be willing to use violence and cruelty to maintain power.

Machiavelli asks the legendary question, Is it better to be loved or feared? And his answer is this: It is best to be both loved and feared; but if just one choice is possible, it is better to be feared. Feelings of love are likely to be fleeting, but fear makes foes and friends (potential foes) cautious in their dealings with the prince. Machiavelli thus advises against relying on idealistic notions of true friendship or shared values as a shield against potential aggression. Power and the fear of power are the prince's ultimate defense.

Like Thucydides, Machiavelli was deeply suspicious of alliances: "When one asks a powerful neighbor to come to aid and defend one with his forces, they . . . are as useless as mercenaries" (Machiavelli 1952, 77). Machiavelli and Thucydides stress state self-reliance as the decisive factor to survival, particularly as it relates to military defense. There is no guarantee that allies will do what they pledge to do. Furthermore, Machiavelli argues that relying on allies makes the prince a prisoner of those allies. The prince becomes vulnerable to the interests and desires of his allies, and the prince's own interests become compromised. Hence, the prince should avoid entangling alliances and pursue his own power.

Thomas Hobbes (1588–1679), a British philosopher, contributed to realist theory through his conception of the nature and the condition of man. Heir to Puritan notions of human nature, Hobbes conceived of men as essentially selfish and evil creatures. In a state of nature, man is pitted against man, and the only rule is survival of the strongest. Writing in the *Leviathan*, Hobbes characterized the state of nature as "continual fear and danger of violent death; and the life of man [as] solitary, poor, nasty, brutish, and short." Hobbes argued that one way to overcome the unsavoriness of human instincts and escape the state of nature is to vest power and authority in a leviathan—an absolute state, particularly a sovereign or king—that can enforce human agreements and protect citizens from each other. This so-called leviathan uses power to control the baser human instincts, allowing citizens to live civilly in a social environment relatively free from violence.

Realists have drawn upon Hobbes's state-of-nature theme, characterizing the international system as anarchy, or absence of higher authority, lacking a world government to enforce agreements or prevent aggression. Without a world government—or in Hobbesian terms, an overall leviathan—international relations can be very dangerous, so states must be prepared for war. Thus, the law of the jungle applies to nation-states existing in this international state of nature. The essence of interstate relations is conflictual and often violent.

Carl von Clausewitz (1780–1831), in *On War*, sees war as the "continuation of political activity by other means." von Clausewitz, a Prussian general who fought in the Napoleonic Wars, stresses the importance of military power for achieving certain political aims. Military power can be an appropriate and useful tool of states to accomplish their goals, especially when political pressure and negotiation prove ineffective. Twentieth-century heads of state have also noted the importance of military power. When told by aides that the pope was displeased with the Soviet treatment of Christians, Joseph Stalin reportedly responded, "How many divisions does the pope have?" And Mao Zedong, the leader of the communist revolution in China, is credited with the saying that "power comes from the barrel of a gun." Realists are noted for their emphasis on military power as the final arbiter of disputes.

Realism also has economic implications. **Alexander Hamilton** (1755–1804), for example, argued for the primacy of politics over economics in his "Report on Manufactures." Hamilton's view is considered an intellectual precursor to **economic nationalism** or neomercantilism (discussed later in this chapter) in its advocacy of a highly diversified economy based on industrial production. A strong, diverse domestic economy is crucial to a nation's security because it enables a state to take care of itself in times of crisis. Hamilton advocates a central role for the government in the development and protection of key national industries and the management of the economy.

Thucydides, Machiavelli, Hobbes, von Clausewitz, and Hamilton are representative of realism's rich intellectual and philosophical heritage. Contemporary realism builds upon their insights, accepting them as foundational assumptions for a theoretical framework that analyzes, explains, and predicts international relations.

Contemporary Realism

Contemporary realism embraces many variations—traditional realism, neorealism, structural realism, mercantilism, and neomercantilism. But whatever their differences, each of these variations rests on four organizing assumptions from which hypotheses, propositions, and generalizations may be deduced regarding the nature of international relations. Let's look at these assumptions in turn.

1. The state is the most important actor in international relations. Since the Treaty of Westphalia (1648), international relations have been based on political units called states. That treaty marked the decline of the transnational authority of the Roman Catholic Church and the rise of distinct territorial entities unified by monarchs who asserted absolute **sovereignty** within a defined territory. That is, states, or representatives of states (the government), have the final say regarding policy within their territorial jurisdictions.

Realists are quick to point out that while sovereignty and autonomy may be considered rights in legal theory, in practice that "final say" within a territory requires the power to deter outside intervention. In other words, autonomy stems from capability. The recognition of the sovereign nation-state in 1648 fundamentally changed the character of international relations. The Church no longer had even the nominal capability to maintain a transnational sovereignty, while monarchs were able to militarily establish territorial states, where they exercised jurisdiction. For realists, international relations since 1648 principally concern the activities and interactions between territorial states.

2. The state is a unitary and rational actor. This is a simplifying assumption, but it is analytically helpful for understanding international relations. Realists recognize that states are not, literally, unitary; they are composed of individuals, groups, and even diverse governmental actors such as legislatures and bureaucracy. However, all of these differing views are ultimately integrated through state structures so that the state speaks with one voice (Viotti and Kauppi 1993, 35). And that single voice speaks for a rational state—a single actor capable of identifying goals and preferences and determining their relative importance. The state is also capable of engaging in a cost–benefit analysis and choosing optimal strategies for achieving its goals.

The realist image of the state as an integrated unit possessing rationality has two advantages. First, analysis of international relations becomes less complicated if the state is viewed as a single actor that interacts with other actors. After all, the goal is to make generalizations and predictions, a goal that cannot be achieved unless the complex set of associations comprising international relations is simplified. Second, it allows analysts to paint the big picture, without getting bogged down in the minutiae of who said/did one thing or another in international relations.

3. International relations are essentially conflictual. While all realists accept this assumption, they differ in assigning reasons for it. Traditional realists

see international relations as inherently conflictual because they are pessimistic in their assessment of human nature itself. Traditional realists, such as Hans Morgenthau and E. E. Carr, are largely Hobbesian. Human beings are, essentially selfish, aggressive creatures prone to base behavior. States are human creations; therefore, states must possess these same characteristics. While some states may strive for goodness and peace, they must always guard against aggression, arming themselves to defend against other states possessing less virtuous motives.

Structural realists point to structural, or systemic, attributes that contribute to international conflict and condition the behavior of states. The international system, according to structural realists, is characterized by anarchy and the **balance of power**—both of which shape state actions. Kenneth Waltz (1959), for example, argues that anarchy is a permissive cause of war because there is no higher authority or world government to prevent aggression. States must resort to "self-help" in order to secure their survival and their national interests. All states want to continue to exist regardless of government type, ideology, or demographic characteristics. All are subjected to anarchy. All behave in the same predictable, rational ways as a result. As Waltz (1959, 201) points out, "States do not even enjoy an imperfect guarantee of their security unless they set out to provide it for themselves. If security is something the state wants, then this desire, together with the conditions in which all states exist, imposes certain requirements on foreign policy that pretends to be rational. The departure from the rational model imperils the survival of the state."

Anarchy compels states to arm themselves for self-defense. However, the acquisition of arms is itself a provocative act. Other states must respond in kind or risk attack or destruction. This response leaves the first state no better off than it was before, so it must acquire even better weapons to counter the threat. Then the other states must respond in kind. And so on. Anarchy leads to arms-racing and arms-balancing behavior on the part of states. States with good and kind leaders will engage in the same kind of behavior as selfish and evil leaders because they exist in the same international environment.

States must also contend with another systemic feature, the distribution of capabilities. More commonly known as the balance of power, the distribution of capabilities affects the power calculation of states. According to structural realists, order and stability are maintained through a balance of power whereby states seek military and other capabilities in order to deter each other from attacking. States may also form alliances; however, those alliances are rarely permanent. For the realist, order and stability mean the absence of war or at least a reduced likelihood. This is achieved through a relatively equal distribution of power. If all states possess enough military capabilities to credibly defend themselves and inflict significant damage on an aggressor, then potential foes are discouraged from making war. Furthermore, the possession of capabilities, both military and economic, often translates into influence that can enable states to get other states to do things that they may otherwise not do.

The distribution of capabilities in the international system is not static, and shifts in the balance of power can threaten international stability. Several factors can disrupt the status quo. Technological innovations can very quickly give one state a significant military or economic advantage over others. The United States was the first to develop and deploy atomic weapons, and after using atomic weapons against Japan during World War II, it became the undisputed military power in the world. But that advantage was short-lived. The Soviet Union exploded an atomic bomb in 1949, and Great Britain and France followed suit shortly thereafter. For those few years, however, every state in the international system was vulnerable to a nuclear attack because they had no credible deterrent.

Uneven economic growth rates can also disrupt the status quo, causing shifts in the balance of power. States and their economies grow at different rates. Some states are rising powers, while others are declining. Consider contemporary China, for example. China's potential for economic growth and development is staggering. China is likely to grow at a faster rate than most other states; this growth can lead to international instability and conflict as other states increasingly feel threatened. States must adjust their policies to account for changes in the balance of power.

4. Security and geostrategic issues, or high politics, dominate the international agenda. Given the hostile international environment and the dire consequences associated with international war, national security is the top priority of states. Traditional realists see the acquisition of power as the principal strategy for achieving national security. States will engage in power-maximizing behavior, particularly as it relates to their military capabilities. Other international issues, including economics, the environment, human rights, and poverty, occupy the realm of **low politics**. States may address these issues but by no means treat them as priorities.

Neorealists modify the traditional realist position by ascribing greater importance to economic issues and using economic, rational choice theory to make realism more scientific. Neorealists emphasize economic issues because they relate to national power and security. The neorealist's economic counterpart is the neomercantilist. These economic theorists evince a realist orientation in their focus on states in the international economy. International political economy is a subfield of international relations that examines on the relationship between markets and states. **Neomercantilists** see participation in a highly interdependent world economy as necessary for attaining and maintaining great-power status. However, interdependence, of necessity, limits the autonomy of the state because states are reliant on each other to varying degrees. Neorealists and neomercantilists argue that interdependent relationships are rarely symmetrical. States foster dominant, asymmetrical interdependent relationships with others and manipulate these relationships to their advantage. States also seek to minimize interdependent relationships in which they are vulnerable. Furthermore, states intervene in the domestic and international economy to protect industries that contribute to their wealth and power.

Neorealists/neomercantilists see certain types of economic activities, especially industrial production, as crucial to the power and security of the state. They also recognize that quests for military power and economic development are not necessarily compatible. The **trade-off hypothesis** posits that excessive spending in the military sector can compromise economic health. Also known as the "guns *v.* butter" hypothesis, the trade-off hypothesis suggests that states will seek to maximize security, not power. The acquisition of power is not the principal goal of states, as traditional realists suggest. Rather, neorealists/neomercantilists argue that states are often willing to satisfy, not maximize, military security, exchanging some military power for robust economic health.

Neorealists do not consider all types of economic activity to be equally important. They are not concerned with the international trade in potato chips or shoes or basketballs. Neorealists are interested in industries in leading sectors of the economy—those sectors that spur economic growth and generate spin-off industries. In the past, leading sectors included textiles, steel, durable goods (refrigerators, stoves, etc.), and automotives. Durable goods and automotives remain important today, but computers, technology, and telecommunications have also emerged as leading sectors. Neorealists/neomercantilists advocate industrial policies that promote a state's competitiveness in leading sectors because they foster diversification and development, thereby enhancing state wealth and power.

In sum, contemporary realism is a mixture of variations of political realism and economic realism (mercantilism and neomercantilism). This worldview shapes the way realists see international organizations in international relations. In the next section, we examine realist explanations for the nature of international organizations—why they are created and how they work—in the context of sovereign states struggling for power in a hostile international environment.

Realism and the Nature of International Organizations

Realists argue that no hierarchy of authority exists in international relations. The international system is characterized by anarchy, where authority resides with each individual state. No international entity exercises jurisdiction over states or reviews their domestic or foreign policy decisions. Anarchy, however, does not mean chaos. The international system is, in fact, quite orderly because a power hierarchy does exist among states. Some states are endowed with a plentitude of resources and, through design or chance, have attained great-power status. Realists tend to classify states in terms of this hierarchy as super, great, middle, or lesser powers. And it is through this power hierarchy that the creation and nature of international organizations is explained.

Hegemonic stability theory is a widely accepted explanation for the creation and behavior of international organizations. According to Robert Gilpin,

> An international system is established for the same reasons that any political system is created; actors enter social relations and create social structures in order to advance particular sets of political, economic or other interests. Because the interests of some of the actors may conflict with those of other actors, the particular interests that are most favored by the social arrangements tend to reflect the relative powers of the actors. (Gilpin 1981, 9)

International organizations and law thus represent the social arrangements among states whereby the interests of the powerful are institutionalized.

One type of power distribution is a unipolar, hegemonic system in which "a single powerful state controls and dominates lesser states in the system" (Gilpin 1981, 29). The dominant state, or hegemon, creates international organizations and regimes to further its own interests and values in the international system. The hegemon uses its wealth and dominant power to create international organizations and bears the costs of maintaining them. The hegemon also provides incentives, such as security guarantees or economic assistance, in order to get other states to join. Once the international organization is established, the dominance of the hegemon and the tangible incentives it offers encourage other member states to defer to the hegemon's leadership.

Realists tend to focus on international organizations that are intergovernmental and public in nature. Since states are the most important actors in international relations, the organizations to which they belong become the subject of analysis. Adherents of hegemonic stability theory see international organizations as an extension of the hegemon. The effectiveness of international organizations is directly related to the hegemon's power. As the power of the hegemon declines, so does its support for the international organizations it has created. The diffusion of the hegemon's power also emboldens those who stand to benefit from a change in the status quo. These states will challenge existing institutions and norms, and ultimately seek to overthrow the existing order. For many realists, hegemony is required for the formation of international organizations, and their maintenance requires continued hegemony (Keohane 1984, 31).

Consider the creation of the United Nations in 1945. Its principal sponsor in terms of political leadership and finance was the United States—the only victor to emerge from World War II virtually unscathed, both geostrategically and economically. Moreover, the United States was in sole possession of atomic weapons. Clearly, it was the most dominant state, a hegemon, a world leader. The UN Charter outlines several purposes for the institution, purposes that were directly linked to U.S. interests. First, the UN was charged with maintaining international peace and security. This task was given to the UN Security Council, which then consisted of five permanent and six nonpermanent members. (In 1965, the nonpermanent membership in the UN Security Council was expanded to 10 to reflect the overall increase in UN membership.) The permanent members were the World War II victors, the United States, Great Britain, France, the Soviet Union, and China, each of which had an absolute veto over Security Council decisions.

During the early years of its operation, the Council both considered and adopted U.S. initiatives. And, in its first three years, when the Security Council held more than 130 meetings, it was widely considered to be an effective instrument of international governance (Bennett 1995, 63). In 1949, however, two events signaled a dramatic shift in the global balance of power. First, the Soviet Union exploded an atomic bomb. Second, control over mainland China was seized by communists led by Mao Zedong. The nationalists, led by Chiang Kai-shek, were exiled to Taiwan, an island off the coast of the mainland. This shift in the global balance ended the effectiveness of the Security Council in international security affairs.

Tension between the communist, totalitarian Soviet Union and the capitalist, democratic United States was evident prior to 1949; however, the power differential minimized the likelihood of conflict. After all, the Soviet Union had been ravaged by war. It had lost more than 25 million people and was economically devastated. But a few years of relative peace and the acquisition of nuclear weapons put the revisionist Soviet Union in a position to challenge U.S. world leadership. The Soviet veto made it difficult to reach UN collective security decisions. The Security Council also lost credibility in the developing world because the United States refused to recognize communist China. Until 1971, it was Taiwan that represented China on the Security Council. The idea of UN collective security under U.S. leadership was dead. Thus, the United States turned to the North Atlantic Treaty Organization (NATO), which was created that same year. Used as a limited collective security provision for Western Europe, NATO was dominated by the United States.

Collective security under the UN Security Council between 1949 and 1990 was virtually nonexistent, with one notable exception. In 1950, the Security Council authorized the use of force by member states to repel a North Korean attack on South Korea. The Security Council resolutions passed only because the Soviet Union was boycotting the Council in protest against communist China's being denied UN membership and a permanent seat on the Council. During this Cold War period, threats to international peace and security came largely from one or more permanent members of the Security Council, each of which could impose unilateral force. Moreover, these members could veto any condemnation or response to their action. The British/French/Israeli invasion of Egypt (1956), the Soviet invasion of Afghanistan (1979), and the U.S. invasion of Grenada (1984) illustrate the signal failure of UN collective security to deter aggression and maintain peace and security. If great powers wish to use force, no organization is going to stop them.

The UN's failure was rooted in power politics and the underlying political order. That is, UN collective security measures work only when the powerful states want them to work. UN successes in collective security (discussed extensively in Chapter 5) were a result of a congruence of great-power interests, a congruence that was short-lived. The balance of power in the post–Cold War era has changed rapidly. The United States is widely considered a declining hegemon and has been unwilling or unable to provide financial support for the UN or its activities. It is slow to pay its dues and often seeks to use its financial contributions as leverage to manipulate the UN. The United States, for the most part, fought the Korean War and paid for it. Forty years later in the Persian Gulf, the United States was forced to go, hat in hand, to its allies and ask them to pay for the use of U.S. military force. The decline of U.S. capabilities undermines its ability to lead. In other words, the United States either cannot or will not bear the costs of supporting its own creation. The inability of the United States to get UN authorization for its war against Iraq in 2003, largely because of the opposition of other great powers—France, Russia, and China—demonstrates the weakness of the United States and the growing importance of other states and their willingness to challenge it.

Realists also recognize that international organizations can be formed without the benefit of a hegemon or world leader. International organizations can be created when states have common interests or common problems. For example, after the end of the Napoleonic Wars, the Congress of Vienna (1815) established the Concert of Europe in an effort to keep the peace in Europe. The great powers were willing to collude because each had an interest in avoiding war with the other, and hence in preventing any single state from gaining too much power. Europe in 1815 was a multipolar system; but instead of generating conflict, the great powers cooperated to avoid another continental war. And, arguably, the Concert of Europe succeeded in keeping the peace until World War I. However, when the balance of power shifted, the great-power interests changed, too, together with the efficacy of great-power cooperation.

Contemporary realist analyses of international organization and cooperation often employ game theory as a tool to explain why cooperation is difficult under conditions of anarchy. Since game theory is utilized by both realists and liberals to explain cooperation, or the lack thereof, it deserves a brief overview here.

On Game Theory

Game theory, which is a variation of rational choice theory, originated with economists who were trying to explain choices among actors participating in a market. Although game theory employs jargon that can daunt nonspecialists, that jargon can readily be translated into more familiar language. Students, then, need not fear the logic of game theory nor shy away from some of the explanations that logic generates. In simple terms, game theory seeks to explain economic and political choice by placing that choice in the context of a game—a game based on several governing rules or assumptions.

The first of game theory's assumptions is that rational actors seek absolute gain when choosing among strategies. That simply means that actors choose the best possible outcome for themselves, no matter what other actors might gain. This assumption is important for game theorists because they expect egoistic actors to think only in terms of their own gains—and not to think in relative terms, weighing their gains against those of others. Another assumption, at least for a simple game, is "perfect" information. This means that all the actors know all the payoffs (the possible outcomes) and all the possible strategies of other actors. In more complex games, this assumption is relaxed to include imperfect information. In this case, payoffs and actors may not be known, so probabilities have to be assigned. Fortunately for us, simple games are most often utilized to explain the behavior of states in international relations.

Many traditional realists and mercantilists see international relations and economics as a zero-sum game. In a zero-sum game, the interests of players are diametrically opposed, and one player's gain is balanced by another player's loss (Binmore 1992, 237). Chess is a zero-sum game, as is backgammon: One player wins while the other loses. What does this mean in the context of international relations? When one state gains a greater degree of security, the security of other states is lessened by that degree. That's a zero-sum game. Under such conditions, a state has no incentive to cooperate with others or even modify its behavior. The state's goal is to maximize its own power and security even if it is at the expense of other states.

Traditional realists and mercantilists are criticized for characterizing all international relations as strictly zero-sum. International relations may be competitive, but they need not necessarily be zero-sum. In fact, incentives to cooperate often exist. Realists respond that the security dilemma that states face in an anarchical environment is a **Prisoners' Dilemma**. The Prisoners' Dilemma is a simple game, but it clearly shows why cooperation is difficult to achieve even in non–zero-sum situations.

The Prisoners' Dilemma works like this. Two armed-robbery suspects, A and B, are in police custody. They have, in fact, committed the crime, but the only evidence is a gun the police found in their car. The police separate the prisoners and then question each one in a separate room—"the box." There, the police present each one a choice among four possible scenarios:

Scenario 1: Confess to armed robbery and rat out your buddy. Then you walk and your buddy goes up the river for twenty years.

Scenario 2: Clam up and let your buddy rat you out for armed robbery. Then you go up the river for twenty years and he walks.

Scenario 3: You both confess to armed robbery. Then you both get a deal—just ten years.

Scenario 4: You both clam up. Then the armed robbery goes away, but you both get three years for illegal possession of a firearm.

Surprisingly, Scenario 3 is the option of choice. Both prisoners confess to armed robbery and each receives a ten-year sentence.

What? Wouldn't it make more sense if both remained silent? Surely, being convicted of illegal possession—and getting a three-year sentence—is more rational than confessing to the greater crime. But the decision to confess is also rational. Here's why. Recall that the rules of game theory say that each player is seeking absolute gains. That is, each player wants to get the best possible outcome for himself. The other rule is that each player knows all the possible strategies (moves) the other player can make. Not that each player knows what the other player will actually do—but each player can predict the move on the basis of what is rational from the other player's standpoint. Now consider the logic from Prisoner A's standpoint—"If I clam up and my buddy rats me out, I get the worst possible outcome—twenty years. If I rat him out and he clams up, then I get the best possible outcome—the walk." So Prisoner A has an incentive to confess. But what Prisoner A gets depends on what Prisoner B does. Prisoner B is going through the same rational, clam/rat thought process. So Prisoner B has an incentive to confess, too.

At this stage, each prisoner is inclined to confess, even though the outcome—ten years for armed robbery—is clearly not the best possible for the two of them. In fact, it would be optimal for both if each were to remain silent; that way, each would get just three years. So why wouldn't both prisoners just keep mum? The trouble is that that choice is not rational. If Prisoner A knows that Prisoner B will stay silent, then Prisoner A could "cheat," or defect: He could confess and get the walk. After all, a walk would be optimal for A, much better than serving three years. But that option isn't available because Prisoner B is considering this same strategy . . . and Prisoner A knows that. So, the only solution to the Prisoners' Dilemma is for both suspects to confess, each one anticipating the other's confession.

The Prisoners' Dilemma demonstrates how rational behavior can lead to suboptimal outcomes and why cooperation is difficult to achieve. This is why realists argue that even in positive-sum games, where all parties can achieve gains, cooperation remains unlikely. The security dilemma faced by states is quite similar to the dilemma faced by the suspects in the box.

Realists have never argued that international cooperation does not occur. Situations do exist in which states must coordinate their policies by agreeing on international rules to avoid undesirable outcomes (Krasner 1991, 338). However, these situations tend to reside in the realm of low politics. While cooperation may occur in such international issue areas as transportation and telecommunication, international and national security are not conducive to such cooperation. The overriding significance of security, together with rapid technological developments, forces states to be vigilant. Furthermore, as Susan Strange (1983, 345) states, "All those international arrangements dignified by the label regime are only too easily upset when either the balance of bargaining power or the perception of national interest (or both together) changes among those states who negotiate them."

For realists, international organizations are either created by a hegemon or formed through great-power cooperation. Realists tend to conceive of international organizations as intergovernmental organizations (IGOs) that serve as extensions of the hegemon or function as great-power directorates. Their activities are directly tied to the powerful states that control them. As a result, international organizations are no more than the sum of their member states; hence their behavior or lack of effectiveness can be explained by the underlying power distribution in the international system.

Realism and the Role of International Organizations

The explanations generated by realism regarding the creation of international organizations suggest that these organizations play one of two roles in the realist world. One role is a marginal one. International organizations matter only at the fringes of world politics (Mearsheimer 1994/1995). They may foster cooperation in noncontroversial issue areas where states have common interests. However, they rarely constrain state behavior in issue areas where interests are diverse and opposed. In other words, international organizations play little or no role in maintaining international peace and security. Rather, balance-of-power realities dictate whether or not war will break out.

International organizations can also play an intervening role in great-power calculations. These organizations are used by the hegemon and great powers to further their interests in the international system (see, e.g., Foot et al. 2003). Other non–great-power states may also use international organizations to attain goals and to have a voice within the existing system. But, in terms of constraining state behavior, international organizations have little influence. States will bypass or ignore international organizations if their immediate security or important national interests are at stake.

In spite of this rather pessimistic view, international organizations do matter in the realist world. Schweller and Preiss (1997) point out that international organizations perform several important functions. First, international organizations provide a mechanism for great-power collusion. Great powers usually benefit from the existing order and have an interest in maintaining it. After all, the fact that they are great powers suggests that they are doing well under existing rules and institutions. International organizations may not be useful if great-power interests collide, but do permit great powers to control other states in international systems. Second, international organizations are useful for making minor adjustments within the existing order, while the basic underlying principles and norms remain uncompromised. An enduring international order must be flexible to account for changes in national interest and for rising and declining states. Third, international organizations can be agents of international socialization. International organizations legitimize the existing order, thereby gaining the acceptance of the status quo by those who are dominated. Finally, "international institutions are the 'brass ring' so to speak: the right to create and control them is precisely what the most powerful states have fought for in history's most destructive wars" (Schweller and Preiss 1997, 13).

REALISM AND INTERNATIONAL LAW

The role of international law in the world of the realist is twofold. Traditional realists see international law as largely irrelevant (see, e.g., Barker 2000, 70–76 and Setear 2005). International law is made by states when it is in their interest and it is broken by states when it is in their interest. Enforcement of the law is nonexistent and the only law that really matters in world politics is the struggle for, and the maintenance of, power (Slaughter-Burley 1993, 207). International relations and global problems revolve around "political" dilemmas and questions, which, even in the most legalistic society, do not lend themselves to a legal or judicial solution. Contemporary realists argue that international norms and agreements result from states acting in their self-interest, but acknowledge that the law can play a meaningful role under limited circumstances (Posner 2009, xv). They acknowledge that international law and courts exist, but reject the idea that international law somehow transcends states. States create and enforce international law because they have self interest in regularized, predictable behavior. Yet, self-interest also means that international collective action and cooperation in important areas will remain rudimentary and sporadic. The proliferation of international law and organizations in the last twenty years is more the result of state dissatisfaction with the existing rules and institutions rather than evidence of a global legalism governing an increasingly interdependent and law abiding international community (Posner 2009, 105–106.) As we will see in subsequent chapters, realists caution against what they see as the idealistic belief that international law and organizations can solve the world's most pressing problems.

Criticisms of the Realism

Realism as a theory has several advantages. It is parsimonious, which means it is a simple and lean framework. At the same time, realism has extraordinary explanatory power regarding international relations and world politics, particularly as it relates to war and violent conflict. Given the complexities of world politics, realism's parsimony and insights have contributed to its popularity and longevity.

But realism is not without its critics. Liberalism, Marxism, feminism, and constructivism mount challenges to many realist explanations of international relations and analyses of international organizations. However, a specific criticism of realism is its conceptual imprecision. Realism is based on the concept of power. After all, realism is power politics. But what is power? Very little consensus exists regarding a precise definition of power. Some see power as tangible, concrete military capabilities. Power is measured by the number of tanks, planes, and nuclear weapons a state has. Others see power as including potential. Japan and Germany are considered powerful, even though they do not possess any significant military capability. Their economic and technological prowess indicates that they could put forth a formidable military. And what about states that do have formidable militaries, but do not have the will to use them? Thus, many realists conceive of power as a thing—a thing that includes both tangible and intangible elements.

Power is also conceived of as influence. Influence means the ability to get other actors to do what they would otherwise not do. This definition of power is problematic because we rarely know what an actor would have done in the first place. Analysis also becomes complicated because power is linked with authority. The pope is a powerful man, not because he has any divisions but because he commands moral and religious authority. Is U.S. hegemony based on its tangible capabilities, or has it been able to influence others through the power of its ideas regarding democracy, equality, human rights, and self-determination?

Another imprecise concept bandied about by realists is national interest. States seek power in the international system to secure their national interests. States create international organizations to further their national interests. States make political calculations based on their national interests. Outside of state survival, defining the national interests of states is next to impossible. Interests vary, and claims of national interest have been used to justify almost every kind of state behavior. This leads to a circular logic. Realists assume rational states act in the national interest. Yet, national interest is measured by state action. Hence, anything the state does is, by definition, in the national interest. So, when the United States participates in the UN, it does so because it is in the national interest to do so. And if the United States ignores the UN, it does so because it is in the national interest to do so. Realism, thus, becomes one big tautology: Because the national interest can be construed to mean anything, it explains nothing.

In spite of these conceptual shortcomings, realism retains a great deal of value in explaining international relations and the behavior of international organizations. Realism paints a rather bleak picture of international relations as hostile, conflictual, and warlike. Realists are not very optimistic about the independent role international organizations play in preventing war and violent conflict. International organizations are tools of the great powers to control lesser states without dominating them by force. They are agents of the dominant power(s) and serve great-power interests at the expense of others. International organizations do not promote some idealized notion of the "collective good." For realists, the so-called collective good is defined by the dominant power(s)—in effect, what is good for me is good for the collective. The behavior and priorities of international organizations are to be understood in terms of the motivations and priorities of leading member states.

LIBERALISM

Liberalism challenges the pessimistic worldview of realism by painting a more encouraging picture of the relations between societies. Liberals see international relations as a mixture of cooperation and conflict and argue that international organizations can play a positive, constructive role in promoting international stability and global welfare. For liberals, the nature of international relations has fundamentally changed during the latter half of the twentieth century for three substantive reasons. First, the importance of military force in international relations has waned. Conventional weapons have evolved, becoming so destructive that their usefulness for achieving foreign policy goals has declined. Weapons of mass destruction (chemical, nuclear, and biological) function as effective deterrents, but are not practical for war fighting. Second, the spread of democracy has instilled values of compromise and the rule of law in governments—values that inhibit decision makers from resorting to war to settle disputes. Third, societies are not as isolated from each other as they were in the past. Societies are linked together by global markets and global production. States are linked together by instantaneous mass communication, rapid transportation, and the

Internet. Societies are increasingly seeing themselves as part of a greater whole rather than as ships of state navigating the treacherous waters of war. International relations today is significantly different from the geostrategic power game played earlier in the twentieth century on the European continent. Liberals, then, are much more optimistic about the prospects for international peace.

"Liberalism" is a term that has different and often contradictory meanings. In the United States, many journalists use the word "liberal" to indicate a position along an ideological spectrum. Liberals on this spectrum are to the left of conservatives and tend to favor government policies that promote social welfare, health care, and civil rights. Conservatives, on the other hand, tend to favor government policies that promote business, prisons, and the military. Hence, Speaker of the House Nancy Pelosi (D-CA) and activist Jesse Jackson are considered liberals, while former president George W. Bush and commentator Rush Limbaugh are considered conservatives. This journalistic usage of "liberalism," especially in the United States, suggests a political position that is rather leftist in nature.

However, liberalism means something quite different to economic and political theorists. Liberalism in economics refers to a belief in capitalism and its emphases on profit, private property, and a free, self-regulating market. In political theory, liberalism means a belief in individual equality, individual liberty, participatory democracy, and limited government. Both these definitions represent classical liberalism. Former presidents Ronald Reagan and George W. Bush, both conservatives in a journalistic sense, are classical liberals. Students should recognize that the majority of policy makers in the United States regardless of political party have a liberal worldview because they have been socialized by liberal ideas. The political and economic systems of the United States are based on liberal principles that are institutionalized in the U.S. Constitution and in the nation's laws. As a result, most citizens in the United States, including policy makers, have a liberal orientation (although they may disagree regarding the necessity and the extent of government regulation).

Liberalism emerged out of the Anglo-American experience of political and economic development. Both Great Britain and the United States evolved into capitalist democracies, and both have been the world leader or the hegemon in international relations. Both have promoted a liberal vision of world order (limited politics/emphasis on free trade) since 1850, largely because of their disillusionment with the politics and economics of continental Europe. Through example and incentives, a hegemonic Great Britain (1815–1917) established free trade (reducing tariffs) and a stable monetary order (the gold standard). The political interests of states were subordinated to international economic stability and market considerations. Both the United States and Great Britain benefited extensively from free trade of wealth and economic diversification.

World War I marks a turning point in modern international relations and is considered by many to be a senseless and irrational war because states fought for no identifiable geostrategic reason (Tuchman 1984). Rather, alliances and virulent nationalism drew states into "accidental war." After the war, President Woodrow Wilson stated that U.S. foreign policy would support democracy, anticolonialism, and self-determination internationally. Woodrow Wilson was the principal sponsor of the League of Nations, and these values were incorporated in the League Charter.

Unfortunately for international stability and the League of Nations, the United States was unwilling to assume a liberal leadership role. Domestic politics and a resurgence of isolationist sentiment resulted in the U.S. Senate refusing to ratify the League of Nations Charter, leaving the League with no capable leadership. Great Britain was willing, yet unable of bearing the costs of sustaining the liberal international economic order as it had in the past. World War I nearly bankrupted Great Britain and weakened it politically, economically, and socially.

Absent effective leadership, states reverted to nationalistic, mercantilist policies. Capitalism for all intents and purposes collapsed, and the resulting Great Depression gave rise to the very illiberal ideology of fascism. The world once again was at war in 1939. World War II ended in 1945, and the United States emerged from the war as the dominant state in terms of military and economic capabilities—in a position, politically and economically, to shape world order and to fashion a system in which it and other states could mutually benefit. The United States institutionalized liberal rules and norms in international politics through the creation of international organizations and a capitalist international economic order.

Liberalism is rooted in an intellectual tradition that is as rich and respected as realism. In the following section, we examine the liberal philosophical tradition. Then we outline the assumptions of liberalism as a theory to provide a different perspective regarding the nature of international organizations in a liberal world. Like realism, liberalism has several variations that have both political and economic influences. And, like realism, liberalism generates compelling explanations about the dynamics of world politics.

Philosophic Roots of Liberalism

Hugo Grotius (1583–1645) is considered to be the father of international law. In *The Law of Prize and Booty* and *The Law of War and Peace*, Grotius identifies international norms and rules that states have agreed upon, either explicitly through treaties or implicitly through practice. He argues that states need to abide by their agreements in order to foster cooperative international relations. For Grotius, international relations includes economic and political transactions. The rules that emerged to govern those transactions shaped the way states interact with one another. Grotius's contribution to liberal international relations theory is his acknowledgment of the cooperation that occurs among states in an anarchical environment. Grotius also articulates how formal and informal rules governing international relations are in the self-interest of states.

John Locke's (1632–1704) *Second Treatise of Government* is considered the seminal work of liberal political thought and has had a significant, albeit indirect, influence on liberal international relations theory. John Locke focuses on the kind of government that is conducive to the happiness and well-being of its citizens. For Locke, individuals and individual happiness are the keys to a productive society. Human beings possess rights, rights that exist in nature and belong to individuals by virtue of their humanity. These natural rights include the right to life, liberty, and the pursuit of private property. They also include the right to political equality, equality under the law, and self-government.

Locke emphasizes the importance and value of the individual to society and prescribes a very limited role for the government. Locke's more important contributions to liberal international relations theory are his view that human beings are essentially cooperative and the idea of limited government composed of, and influenced by, those governed. In the state of nature, human beings are essentially cooperative; however, the condition of scarcity compels individuals to act in a self-interested manner. In order to create a society, a government must protect private property and arbitrate disputes between individuals. With private property rights protected and legal mechanisms for settling disputes in place, individuals are free to realize their rights and potential to the fullest. For Locke, the best government is the government that "governs least." The best way to ensure good government is to allow individuals to participate in politics through voting and holding public office.

Similarly, **Adam Smith** (1723–1790) in *The Wealth of Nations* addresses the essence of human beings and the role of government in society. According to Smith, human beings have a natural inclination to "truck, barter and exchange one thing for another." Human beings are essentially economic creatures driven by a quest to acquire and dispose of property. Society is born out of economic exchange between individuals. Smith argues that self-interest motivates individuals to act, yet this selfish behavior can have a surprising result—social harmony. Unlike Hobbes, who argues that selfish behavior makes life particularly nasty, Smith argues that the "market" can harness the selfish impulses of individuals and propel a society to progressively higher levels of development. How does the market mechanism do this? According to Smith, the market is governed as if by an "invisible hand" that regulates the behavior of individuals in a society. Self-interested individuals interacting with other self-interested individuals will create competition to generate the goods and services a society needs and wants at a price it is willing to pay (Heilbroner 1986, 55). Goods and services are not produced out of kindness and goodwill. They are provided out of the self-interest of the producer. Competition ensures that no one provider will artificially raise prices to take advantage of consumers, because a competitor will offer the same good or service at a fair price. For Smith, this self-regulating market promotes the welfare of individuals and societies.

Smith recognizes that human nature is complex and that individuals could be driven by other passions, such as racism, nationalism, and religious devotion. Smith thought that these other passions could be held in check if the instinct for economic self-interest was developed. In other words, economic self-interest would not only promote social harmony but also override other human passions that give rise to violent human conflict.

The writings of Adam Smith support Locke's idea of a limited government. The idea of society's being self-regulating because of the market's invisible hand suggests a limited role of the state in the market. Borrowing the term *laissez-faire* from the eighteenth-century French physiocrats, Smith argues that the government should not interfere in the market, lest it disrupt the market's natural tendencies toward equilibrium. Smith also contributes the idea that economic self-interest produces social harmony, while passions such as racism and nationalism promote conflict and violence. Smith sees economics as being strongly associated with peace, and politics as associated with war. This separation of politics from economics represents a shift away from the mercantilist idea that economic activity should enhance the national treasury and serve the power interests of the state. For Smith and other liberals, the economic interests of individuals should determine the politics of the state. The "wealth of nations" results from the economic self-interest of individuals.

David Ricardo (1772–1823) builds on the work of Adam Smith and highlights the importance of international trade for states in his classic work *The Principles of Political Economy and Taxation*. International trade is important to states because domestic economies are constrained by limited resources and conflicting interests, while the international economy provides additional avenues for growth and expansion (Crane and Amawi 1997, 57). States benefit from international trade by exporting products in which they have a comparative advantage. "The theory of comparative advantage holds that nations should produce and export those goods and services in which they hold a comparative advantage, and import those items that other nations can produce at a lower cost" (Balaam and Veseth 1996, 450). Through comparative advantage, global resources and welfare can be maximized. For example, the United States produces computer chips efficiently and at a much lower cost than other states. The United States also produces potato chips, but not as efficiently as Poland. Poland can produce computer chips, but at a much higher cost. The theory of comparative advantage would prescribe an international division of labor in which the United States would export computer chips and Poland would export potato chips. This division is the most efficient way to allocate resources. The principal beneficiaries, of course, would be individual consumers, who would have both computer chips and potato chips for the least possible cost.

Immanuel Kant (1742–1804) incorporates Locke's view of representative government and addresses the issue of individuals who are organized into territories. Kant argues in his classic *Perpetual Peace* that states need to form a federation whereby they can peacefully resolve their disputes. The formation of a world republic is part of the natural evolution of human society. Kant argues that the world republic should be composed of nation-states that are constitutional democracies. Peace and cooperation would be easier to achieve because the decision of whether or not to go to war would lie with the people. Kant's political philosophy is informed by the liberal writing of Smith and Ricardo in that he assumes that the economic self-interest of individuals contributes to peaceful relations among nation-states.

Jeremy Bentham (1748–1832) is commonly associated with a group of thinkers called the "utilitarians." The utilitarians see individuals as rational creatures, capable of engaging in a cost–benefit analysis and deciding for themselves what their wants and needs are. The utilitarian principle is that laws and institutions of a society should produce "the greatest good for the greatest number." Bentham reinforces the liberal ideas that the institutions of limited, representative government and the market generate a great deal of wealth for a great many people.

Grotius, Locke, Smith, Ricardo, Kant, and Bentham have influenced, both directly and indirectly, the evolution of liberal international relations theory. For all of these thinkers, the relationship of politics and economics is a crucial one. Normatively speaking, economics should determine politics. Economic behavior is seen as the path to social harmony, or at the very least, as promoting cooperation through interdependence and shared values. This view shapes the expected behavior and policies of international organizations. In the following section, we'll look at the organizing assumptions of contemporary liberal theory.

Contemporary Liberalism

The liberal theory of international relations is based on four assumptions. The first assumption is that both state and nonstate actors are important in international relations. The philosophic tradition of liberalism places a great deal of value on individuals, meaning that individuals matter as well as the social, economic, and political organizations to which they belong. As a result, liberals focus on individuals, households, firms, interest groups, governments, and international organizations. Substate actors such as individuals and interest groups can have important effects on international affairs, both directly and indirectly. Bill Gates, chairman of Microsoft, can shape global information networks by determining how and what kind of information is accessed. Interest groups can lobby governments for foreign policies that help them achieve some or all of their goals.

Liberals also see international and transnational actors as shaping the international landscape. International organizations include not only IGOs but also nongovernmental organizations (NGOs) that can have both public and private functions. The activities of multinational corporations (MNCs), drug cartels, and terrorist organizations also influence international affairs. Contrary to the realist assumption that the state is the most important actor, liberals see nonstate actors as important because these actors have independent, as well as indirect, influences on the domestic and foreign policies of states.

The second assumption of the liberalism holds that the state is not necessarily a unitary and rational actor. Governments are composed of individuals, bureaucratic agencies, and judicial and legislative bodies that can have differing and competing interests. As a result, what may be rational from the standpoint of a unitary state may not be rational from the standpoint of a government official, like the president or the secretary of state, or of an agency like the Department of Defense. While choices are still made on the basis of self-interest, what is considered "self" is determined by the level of analysis that affects the perception of rationality. This disaggregation of the state expands analyses of governmental decision making and can explain why governments make the policy choices that they do.

In addition to being disaggregated, the state, as seen by liberals, is a much more fluid entity comprising competing interests that seek to either control the government or lobby the government to achieve their policy objectives. In other words, the state is not autonomous, and it can be swayed by internal, as well as external, influences. The government may be controlled by any group (party) or coalition of groups (parties) at any given time.

The third assumption of liberalism is that the nature of international relations is a combination of conflict and cooperation. This assumption stems from the liberal view of human nature as self-interested yet cooperative. Smith and Ricardo thought that self-interested economic behavior in a market led to social harmony. Most contemporary liberals are not this idealistic. However, modern liberals claim that self-interested market behavior creates wealth and leads to increased international transactions. These international transactions also generate **complex interdependence**, whereby states and other actors within societies are interconnected through trade and finance. Complex interdependence provides incentives to state and nonstate actors to cooperate with each other because they rely on each other. Liberals acknowledge that mutual reliance is by no means symmetrical. Nevertheless, they see complex interdependence as fostering cooperation and reducing the likelihood of violent conflict. Complex interdependence is a defining characteristic of the international system—a characteristic that conditions the behavior of state and nonstate actors.

Many liberals argue that the proliferation of shared norms and values, brought about by the proliferation of representative, democratic governments, has also created a kind of moral interdependence. Societies organized around such democratic principles as individual rights, equality under the law, majority rule, and minority rights are predisposed to the peaceful settlement of disputes, collaboration, and compromise. Simply put, democratic societies identify with each other because of shared norms and values. Even when conflict persists, the conflict is not prone to violence because the decision to go to war does not rest solely in the hands of a single individual or small group. Decision makers in democratic societies are accountable to their citizens. Hence, democracies rarely make war on each other (Nincic 1992; Oneal and Russett 1997; Russett 1993). Coupled with the economic and political costs of unilateral action, this type of moral interdependence promotes international coordination and cooperation under existing international laws and organizations.

The fourth assumption of liberalism is that a variety of issues can come to dominate the international agenda. Unlike realists, who see security and military issues at the top of the agenda, liberals point to the fact that economic, social, and environmental issues are also important to governments and societies. Hence, Iran's nuclear capabilities might be important one week, typhoon-ravaged Myanmar another week, and a crisis in the subprime mortgage market in yet another. Issue areas will involve multiple actors, from states to IGOs and NGOs, and each will pursue its own strategies and goals (Keohane and Nye 1977, 37). For liberals, there is no hierarchy of international issues; consequently, international goals and interests are increasingly difficult to define.

Liberalism and the Nature of International Organizations

Liberal theory emphasizes several different kinds of international organizations—the IGO, the NGO, the MNC, and the regime. Hence, several different explanations regarding the origins and the essence of these organizations exist. Functionalism and institutionalism are two prominent liberal explanations regarding IGO and regime creation. According to Bennett (1991, 15), "The functionalist believes in the efficacy of a gradualist approach to world order with the attainment of political federation by installments." IGOs are created because of a basic need for them. The increase in transnational ties has led to integration and interdependence, which in turn has led many societies to share common problems. Many of these problems can be managed only through international cooperation, necessitating the creation of specialized international agencies with technical experts (Haas 1964; Mitrany 1948, 1966). IGOs are formed because, in effect, they "demand jurisdiction over preexisting national states" (Haas 1958, 16).

Functionalists recognize that state sovereignty is a well-entrenched principle in international relations. However, they argue that cooperation in narrow, nonpolitical (economic and social) issue areas leads to a "spillover" into larger, more politicized issue areas such as defense or monetary policy. Cooperation in economic and social spheres leads to confidence building, which promotes cooperation in more highly charged issues. IGOs socialize elites into recognizing that it is in their states' interest to join and participate in international organizations. As cooperative behavior becomes institutionalized, IGOs can evolve into supranational organizations such as the European Union (EU) or the World Trade Organization (WTO). The authority of the nation-state would be displaced incrementally by supranational institutions.

Institutionalism, which represents the most recent research in the liberal tradition on the study of international organization (IGOs and regimes), is a hybrid of realism, game theory, and functionalism. Robert Keohane's seminal work *After Hegemony* (1984) examines how IGOs can assist egoistic state actors in overcoming collective action problems and encouraging cooperation under conditions of anarchy. Like realists, liberal institutionalists argue that a hegemonic power is necessary for the creation of IGOs and regimes. Like realists, institutionalists see the state as a unitary, rational actor interacting in a dangerous and uncertain world. Liberal institutionalists have been charged with being "realist by any other name" because of their adoption of realist precepts and assumptions (Mearsheimer 1995).

Unlike realists, however, institutionalists are more optimistic about the importance of international organizations when a hegemon is in decline. Recall that realists who adhere to hegemonic stability theory argue that when a hegemon's power begins to wane, disorder and the decline of international organizations are the likely result. Liberal institutionalists argue that IGOs and regimes serve several purposes in addition to promoting the interests of the hegemon. IGOs and regimes reduce **transaction and information costs to member states.** They also regularize state behavior and promote **transparency.** Under conditions of complex interdependence, IGOs and regimes become valuable assets to states. They provide tangible benefits to members, who then become willing to share the cost of maintaining IGOs and regimes "after hegemony." This idea has been expressed in a game theoretic context using the concept of a *k group*. A *k group* consists of actors that would still benefit by providing for a public good (in this case, an IGO or regime) even if they have to bear the costs solely. A cost–benefit analysis of the payoffs between having an international organization and not having one suggests that the great, but nonhegemonic powers would find it rational and in their self-interest to maintain existing IGOs and regimes (Gowa 1988, 316).

Both liberal institutionalists and realists use game theory to explain the behavior of states, though institutionalists are more encouraging about the ability of international organizations to temper the ill effects of anarchy and the suboptimal outcomes it can yield for egoistic actors. By linking cooperation in one area to cooperation in another, states become accustomed to using IGOs and regimes to achieve their goals and settle their disputes. This, coupled with the effects of complex interdependence, prompts states to abandon power-maximizing behavior and immediate self-interest for long-term stability.

The key to understanding the optimism of institutionalism and functionalism lies in their liberal identity. The world order the United States sought to institutionalize after World War II was based on economic and political liberalism. For many liberals, the key to U.S. hegemony is not so much economic or military as it is ideological. The United States possesses "soft" power, or the power of ideas (Nye 1990). The United States has been able to convince the world of the value of free trade and markets and has promoted the ideas of human rights and democratic government. **Antonio Gramsci** (discussed in Chapter 4) identifies "ideas" as central to understanding **hegemony.** Hegemony is not simply based on material capabilities to coerce others. Hegemony is based on powerful and compelling ideas. Liberal ideas have become so pervasive internationally that they are widely perceived as economic and political "truths." Even though the United States has declined materialistically, the liberal world order it created will continue because it is based on time-tested and accepted ideas.

Both institutionalists and functionalists see IGOs and regimes as becoming something more than just the sum of their member states (see, e.g., Moore and Pubantz 2006). Both see IGOs as important and influential actors in their own right, although they differ as to the degree of influence. Institutionalists do not see IGOs as displacing the nation-state. IGOs enable states to reach mutually beneficial outcomes in international relations (Schweller and Preiss 1997, 3). States may be willing to cede some sovereignty to international organizations in some areas, such as trade, in exchange for the benefits provided by an autonomous organization. However, the state remains an important actor in international relations and still jealously guards most of its sovereign prerogatives. Some liberals see the internal bureaucratic workings of IGOs as important in understanding the behavior of international organizations (Alvarez 2005; Barnett and Finnemore 2004). The culture of international organizations, coupled with internal norms and folkways, affects the ability of international organizations to assess situations and conditions their response. International organizations are also important for promoting democratic values and international law (Alvarez 2005; Zweifel 2006).

In sum, the creation and nature of IGOs and regimes are explained by liberals in two ways. Institutionalists argue that hegemonic power is necessary for the creation of international organizations, but hegemony is not required for their continued maintenance. IGOs and regimes are collective goods that help promote the common interests and development of shared values. As a result, they are valuable to states and will be continued absent a hegemon. Hegemony is not required for functionalists. Issues and their complexity determine the need and creation of IGOs. Like-minded individuals and governments create organizations to manage complex problems.

MNCs are important international organizations for liberals because they see the private sphere as the locus of economic, social, and political innovation. MNCs are private, economic entities that are spawned by an expanding and increasingly efficient market. MNCs achieve global economies of scale, whereby they have control over, or access to, labor, production facilities, sales, and markets. For many liberals, MNCs are benign in nature. They are motivated by the profit motive, as are all individuals and firms participating in the market. The self-interest of shareholders drives MNCs toward greater and greater efficiencies, and their activities propel international society to progressively higher levels of development. MNCs are the innovators of new technology and industrial organization. They create jobs and promote efficiency. More importantly, they bring high-quality goods and services to the world's consumers at a price they are willing to pay. MNCs are global citizens that respond to and serve the needs of an expanding market.

MNCs are also local and global citizens that serve their communities in more than just economic ways. They participate in partnerships with NGOs, universities, and individuals that contribute to governance and the development of knowledge, particularly in the area of environmental management and protection. For example, the Marine Stewardship Council (MSC) was created in 1999 as a result of a partnership between the World Wide Fund (WWF) for Nature and Unilever for ensuring the long-term viability of fish stocks. In spite of the divergent organizational missions, the partnership helped both organizations develop "the shared perception of the added value of the partnership, over and above what each organization could achieve on its own" (Fowler and

Heap 1998). This and other types of collaborative teams help "promote a more sustainable use of natural resources, improved economic opportunities for local communities and provide workable solutions for environmental problems" (Kennedy et al. 1998, 32).

Liberalism and the Role of International Organizations

Liberalism is more optimistic than realism about the contributions and independence of international organizations in international relations. Five interrelated roles can be discerned from liberal theory. First, international organizations help states overcome **collective action problems**. Recall the Prisoners' Dilemma. Had the prisoners acted together (collectively) and kept silent, both would have achieved the optimal outcome, a light sentence. Yet, the uncertainty about what the other was going to do, plus uncertainty about what evidence the police had, provided incentives for both prisoners to confess. The result was a suboptimal outcome for both players. Liberals, particularly institutionalists, argue that international organizations can change the rules of the game. With respect to the Prisoners' Dilemma, international organizations can function as figurative lawyers who advise their client(s). After all, the interests of the prisoners are not fundamentally opposed, especially in light of the consequences if both should confess. The prisoners could overcome their collective action problem if they had a lawyer or some kind of mediator/arbitrator.

Realists use the Prisoners' Dilemma to explain the security dilemma faced by states in an anarchical environment. The consequences associated with cooperation and defection are so dire for states because, in reality, security is no game. It means life or death for a great many people. Rational states really have no choice but to unilaterally pursue their own security interests, even if it means suboptimal outcomes for all states. Liberals point out that theory and practice can be quite different from each other. The pursuit of power and immediate self-interest has led to war, not to stability, as realists suggest. States that do not have significant military capability, such as Sweden, Switzerland, and Costa Rica, have maintained their territorial integrity and avoided war. Alliances have worked to deter attacks on member states by credibly demonstrating that an attack on one member is an attack on all the members. For example, NATO is credited by institutionalists for preserving the peace in Europe during and after the Cold War (Duffield 1992, 1994a, 1994b). NATO was instrumental in building confidence and trust among historical adversaries and serves as the anchor for the EU. EU and NATO membership is sought by a number of states willing to cede sovereignty and autonomy for the benefits of membership. For liberal institutionalists, NATO is the exemplar, the quintessential example of how egoistic states can overcome the most difficult of collective action problems—security. If each member state were seeking to obtain this goal unilaterally, it would bear enormous costs; moreover, such unilateral strategies would likely lead to suboptimal outcomes. By cooperating, each member state saves on cost and avoids the worst possible outcome—war.

Collective action problems exist in other issue areas ranging from the economy to the environment. The most difficult is the **"free rider"** problem. A free rider is an actor that benefits from the provision of a public good without contributing anything to providing that good. **Public goods** are "goods or services that, once provided, generate benefits that can be enjoyed by all simultaneously" (Balaam and Veseth 1996, 458). For example, liberals consider free trade a public good that is provided by the hegemon. The hegemon bears the costs of creating and maintaining the free trading system. In this case, a free rider is a state that benefits from the open markets of other states while at the same time keeping its markets closed to foreign competition. The hegemon usually carries a free rider because the gains associated with the free trading system outweigh the costs of the free rider. However, the balance of that equation shifts as the hegemon's capabilities decline. International organizations can help counter the free rider problem absent the hegemon by identifying unacceptable barriers to trade and providing a neutral forum for settling trade disputes. International organizations can, in a neutral manner, decide when it is permissible to discriminate against foreign goods. Under hegemony, a free rider gets away with free riding because a hegemon is willing to bear the costs. After hegemony, the free rider's position is increasingly untenable and international organizations provide a mechanism for discouraging such behavior.

⌐A second role of international organizations is to promote economic prosperity and global welfare⌐ Ideologically speaking, liberals argue that the world's goods, services, and resources should be distributed by the market. Liberals argue that the market yields the most efficient use of natural resources and the most efficient production of goods and services. Private ownership and private property rights are also important because private citizens and firms are more directly influenced by and can more easily adjust to market changes. Private citizens and firms are also more innovative and dynamic. Through the development of a global market based on comparative advantage, the welfare of the world can be maximized by improving the lot of individuals regardless of their nationality. International economic institutions, like the IMF and the WTO, exist to promote these goals.

International economic institutions have pursued several strategies in order to promote economic prosperity and global welfare. They have sought to reduce barriers to trade through multilateral negotiations. They have sought to eliminate protectionist measures by states, thereby forcing industries to either become efficient or lose out as casualties of the market. They have encouraged states to privatize industries and reduce their regulation of the market. They have development programs that encourage direct foreign investment by multinational corporations. They have provided funding for the creation of export industries that promote economic growth and development. They even help states adjust their economies to the new, global market realities. When international organizations promote global markets, trade, and investment, they are also promoting complex interdependence. Complex interdependence reduces the likelihood of war because the utility of military force in achieving national goals or settling disputes is greatly reduced.

A third role of international organizations is to help societies develop shared values and norms (Alvarez 2005; Zweifel 2006). Interdependence may reduce the chances of violent conflict; however, the problems associated with interdependence cannot be managed or solved unless societies have some common ground. International organizations foster certain values and help to establish certain norms that are conducive to the peaceful settlement of disputes, such as compromise, reciprocity, multilateralism, and the rule of law. International organizations promote democracy and democratic institutions. They promote and protect individual human rights. They promote values associated with a liberal international economic order based on neoclassical economic principles, such as private property rights and limited state involvement. But these values and norms are not universal, nor are they self-evident within or between societies, contrary to the writings of liberal writers. Some societies put the needs of the community over the needs of the individual. Some see the separation of church and state as a bad idea. For others, the state should eliminate private property or at least be responsible for caring for citizens "from cradle to grave," even if it means public ownership of industries or expensive welfare budgets.

For liberals, values and norms must compete in the "free marketplace of ideas" and evolve over time. Many liberal values and norms have withstood the test of time, generating unprecedented levels of prosperity and individual freedom. Contemporary international organizations are agents of socialization for a political and economic order through which everyone can benefit. This liberal view contrasts slightly with the realist notion of international organizations of agents of socialization for an international order whereby one state or a group of states dominates lesser states in the international system.

A fourth role of international organizations is integrative and is performed principally by MNCs. MNCs are seen as a figurative needle and thread that binds societies together through the formation of a common global market. The activities of MNCs benefit societies because they bring jobs, industries, managerial skills, and technologies to societies. They are private economic organizations that transcend national boundaries and are responsible only to international stockholders. MNCs are a strong force for economic liberalism in the global economy (Goldstein 1996, 376). They command significant resources and have the ability to influence governments and IGOs. MNCs are interested in limited government involvement and the right to freely move capital to areas where it can be utilized more efficiently. MNCs are committed to capital mobility, and wherever they go they bring liberal ideology and a commitment to human rights with them.

A fifth role performed by international organizations in the liberal world is to provide assistance to the "victims of international politics." These victims include the abject poor, refugees, and those who have experienced environmental disaster, medical epidemics, and war. Liberals see many of these kinds of crises as being man-made. Choices are made by governments that have important consequences for their citizens. While environmental and medical emergencies may be influenced by nature, the policies and the reactions of governments play a decisive and often aggravating role. International organizations (IGOs and NGOs) seek to provide immediate relief to the victims of such "politics" and to find durable solutions.

In sum, international organizations are prominent features in the liberal landscape. International organizations help states overcome collective action problems and promote economic prosperity and global welfare. In addition, international organizations foster shared norms and values among societies and further economic interdependence. Lastly, international organizations aid the victims of international politics. Rather than being marginal actors, international organizations are at the forefront of international governance.

LIBERALISM AND INTERNATIONAL LAW

For liberals, the rule of law is the foundation of society and international law is the foundation of global society. Liberals view international law as a major force in world affairs that conditions and frames the actions and reactions of states and government officials (Koh 1997). Liberal international lawyers see international law as serving important functions in international relations. According to Slaughter-Burley (1993, 220), international law provides the rules of the game for states, stabilizing expectations. It establishes baseline expectations and helps states avoid constant renegotiations over basic issues. International law provides the criteria by which state and nonstate actors can judge behavior as reasonable and justified. It also provides a process for communication in a crisis and creates opportunities for intermeshing international and national bureaucracies. More importantly international law enhances compliance by embedding international agreements in domestic political systems. In short, international law can help state and nonstate actors solve global problems through the legalization of international relations.

International law works particularly well for liberal democracies because they share the "value" that law made through agreed-upon democratic procedures will be accepted by those governed because the people have a say in what the law is. If law can help liberal democracies overcome collective action problems domestically, it can help them overcome collective action problems internationally. For illiberal states, international law can help socialize states regarding the utility of international law and compliance, especially if the law is effective at addressing global problems. Liberals also argue that the international system is moving away from a system where states make the law to a more cosmopolitan legal order where nonstate actors participate in creating the law (Roach 2009).

Liberalism and Its Critics

Liberal theory to international relations and international organizations is widely criticized as **ethnocentric** (Strange 1983; Viotti and Kauppi 1993). The liberal worldview is widely held by American and British scholars. Their argument that the contemporary liberal order is beneficial to all is influenced by their own bias that their societal organization is superior to other kinds of organization. This bias is perpetuated in that international relations as a discipline is dominated by English speakers from Canada, Great Britain, Australia, and the United States. The normative bias in liberal arguments is evident—democracy is a "better" form of government and capitalism is a "better" mode of production.

Ethnocentrism compromises the ability of liberal scholars to adequately assess and criticize the liberal order that they are describing. Take, for example, the idea that free trade is a public good. It is a mighty bold statement to say that free trade benefits all. Liberals claim that consumers benefit because free trade widens the range of consumer choice. However, consumer choice means very little if the consumer's job has been lost because foreign competition has driven the domestic employer out of business. Liberals also tend to focus on absolute rather than relative gains. In other words, they only ask whether societies are better off (in terms of prices and consumer choice) than they were before. Liberals do not consider relative gains, nor do they recognize that "development" is itself an ethnocentric concept. Why do liberals unconsciously assume that other societies want to be like the United States and the Western democracies?

A second criticism of liberalism is that "blame" for underdevelopment and poverty is often placed on the individual, firm, or government. Individuals are poor because they did not make the right choices in order to effectively participate in the market. They did not seek the right education or occupation that would provide them with an acceptable standard of living. Similarly, if societies are poor, it is because governments were corrupt or pursued irrational state policies that contributed to economic problems. Irrational state policies include subsidizing industries that do not have a comparative advantage, import substitution, state ownership of industries, and protectionism. Liberals rarely emphasize the fact that capitalism can create both winners and losers and that what determines a winner or loser has nothing to do with economic factors. Rather, it has to do with resources and existing power positions.

A third criticism of liberalism is that it assumes that all interests are able to compete effectively in the political arena. Interest group theory holds up only if all interests have relatively equal opportunity and enough resources to influence government. If only big-money interests dominate the political process, then only their interests will be represented in the political process. Considerable evidence suggests that small, private-business interests are better able to influence governments than are large public-interest groups (Welch et al. 1997). After all, it is easier to stop legislation than it is to enact it. Private interest groups seek to reduce or impede government regulation. Public interest groups, such as environmental groups, seek government regulation of industry and consumers to protect the environment.

A fourth criticism of liberalism is its reliance on the market and economic considerations. Liberals argue that economics should determine politics. The state should not intervene in the market, absent a market failure. However, the market is driven by expansion and efficiency. Societies are compelled to adjust to market changes. Thus, in the United States, for example, the inefficient family farm is displaced by large corporate farms, and high-paying manufacturing jobs are relocated to countries with lower wages and less rigorous environmental standards. And in Paris, the sidewalk cafe and boutique are giving way to McDonald's and T-shirt shops. Critics of liberalism argue that societies have other values in addition to efficiency. They cherish traditional institutions that reflect their moral, familial, national, and religious heritage as well. The global market fosters crass commercialism in which businesses must appeal to the lowest common denominator to reach the widest audience.

Relatedly, liberals assume that the market is apolitical. That is, the market is driven solely by the laws of supply and demand and the price mechanism. However, irrational market behavior, such as price-fixing or racial/gender discrimination, occurs all the time. The liberal response to racial or gender discrimination is that markets are the solution, not the problem. Discrimination may exist in the social and political realms; however, in the economic realm, markets erode discriminatory practices because such practices are unproductive and inefficient.

Like realism, liberalism is plagued by tautological arguments. Liberals assume that markets lead to optimal outcomes; therefore, when suboptimal outcomes emerge, they must be caused by something other than the market. The suboptimal outcomes are the result of poor choices on the part of individuals, firms, and government. If the outcome is optimal, then the market was able to work its "magic." Assuming a conclusion rarely contributes to analysis. Liberals never seriously consider whether markets and capitalism cause international conflict and contribute to global inequality.

For liberals, the nature of international relations has fundamentally changed during the latter half of the twentieth century. The world has been tied together through economic, political, social, and moral interdependence, making effective international governance a necessity for nation-states. International organizations play an important and constructive role in international governance. Some liberals see international organizations as the pillars of a nascent new world order. Others see international organizations as assisting states in overcoming collective action problems. The liberal theoretical framework provides a mechanism for understanding the role of state and nonstate actors in the governance of international affairs and highlights the role of the market in promoting international change, economically, politically, and socially.

KEY TERMS

great-power concert   44
Thucydides   44
might makes right   45
Niccolo Machiavelli   46
Thomas Hobbes   47
anarchy   47
Carl von Clausewitz   47
Alexander Hamilton   47

economic
   nationalism   47
state   48
sovereignty   48
unitary and rational
   actor   48
structural realists   49
balance of power   49

high politics   50
low politics   50
neorealists   50
neomercantilist   50
trade-off
   hypothesis   51
hegemonic stability
   theory   51

SUGGESTED READINGS

Axelrod, Robert, and Robert Keohane. 1986. Achieving Cooperation Under Anarchy: Strategies and Institutions. pp. 226–260 in *Cooperation Under Anarchy*, ed. Kenneth Oye. Princeton, NJ: Princeton University Press.

Gilpin, Robert. 1981. *War and Change in World Politics.* Cambridge, UK: Cambridge University Press.

Grotius, Hugo. 1984. *The Law of War and Peace.* Birmingham, AL: Legal Classics Library, Division of Gryphon Editions.

James, Patrick. 2002. *International Relations and Scientific Progress: Structural Realism Reconsidered.* Columbus, OH: Ohio State University Press.

Keohane, Robert O. 1986. *Neorealism and Its Critics.* New York: Columbia University Press.

Keohane, Robert O., and Joseph M. Nye, Jr. 1977. *Power and Interdependence: World Politics in Transition.* Boston, MA: Little Brown.

Milner, Helen. 1991. The Assumption of Anarchy in International Relations Theory. *Review of International Studies* 17 (January): 67–85.

Morengthau, Hans. 1967. *Politics Among Nations.* 4th ed. New York: Alfred Knopf.

Ricardo, David. 1965. *The Principles of Political Economy and Taxation.* London: Dent; New York: Dutton.

Posner, Eric A. 2009. *The Perils of Global Legalism.* Chicago, IL: University of Chicago Press.

Smith, Adam. 1971. *The Wealth of Nations.* New York: Dutton.

Thucydides. 1963. *The Peloponnesian Wars*, trans. Benjamin Jowett. New York: Washington Square Press.

Waltz, Kenneth N. 1959. *The Man, State and War: A Theoretical Analysis.* New York: Columbia University Press.

Critical Theories and Approaches

Critical theories and approaches to international relations are useful for reevaluating commonly held views and beliefs. Marxism, feminism, and constructivism offer alternative ways of understanding and assessing the role of international organizations in world affairs. Marxism, feminism, and constructivism can be seen as critical reactions to the putative universality of realism and the ethnocentrism of liberalism. Like the mainstream approaches, critical theory and approaches have philosophic origins and underlying assumptions that shape a particular kind of worldview.

MARXISM

Marxist theory makes several important contributions to the study of international relations. First, Marxism challenges the realist assertion of the primacy of politics over economics and the liberal assertion that the expansion of global markets is beneficial to international peace and stability. Second, Marxism offers a comprehensive critique of capitalism as a mode of production. Marxist analyses of capitalism have identified issues that lead to genuine conflict within and between societies. Third, Marxism articulates significantly different roles for current international organizations. For Marxists, such organizations are neither great-power directorates nor relatively independent actors promoting the international public good; rather, they are tools of capitalists that help them undermine and exploit subordinate classes and states.

As an ideology, Marxism carries with it many negative connotations. Some people in the United States feel that American Marxists are traitors. Others see them as idealistic and misguided. Marxist-Leninist ideology is associated with brutal communist governments in the former Soviet Union, the former Eastern Bloc states, Cambodia, and China. Marxist ideology has also been at the heart of many social and political movements in the developing world, movements that were hostile to the United States and its interests. As a result, many tend to dismiss Marxist or Marxist-influenced explanations without considering whether or not they have any validity or provide any insight. Such a tendency is ill-advised because it narrows the scope of analysis. It is analogous to dismissing liberal ideas about representation and democracy because the United States practiced slavery and Thomas Jefferson and George Washington owned slaves. Ideas can have merit even if their practice is sometimes offensive.

Marxist analyses have generated insights and explanations that are useful in understanding contemporary international relations. Marxist insights regarding the drawbacks of global capitalism have been used by former presidential candidates Ross Perot, Patrick Buchanan, and Ron Paul, none of whom is considered a Marxist. Many environmental groups and labor unions accept Marxist explanations without necessarily embracing Marxist ideology. Many in the developing world have a worldview that is a mixture of realism and Marxism. They are realists in that they are concerned about state sovereignty. After all, most developing states have experienced colonialism and have been formally independent only for the last couple of decades. Their relative weakness vis-à-vis the great powers has resulted in numerous interventions, and they understand the consequences of being a lesser power in an anarchical environment. They also have Marxist leanings in that they are poor and economically disadvantaged. Their colonial history only reinforces their distrust of capitalism as their experience with capitalism is one of poverty, malnutrition, disease, and even violent death. Marxism as an ideology has made a comeback in Latin America with leftist governments being elected in Venezuela, Brazil, Bolivia, and Chile; and radical Islam, while not seeking to establish socialism, has adopted Marxist ideas associated with imperialism, oppression, and the corruption of elites in Muslim countries. As a result, Marxist thought continues to be relevant today.

Philosophic Roots of Marxism

Socrates (470–399 B.C.), the Athenian philosopher, may seem an unlikely contributor to Marxist thought; however, he has influenced many different kinds of theorists, not to mention lawyers, through his method of inquiry. Known as Socratic inquiry, this method is a process for discovering truth by juxtaposing two contradictory ideas. By pitting a thesis against its antithesis, we reveal a new truth—a synthesis. The synthesis then becomes the new thesis, which is pitted against its antithesis, whereupon the process starts all over again. For Socrates, progress and knowledge are promoted by using this method of questioning alleged truths.

Georg Wilhelm Friedrich Hegel (1779–1831) was one of the many theorists influenced by the Socratic method. In *The Philosophy of Right*, Hegel uses a dialectic, a process quite similar to Socratic inquiry, to pit competing ideas about social and political relations against each other. Hegel departs from the liberal, social contract thinkers of his time in that he sees human beings as essentially social rather than economic creatures (Cahn 1997, 734). For Hegel, human beings were not merely individualistic and solitary creatures who enter into society merely to "truck, barter and trade." Rather, the highest form of freedom for individuals is participating in a politically organized community, or the state (Cahn 1997, 734). The central difference between liberal thought and Hegel's communitarian ideas is that liberals place value on the individual. If the individual is happy, then so is society. Hegel places value on the society so that the individual can be happy. Hegel's contributions to the Marxist theory to international relations are his use of the dialectic and his emphasis on the environment/context in which individuals and groups interact.

Karl Marx (1818–1883) is, obviously, an intellectual precursor to Marxism. Marx's central work *The Communist Manifesto* was written with his collaborator, friend, and benefactor, Friedrich Engels. In that work, they argue that history and progress can be seen dialectically as societies shift from one mode of production to another. A **mode of production** is simply the way goods and services are provided for a society. Slavery, feudalism, capitalism, and socialism are examples of ways in which goods and services can be produced. According to Marx, society is shaped by a mode of production and is organized around **economic class**, where the classes are based on an individual's relationship to the means of production. The means of production are the resources that are needed to provide goods and services. For example, under feudalism, the economy was, in large part, agriculturally based. The means of production were the land and the tools needed to work on and farm the land. Feudal society was based on two principal classes, the aristocracy and the serfs. The aristocracy consisted of the lords and their families, and they owned the land. The serfs worked the land in exchange for protection, food, and a place to live.

Marx sees economics, not ideas, as the driving force of society and politics. He argues that each mode of production contains within itself the contradictions that will eventually lead to its collapse. Again, using feudalism as an example, we can see that its own contradictions undermined its dominance. These contradictions resulted from the clash among the social arrangements associated with feudalism coupled with technological advances. Emerging industrial technologies provided alternative ways for people to make a living and also created surpluses of goods. Under feudalism, land was passed down from father to the firstborn son, so that estates could be kept intact. Second, third, and fourth sons usually had some money, but no inherited land. Once the father died, these sons often went off to the cities, investing in new technologies and starting new enterprises. Ironically, they became the foundation of a new class, the merchants. As these contractions became too great, feudalism collapsed, and in its wake a new, dominant mode of production emerged—**capitalism.**

As capitalism emerges, the nature of society fundamentally changes. New classes arise. The **bourgeoisie** are capitalists who own the factories, hire workers, and control most of the money. The **proletariat** are wage workers and managers who sell their labor for a salary. Society reorganizes itself around this new mode of production, and social and political institutions reflect the underlying economic order. Just as aristocracy reflects the interests of a dominant class under feudalism, democracy reflects the interests and needs of the bourgeoisie. Legitimacy to govern is no longer based on the idea of heredity. Rather, the liberal ideas that all men are created equal and have the right to political participation form the foundation of legitimate governance under capitalism. Democracy is based on the rule of law—law that was made by the majority rule of consenting men (initially, white men who owned property). Liberalism undermines the political authority of the aristocracy and legitimizes the new political structures, which favor the interests of the bourgeoisie.

Marx predicts that capitalism will also collapse under the weight of its own contradictions. Marx identifies many contradictions of capitalism that would impoverish the workers to such an extent that they would rise up and seize the means of production. Three of these are discussed here. Note, however, that Marx did not invent these contradictions. They were real problems—the pressing issues in the political economy of his day—which were also addressed by the likes of Malthus, Mill, and Ricardo. With the exception of Malthus (who was nothing if not "dismal"), these liberals are considerably more optimistic than Marx about the ability of the market to deal with the problems faced by capitalism. Marx described these problems as contradictions leading to market failure and showing, at the very least, that capitalism is unstable and prone to crises.

The first problem is the tendency of the market toward the **concentration of capital**. Capitalists operating under market forces are driven toward greater and greater efficiency in the production of the goods and services. Competition and efficiency demand that capitalists reduce the cost of producing goods and services for markets. Inefficient and uncompetitive enterprises are driven out of market, which leads to oligopoly and monopoly and the accumulation of wealth in the hands of the few. The consequences of this contradiction are serious for both workers and consumers. Efficient production ultimately translates into reducing labor costs because labor accounts for the lion's share of production costs. The masses are impoverished, owing to the resulting decline in wages and increased unemployment. When the market becomes dominated by a few firms (oligopoly) or one firm (monopoly), the remaining bourgeoisie can demand high prices. Once competition ceases to exist, so does capitalism.

A second contradiction of capitalism is the tendency toward **overproduction**. Liberals argue that the interaction of supply and demand, coupled with the price mechanism, prevents overproduction. Marx argues against this belief in the inherent equilibrium of the market, claiming that capitalism is prone to overproduction because greater efficiency allows capitalists to make more of the same good for the same or lesser cost. Demand for these goods also declines because the workers cannot easily afford them. As a result, the market is flooded with a surplus of goods and services.

A third contradiction is the **falling rate of profit**, which leads to oversavings on the part of capitalists. As capital accumulates, the rate of return on capital investments declines. Capitalists have less incentive to invest in productive enterprises and instead save their excess wealth. In other words, capitalist development is finite. Capital accumulation leads to a decline in investment returns until, finally, a point is reached when investment ceases. These contradictions lead to great disparities between rich and poor, the capitalists and the workers. The immiseration of the working class eventually leads to a socialist revolution, for the workers would have "nothing left to lose but their chains."

John A. Hobson (1858–1940), a British economist, indirectly provides an explanation as to why capitalism did not, in fact, collapse. His answer? **Imperialism**. Decidedly a non-Marxist, Hobson argues in *Imperialism* that overproduction, underconsumption, and oversavings force capitalists to seek new markets in order to sell their surplus goods and to find new outlets for investment. Hobson defines imperialism as "the endeavor of the great controllers of industry to broaden the channel for the flow of their surplus wealth by seeking foreign markets and foreign investments to take off the goods and capital they cannot sell or use at home" (Viotti and Kauppi 1993, 453). Hobson sees imperialism as a cause of war in that capitalist societies force their way into markets and even fight each other in order to gain access to new markets, cheap labor, and raw materials. Hobson might be considered a neomercantilist or economic nationalist in that he saw wars of imperial expansion as benefiting only certain segments of society (e.g., export capitalists, bankers) and not the nation as a whole.

Vladimir Ilyich Lenin (1870–1924) argues that the demise of capitalism, as predicted by Marx, was only postponed by imperialism. In *Imperialism: The Highest Stage of Capitalism*, Lenin argues that the contradictions of capitalism—overproduction, underconsumption, and oversavings—were temporarily resolved by the colonial expansion of capitalist states: "The acquisition of colonies had enabled the capitalist economies to dispose of their unconsumed goods, to acquire cheap resources and to vent their surplus capital" (Gilpin 1987, 38). Lenin argues that the expansion of capitalism through colonialism contributes to economic development internationally; however, that development is uneven. That is, capitalist powers develop unevenly, which leads to economic instability, political conflict, and war. Note that this explanation is quite similar to one type of realist explanation regarding the cause of war. Realists argue that uneven growth rates cause shifts in the balance of power and that can lead to war. However, Lenin emphasizes the underlying economic causes of conflict, whereas realists stress the political causes.

Antonio Gramsci (1891–1937), an Italian Marxist, contributes to Marxist theory through his criticism of "**economism**"—the idea that economic and technological advancements account for change, while politics is merely a reflection of the underlying economic order. According to Marx, capitalism is advancing toward economic collapse as the contradiction between the forces and the relations of production become greater. Gramsci maintains that the notion of economism is a defect in Marxist theory because it encourages the working class to remain passive, just waiting for the inevitable capitalist crisis

(Simon 1982, 11). Gramsci conceives of society as a series of relations between different groups and classes. To understand the power of the bourgeoisie in capitalist society, it is necessary to bring politics back into the analysis.

According to Gramsci, politics is "the entire complex of practical and theoretical activities with which the ruling class not only justifies and maintains its dominance, but manages to win the active consent of those over whom it rules" (Hoare and Smit 1971, 114). The ruling class develops "hegemony," a concept originally articulated by Gramsci. Hegemony "has to do with the way one social group influences other groups, making certain compromises with them in order to gain their consent of its leadership in society as a whole" (Sassoon 1982, 13). This concept of hegemony is different from the one of sheer domination employed by some realists, liberals, and Marxists. Hegemony for Gramscian Marxists is the relation of consent to political and ideological leadership, not domination by force (Simon 1982, 11). This relation is based on compromise and incentive only to the extent of achieving deference. The core values of the ruling class, however, remain intact.

Gramsci provides another distinction between hegemony and dominance (Hoare and Smit 1971, 56–57). Domination results from the state's monopoly on the means of violence and its role as the final arbiter in all disputes. Hegemony, on the other hand, requires deference on the part of those who are led. Only weak states rely on force or domination to rule. Strong states rule through hegemony. A proletarian revolution would require an alternative hegemony that could displace the hegemonic relationship that already exists between the bourgeoisie and the masses.

Gramsci's contribution to Marxist thought (as well as to neoliberal and neorealist thinking) about international relations lies in the relevance of ideas to power. For Gramscian Marxists, the power of the bourgeoisie does not result solely from its control of the state and brute force. Any number of groups or coalition of groups can control the government. Power results from developing an ideology or hegemony where the interests of the dominant class or state are inextricably tied to the interests of subordinate classes, and workers buy into the system even though they are being exploited. The well-being of the firm is directly related to the well-being of the workers. Workers who question working conditions, seek to unionize, or try to improve wages are seen as threats not only by the bourgeoisie but also by other workers. Hence, labor leadership seeks reform within the system but refrains from trying to replace it. Social and political pressure is exerted on dissatisfied members of subordinate classes to make them conform to existing bourgeois norms and values. Violence is employed only as a last resort.

Socrates, Hegel, Marx, Hobson, Lenin, and Gramsci—all have influenced Marxist theory. Socrates contributes dialectical reasoning. Hegel adds the idea of the context in which economic, social, and political relations take place. Marx provides an alternative view regarding class formation and identifies contradictions that threaten the stability of capitalism. Hobson and Lenin bring to the fore the economic causes and the political consequences of colonialism. Gramsci shows how ideas relate to power and the dominance of one class by another with their active consent. These influences are evident in the following section detailing the assumptions of the contemporary Marxist theory in understanding international politics and international organizations.

Contemporary Marxism

Marxist perspectives of international relations consist of many different perspectives. These perspectives are distinguished by their emphases on economically determined classes, the international division of labor, and economic forces as critical for understanding international relations. Like realism and liberalism, Marxism rests on several underlying assumptions. The first assumption is that global capitalism determines the position and behavior of actors in international affairs. For the Marxist, the defining characteristic of the international system is not the anarchy of realism or the interdependence of liberalism, but capitalism. Capitalism as a global mode of production is the systemic feature that explains the dynamics of international relations. The world capitalist economic system imposes constraints on actors and motivates their behavior. Private property, the profit motive, and the exigencies of the market affect economic actors and the societies in which they operate.

The assumption that capitalism as a global mode of production matters is not particularly divergent from realist and liberal systemic assumptions. The neorealist sees participation in the global economy as the key to great-power status. Having power enables states to pursue national security and interests under conditions of anarchy. The global economy currently happens to be capitalist. The liberal argues that interdependence results from interaction between private individuals in the market. The Marxist lens simply shifts the focus slightly and emphasizes global capitalism.

The second assumption of the Marxist theory is that the principal unit of analysis is economic class. Marxists see the actors in international relations as being defined by economic class. International relations are driven by economic production; therefore, the principal actors are distinguished by their role in the global production of goods and services. Two of the most prominent Marxist theories, **dependency theory** and **modern world system theory**, vary slightly regarding the role of class. Dependency theorists tend to take a traditional Marxist view on class and apply it to the international system (e.g., Amin 1977; Cardoso and Faletto 1979; Evans 1979; Packenham 1992; Valenzuela and Valenzuela 1978). These theorists seek to explain why economic development has not occurred in many Third World states, particularly those in Latin America. They argue that neocolonialism, capitalist expansion, and the creation of grossly asymmetrical interdependent relationships are responsible for under- and maldevelopment in the Third World.

Dependency theorists explain that underdevelopment in the Third World must be understood in historical context. The majority of Third World states were once colonies of the Western capitalist powers, serving both as captive markets and as sources of raw material and cheap labor. After decolonization, the international bourgeoisie continued to control these newly independent states through more subtle means. Whereas colonialism refers to territorial domination by force, neocolonialism refers to the nonterritorial, economic controls exercised by capitalist states over the developing world.

Neocolonialism represents a more sophisticated exploitation. The military conquest and the subjugation of a population are expensive endeavors. Colonial powers have to administer the affairs of the colonies, thus incurring great costs. Recall Hobson's critique of imperialism, that it was a drain on state resources and benefited only those earning profits from international economic transactions. Under neocolonialism, newly formed Third World states possess sovereignty in legal principle; in practice, however, the colonial powers retain *de facto* control over the raw material, market, and labor. Within the Third World itself, the ruling class, composed largely of willing collaborators who helped administer the colonies, retained control after decolonization. Termed the *comprador class* by dependency theorists, this group of elites became a domestic bourgeoisie, whose role was to aid in the exploitation of their own society by international and transnational capitalists (Viotti and Kauppi 1993, 458). The interests of the comprador class are tied to the interests of global capitalism, not to the development and progress of their own societies.

Dependency theorists analyze the impact of capitalism on developing states; hence, it is fair to say that they consider states as important in international relations. Nevertheless, they see the state as a reflection of the dominant-class interests, the domestic bourgeoisie. The state is subordinated to the bourgeois class that controls it. Seen in its best light, the state reproduces the necessary elements of capitalism (infrastructure, an educated workforce, and so on) and also enforces contracts and property rights. At worst, the state is the "executive committee of the bourgeoisie," which uses the state's coercive authority to further its own interests and exploit subordinate classes.

Modern world system theorists take a similar state-centric approach to international relations, viewing the system as one organized around nation-states. But they see these states as classes of states—each class being determined by a state's place in the international division of labor in a world capitalist system. Immanuel Wallerstein (1980) identifies three such classes, categorizing them as **core, periphery, and semiperiphery**. The core consists of industrialized states, which provide capital to the global economy, as well as highly skilled and well-paid labor. The periphery provides inexpensive, unskilled labor and raw materials. The semiperiphery represents the newly industrializing countries (NICs), which provide cheap, skilled, and semiskilled labor to the global economy. Put another way, the core represents the global bourgeoisie, while the periphery and semiperiphery represent the global proletariat.

The systematic exploitation of the periphery by the core has occurred over the last five-hundred years, although the character of the exploitation has changed significantly. From around 1500 until 1945, core exploitation of the periphery came in the form of (territorial) colonialism. After 1945, the pattern of exploitation shifted from territorial to economic means. Instead of forcibly extracting raw materials using cheap unskilled labor for use in the core, the core either leased the resources or purchased them cheaply on the open market. These resources were brought to the core for the production of highly valued manufactured goods. The manufactured goods were sold in the core, and any surplus was exported to the periphery for sale.

This pattern of exploitation leads to bad terms of trade, meaning the ratio of the value of imports is much greater than the value of exports. Ideally, these values should be equal. But if the value of imports exceeds the value of exports, a state loses wealth because it must pay for imported goods with foreign currency—currency it can get only by borrowing or earning it through the export of its goods. Under bad terms of trade, not enough wealth and capital can be accumulated to form the critical mass necessary for spurring sustained economic growth. Thus, bad terms of trade can be quite detrimental to development. The globalization of production has changed the pattern of exploitation again. The periphery still provides raw materials and unskilled labor; however, the semiperiphery, which includes NICs such as Malaysia, Mexico, Brazil, and Hong Kong, has emerged as an intermediary in the production process. The semiperiphery serves two key purposes for global capitalism. First, it serves as a safety valve when wages become too high in the core. Second, it is the locus for manufacturing as the core economies shift to more service-oriented enterprises such as banking, insurance, and telecommunications.

The pattern of capitalist exploitation has shifted economic analysis away from conceptualizing core/periphery/semiperiphery relations as state-based relationships—say, for example, the idea that France as a core state benefits from the economic exploitation of Algeria, a periphery state. Global production activities have increased the utility of using economic classes as a unit of analysis. Increasingly, workers throughout the core are experiencing either high unemployment or declining real wages. Core/periphery/semiperiphery relations can be characterized by an international bourgeoisie (which just happens to be French or British or American) that benefits at the expense of workers everywhere.

Both modern world system theory and dependency theory see class and the state as part and parcel of each other. Dependency theorists tend to view the state as a reflection of the dominant economic class. Modern world system theorists view the state and the nation-state system as necessary for capitalist accumulation: "A balance of power among a number of leading states inhibits the development of a single overarching political authority that could subvert international production and exchange" (Crane and Amawi 1997, 142). The capitalist accumulation process, of course, benefits the international bourgeoisie.

Marxist views of the state contrast with the realist and liberal views. Realists and liberal institutionalists see the state as a unitary, rational actor seeking to maximize the national interest. Other liberals tend to see the state as a disaggregated entity composed of a congeries of competing interests that results in the maximization of individual welfare. Marxists also see the state as a disaggregated entity composed of classes. In the Marxist worldview, however, one class, the bourgeoisie, usually dominates the government.

A third assumption of Marxist theory is that international relations are essentially conflictual. Exploitation breeds conflict within and between societies.

Capitalism fosters violence as well as economic, social, and political inequality. For Marxists, as long as capitalism (or any other mode of production based on exploitation) dominates international economics, international conflict will continue. International conflict manifests itself in the form of interstate wars, terrorism, and intrastate violence such as government repression or civil war. In an era of global production and the interdependence it breeds, violence within a society often has international and global causes and implications.

A fourth, related assumption is that economic, not political or strategic, factors are most important to understanding international affairs. Issues that appear to be geostrategic and military in nature are rooted in capitalist accumulation and exploitation. After all, military capability and other elements of power are directly related to economic capability. Wars between great and lesser powers have occurred because of colonialism. In the postcolonial period, wars have occurred because of access to markets, labor, and resources. Hegemonic or great-power wars such as World Wars I and II were as much about how the world was going to produce things as about who would be the world leader. The Cold War was not the product of the Soviet Union's posing a serious military threat to the West. Rather, it was the result of the U.S. quest for a capitalist economic empire (Kolko and Kolko 1972).

Marxism and the Nature of International Organizations

Like many liberals and realists, Marxists argue that international organizations are created through hegemony. However, traditional Marxists and Gramscian Marxists have diverging notions of hegemony, notions that lead them to different conclusions regarding the nature of international organizations. Traditional Marxists tend to equate hegemony with military and economic dominance. International organizations are created, then imposed on the rest of the world. International organizations reinforce and promote the capitalist mode of production whereby the dominant position of the core and the subordinate positions of the semiperiphery and periphery are institutionalized (see, e.g., Bennis 1996). International organizations are mechanisms of capitalist domination and exploitation. The international order established by the United States after World War II was a capitalist system in which the United States had a competitive advantage in industrial production. An international system based on liberal (capitalist) economic principles would allow American businesses to penetrate markets worldwide. For traditional Marxists, the root of U.S. hegemony was its ability to impose its capitalist vision. Political, economic, and social organizations reflect the underlying economic system. Contemporary international relations and organizations are shaped and informed by and are reflective of contemporary world capitalism.

Gramscian-inspired Marxists differ from traditional Marxists and realists in that they have a broader conception of hegemony. Recall that Gramsci links ideas to power, claiming that hegemony is the relation of consent to political and ideological leadership (Simon 1982, 11). How does the ruling class (or class of states) get subordinate classes (or classes of states) to consent to their own domination and exploitation? The answer is this: by linking the dominant-class interests to the interests of subordinate classes. For example, the international order created by the United States was based on several principles—principles that developed U.S. hegemony in the Third World. First, the United States insisted on the end of colonialism and charged the UN with assisting in the decolonization process. Decolonization was based on the Wilsonian idea of "self-determination," the idea that each society has the right to decide for itself the type of government it wants as well as the right to chart its own course in international affairs. Self-determination is a very powerful idea, particularly to societies under the yoke of European colonialism. The United States then represented these colonies' opportunity to become self-governing. However, decolonization also meant that U.S. corporations would finally have access to the markets, resources, and labor that had previously been denied by the Europeans. By tying U.S. interests to the interests of developing states, the United States was able to gain consent to its domination. International organizations like the UN facilitated this linking of interests and promoted U.S. leadership.

In other Gramscian Marxist perspectives, international organizations are seen as instrumental in the development of modern capitalism (see, e.g., Murphy 1994). International organizations are crucial for linking evolving capitalism to evolving nation-states. Thus, global governance by international organizations guides nation-states through the rough waters of global industrial change. International organizations facilitate and manage industrial change by conditioning the impact of states on changing markets and vice versa. These Marxists acknowledge contemporary international organizations as reflections of the underlying capitalist order, but they also attribute to international organizations a pivotal role in shaping the development of liberal ideology together with the development of capitalism.

Marxist, realist, and liberal explanations regarding the creation of international organizations are not wholly dissimilar, although their differences lead to different conclusions about the nature of international organizations. Many Marxists, realists, and liberals see hegemony as requisite for the creation of international organizations. Realists and traditional Marxists conceive of hegemony as military, political, and economic dominance. Liberal institutionalists and Gramscian Marxists not only view hegemony as domination but also seek to understand why others would consent to domination. Liberal institutionalists see that hegemony benevolently gains deference to its leadership by providing public goods and making side payments. Gramscian Marxists argue that hegemony involves more than just buying off subordinate classes or lesser powers. It involves developing a coherent set of values that transcend class and national boundaries but never compromise the position of the dominant class.

The nature of international organizations, therefore, varies by theoretical approach. Realists see international organizations as no more than the sum of their member states. International organizations are largely intergovernmental, great-power directorates susceptible to great-power manipulation. The behavior of international organizations can be explained by the interests of the great powers and the underlying balance of power. For liberals, international organizations can be IGOs, NGOs, MNCs, or regimes. They can be relatively independent agents that help states overcome collective action problems and create an international environment conducive to economic prosperity. Marxists see international organizations as both public and private, consisting of state and nonstate actors. They conceive of these organizations as mechanisms of capitalist domination, both reflecting and legitimizing the underlying economic order. Each theory provides a slightly different focus, which leads to different explanations and understandings of international organizations.

Marxism and the Role of International Organizations

Marxist theory suggests three interrelated roles for international organizations. For IGOs like the UN, they are political complements to capitalism. Financed and controlled by the capitalist states, they promote a capitalist agenda. The political institutions of the UN, such as the Security Council and the General Assembly, are hobbled by procedural rules that make them ineffective as organs of international governance. This enables capitalism to expand unchallenged. In an environment of interstate competition and rivalry, capitalists are unfettered by significant international restriction—they are free to seek new outlets for goods and new sources of raw materials and cheap labor. The principles of sovereignty and nonintervention allow the capitalist states to pick and choose when, where, and how the "international community" will act against a state. International intervention usually happens only when there is a compelling economic interest.

The only realm in which "supranationalism" is evident is the economic realm. Supranationalism simply means that international organizations exercise authority over states. IGOs such as the EU and the WTO possess the legal authority to override the policies of states that impede the free flow of goods and services across national boundaries. The interests of international and transnational capitalists are furthered at the expense of national capitalists and labor, whose interests are largely tied to national economies. Should a government seek to protect the latter's interests, the legal framework exists to nullify state policy.

The independent economic agencies of the UN, such as the IMF and the World Bank, impose capitalist features such as private property and wage labor on developing societies. These societies are forced to accept the market, which is easily manipulated by financial and corporate elites, as the mechanism for distributing wealth, resources, and values. As long as the market distributes wealth, resources, and values, the owners of the means of production will always benefit at the expense of wage earners. In the context of modern world system theory, the core will always benefit at the expense of the periphery. As long as the IMF and the World Bank continue to demand market reforms in exchange for development and stabilization loans, periphery states will see, at best, maldevelopment and, at worst, chronic underdevelopment.

The lending and development policies of the IMF and the World Bank are grounded in neoclassical economic thought, that is, they are neoliberal or capitalist institutions. On the basis of comparative advantage, the liberal sees specialization as the key to maximizing global economic growth. However, in periphery states, the comparative advantage consists of providing raw materials and cheap unskilled labor to the global market, an "advantage" that cannot generate the same kind of wealth and income that comes from producing durable and highly valued manufactured goods. Producing potato chips is not as advantageous or lucrative as producing computer chips, and potato chip production does not generate the kind of income that enables the vast majority in the periphery to buy products containing computer chips. Periphery states will lose wealth and remain underdeveloped because they have chronic balance-of-payments problems resulting from their bad terms of trade.

A second, related role of international organizations is that of mechanism of domination. International organizations are tools that core states use to exploit and control the weak. Periphery societies are controlled politically because they are given a voice in organizations like the UN in which that voice carries very little weight. The decolonization process provided periphery states with the trappings of sovereignty. The newly formed states thus have the right to govern themselves but not the means. Their ruling classes are collaborators with the core states, and their interests are tied to the core. The ruling class controls the government, and that government is what is represented at the UN. Hence, many UN officials are the elites of periphery states. Their constituencies often include the ruling classes and are committed to capitalist values.

Self-determination is a principle that is recognized only when societies determine for themselves that they will embrace capitalism. Developing states that do not embrace capitalism or who threaten core economic interests are subject to intervention. The UN paid only lip service to the principle of nonintervention when the United States invaded the Dominican Republic, Grenada, and Panama and while intervening covertly in Iran, Guatemala, Cuba, Chile, and Nicaragua. All of these states had one of two things in common. Their governments were guided by nationalist or populist sentiments and/or they sought to embrace a different mode of production—socialism or communism. Most of these had democratically elected governments, and those that were not had overthrown extremely brutal dictators or military regimes. Yet, the UN did nothing, hobbled by its own rules and procedures.

Economically, international organizations have a more direct role in dominating weak societies. Private international banks have entangled developing states in a web of debt that permits their continued exploitation. The IMF and the World Bank provide just enough assistance to keep them from defaulting on their loans. Developing states are forced to borrow more just to pay on the interest. The result is a debt crisis that the majority of developing states now face. According to Marxists, this crisis is the inevitable consequence of global capitalism. Multilateral and international banks exercise a great deal of leverage and can force compliance with capitalist mandates.

For Marxists, the MNC is a classic example of an international organization as a tool of exploitation and a mechanism of domination that fosters underdevelopment. The drive for market efficiency leads MNCs to states that have lax environmental and labor standards. Many MNCs will use child and prison labor if it reduces costs. They will locate where labor is not represented by unions or any type of collective bargaining to order to keep their labor costs down. Where the liberal sees that the MNCs are providing jobs, Marxists see those same MNCs as exploiting global competition for jobs to drive down wages to subsistence levels or even below.

MNCs can also directly and indirectly challenge sovereignty. MNCs are exceptionally wealthy entities; thus, they can directly compromise a host state's sovereignty through bribery and even private armies. Moreover, most MNCs are headquartered in core states, where they possess all the rights and privileges of citizens. Hence, they can also challenge a host state's sovereignty by appealing to their home governments for intervention when their interests are threatened. International Telegraph and Telephone (IT&T) and United Fruit, for example, were integrally involved in U.S. intervention in Chile and Guatemala, respectively. And British Petroleum (BP), Shell, and a consortium of U.S. oil companies were linked to Cold War interventions in Iran and Egypt.

State sovereignty can also be compromised indirectly because the competition for capital gives MNCs significant leverage over governments. All states—core, periphery, and semiperiphery—seek to attract capital for development. This enables MNCs, effectively, to play governments off each other to get the best possible "location package." Such packages usually entail promises of infrastructure for the MNCs such as roads and utilities. More important, MNCs are able to negotiate significant tax concessions from local and national governments. These concessions usually entail allowing the MNCs to operate tax-free for an extended period of time, sometimes indefinitely. The power to tax is the defining indicator of a sovereign government. When a government cannot or will not tax its subjects, its authority over them is considerably weakened. Of the two proverbial certainties—death and taxes—MNCs seem able to elude at least one.

Many observers have pointed out that the activities of MNCs are not necessarily beneficial to the home states (Biersteker 1978; Cohen 1986; Reich 1991). The credo of the 1950s, "What's good for General Motors is good for the U.S.A.," is no longer true. What's good for General Motors is profits—profits that can be increased by locating in areas where labor is cheaper. For the United States, that means a loss of high-paying jobs and a reduction of the tax base. Entire communities are devastated, and families are forced to pull up roots, moving to find jobs that pay a fraction of their previous wages or salaries. MNCs can also displace exports and domestic industries. Businesses that rely on domestic labor and resources cannot compete with MNCs operating with global economies of scale. National businesses are driven out of the market, causing unemployment and a further reduction of the tax base.

A third and closely related role of both private and public international organizations is as developers of hegemony. Traditional Marxists have tended to view hegemony as sheer domination. Hence, international organizations reflect, reinforce, and impose capitalism. However, coercive domination is not an effective means of control, at least in the long run. Effective control comes from the consent of the dominated. Gramscian Marxists see international organizations as important instruments for selling capitalism, an economic mode of production under which the vast majority of the world's people are impoverished, malnourished, and exploited. A tough sell? Not really—not when capitalism is coupled with the ideas of self-determination, human rights, and democracy and is, besides, the only game in town. The implementation of these ideas in the real world suggests that they take a backseat to market capitalism and are sacrificed if they interfere in any significant way with capitalist accumulation. Nevertheless, the ideas are important selling points.

The evolution of the market from local, to national, to international, and now to global suggests that hegemony must also evolve. The dialectical nature of this evolution suggests that new selling points must be developed, and that the dominant class must ensure that its interests become the interests of subordinate classes. Many observers have pointed to the increasing preeminence of the transnational capitalist class (e.g., Cox 1987; Gill 1991; van der Pijl 1984). Public international organizations (e.g., the UN, IMF, WTO, EU, and NATO) and private international organizations (e.g., the Trilateral Commission, the International Chamber of Commerce, and MNCs) serve the dual purpose of fostering class consciousness (identity) among the transnational bourgeoisie and delegitimizing nationalist interests (labor and national capital) in both developed and underdeveloped societies.

Transnational capitalists are committed to the globalization of production and capital mobility (Gill 1991, 55). Global production requires the free flow of goods and services across national boundaries. Capital mobility requires the ability and the right to move capital from one national jurisdiction to another. The principal obstacles to achieving these transnational goals are governments seeking national goals, such as full employment and economic development at the expense of transnational interests. Hence, transnational interests are pitted against national interests—the antithesis of the Cold War experience when these interests were synonymous within the core states. Politics in Europe and the United States reflect this antithesis—whether or not to join the EU or the WTO, organizations that formalize the dominant position and interests of transnational capital. Transnational capital seeks to tie its interests to subordinate interests, namely national interests. It is in the "national interest" of these states to join, even though clearly transnational capital will gain and national capital and labor will lose. The world economy is really run by transnational capitalists who congregate in five-star hotels in the world's capitals and collude annually in Davos, Switzerland.

A final role of international organizations is to help states (which are controlled by the bourgeoisie) sustain global capitalism in the face of recurring financial and economic crises. The global financial crisis, which began in 2008, required trillions of taxpayer dollars to keep wealthy multinational banks solvent. This required global coordination under the auspices of the G-20 (a group of the 20 largest economies), the IMF, and the World Bank. Taxpayers, in essence, paid to bailout banks and have borne the cost of having lax financial regulations. Yet, both nationally and internationally, financial MNCs resist even modest attempts to regulate their activities.

Marxism and International Law

International law provides the legal structure for promoting the rules and the values associated with the capitalist mode of production. The law is transnational in nature and governs trade, investment, and finance (Cutler 2008, 200). Far from being laissez faire, global capitalism is full of formal rules and regulations about what states and other actors can and cannot do in relation to private capital. Laws favor transnational capitalists and their ability to make profits across national boundaries without undue interference by others. International law relating to the acquisition and the expropriation of property favors those who possess the property regardless of how that property was obtained. The right to property is considered a basic human right, whereas the rights of workers to organize, collectively bargain, and to work for a living wage, if even accepted as human rights, are subordinate to other rights. Increasingly, international law is being used to displace the welfare state and promote economic liberalization, which benefits transnational capital accumulation. Transnational economic law is one of the few areas where the law is routinely enforced by states and international organizations.

International law is also made by the strong Western capitalist countries to control weak peripheral countries (Snyder and Sathirathai 1987). Customary international law, which most developing states had no part in forming because of their colonial past, is still binding on them. When developing states tried to use international law to create a more equitable system called the New International Economic Order (NIEO); they were rebuffed by the core states. The NIEO tried to formalize important ideas such as the right of economic self-determination and sovereignty over natural resources, but to no avail. International law in the twenty-first century reinforces the existing international division of labor, maintaining the privileged position of the West.

For Marxists, the development of international law parallels the development of the world market from its beginnings in the 1400s until today (Mieville 2006). International law has legitimized different modes of production from slavery to capitalism. While formal slavery has since been outlawed by international law, the working conditions in some parts of the world approximate slavery in its many dimensions. International law is imperialism because it imposes values and rules on subordinate states and classes. At the same time, the belief in law reinforces the dominant position of the transnational bourgeoisie because subordinate classes have internalized the value of legalism, without critically assessing what the law is and how it justifies the gross inequalities in international relations.

The Critics of Marxism

There is no shortage of criticism for Marxist theory. First, Marxists tend to rely on economic factors to explain political behavior (Viotti and Kauppi 1993, 464–465). The idea that war and the foreign policies of states are principally driven by economics ignores the fact that war existed before capitalism. The foreign policy of states is indeed influenced by geostrategic security and other factors such as nationalism or religion. Marxists are hard-pressed to explain how the intense violent conflict over such barren territory as the Gaza Strip or the West Bank is economically motivated. Similarly, it is difficult to explain Islamic fundamentalism as simply a function of class conflict.

Second, Marxist analyses tend to be deterministic. Just as liberals see underdevelopment and poverty as the result of poor choices on the part of individuals and governments, Marxist see capitalism as the root of these problems. For liberals, the market is the solution, never the problem. For Marxists, capitalism is the problem, never the solution. Liberals blame the individual, and Marxists blame the system. This makes the arguments of liberals and Marxists tautological because, in effect, they assume their conclusions.

In sum, Marxists posit different roles for international organizations in international relations, and they have a very different notion of global governance. International organizations are tools of the dominant class that emerges with capitalism—the transnational bourgeoisie. They impose and reinforce the capitalist mode of production and facilitate capitalist exploitation. In terms of global welfare, capitalism generates enormous wealth for the few and poverty for the many. International organizations also serve as mechanisms for developing hegemony of transnational capitalists. Transnational capitalists, who are accountable only to their shareholders, are committed to the erosion of governmental regulation of the market and the mobility of capital. The consequences for the vast majority of individuals are continued exploitation, lower wages, and job insecurity.

FEMINISM

Feminist theory is relatively new to international relations. Its central purpose is to understand how "**gender**" affects international politics and our understanding of international processes. In this case, gender is defined as a social construction that indicates what it means to be masculine or feminine. Thus, gender is different from **sex**. While sex is the obvious anatomobiological difference between men and women, gender refers to societal norms and expectations regarding appropriate masculine and feminine behavior. For example, men are expected to engage in war and women are not. Women are expected to care for children, while men are expected to work outside the home. Gender roles might be rooted in biological differences, but they are not necessarily "natural." That is, just because only females can bear children, it does not follow that only females can care for children. The feminine gender role of women as caregivers stems from their sex difference, but societal expectations are such that women are also expected to take care of the children. Gender analyses examine what it means to be masculine or feminine beyond the obvious anatomical differences. Feminist scholars argue that political, economic, and social relations are ordered around gender identities.

The use of gender as a lens provides important insights as to what is known about international relations and how it came to be known. In the 1980s, feminist scholarship emerged to challenge the hidden assumptions embedded in the traditional theoretical approaches of realism, liberalism, and Marxism. These theories of international relations rest implicitly on universality. International conditions such as anarchy, interdependence, markets, and global capitalism are assumed to affect men and women in the same manner. They assume that men and women will respond to these conditions in the same way and that the concepts and language used to describe and analyze international relations are gender-neutral. Feminists argue that gender is a useful category for examining global politics and criticizing mainstream theories. Gender allows scholars to examine the impact of international relations on women and the role women play in those relations. Scholars can examine gender as a "power relation" also. That is, they ask, "Why are women as a social category almost always underrepresented in relations of power?" (Pettman 1998, 488). Both the theory and the practice of international relations are "gendered," and that has consequences for men and women alike.

Feminism as a worldview has been under attack by conservatives in the United States and elsewhere because it challenges status quo beliefs. Sometimes referred to as "femi-nazis" by such talk-radio commentators as Rush Limbaugh, feminists are excoriated for their staunch support of equal rights for women and the right of women to abort an unwanted pregnancy. Many conservatives see equal rights for women as destructive of the family, and abortion as the equivalent to a holocaust of children perpetrated by feminists. Feminists have also been stereotyped as crew cut, man-hating "bull dykes." That way, it is easy to dismiss feminist insights. But such negative stereotypes or religious beliefs that run counter to feminist issues should not deter students from engaging those insights critically. Just as students can learn from Marxism without becoming Marxists, students can learn from feminism without becoming feminists. Feminism simply looks at the world through the lens of gender. What feminism discovers through this lens challenges traditional, status quo understandings, and that disturbs many conservatives in political as well as academic circles. But such disturbances are also, quite literally, thought-provoking. Not, all in all, a bad thing.

The international relations discipline has traditionally been populated by male scholars studying issues that have historically concerned men—war, politics, economics, and the like. Discussion of women's roles, contributions, and issues are rare and tend to be trivialized because the female experience is not as valued as the male experience. Feminist international relations theory is controversial among scholars within the discipline, and its analyses are widely viewed with skepticism. Is feminist theory marginalized because it represents the scholarship of women, or is it just poor scholarship? Who gets to decide what is good scholarship? These questions will continue to be debated in academia for years to come. At the very least, feminist theorists have challenged realist, liberal, and Marxist theorists to reexamine their respective frameworks and revisit their conclusions (Keohane 1989; Niva 1998; Smith 1998).

Here we examine the contributions of feminist scholarship to understanding international relations and international organizations. Feminist theory enhances our understanding of the nature and behavior of international organizations in two meaningful ways. First, the lens of gender focuses on aspects of international relations and organizations that are often overlooked by the traditional approaches. Different questions are raised: How does war or the market affect women? How are women represented in international organizations? What impact do women have on policies of international organizations and vice versa?

Second, feminist theorists highlight the **masculinity** inherent in realism, liberalism, and Marxism and show how that bias influences conventional explanations regarding the behavior of actors participating in international politics. Feminists maintain that international relations theory is, in fact, gender biased and, as a result, so too are the usual analyses of international organizations. The feminist epistemological contribution lies in recognizing that what we know and how we know it is shaped by societal norms and expectations about what it means to be male or female.

Feminist Influences

No rich intellectual or historical tradition prefigures feminist theory, at least in the conventional sense. Some argue that, historically, women were not scholars, writers, or philosophers, so it is not surprising that they have contributed little to academic tradition, much less to feminism. No woman is considered a significant contributor to realism, liberalism, or Marxism because few, if any, women were scholars at the time. Feminist scholarship did not become prominent until the 1970s, as more women entered academia. This kind of explanation for the absence of women in international relations theory can be controversial because it assumes that feminism is strictly associated with the increase of women in academic roles. Feminists argue that while sex influences gender, it is gender (societal expectations) that explains why women have been excluded from scholarly analysis, either as academics or as analytic categories.

Feminist theory has been indirectly influenced by the **international women's social movement** (Rupp 1998). A social movement is a concerted effort among groups to achieve political, social, and economic change. In the United States, the women's movement has been closely related with the civil rights movement, which seeks equality of rights regardless of race, sex, creed, or culture. The civil rights movement began in the nineteenth century with efforts to abolish slavery. Slavery was a glaring contradiction to the Enlightenment philosophy, which had given rise to such liberal principles as "all men are created equal" and "all men were born with certain inalienable rights." Women began to appear on the political landscape, first as abolitionists and then as advocates of women's rights. Women in the United States finally gained the right to vote with the Nineteenth Amendment in 1920.

The early suffrage movements in the United States and Europe were facilitated by several international organizations. Such organizations included the **International Council of Women** founded in 1888, the **International Women's Suffrage Alliance** founded in 1904, and the **International Women's League for Peace and Freedom** founded in 1916. The early suffrage movements highlighted the gender roles of women in Western societies during that period. The gender roles of women in large part relegated them to the home, the most private area of private life. The venture of women into the public sphere of politics by seeking the right to vote has contributed to societies' changing notion of gender. Women's right to vote was once thought of as a revolt against nature, whereupon women would grow beards and lose their babies (Welch et al. 1997, 174). Today, such fears are hardly taken seriously.

The women's movement and the civil rights movement did not end with the right to vote. An international women's movement has evolved and has been facilitated by IGOs and NGOs geared toward improving the status of women globally. This movement is characterized by a series of struggles to gain equality of rights in fact as well as in law. Women in many developing countries do not even have the trappings of legal equality. In the developed world, women have formal equality, but are still denied equal access to schools, jobs, housing, and pay. The international women's movement affected feminist theory in two ways. First, it enabled women to venture outside of their traditional gender roles, becoming lawyers, professors, and politicians. Second, the women's movement demonstrated how powerful social constructions are in shaping our understanding of the social, political, and economic worlds. Even after formal and legal barriers have been removed, women still do not receive equal pay for equal work. Women are still underrepresented in positions of economic and political power. Something other than legal impediment is at work to account for the differences in power between men and women. Feminist theory shows that we often understand the world in gendered ways and, consequently, how the female experience is easily ignored or trivialized by history, political science, economics, and even the physical and biological sciences.

Feminist scholarship considers the ways in which gender has shaped our understanding of international relations. Consider the intellectual precursors to realism, liberalism, and Marxism. The gender lens magnifies the masculine nature of their contributions. Every one of the philosophers we discussed is a man speaking about men. These philosophers focus on the activities and the nature of men, which leads them to describe events in very masculine terms. The idea that Hobbes and Smith were theorizing about "human nature" is misleading. They were theorizing about the condition of men—masculine nature. Women, thought to be softer and more docile, were possessed of a more delicate and accommodating nature. The translation of historical writings into gender-neutral language does not eliminate their masculine bias. Rather, it essentially universalizes masculine behavior.

The philosophical roots of realism demonstrate how masculine behavior becomes universalized in theory. Thucydides focuses on the dialog between Athenian men and Melian men. Hobbes's Leviathan is clearly male, possessing very masculine characteristics. Machiavelli writes about a prince, not a princess. These great thinkers were men writing about men and the experiences of men. Contemporary realists use these insights to show how the "real" world is and how responsible leaders should behave.

Feminists point out that it is not the sex of the actors, it is their expected behavior. The social expectations created by the early realist thinkers are behaviors that are definitely masculine. International relations for the realist boils down to an ability to impose one's will physically and forcibly. Is imposing one's will physically and forcibly considered feminine behavior? No. To be feminine means having to take it, to be forced to accept the will of others. The masculine–feminine relationship is one of dominance and subordinance, of superiority and inferiority. Margaret Thatcher was able to impose her will militarily on the generals of the Argentine junta during the Falkland Islands War (1982). Margaret Thatcher, though female, was behaving in a masculine way, and the generals, though male, were in a feminine position. Hobbes's Leviathan could be a woman, although she would be expected to behave in a violent, dominating, and threatening fashion.

Liberal philosophers are equally masculine in their approach, and their objects of study are principally men. Adam Smith argues that society is based on economic exchange. Social relationships are formed when men exchange goods and services with each other. Smith assumes that men emerge as fully formed and rational adults, ready to truck, barter, and trade. He ignores that other social relationship—the family. By ignoring the social relationships in the family, where women have influence, he is trivializing the feminine in economics. Smith's market, like the actors within it, is endowed with very masculine characteristics. The market is disciplined, logical, and unbiased; the actors are rational and self-interested. Being undisciplined, illogical, biased, irrational, and caring of others are feminine stereotypes and, as such, make up no part of Adam Smith's world.

Liberal political thinkers are uncomfortably quiet on the topic of women's rights, although John Stuart Mill did write on the status of women in *The Subjection of Women* (1858), in which he opposes the legal subordination of women (Cahn 1997, 929). Others are not so progressive. Kant argues that women should not be enfranchised because they are economic dependents and unequal to men. John Locke ignores women altogether, stating that men are entitled to their own private dominions where no government may interfere. This distinction between private and public is important because the private—the household—is where the women are.

Early Marxist influences also ignore women in their writings, although Marx and Engels did argue that the subjugation of women is property-based. Women were unequal because they could not own property; but once private property was eliminated, the inequalities between men and women would be rectified. For feminist Marxists, class analysis is insufficient for explaining gender inequalities or the kinds of work that are considered feminine. Marx emphasizes the condition of industrial workers, most of whom are men, and their exploitation by the bourgeoisie. Class analysis ignores unpaid "women's work" in the homes of the bourgeoisie and the proletariat.

The philosophical influences on the feminist theory in international relations are indirect. Feminist theory has been influenced by the women's movement, which has enabled more women to enter professions that allow them to speak authoritatively on issues. The theory has also evolved as a reaction to the masculine nature of realism, liberalism, and Marxism. This reaction offers substantially more than a critique of men for speaking about men and criticism of masculine issues. It involves identifying the hidden, gender-biased assumptions embedded in these theories and providing an alternative for examining and explaining international relations and organizations.

Contemporary Feminism

Feminist international relations theory does not speak with one voice. Just as realism has traditional, neo, and structural variations, feminism also has several variations. According to Ferber and Nelson (1993, 38–39), one strand of feminism emphasizes the exclusion of women from traditionally male activities and institutions, while other strands emphasize the ways in which traditional feminine activities and traits are devalued, trivialized, and associated with low reward or status. The former strand, or **"traditional feminism,"** sees men and women as basically equal, attributing any inequality to gendered stereotypes. Thus, the inclusion of women in traditionally masculine roles will erode gendered perceptions and beliefs. Among the latter varieties of feminism, there is the **"neofeminism"** strand, which valorizes feminine traits. These feminists, also known as essentialist feminists, tend to see the biological differences between men and women as accounting for many gender traits. Women are seen as more cooperative, sensitive, intuitive, and nurturing than men. However, these traits are denigrated, either through their exclusion from analysis or through their dismissal as insignificant elements of international politics. Another strand of feminism, **"postmodern feminism,"** emphasizes the gender-laden language and gendered concepts used to describe international relations. Adding gender or women as a category of study is not enough to dispel gender bias as they often appear as "victims" or as a residual category of the nonadult male. Hence, many feminists include the trials of women in the context of the ill-effects on women and children, which reinforces gender responsibilities and expectations regarding who is to be protected. Postmodern feminism challenges not only the substance of international relations but its methods of research as well.

These different strands of feminism also have liberal and Marxist variants. For example, traditional, **liberal feminists** focus on equality between the sexes and highlight exclusion of women from the political process. They see the empowerment of women as the key to improving the status of women. They differ from liberal neofeminists in that they do not think that men and women behave differently. For the liberal neofeminists, the inclusion of women will fundamentally change the political environment. Similarly, **Marxist feminists** challenge the idea that capitalism is beneficial for women either within or outside of their traditional gender roles (Bergeron 1999). Also, because of the international division of labor, women do not necessarily have uniform interests. The interests of women in war-ravaged Congo are quite different from female factory laborers in China and professional women in the United States.

In spite of their differences, traditional, neo, and postmodern feminism strands and their theoretical variants are based on four interrelated assumptions. The first assumption is that gender matters. Gender can be biologically based, but the social meanings of gender are also important for understanding international relations. Gender as the principal unit of analysis increases the purview of international relations issues. Wars are not just about troops, tanks, weapons, and battles. Wars include women engaging in traditionally male activities—as soldiers, guerrillas, heads of state, ambassadors, and reporters. Wars also include women operating in traditionally feminine roles—as mothers, nurses, prostitutes, and pacifists. Gender also refocuses on aspects of war that have not been systematically addressed, such as the close relationship between sex and violence, the role of rape in war, and the dire consequences of war for women and children.

In addition to expanding analysis, gender permits a reexamination of the language and concepts commonly used to describe international relations. Consider realists' emphasis on the state or liberals' emphasis on the individual. Both are considered rational. On the surface, this characteristic seems neutral enough, although scrutiny through the lens of gender shows that the state and the individual are quite masculine. To realists and liberals, "rational" means self-interested. Self-interested behavior for the realist is indicated by power- or interest-maximizing behavior. For liberals, individuals engage in self-maximizing behavior in the market. This kind of behavior is contrasted with altruistic behavior, which is feminine in nature. According to realists, altruistic behavior can rarely take place, and according to liberals, it occurs only within the household. Liberals are able to bridge the gap between selfish behavior and the collective good by arguing, in a very rational way, that being selfish leads to social harmony.

A postmodern feminist interpretation might see debate between realists and liberals as a version of *quien es mas macho*. Both posit rationality, but offer competing versions of masculinity. The realists focus on military force and other elements of coercion. Liberals focus on economic prowess and the ability to offer positive and economic inducements. The debate between realists and liberals first manifested itself as a debate between realism and idealism. This debate has a gender bias in that realists somehow understood the "real" world, while the idealists (liberals) maintained a utopian outlook. A postmodern feminist translation might argue that this is another way of saying that women can afford to be idealistic because they don't have to worry about the day-to-day realities that "real" men face. Realists trivialize liberal insights regardless of the merit of their arguments. Conversely, liberals have portrayed nationalism as irrational (feminine) and realism as something other than utilitarian. In other words, scholars are more than willing to use gendered language and methods to trivialize competitors from other paradigms.

A second assumption of the feminist theory is that the nature of international relations is essentially conflictual. Conflict results from the **superior–subordinate nature of gender relationships.** Biology may account for many differences between men and women (essential feminists), but the determination of whether "masculine" or "feminine" differences are superior or inferior is socially constructed. This assumption extends the analysis of international conflict to women in order to explain women in war and how and why their experience differs from men. It also allows scholars to explain exploitation that extends beyond the market or economic class.

In addition to expanding analysis, the idea of gendered conflict allows for a reexamination of conflict in traditional international relations theories. These theories focus on one of the following: Realists ascribe a central role to geostrategic conflict in which states are maximizing their self-interest; liberals focus on individual and group conflict, but allow for the resolution of that conflict by democratic institutions and processes (market forces) that maximize the global welfare; Marxists shift the focus to class conflict, which emerges from market-based, capitalist economies; and feminists argue that conflict, as conceptualized by these theories, has a masculine bias in that it ignores women. Thus, conflict, while pervasive in other paradigms, is based on attributes other than gender.

A third assumption of feminist theory is that international relations is characterized by **patriarchy.** Patriarchy, or male dominance, pervades almost every political, social, and economic organization and institution, whether domestic or international. These include government agencies, legislatures, courts, firms, universities, secondary schools, NGOs, IGOs, MNCs, and regimes. Feminists argue that male dominance has built into these organizations a bias toward masculine values and behaviors. The assumption of patriarchy "problematizes" the masculinity and the hegemony of men (e.g., Zalewski and Parpart 1998, 1). That is, the problems in international relations might be rooted in what is masculine about the world. Patriarchy is so prevalent within and between societies that it would be academically irresponsible not to explore the possible relationship between male dominance and social problems.

The fourth assumption of the feminist theoretical framework is that international issues are ranked in a gendered fashion. International issues traditionally considered feminine in nature—education, health, poverty, the environment, and justice—occupy low positions in the international agenda. Efforts to manage and find durable solutions to the problems associated with these issues are underfunded and subordinated to state or market interests.

Feminism and Theories of International Organizations

Feminist theory uncovers the hidden masculine biases of realist, liberal, and Marxist interpretations of international organizations. The lens of gender focuses on the masculinities associated with conceptualizing the behavior and nature of international organizations. Realism, liberalism, and Marxism are similar in that they see international organizations in largely mechanical terms. International organizations are "tools," either to dominate other states or classes or to overcome collective action problems. The differences between theories can be interpreted through degrees of masculinity. Several scholars have pointed out that contemporary realism is extremely masculine in nature (Peterson 1992; Runyan and Peterson 1990; Tickner 1988). Realist concepts such as "state," "anarchy," and "high politics" all have masculine biases. For realists, the state is an entity that possesses sovereignty; that is, it has the final say within its territorial jurisdiction. The state determines what public policy will be, and no higher authority exists to review state decisions. The realist conception of the state as a unitary rational actor possessed of sovereignty smacks of the conventional (sexist) wisdom that a "man's home is his castle" and that "he is master of the house." No man has the right to tell another what he can do in his own home. Sovereignty also implies autonomy, another masculine attribute. Psychologically, men see themselves as separate from others, whereas women tend to see themselves as part of a collective (see, e.g, Goldstein 1996, 111–112). Relatedly, the idea of anarchy, or the absence of a higher authority, is quite masculine; it conjures up images of individuals interacting in a state of nature that reduces to survival of the fittest. Brute force is the final arbiter of disputes. This is why "high" politics focuses on geostrategic and military issues. These are male issues. "Low" politics consists of issues that are deemed feminine, like the environment, human rights, poverty, and education.

The masculine bias of realism leads to biased interpretation of international organizations in terms of which kinds of organizations are important in international relations and what their role should be. Realists argue that international organizations are little more than the sum of their member states. They are tools by which the great powers dominate lesser states. International organizations are subordinate to the state and dependent on the largesse of states. International organizations are feminized by realist theory in two ways. First, international organizations are objects to be used by states to further their interests in world politics. They have no significant independence. At best, they might function as the "wife" of the state, who exerts some influence in some areas but would not challenge the primacy of state sovereignty. Like the traditional wife, international organizations are dependent on states for their identity, direction, and income. Second, realists emphasize the IGO; NGOs (organizations in which women are more likely to participate) are excluded from realist analyses altogether. NGO activity in international relief and development efforts is trivialized by being relegated to the realm of low politics.

Liberalism has a different masculine bias, although it does allow for consideration of feminine issues. Liberals see the state as an aggregation of competing interests within a society. Assuming equality of resources (a questionable assumption), any group or coalition of groups can come to dominate the government. In this sense, women can have an important influence on government and public policy. Consequently, feminine issues (e.g., poverty, education, and environment) can come to dominate the domestic and international agenda. Liberal institutionalism, a variation of liberalism, does conceive of the state as a unitary and rational actor, thus displaying the same masculine bias as realism—the autonomous state reacts rationally (self-interestedly), not in an intuitive or emotional manner.

Liberalism also emphasizes interdependence as an attribute of the international system. That is, states rely on each other mutually, although not necessarily in the same ways. Liberal international relations theory has feminine characteristics in that it accentuates the interconnectedness of societies and the idea that national security might best be obtained through collective, or multilateral, means, rather than unilaterally.

In spite of the liberal emphasis on interconnectedness and equality, the central underpinning is masculine. The market is the key organizing concept, one that is masculine. Neoclassical economics, which provides liberalism with its understanding of the market, is based on mathematical models and proofs. According to Nelson (1996, 20–21),

> The idealized market is a place where rational, autonomous, anonymous agents with stable preferences interact for the purposes of exchange. The agents make their choices in accordance with the maximization of some objective function subject to resource constraints, and the outcome of their market interactions is the determination of an efficient allocation of goods along with a set of equilibrium prices. The prototypical market is one in which tangible goods or labor services are exchanged, with money facilitating transactions in which the agents are individual persons. The prototypical scholarly work in economics is an article that studies market behavior using sophisticated mathematics to formalize the model in the "theory" section, accompanied by econometrics analysis of data in an "empirical" section.

Liberals emphasize that the individual, household, or firm is operating in a market. In this sense, the liberal world is just as masculine as the realist's anarchic world. The debate between realism and liberalism is often gendered in that each tries to portray the other as feminine. For the liberal, the market is unbiased, governed by objective laws of supply and demand. The market becomes unpredictable (feminine) when it is disrupted by irrational (feminine) behavior that may be motivated by nationalism or religion. The state is feminized by liberalism, particularly if it governs too much. The state is fiscally irresponsible (feminine) and is incapable of carrying out complex tasks. States engage in irrational policies such as protectionism or economic nationalism that undermine the long-term national interests.

Realists portray liberals as idealistic (feminine) for insisting that economics can overcome most kinds of international conflict. Liberals are behaving irrationally if they conceive of national interest as anything other than narrow self-interest. The market can function only if a hegemon provides effective protection (masculine). Simply put, realists and liberals offer competing versions of masculinity while effectively denigrating the other as feminine (Ashworth and Swatuk 1998, 82–83).

Liberal understandings of international organizations provide such organizations with a positive and constructive role in international relations. International organizations offer a mechanism for states and other actors to settle their disputes peaceably. But the strategies for settling those disputes remain masculine, though not as masculine as physically assaulting an adversary.

Liberals see the market and economic competition as a substitute for war and other forms of violent conflict. Put another way, men don't need to prove themselves on the battlefield if they can dominate the market and the boardroom. According to liberals, contemporary international organizations should seek to minimize the influence of the state in domestic and international markets. Liberals also place significant emphasis on the difference between public and private spheres. Normatively speaking, liberals believe that goods and services should be provided and distributed within a society and between societies by private or market mechanisms, not authoritatively by states or international organizations. For feminists, liberal international economic organizations, such as the WTO, IMF, or the World Bank, serve market interests and ignore the subordinate position of women and minorities in the so-called unbiased market. The market is seen as the solution to the problems faced by women and minorities and is rarely, if ever, seen as the problem.

Marxist theory is least masculine because it emphasizes exploitation and the consequences for collective society. Marxist and Hegelian approaches underscore societal development as critical to individual development. A society's mode of production shapes political and social arrangements. However, class analysis and capitalism cannot explain gender or racial discrimination. Marxist theory is very mechanical in that it argues that the subjugation of women and minorities will disappear when capitalism is eliminated. Marxist theory also focuses on dependency, a condition that creates a superior–subordinate relationship, rather than interdependency, which implies more benign and mutual relations. The superior–subordinate relationship between classes and classes of states is analogous to the superior–subordinate relationship between men and women, the masculine and the feminine. This kind of relationship leaves plenty of room for exploitation and abuse. It also leaves room for inattention and marginalization. Feminists see Marxist and realist theories as prevalent in developing states because they are in a subordinate (feminine) position, a position that is not very desirable. Marxist and realist theories prescribe certain kinds of state behavior that will eliminate the subordinate role or minimize its ill effects. The hidden assumption is that being dependent (feminine) is not desirable while being independent or autonomous is.

The Marxist view of international organizations as mechanisms of capitalist domination or as tools for developing transnational hegemony has a masculine bias because it assumes that the impact of international organizations is the same for men and women. Actions taken by, or on behalf of, international organizations disproportionately affect women, often adversely. Consider the effects of military force, economic sanctions, or structural adjustment programs, which burden women and children in different and perhaps more serious ways. When international organizations ignore women and trivialize gender issues, they reinforce their own patriarchal tendencies, legitimizing the subjugation of women. Feminist theory enhances contemporary understandings of international organizations by pointing out the overt and hidden biases of realism, liberalism, and Marxism. The gender lens accentuates the subsumed masculinities associated with conceptualizing the behavior and the nature of international organizations.

Gendering International Organizations

The feminist theory genders international organizations in several ways. First, the theory critically examines the role and contributions of women in IGOs (Goetz 1997; Heyzer, et al. 1995; Karl 1995; Meyer and Prugl 1999; Staudt 1997; Whitworth 1994; Winslow 1995). In terms of employment, women are largely excluded from traditional positions of power and are often missing from the decision-making elite in the UN. This includes UN ambassadors, top management, and senior staff. The United States, which prides itself on its record for the advancement of women, did not have its first female ambassador to the UN until 1980, when President Ronald Reagan appointed Jeanne Kirkpatrick.[1] Since then only two women, Madeline Albright and Susan Rice, have held the position. Women still tend to occupy the clerical and support positions at the UN. After more than a decade of systematic review of UN hiring practices, the question still remains as to whether women workers in the UN have moved from "margin to mainstream" (D'Amico 1999, 19–40). Feminist theory highlights these kinds of gender inequities within IGOs.

Women who do occupy decision-making positions tend to lead agencies that are traditionally concerned with feminine issues. For example, women have headed the UN Fund for Population Activities (UNFPA) and the UN Development Fund for Women (UNIFEM). Higher proportions of women are involved in agencies such as the World Health Organization (WHO) and the United Nations Children's Fund (UNICEF). Feminist scholarship also highlights the contributions of women operating within traditional gender roles and the accomplishments of "feminine" agencies within the UN system. More recent studies have shown that the UN and its related agencies have taken the gender questions seriously and have attempted to adjust their policies to promote equality with varying success (Alleyne 2004; Bessis 2004; Quinn-Maguire 2003).

Second, feminist scholarship also spotlights the activities and strategies of NGOs (Connors 1996; Cook 1997; Gelb 2002; Penrose and Seaman 1996). These kinds of international organizations are involved with helping people (mostly women and children) at the grassroots level (Aubrey 1997; Eldridge 1995). Women are involved in social and revolutionary movements. They are active in NGOs that provide legal and medical assistance in issues that affect women and to those that seek to promote change in extremely patriarchal societies.

NGOs are often the only groups willing to challenge state and IGO practices that have a significant impact on women. For example, Human Rights Watch released an extremely controversial report, "Hidden in the Home: Abuse of Domestic Workers with Special Visas in the United States," which

---

[1]Not all feminists regard the appointment of Jeanne Kirkpatrick as UN ambassador as a particular advance for women. The Reagan administration did little to hide its contempt of the UN and was more than willing to act unilaterally in international affairs. Moreover, Kirkpatrick's outspoken criticism of the UN and support for brutal dictatorships in Latin America denote masculinity, her female sex notwithstanding.

charged that many diplomats and employees at the UN, World Bank, and the Organization of American States have abused the rights of their domestic workers by paying far less than minimum wage and even engaging in forced labor and physical abuse (Greenhouse 2001, A16). Human Rights Watch was willing to ask the tough questions when the U.S. government claimed that diplomats had special protections, and IGO officials lamented the difficulties of taking action because "they are the employees of our employees" (Greenhouse 2001, A16). NGOs and transnational networks of women are often the only voice for the most vulnerable in global society, especially when life-altering decisions are made at the international level (True 2008).

Third, feminist theory examines the effects of patriarchy, or male dominance, in contemporary international organizations. Attitudes, policies, methods, and approaches that neglect women or treat them as insignificant contribute to gender inequities (Alvarez 1997; Campbell and Stein 1992; Staudt 1997; Vuorela 1992). World Bank and IMF officials who make decisions based on neoclassical economic theory and models are perpetuating gender inequalities because these models assume away gender and rely on methods that demand "hard" facts and documented evidence. For example, feminists and Marxists have charged that structural adjustment loans hurt women more than men. How does one measure "hurt"? World Bank and IMF officials measure structural adjustment effects in terms of lost jobs, declining wages, and economic stagnation, all of which particularly impact men. But the IMF and World Bank cannot track the effects of structural adjustment on women because they reside in the home or serve in the ranks of unpaid or unofficial labor. As a result, there is no "reliable" documentation that women are also hurt, in which case the World Bank and the IMF cannot conclude that their structural adjustment programs are "more" harmful to women. Feminists point out that the IMF is concerned about the market (masculine) effects and not the social (feminine) effects of structural adjustment. Neoclassical economic thought, which currently dominates multilateral financial and development institutions, imposes a masculine economic world order.

The impact of policies emanating from IGOs, particularly in combat zones, has also been examined by feminists. Military action in Afghanistan in 2001 had a different impact on Afghan women in that it was a continuation of violence and instability that women had been experiencing for the last 30 years. Rather than benefiting women, the U.S. attacks represented a continuation of gender insecurity (Hans 2004, 232–248; Khattak 2003, 367–370). Furthermore, the operation of refugee camps and safe haven zones, along with reconstruction, has gender dimensions in that women face different challenges and threats than their male counterparts (Alwis 2004, 213–231; Hyndman 2004, 193–212; Klein 2004, 273–300). By taking gender into account, the female experience is recognized and alternative courses of action are considered.

Feminism and International Law   Feminists argue that "the absence of women in the development of international law has produced a narrow and inadequate jurisprudence that has, among other things, legitimated the unequal position of women rather than challenge it" (Charlesworth and Chinkin 2000, 1). Liberal feminists point out that international law is made by states and that states speak for the women within their territorial jurisdiction. However, women are not represented in positions of power within states and therefore their interests are not reflected in international law. States are subjects of international law and individuals objects of international law, but as a practical matter international law is made by individuals and it governs what individuals can and cannot do in the name of the state. With the dearth of women at the table in its formulation, international law contains many "silences" as it relates to women and global gender issues (Brooks 2002; Buss and Ambreena 2005). International law provides no mechanisms to sanction states for systematically discriminating against women or denying them equal rights. Nor does the law hold states accountable for systematic violence against women perpetrated by "private actors" such as fathers, brothers, husbands, or self-appointed dignity police. Such matters are, in large part, considered part of the domestic jurisdiction of states.

Feminist critiques of specific areas of international law (laws of war, refugee law, human rights law, and international criminal law) have made some progress in getting some officials to consider how laws affect women; however, little headway has been made to develop an alternative, "feminist" jurisprudence. Fellmeth (2000, 681–686) argues that the UN Charter model of international law improves upon the Westphalia model because it allows more room for individuals to challenge the rights of the states under international law. Women have had a demonstrable impact on certain areas, like international criminal law, and proliferation of courts demonstrate the commitment of states to punish individuals for war crimes. "The solution to gender bias in international law is . . . not only to increase the representation of women in international organizations, but to augment their political and economic power in the states that comprise the international community" (Fellmeth 2000, 731).

The Critics of Feminism

Feminist is widely criticized, informally, as poor scholarship, lacking both rigor and precision. Moreover, it lacks the status of a "worldview" except in the minds of feminists. It consists of traditional feminism, neofeminism, liberal feminism, socialist feminism, and postmodern feminism—variations that often contradict each other and raise questions about the utility of the feminist endeavor. As Genest (2003, 265–266) points out, "feminist theory does not supply the explanatory and theoretical tools to conduct a thorough analysis." As such, the usefulness of feminist theory to systematically analyze international organizations is called into question. Few scholars have been willing to challenge feminist analyses of international relations; rather they are more likely to simply ignore their analyses or dismiss them. The reasons may well have to do with the politics of academia; however, readers should be aware that feminist theory is undoubtedly contested. It is included in this text because women constitute half of the world's population and ignoring their role in international organizations and the effects of male-dominated international organizations on their lives does a disservice to those wishing to understand the role of international organizations in global governance.

CONSTRUCTIVISM

The constructivist approach to international relations began in earnest in the 1990s. Constructivism is not a theory, per se, as it says nothing about international relations. Rather, it is a process of uncovering how the world we know is **socially constructed**. When something is said to be "socially constructed," it means that its existence, meaning, and value were created by individuals and groups within the society. Individuals and groups assign meanings and values to concepts and institutions. Take, for example, the concept of "race." For constructivists, race is not an objective fact but rather a social construction created by society, and its meaning has changed over time. In the early twentieth century, U.S. Irish immigrants where considered "black" and of a different race by many white Americans. As the relationship between Irish immigrants and other segments of society evolved, the notion of race changed and the Irish became whites. Constructivists seek to uncover how "what we know" is shaped by our group and social affiliations. They also seek to analyze how "what we know" changes over time.

As applied to international relations, constructivists seek to understand the social construction of the international system and the norms and rules associated with global governance. This invariably involves critiquing the theories of realism, liberalism, Marxism, and feminism (although some feminists do highlight the social construction of gender). These theories assume an "objective reality" to the international system (characterized by anarchy, complex interdependence, capitalism, or patriarchy) that explains much of what happens in international relations and shapes the nature of global governance. Constructivists seek to show how this assumed reality is socially constructed and how it is constructed differently by different states, groups, and individuals through their complicated social relationships.

Constructivist Influences

Constructivism is a relatively new approach to the social sciences and has been influenced by the postmodern and post-structural movement of the 1960s. Perhaps the most important earliest influence on the constructivist approach to international relations is Berger and Luckmann's (1966) classic *The Social Construction of Reality*. The central point of this book was to show "how objectivity of the institutionalized world, however massive it may appear to the individual is . . . humanly produced" (Berger and Luckmann 1966, 60). Over time, institutions become so much a fabric of society that individuals relate to them as if they were part of the "natural" or "real" world. In short, we forget that we constructed these institutions, ideas, and identities and, therefore, can change them.

In the study of international relations, one of the first groundbreaking constructivist works was Onuf's (1989) *A World of Our Making: Rules and Rule in Social Theory and International Relations*. Onuf makes the case that theorists need to break down the boundaries between international relations and other disciplines. By applying social theory to the study of international relations, we can begin to understand how international institutions, values, norms, and identities are humanly created and how we change them over time. Onuf argues that social interactions can explain the preferences and interests of international actors. Wendt (1992), in "Anarchy Is What States Make of It," explains that the mainstream approaches of realism and liberalism are "rationalist" in that they take the identities and the interests of states as a given. He argues that identities and interest are not given but rather shaped by the social interaction of individuals and states. Anarchy does not automatically lead to a security dilemma and self-help. Rather, the social interactions of states define what states think about anarchy. For example, anarchy has not led to an arms race between the United States and Canada because the social interactions between the countries have shown that Canada has very little to fear from its nuclear armed neighbor. The social interactions between the United States and Iran, however, may explain why Iran may be seeking to acquire nuclear weapons. By examining social relations and group identities, we can add another dimension to the study of international relations.

The Constructivist Approach

Although not a formal theory or meta-theory, the constructivist approach rests on several assumptions (Genest 2003, 260–261). First, ideas, beliefs, and identities of individuals and states are important for understanding international relations. Second, those ideas, beliefs, and identities are socially constructed by their group affiliations. Third, social factors are more important than material factors in understanding international relations. Social relations define how we view, understand, and evaluate material factors such as military power or economic wealth. Fourth, cooperation and/or conflict between state (and nonstate) actors are the result of intersubjective relationship of the actors. The actors' views and ideas about each other at any given time (and over time) affect the nature of their relationship. Finally, the constructivist approach is centered on explaining change, showing how key concepts used to explain international relations have changed over time.

The Constructivist Approach to International Organizations

The constructivist approach has made many important contributions to the study of international organizations. One strand of research focuses on how international norms affect state behavior and vice versa (see, e.g., Finnemore 2004; March and Olsen 1998). For example, a constructivist would be interested in how the norm of the "nonuse of force in international relations" affected the decision of the United States to go to war with Iraq, and conversely, how the U.S. invasion of Iraq shaped and changed that norm (and its understanding) for other actors, which invariably involved the interaction of UN officials and the individuals involved in decision making at the time.

A second, related strand of research centers on the socialization of international actors. How do international organizations socialize states and decision makers about their appropriate expected behavior in world or regional politics (see, e.g., Checkel 2000, 2005; Eaton and Stubbs 2006; Narine 2006)? This can affect any issue area from security to immigration to deficit spending. How are norms, values, and identities created in international organizations? How are these norms, values, and identities diffused to other groups and individuals? Conversely, what factors and agents socialize international organizations and their personnel?

A third strain of constructivist research looks at the institutional values, group identities, and social interaction within an international organization. How do bureaucratic values and expected behavior shape an international organization's response to a crisis (see, e.g., Barnett 2003)? How do the values and norms of a particular organization change over time? Given the nature of constructivism, the answers to these questions yield as many interpretative answers as there are constructivist scholars.

Constructivism and International Law Constructivists explore how international law is created by examining the ideational factors (norms, rules, and inter-subjective beliefs) associated with the law. The approach details how law is legitimized and the processes by which other factors, such as the international morality and specificity of legal rationality, contribute to the law's acceptance (Brunee and Toope 2000). Constructivists also detail how law affects the normalization of relations between states and bureaucracies such that they internalize the routine use of international law to define problems and solve disputes. Norms can be created (e.g., participatory development as a legal human right or the right to water as a basic human right) by NGOs that are then internalized by IGOs (Totaro 2006, 743–749). Constructivists also seek to explain how and why international organizations are created even without the support of United States and other important states (Fehl 2004). In short, international law reflects the world that is being constructed by individuals and state and nonstate actors.

Criticisms of the Constructivist Approach

The central criticism of constructivism is that it is not really a theory but an approach that mainly criticizes other theories (Genest 2003, 267). It does not really describe, explain, analyze, or predict anything about international relations other than positing that everything we and others think we know about international relations is socially constructed. Constructivists counter that their main contribution is that it isn't a grand theory explaining but a more inductive process that allows us to explore questions ignored by the other theories. Moreover, constructivism can act as a bridge between the different theories and provide a middle ground for analysis (Adler 1997).

A second criticism of the constructivist approach is that it generates a multitude of interpretations with no systematic way of evaluating them. How are we to assess whether one constructivist interpretation of norm creation at the UN is more rigorous than another? It has no particular methodology, and many claim that it is antipositivist and antiscientific (Hopf 1998). At best, it is a loose paradigm of multiple interpretations (Jackson and Nexon 2004). Constructivists counter that their approach, and ultimately their theory, is evolving. Several scholars are pushing constructivists to develop a meta-theory that will more systematically address the nature and particulars of international relations (Checkel 1998; Guzzini 2000; Klotz and Lynch 2007). Also, constructivism has many variations, some of which are more scientific and quantified, while others are more postmodern in orientation.

A third criticism is that constructivists are really liberals using theories from the discipline of sociology. The issue areas that constructivists tend to focus on are human rights, multilateralism, and "security communities" (Steele 2007, 26–28). Moreover, constructivists often seem to be prescribing ways to promote these values without serious self-criticism. Constructivists tend to ignore how malevolent or harmful interests, values, and institutions are socially constructed (or why we may see them as malevolent while yet other societies or social groups may not). In terms of international law, constructivists often ignore the social context, like the structured system of inequality and hierarchy in which law is created and implemented (Kurki and Sinclair 2010). In spite of these criticisms, the continued utility and the proliferation of the constructivist analyses make constructivism an important approach to consider when studying international organization.

KEY TERMS

Socrates   77
Georg Wilhelm Friedrich Hegel   77
dialectic   77
Karl Marx   78
Mode of production   78
economic class   78
capitalism   78
bourgeoisie   78
proletariat   78
concentration of capital   79
overproduction   79
falling rate of profit   79
John A. Hobson   80
imperialism   80
Vladimir Ilyich Lenin   80

Antonio Gramsci   80
economism   80
hegemony   81
dependency theory   82
modern world system theory   82
neocolonialism   83
comprador class   83
core   83
periphery   83
semiperiphery   83
gender   92
sex   92
masculinity   94
international women's social movement   94
International Council of Women   95

International Women's Suffrage Alliance   95
International Women's League for Peace and Freedom   95
traditional feminism   97
neofeminism   97
postmodern feminism   97
liberal feminists   97
Marxist feminists   97
superior–subordinate nature of gender relationships   99
patriarchy   99
socially constructed   106

SUGGESTED READINGS

Berger, Peter L., and Thomas Luckmann. 1966. *The Social Construction of Reality: A Treatise in the Sociology of Knowledge.* New York: Doubleday.

Ferber, Marianne, and Julie A. Nelson. 1993. Introduction: The Social Construction of Economics and the Social Construction of Gender. pp. 1–22 in *Beyond Economic Man: Feminist Theory and Economics*, ed. Marianne Ferber and Julie A. Nelson. Chicago, IL: Chicago University Press.

Hawkesworth, Mary E. 2006. *Globalization and Feminist Activism.* Lanham, MD: Rowman and Littlefield.

Marx, Karl, and Friedrich Engels. 1965. *The Communist Manifesto*, ed. Joseph Katz. New York: Washington Square Press.

Mieville, China. 2006. *Between Equal Rights: A Marxist Theory of International Law.* London: Haymarket Books.

Pettman, Jan Lindy. 1998. Gender Issues. pp. 483–497 in *The Globalization of World Politics: An Introduction to International Relations*, ed. John Bayliss and Steve Smith. Oxford, UK: Oxford University Press.

Wallerstein, Immanuel. 1980. *The Modern World System.* New York: Academic Press.

Wendt, Alexander. 1992. Anarchy Is What States Make of It: The Social Construction of Power Politics. *International Organization* 46 (Spring): 291–424.

Security

Traditionally, the issue of security has centered on the security of the state and the perennial problem of war. War has ended the lives of hundreds of millions of people and left once thriving societies in ruins. With respect to the central issue of **international security**, then, it is legitimate to ask how and why international organizations respond to war and threats of war. Can international organizations prevent war? If so, how? And how do international organizations identify international aggression, diplomatically referred to as "breaches of the peace" or "threats to international peace and security"? The causes of war are numerous and intertwined. Societies fight for tangible reasons—territory and resources. They also fight for intangible reasons—ideology, nationalism, and religion. Yet the solutions to war are few and frustratingly elusive. A true balance of power might deter aggression; but if history is any indicator, a straight balance-of-power approach is flawed and prone to failure.

The causes of war have become increasingly complicated and its effects ruinous. Contemporary wars tend to have both internal and external sources, and sophisticated weapons are readily available to any party with money or credit enough to buy them. And though fighting itself may be confined within states, its consequences are felt elsewhere, often having international repercussions. International organizations and member states attempt to manage the ill effects of war and seek mechanisms that may prevent war in the future.

International security generally has meant the **security of states**; however, many international organizations have sought to reconceptualize security in terms of "**human security**" (MacFarlane and Foong Khong 2006; Oberleitner 2005, 185–203; Ogata and Cels 2003; Paris 2001; Peou 2002; Pettman 2005; Wedgewood 2002). Human security is a people-centered approach that focuses on physical threats to individuals. Such threats include not only war and other forms of violent conflict but also hunger, disease, environmental disaster, or extreme poverty. Physical threats to individuals may emanate from their government or from other groups within a society. In this chapter, we examine the role of the UN Security Council and other UN bodies carry out the important assignment of identifying, defining, and responding to threats to international peace and security. We outline the legal framework and the historical evolution of UN responses to the perennial problem of war, and we detail the origins of collective security and human security as well as peacekeeping and peacebuilding. Then we apply realism, liberalism, Marxism, feminism, and constructivism to the case study of Iraq in order to interpret the dynamics of collective security. In the second part of this chapter, we examine another pressing security issue, the spread of nuclear technology and weapons. We look at the nuclear nonproliferation regime with special emphasis on the **Nuclear Nonproliferation Treaty (NPT)** and the **International Atomic Energy Agency (IAEA)**. The theoretical lenses are then focused on the case study of Iran to highlight the differing perspectives regarding the effects of international law and organization on this important security issue.

THE UNITED NATIONS

In 1944, representatives of the "big three" (i.e., the United States, UK, and USSR) fleshed out the framework for the UN at the Dumbarton Oaks Conference (Hilderbrand 1990). The UN's *raison d'être*, its reason for being, is identified in Article 1(1) of the Charter:

> To maintain international peace and security and to that end: to take effective collective measures for the prevention and removal of threats to the peace, and for the suppression of acts of aggression or breaches of the peace, and to bring about by peaceful means, and in conformity with the principles of justice and international law, adjustment or settlement of international disputes or situations which might lead to a breach of the peace.

The devastation of World War II, coupled with the advent of nuclear weapons, brought about a renewed sense of urgency in preventing future wars. To bolster this mission, **Article 2(4) of the UN Charter** explicitly forbids member states from threatening or using force in their international relations. The exception to this prohibition is found in Article 51. Member states are permitted to use force only in cases of self-defense or for collective self-defense. The international peace and security interests of all member states could be served by effectively outlawing war as a legitimate option of international diplomacy.

Article 2(1) of the UN Charter recognizes the principle of state sovereignty and the territorially based state. Only states may be full members of the UN, and all states are equally sovereign in that their representatives (the governments) have the final say within their own territories. Article 2(7) reinforces the principle of state sovereignty by limiting the jurisdiction of the UN: "Nothing contained in the present Charter shall authorize the United Nations to intervene in matters which are essentially within the domestic jurisdiction of any state or shall require the Members to submit such matters to settlement under the present Charter; but this principle shall not prejudice the application of enforcement measures under Chapter VII." Chapter VII refers to the authority of the Security Council to issue decisions that are binding on all UN members.

The architects of the UN sought to strike a balance between the status quo of territorially based sovereign states and the need for global governance and stability. Governments retained sovereignty domestically and agreed to the peaceful settlement of their disputes internationally. This balance is a precarious one. International peace is not necessarily an interest of all states at all times. From ancient Sumer to modern-day Baghdad, violence has proven to be an effective form of leverage, and the threat of violence a useful tool for obtaining foreign policy goals. Violence has often been the decisive mechanism of change and the final arbiter of international disputes. Thus, the UN Charter is revolutionary: It challenges the long-established international practice by outlawing both the threat and the use of force and by creating a higher authority to maintain international peace as security. The UN Security Council is that higher authority.

The Security Council

Chapter V, Article 24, of the UN Charter gives the Security Council the responsibility for preventing and responding to war: "In order to ensure prompt and effective action by the United Nations, its Members confer on the Security Council primary responsibility for the maintenance of international peace and security, and agree that in carrying out its duties under this responsibility the Security Council acts on their behalf." As identified in Chapter V, the five permanent members of the Security Council are the United States; the United Kingdom; the USSR, now Russia; France; and China. These states were the allied victors of World War II and their status enabled them to take on a special responsibility for providing international stability in the postwar period. As permanent members, the states retain a continuous seat from session to session; moreover, each possesses an **absolute veto**, meaning that each can nullify a decision without further discussion.[1] The veto provision was a controversial feature of the UN Charter as it violates the principle of the sovereign equality of states. That is, the permanent members are more sovereign than others: Their veto renders UN action against any permanent member impossible and keeps the UN from taking any other action without their consent. But many observers argue that the veto provision was simply necessary. It was there to prevent the UN from starting an enforcement action it could not finish or invoking the name of the UN to use force over a great

---

[1]An absolute veto is the ability to nullify legislation or decisions without any further discussion. A qualified veto can also nullify legislation or decisions but can be overridden, usually with a qualified majority of voting members.

power's objection, thereby quickly raising a local conflict into a global one (Riggs and Plano 1994, 57). In essence, the structure and the decision-making procedure of the Security Council are fully informed by a strong dose of political pragmatism.

Chapter V also mandates that the General Assembly elect the ten nonpermanent members of the Security Council. These ten nonpermanent members are elected for two-year terms, and retiring members are not eligible for immediate reelection. The architects of the UN wanted the Security Council to represent the entire international community, not just the victors of World War II. By granting the General Assembly the power to elect the remaining members, they provided for a diverse membership in the Security Council, thereby ensuring that alternative viewpoints would be represented. The presidency of the Security Council rotates monthly among members alphabetically (English). The task of the UN architects was to construct the Security Council as an organizational mechanism that would permit member states to act collectively to deter international aggression and provide a framework for a collective military response should deterrence happen to fail.

The UN Charter contains several provisions for maintaining international peace and security. First, Chapter VII requires member states to abide by Security Council decisions and to contribute to UN enforcement in general. Second, and more specifically, Article 43 of Chapter VII requires member states to make armed forces available to the Security Council. Article 47 establishes a Military Staff Committee to advise and assist the Security Council in matters relating to military enforcement of Security Council decisions.

Through these provisions, "**collective security**" was institutionalized, at least on paper. Collective security is based on the notion that an attack on one member is an attack on all. Potential aggressors would then be deterred by a credible threat of retaliation by the international community. Collective security arrangements are based on universal membership, and there is no presumptive aggressor (Goodby and O'Connor 1993). All states, especially members of the Security Council, must be willing to refrain from using force to further their own interests and at the same time be willing to intervene collectively in situations where they have no compelling strategic, military, or economic interests. But the architects of the UN Charter could not change world politics. The Cold War, which pitted two of the most influential of the permanent members against each other, rendered UN collective security arrangements ineffective. UN membership is diverse. Democracies, dictatorships, markets, and command economies exist side by side, making it difficult to develop cohesion. The Military Staff Committee and the security force envisioned in Chapter VII died shortly after their inception. Other security initiatives designed to stabilize the immediate postwar environment also met an early demise. Early efforts to control the spread of atomic weapons, such as the UN Atomic Energy Commission, the U.S.-sponsored Baruch Plan, and the USSR-sponsored Peace Offensive became little more than propaganda tools in the emerging Cold War. The veto provision led to near-complete paralysis of the Security Council in matters of international security. Thus, collective security and arms control gave way to alliances, balance of power, and arms races.

Why did UN collective security falter so dramatically after its inception? According to Riggs and Plano, three factors—**consensus, commitment,** and **organization**—are necessary for collective security to work (1994, 100). The UN Charter provided member states with the organization, but consensus and commitment among the Security Council's permanent members were clearly absent. The lack of consensus was based not merely on practical questions—who contributes what and how much—but on fundamental differences as to how the world ought to be ordered. Perceptions of right and wrong are rarely negotiable. The United States and the USSR and their respective allies had essentially different worldviews, making any consensus fleeting at best. And, without a consensus, commitment is hard to establish. Member states must be willing to contribute to enforcement actions, even when those actions run contrary to their national interests. They must also be willing to refrain from using force unilaterally.

The lack of consensus and commitment to collective security is less a problem in principle than the question as to what constitutes **aggression.** Is a state that funds and arms a national liberation movement in another state engaging in aggression? What if states finance suicide bombers and their families? A general agreement on this point is important because it is, presumably, an aggressive act that should trigger a collective response. In writing the UN Charter, its architects wanted to prevent another world war—a conflict like World War II, in which the character of aggression was a fairly unambiguous land grab, involving the use of clearly identifiable, regular military forces. In that sense, a state would be clearly an aggressor, in which case the UN could step in militarily to restore the status quo. After World War II, however, aggression became ambiguous, and the use of force more limited and nuanced. States did not try to conquer new territories. They used force to change governments or to help national liberation movements. Violent international conflict took several new forms, including proxy war, insurgency, covert military operations, anticolonial rebellion, subversion, and terrorism. State and nonstate actors used violence, each claiming a legitimate right to use force.

According to the UN Charter, the only permissible use of force is self-defense. Does this mean force cannot be used against colonial or racist regimes or governments committing genocide against their own people? Does this mean a state must wait to be attacked before it can act to prevent imminent hostilities? Does this mean that a state must sit idly by while its citizens are *in extremis* abroad? International efforts to define aggression have met with little success. And if defining aggression is difficult, then so is determining an appropriate collective response.

The complexity of the political landscape in the postwar environment doomed the UN experiment with collective security. During the Cold War, the UN Security Council did authorize a military response to the North Korean invasion of South Korea in 1950; however, that response was possible only because the USSR was boycotting the Council to protest the denial of a seat to the newly formed communist Chinese government. When the USSR returned, it used its veto to block any more Security Council decisions.

The Cold War record of the UN Security Council in providing for collective security is, by most accounts, quite poor. However, the UN's *raison d'être* was not completely abandoned. The prevention of violent conflict involves more than just a credible threat of a collective violent response. Breaches of the peace can be prevented through airing of grievances, diplomatic negotiations, mediation, arbitration, confidence building, and other forms of nonviolent conflict resolution. The Security Council, the General Assembly, and the Secretary-General have improvised to approximate the UN's central mission in spite of political exigencies that prevented successful collective security. It may not be able to prevent war, but it still has a role in preventative diplomacy, and if violence breaks out, in managing the conflict. The UN can also help with post-conflict reconstruction.

The General Assembly

The General Assembly's influence in the realm of international security stems from two Charter provisions—the authority to make recommendations regarding international security issues (Articles 10 and 11) and control of the UN budget (Article 17). During the Cold War, the General Assembly stood as a voice against aggression by condemning illegal uses of force through resolutions. Such resolutions fell far short of the expectations generated by the ideals of collective security and peace enforcement because the General Assembly had neither the authority nor the resources to do anything about breaches of the peace. Nevertheless, they expressed the conscience of the community and served as a reminder of the main purpose of the UN. The General Assembly also supported "peacekeeping" by establishing it as a budget priority. Peacekeeping, discussed in more detail later, developed as an alternative to collective security and has been an important feature of international conflict resolution.

The General Assembly's first foray into international security came on November 3, 1950, with the **"Uniting for Peace" resolution** (UNGA RES 377):

> If the Security Council, because of lack of unanimity of the permanent members, fails to exercise its primary responsibility for the maintenance of international peace and security in any case there appears to be a threat to peace, breach of peace, or act of aggression, the General Assembly shall consider the matter immediately with the view of making appropriate recommendations to Members for collective measures including in the case of a breach of the peace or acts of aggression the use of armed force when necessary, to maintain or restore international peace and security.

This U.S.-sponsored resolution expanded the mandate of the UN General Assembly by giving it a more active role in international security matters when the Security Council was too paralyzed by politics to act. It even allowed for the UN General Assembly to be called into emergency session at the request of seven Security Council members. While originally designed to circumvent the Soviet veto, this resolution has been used by the General Assembly nine times, several of which were in response to armed aggression by France, Great Britain, and the Soviet Union (Howard 1990). No armed response has ever been recommended, although the General Assembly did express the majority sentiment of the international community. Through this resolution, members were reminded of their commitment not to threaten or use force in their international relations. Postwar relations would not be business as usual, and aggressive war would not go unchallenged, even if it could not be challenged forcibly.

The Secretary-General

The role of the Secretary-General in international security is complicated and difficult to understand without understanding this position in the overall UN organization. The Secretary-General is the chief UN diplomat and the head of the Secretariat. The Secretariat is the professional bureaucracy that administers UN programs and executes UN policies. The Secretary-General is selected for a five-year, renewable term through an elaborate process whereby the Security Council makes a recommendation to the General Assembly, which must then approve the nominee with a two-thirds majority. The selection process is highly politicized because any recommendation is subject to the Security Council permanent member veto. Furthermore, the candidate must be acceptable to two-thirds of the members of the General Assembly. Hence, it is not surprising that the selection of the Secretary-General is an arduous and difficult process shot through with conflicting interests and rivalries.

Once in office, the Secretary-General must perform a balancing act, representing the UN on the one hand and responding to member states on the other. The Secretary-General's role as head of the Secretariat means that he is the chief bureaucrat. He must foster neutral competence in the international civil service so that the UN can develop a reputation of professionalism, expertise, credibility, and impartiality. This entails developing bureaucratic loyalties that extend beyond national loyalties. At the same time, the Secretary-General must answer to member states. The United States, for example, succeeded in derailing the reelection of former secretary-general Boutros Boutros-Ghali because it was dissatisfied with perceived UN excesses and Boutros-Ghali's penchant for expanding UN peacekeeping missions without Security Council authorization.

The Secretary-General plays a key role in identifying threats to international peace and security and attempting to resolve violent conflicts. However, the UN Charter is not specific about the Secretary-General's role in the maintenance of international peace and security. Article 99 states that the Secretary-General "may bring to the attention of the Security Council" matters that threaten international peace and security, but this provision has rarely been used. The Secretary-General's role is subtler than that. He exercises considerable influence over fact-finding activities, and he is responsible for carrying out UN policy with regard to international security. In short, "it's all in the execution," meaning that the way in which a policy is implemented profoundly shapes the policy itself, not to mention its outcome. The Secretary-General, together with the appropriate Secretariat agencies, is responsible for evolving and developing what has emerged as the alternative to collective security—peacekeeping, peacebuilding, and the reconceptualization of international security as human security.

Peacekeeping

The architects of the UN Charter did not envision **peacekeeping**. Former secretary-general Dag Hammarskjöld once joked that peacekeeping was permitted under "Chapter Six and a half" (Goldstein 1996, 279). He was referring to the tacit compromise between the UN's role in diplomatic efforts at conflict resolution as outlined in Chapter VI and its role in collective security under Chapter VII. As collective security arrangements proved increasingly unworkable, the UN's role in nonviolent conflict resolution gained in prominence.

Defining "peacekeeping" is problematic because peacekeeping operations have been developed, implemented, and modified as particular responses to particular situations (Weiss et al. 1994, 48). However, two conditions are essential for traditional peacekeeping: The consent of the principal parties involved and a temporary cease-fire. No UN personnel are deployed until these conditions are in place. The first full-fledged UN peacekeeping operation occurred during the Suez Crisis in 1956, when Egyptian President Gamal Nasser announced that he was nationalizing the Suez Canal, which was jointly owned by Great Britain and France, two former colonial powers in the region. After several months of intense and hostile negotiations, Israel invaded Egypt (with the tacit agreement of Great Britain and France). French and British forces invaded a few days later, purportedly to protect the canal. The United States and the USSR called for an immediate cease-fire, as did the General Assembly. Then the General Assembly created the United Nations Emergency Force (UNEF), which was deployed to operate the Suez Canal and provide stability during the stand-down of hostilities. UNEF consisted of approximately 6,000 lightly armed peacekeepers from ten countries. In order to build confidence within the highly charged political atmosphere, UNEF excluded forces from the permanent members of the Security Council. Later, the mission of UNEF shifted to overseeing the withdrawal of foreign troops and establishing a buffer zone between the Egyptian and the Israeli troops. Unfortunately, UNEF was withdrawn in 1967 at the request of Egypt and hostilities resumed shortly thereafter with the 1967 Arab–Israeli War.

The UN's first experience with peacekeeping generated several important lessons (Taylor 1998, 280). First, it established that peacekeeping operations should be as neutral as possible, using force only if peacekeeping forces are attacked. Second, peacekeeping forces must be deployed with the consent of the host state. Third, the Secretary-General should control peacekeeping forces to bolster the neutrality of the mission. Peacekeeping clearly involves a different dynamic than collective security. With peacekeeping, no aggressor is identified or acted against. The parties involved are not assessed blame. This approach permits parties to disengage from violent conflict without losing face, thereby facilitating more peaceable conflict resolution.

The UN conducted nineteen peacekeeping missions between 1947 and 1989. This figure includes observer missions that monitor cease-fire agreements or election procedures. Peacekeeping can be costly, and such missions have met with varying degrees of success. Most agree, however, that they have saved countless lives, which can have no price tag. Since 1989, UN peacekeeping operations have expanded considerably. UN authorized dozens of missions in more than twenty countries, including Tajikistan, India, Haiti, Bosnia, Kosovo, and Mozambique. The end of the Cold War marks the beginning of a second generation of peacekeeping that extends beyond observer missions and lightly armed multinational contingents. Peacekeeping has evolved to include preventive peacekeeping, supervising cease-fires between irregular forces, assisting in the maintenance of law and order, protecting the delivery of humanitarian assistance, guaranteeing rights of passage, and enforcing sanctions and Security Council decisions (MacKinlay and Chopra 1997, 175–197). These kinds of activities were called "**peace enforcement**" by former secretary-general Boutros Boutros-Ghali.

Peacekeeping during the 1990s also included new activities such as monitoring and running elections, protecting safe havens, and engaging in post-conflict reconstruction of societies (Yilmaz 2005). The UN has taken over many governmental functions inside what have been termed "failed states." For example, the UN has been effectively functioning as the government of Haiti since 2004 and conducted elections in 2006. The UN mission in Haiti has been plagued by violence, riots, and kidnapping, but it has also brought stability to a large number of Haitians. The 2009 earthquake devastated the UN headquarters in Port Au Prince, killing sixteen peacekeepers, including mission head Hedi Annabi. In spite of these losses, the UN played a pivotal role in delivering humanitarian assistance and getting some government services operating again. Similarly, the UN peacekeeping force in Cambodia (UNTAC; 1992–1993) performed many governmental functions, including the administration of health care and education, in addition to negotiating cease-fires and conducting elections. These kinds of peacekeeping missions have been termed "**peacebuilding**" in that they help war-torn societies transition into stable, self-governing states. Unfortunately, these kinds of missions face significant challenges involving money, mandates and military troops, all of which require a sustained and long-term commitment from member states. In terms of contributing personnel, the United States accounts for less than 1 percent of the total UN forces, Russia a little more than 1 percent, Europe 10 percent, China 6 percent, and Japan does not contribute troops (Yilmaz 2005). Most UN troops come from the developing world and some peacekeeping missions are conducted outside of the UN. The African Union has peacekeepers in the Darfur region of Sudan, and NATO continues to operate in Bosnia after taking over from the UN in the late 1990s.

The success of UN peacekeeping is difficult to quantify. In most cases, what would have happened had the UN not become involved is impossible to discern. In some situations, such as the UN peacekeeping mission in Macedonia, the UN may have prevented the spread of ethnic violence from neighboring Balkan states. In other situations, such as Kosovo, the UN has been accused of legitimizing NATO's illegal military intervention and being biased against Serbia and the Serb ethnic minority. Nevertheless, peacekeeping has emerged as an important part of international conflict resolution and represents an important function played by the UN. Currently, nineteen peacekeeping missions are in operation, and over 70,000 soldiers are deployed in the field. And compared with the human costs of today's violent conflicts, peacekeeping is a cost-effective way of dealing with these seemingly intractable problems. Just as the end of the Cold War provided the international community with more opportunities for greater cooperation in peacekeeping, events began to unfold in the Middle East in 1990 that allowed the international community to revisit the idea of collective security.

CASE STUDY 1: IRAQ

The idea of collective security experienced a rebirth during the Iraq–Kuwait crisis of 1990. In August of that year, Iraq invaded Kuwait, quickly occupying and annexing that tiny, oil-rich kingdom. Several factors made this crisis unique among those generated since World War II. First, the Iraq invasion was a textbook land grab, a kind of aggression not witnessed since World War II. The Korean War could be interpreted as a civil war or a war of national liberation. Other invasions involving force had occurred, but they were for reasons other than the occupation and annexation of territories legally belonging to another sovereign state. In this case, however, the Iraqi use of force clearly violated Article 2(4), the key UN provision designed to thwart efforts to change territorial boundaries by force. This kind of "naked" aggression drew condemnation from around the world. Second, the Iraqi aggression occurred during a period of transition in world politics. The USSR had become less obstructionist and was seeking a different role for itself in international affairs under Soviet president Mikhail Gorbachev. The warming of East–West relations and the clear-cut nature of the Iraqi aggression enabled the collective security arrangements of the UN to function in the manner originally intended.

On the date of the Iraqi invasion, the UN Security Council met in emergency session; it condemned the invasion as an unlawful use of force and demanded an immediate withdrawal of Iraqi forces. Iraqi forces quickly entrenched themselves in Kuwait, fortifying their positions along the Saudi Arabian border. The United States immediately moved rapid-deployment combat forces into the region to help defend Saudi Arabia and its strategic oil fields. The United States informed the UN that it was deploying its military in accordance with Article 51 of the Charter, permitting the use of force for collective self-defense. Moreover, both the Kuwaiti government and the Saudi Arabian government had requested U.S. military assistance.

On August 6, 1990, the Security Council passed Resolution 661 calling for mandatory economic sanctions against Iraq. The sanctions were comprehensive although humanitarian and medical supplies were exempted. UN members, bound under Chapter VII of the UN Charter to abide by Security Council decisions, were obligated to honor this resolution. In the past, however, such economic sanctions had not always been enforced; and in this case, supplies and arms continued to flow to Iraq, especially from Jordan and Turkey. On August 25, 1990, the Security Council authorized the use of force if necessary to implement the economic sanctions—this, to ensure the isolation of Iraq and to remind members of their UN obligations.

While the UN was applying diplomatic pressure on Iraq, the United States was putting together a multinational force dubbed Desert Shield. Although composed largely of U.S. army, air, and naval forces, Desert Shield also included military units from the Arab League states, Great Britain, and France. On November 29, 1990, the Security Council passed Resolution 678, authorizing "all means necessary" to extract Iraq from Kuwait and setting a deadline of January 15, 1991, for the Iraqi withdrawal. On January 16, 1991, Operation Desert Storm, a U.S.-led, UN-sanctioned military response, was launched to force Iraqi troops from Kuwait. The Iraqi invasion was effectively reversed on March 16, 1991, when Iraq, having been driven from Kuwaiti territory, agreed to a cease-fire.

What factors precipitated the Persian Gulf Crisis? Was the UN role constructive, scripting a leading role for the UN on the stage of world politics? Who was affected by the UN action, and how? Was the Gulf Crisis an important precedent for collective security? The answers to these questions depend on your theoretical orientation or your worldview. Understanding the role of the Security Council in the Gulf crisis and afterwards is conditioned by the tools that analyze it.

A Realist Cut

Recall that realists tend to see international organizations like the UN as tools or extensions of great powers. They are usually created by a hegemon or formed through the cooperation of great powers. According to realist theory, international organizations either serve the interests of the great powers or are bypassed in favor of unilateral action if great-power consensus cannot be reached. The Persian Gulf Crisis exemplifies why power politics will always take precedence over, and shape the actions of, international organizations. Realists argue that the Persian Gulf Crisis is a classic lesson in power calculation and miscalculation.

For realists, the Persian Gulf Crisis was the consequence of a very risky Iraqi gamble, one that Iraq lost and continues to pay for today. Iraq has always been a strategic power in the Middle East, playing a balancing role between the East and the West during the Cold War. A virtual client of both the USSR and France, Iraq has historically played a central role in Middle Eastern politics. As an oil producer and a long-time adversary of Iran, Iraq's strategic value was not lost either on the United States or the USSR, both of whom provided arms and assistance to Iraq.

The mainstream U.S. media have largely interpreted Iraq's invasion of Kuwait as the folly of a madman. But, from a strategic point of view, it was a gamble that could have paid off handsomely for Iraq. Consider the decision to invade from Iraq's position. In the twentieth century, Iraq has been a second-rate power at best. First as a colony and then as an independent state, Iraq was overshadowed by the Cold War. Iraq's patron, the USSR, was cutting back on its international commitments. Worse, Iraq's devastating war of attrition with Iran had drained its treasury and left its army demoralized. Meantime, right next door was Kuwait, an unpopular neighbor with impressive oil reserves, a lot of money, and no defenses worthy of the name. Many in the Arab world viewed Kuwait as an arrogant puppet of the United States. During the Iran–Iraq War, Kuwait had reflagged its oil tankers with the U.S. flag and repeatedly exceeded its Organization of Petroleum Exporting Countries (OPEC) quotas, lowering the price of oil in global markets. A successful takeover of Kuwait would make Iraq the power in the Middle East, controlling the largest standing army in the region together with more than a third of the world's oil supply. A quick military action would present the world with a *fait accompli*, which few states could do anything about. And once entrenched, Iraq could be extracted from Kuwait only under very difficult conditions and at extreme cost. The only state capable of such a task was the United States, whose forces in the region were negligible. By Saddam Hussein's calculations, then, a successful military action would raise Iraq to great-power status with one quick, relatively cost-free stroke.

But the UN, and particularly the Security Council, had its own calculations. Its role and behavior can be explained by the interests of the status quo great powers. The Security Council did not ignore the Iraqi invasion; it reacted because it directly threatened the interests of many of the permanent members. If Iraq's aggression were not reversed, there would be a permanent shift in the balance of power in the Middle East, and perhaps the world. Iraq was perceived as dangerous because its population was Muslim, its leaders nationalist, and its agenda aggressive. Middle Eastern oil is crucial to the military and economic security of Europe and the United States. Iraq's control over such a significant portion of the world supplies was an unacceptable risk as it could manipulate oil prices or impose a boycott during times of conflict.

Mere dependence on oil is not sufficient reason for the great powers to intervene militarily. Iraq was challenging the status quo order. It challenged U.S. leadership. U.S. hegemony has depended, to a large extent, on its ability to provide the world with access to oil at relatively low prices. Iraq threatened that ability. The shift in the balance of power would destabilize the Middle East and weaken U.S. leadership capability. Hence, U.S. interests were more directly engaged than those of other powers dependent on Middle Eastern oil.

Was the UN useful? Absolutely. Would the United States have acted without the UN? Absolutely. The UN was useful only by virtue of a rare congruence of interests among the great powers and the permanent members of the Security Council. The USSR, much preoccupied with internal difficulties, was increasingly interested in rapprochement with the West. Although Iraq was an informal ally of the USSR, the USSR was not going to risk Western aid, nor would it court a possible military confrontation with the United States. Similarly, China was seeking to repair its international reputation after the Tiananmen Square incident, and its usual diplomatic style is to abstain in voting situations in which it has no direct interest.

Realists see international organizations as arenas that reflect the existing balance of power (Mearsheimer 1994/1995). At the time of the Gulf Crisis, the West, led by the United States, was able to exercise its power within and outside of the UN, bringing significant force to bear against Iraq. But despite the "global community" and "new world order" rhetoric, the military action against Iraq was far from unanimous. Both France and the USSR were reluctant to authorize military force and hesitated up to, and perhaps beyond, the January 15 deadline. They argued that the sanctions had not had enough time to work and that more time was needed to compel Iraq's withdrawal. Several nonpermanent members of the Security Council also expressed reservations about the use of force. India, Cuba, China, and Yemen either abstained or voted against economic and/or military sanctions. Yemen was punished for its abstentions by the United States, which cut off a planned aid package (Weston 1991, 524).

Key states that did not belong to the Security Council also needed persuading, and/or positive inducements, to support "collective security" action. The United States forgave billions of dollars in loans to Egypt and promised to provide significant military hardware to Saudi Arabia. Israel received then state-of-the-art Patriot missile systems in exchange for their noninvolvement in the conflict in spite of direct Iraqi provocations and SCUD missile attacks. Germany and Japan were pressed to finance the largely American use of force. The so-called united world response to the Iraqi aggression was manufactured through the application of U.S. and Western European economic and military capabilities. The UN was largely a U.S. creation, and the United States used it masterfully to meet its national security interests. The fact that these interests did not conflict significantly with those of other permanent members of the Security Council yielded a unique convergence—the first since 1950. It is also unlikely that such a configuration of interests, circumstances, and events will align again.

The United States manipulated the UN to serve its interests in Iraq. While Operations Desert Shield and Desert Storm were conducted under the auspices of the UN, it was U.S. military capabilities that enforced the economic sanctions and conducted military operations. The UN had no control over the kind of force that was employed, nor could it limit the amount of military force that was used. On several occasions, then secretary-general Javier Perez de Cuéllar disagreed with the United States as to which of the Security Council resolutions authorized military force (Crozier 1991, 40). The United States prevailed, and its position was solidified with Resolution 678, which authorized "all means necessary"—a diplomatic euphemism for war—to restore the sovereignty and the territorial integrity of Kuwait.

The Security Council could only authorize the use of force; it had no military forces it could deploy itself. As long as the UN must rely on the armed forces of member states, only member states that have a compelling interest are likely to volunteer to participate in enforcement action. Thus, in crisis situations, the UN response will always be politicized, reflecting the interests and power calculations of leading member states. In other words, either the UN will behave in a manner consistent with the interests of the great powers, or it will be marginalized. If great-power interests happen to be congruent, the UN can play a leading role because it will represent those interests. But if great-power interests conflict, the UN will be marginalized, and states will act unilaterally or in concert with its allies.

The UN was just one of the many tools in the statesmen's toolbox. The UN provided legitimacy to the largest deployment and use of force since World War II. Yet, it was the United States that provided the military capability, controlled the use of the military, and made all of the command decisions. Several observers have indicated that UN approval enabled the United States to escape condemnation for the excessive loss of Iraqi life and the destruction of Iraqi infrastructures. The extensive levels of destruction, along with the high civilian casualty rates, raise important questions as to whether the UN response was proportional and whether all nonforcible means had been exhausted before military force was applied (Gardam 1993; Weiss et al. 1994, 70; Weston 1991).

The UN had little or no independent influence on the calculations and the interests of states. The UN collective security system did not deter Iraq from invading Kuwait. The UN could not have done anything about the invasion without the consensus (acquiescence) of the permanent members of the Security Council. Even with the consensus of the permanent members, the UN had to rely upon the military capabilities of the United States. The UN served as little more than window dressing to the U.S. exercise of political and military power. At the very best, it facilitated great-power collusion at a rare moment of great-power consensus. At worst, the Persian Gulf Crisis has created a "mirage of global collective security" and instilled "delusions of grandeur" in UN effectiveness (Carpenter 1997).

A Liberal Cut

Most liberals recognize that power and politics remain important features within international organizations (see, e.g., Claude 1993; Keohane and Martin 1995; Weiss et al. 1994). Yet, the principal impediment to UN collective security was the ideological polarization of the Cold War and the U.S.–USSR rivalry (Bennett and Lepgold 1993; Flynn and Scheffer 1990). With the end of the Cold War, a "new world order" based on the rule of law and peaceful relations could be established. According to President George H. W. Bush's Address to the Joint Session of Congress on September 11, 1990, the Persian Gulf Crisis offered the UN a rare opportunity for

> a new era—freer from the threat of terror, stronger in the pursuit of justice, and more secure in the quest for peace—an era in which the nations of the World, East and West, North and South, can prosper and live in harmony. A hundred generations have searched for this elusive path to peace, while a thousand wars raged across the span of human endeavor. Today that new world is struggling to be born, a world quite different from the one we've known: a world where the rule of law supplants the rule of the jungle; a world in which nations recognize the shared responsibilities for freedom and justice; a world where the strong respect the rights of the weak.

These words are not mere rhetoric. They reflect attainable goals. While the UN approach to the Gulf Crisis was flawed, it represents an important landmark in contemporary international relations. For liberal institutionalists, the UN played an instrumental role in the Gulf Crisis for several reasons. First, it provided states and their leadership with a framework for action. Recall that in addition to consensus and commitment, collective security requires "organization" to implement decisions once they are made. The Security Council participated in and oversaw the creation and the implementation of Desert Shield and later Desert Storm. While arm-twisting and side payments were part of the policy-making process, such tactics are common, even central, in most democratic institutions. The Security Council represents a diverse cross-section of nation-states, all of whom had input into the decision-making process.

Second, the UN served the pragmatic interests of governments. Consider the United States. Its economic and security interests were directly engaged, and it probably would have acted unilaterally. However, it would have been a wholly different kind of war if the UN had not facilitated and enforced the embargo of Iraq. Had Iraq continued to receive military supplies and been able to sell its oil, the fight could have been much longer and considerably nastier. In many respects, UN involvement controlled the conflict. This regional conflict did not escalate into a global conflict because UN forums promoted common goals and a common agenda. UN diplomatic efforts were also instrumental in allowing the United States and its allies to deploy their forces, and may even have deterred Iraq from moving against Saudi Arabia. UN negotiators played a very important and independent role in securing the release of Western hostages, whom, according to many, Iraq would use as "human shields" to deter the United States from attacking. Thus, the UN reduces many uncertainties associated with crisis situations and the use of force.

Third, the Security Council helped shield the leadership of the permanent members from internal dissent. The leaders of the member states were able to appeal to their international obligations and the international legitimacy of the UN to support their actions. France and French companies had vested economic interests in Iraq. French oil companies held Iraqi oil leases, which were quite lucrative. The USSR may have been seeking warmer relations with the West, but it could not easily abandon its strategically located client. Domestic constituents within the USSR, such as the military and the KGB, pressured the Soviet leadership to support their *de facto* ally in the Middle East (Crozier 1991, 40). Iraq also owed the USSR billions of dollars in loans. Even the United States, which was leading the world response, had difficulties internally. The Congress narrowly passed a resolution supporting the president's use of force in the region. The vote in the Senate was 52–47. The Security Council enabled the leadership to appeal to international commitments and the idea of collective security to sell the war at home.

The Security Council demonstrates how international cooperation can continue "after hegemony." While the United States had the military capability, it could not finance the Gulf War on its own, as it had done forty years earlier in the Korean War. The financial contributions of Germany and Japan were instrumental in making the collective effort possible. In more theoretical terms, other states become more willing to bear the costs of maintaining international organizations and their operations, when the hegemon is in decline.

A Marxist Cut

The Gulf Crisis from a Marxist perspective highlights the legacy of imperialism and the influence of world capitalism. The crisis must be understood in the historical context of colonialism and the policies of the core, capitalist states toward the entire region in the postcolonial era. The role of international organizations has been to foster, promote, and legitimize the aggressive policies of the leading capitalist states. International organizations under capitalism reflect the underlying economic order. Facilitating the expansion of the market and the reduction of state intervention and regulation furthers the interests of the dominant classes, the national and international bourgeoisie. The UN role in the Persian Gulf Crisis is a rare example of political intervention on the part of the Security Council—an intervention that benefited the U.S. military-industrial complex, multinational oil companies, and the tiny capitalist creation "Kuwait Inc."

The states of the Middle East are largely colonial constructions. The territorial boundaries of virtually all the Middle Eastern states were drawn by French and British diplomats after the end of World War I. During the Great War, Russia, Britain, and France negotiated the Sykes–Picot Agreement, which carved up the Arab world, including areas of North Africa and the Middle East. Great Britain, the leading colonial power, received a territory that encompassed much of present-day Israel, Jordan, Iraq, and Kuwait in the form of a mandate. The British then partitioned this territory into states. While these states were to be technically independent, their borders were artificially created to serve the strategic and economic interests of Great Britain. Political authority was handed over to the native ruling class, the very same people who had collaborated with both Ottoman and British colonial officials. This ruling class was given control over national industries, and a special relationship was created between the local and British authorities. Their economic and political interests remained tied to their colonial benefactors. The division of the Middle East into states really meant that they were colonies in almost every way, except in name. Hence, the era of neocolonialism was born.

The Iraq–Kuwait border dispute began with the creation of that border in 1922 by Sir Percy Zechariah Cox (Nemeth 1990). Iraqi and Saudi Arabian officials claimed Kuwait as a historical province, and Kuwaiti officials claimed that Kuwait was semi-independent under the Ottomans and therefore should become an independent state. Cox settled the dispute by arbitrarily drawing borders defining Iraq, Kuwait, and Saudi Arabia. Saudi Arabia and Iraq formally became independent, while Kuwait became a British protectorate until its independence in 1961. Iraq refused to recognize Kuwait after Kuwait declared independence from Great Britain. Iraq again stated its historic claim to the territory and sent troops to the Kuwaiti border but was forced to acknowledge Kuwaiti sovereignty in 1963 after the British and the Arab League deployed troops in Kuwait to deter any Iraqi military action. All of this occurred long before Saddam Hussein emerged on the political landscape.

The formal creation of Kuwait and its artificial boundaries exemplifies how the traditional colonial powers can continue to control strategic areas without a direct imposition of colonial rule. The colonial powers "came up with a proposal whereby these same areas would be ceded to them by the League of Nations as their 'mandates' under the fiction that these territories were being prepared for self-rule" (Ahmad 1991, 31). The colonial powers carved up the Middle East and structured their mandates in a manner that suited their interests. Kuwait retained the Port of Uqair, which provided strategic access to the Persian Gulf. While oil had not yet been discovered in Kuwait, it was widely believed that the territory was oil-rich. The colonial powers ensured that no rival power could rise out of the Middle East by drawing unnatural borders and fostering economic division between oil-rich and oil-poor Arabs. By creating a variety of oil producers, market forces would keep the price of oil low and political manipulation would keep the supply flush.

Just as the League of Nations served the interests of the colonial powers by establishing mandates, so too did the UN serve the interests of the newly dominant capitalist state, the United States. When the UN was established, another new world order was implemented. This order was based on the end of formal colonialism and support for self-determination, democracy, free trade, and free markets. Through free trade and free market agreements, American and European oil companies controlled almost all of the Arab and Iranian oil by

1954 (Keohane 1984, 151–159). The UN imposed the West's will on Arab countries from the beginning. The creation of Israel in 1948 signaled the permanent U.S. presence through a strategically located client. While Cold War tensions prevented further UN political action, UN conservatism did little to correct the injustices of colonialism. Its very orientation is to maintain a status quo, which is unjust and exploitive of most of the world's population. The UN did nothing, while the capitalist powers attacked developing states, both politically and militarily, when they sought to chart their own courses or deviated from capitalism.

The UN's actions in the Gulf Crisis set several disturbing precedents. First, the initial UN collective security action in the post–Cold War era was used to liberate an antidemocratic, oil-rich kingdom with strong historical ties to the capitalist West. Kuwait Inc., as Kuwait is known both to critics and admirers, is one of the first transnational corporate nation-states. Its national income comes from two main sources: the Kuwaiti Oil Company, which was once a joint venture between Gulf Oil Corporation and British Petroleum, and the Kuwait Investment Office (KIO), which manages an international investment portfolio worth more than $120 billion. After the invasion by Iraq, KIO operations continued almost uninterrupted from its headquarters in London, the capital of its former colonial benefactor (Phillips 1990, 32). Revenues from the KIO are thought to outpace oil revenues, which means Kuwait's economy continued to grow even after Iraq seized its oil fields and refineries.

The Kuwaiti government-in-exile set up operations in the five-star Sheraton Hotel in Taif, Saudi Arabia. Kuwaiti officials, most of whom were members of the royal family, occupied luxurious suites. Very few in the Arab world had much sympathy for either the rulers or the citizens of Kuwait. According to the 1990 Statistical Survey (*Europa World Year Book* 1990), non-Kuwaiti residents (1,463,954) greatly outnumbered Kuwaiti citizens (550,181). Kuwait society was divided into rigid and distinct classes where non-Kuwaitis comprised more than 80 percent of the workforce and occupied lower-paying and lower-status jobs. Palestinian workers in Kuwait supported the Iraqi invasion, sensing that Hussein was the lesser of two evils. Hussein may have been a brutal dictator but he was popular in much of the Arab world because he stood up to the West and represented Arab unity and anti-imperialism (Ahmad 1991; Al-Radi 1995).

Second, the collective security operation, which was sanctioned by the UN and carried out by U.S. military forces, was financed in large part by Kuwait and Saudi Arabia. While much is made of the contributions of West Germany and Japan, their contributions accounted for only a third of the reimbursement to the United States. Kuwait and Saudi Arabia paid the remaining two-thirds (Clark 1995). Collective security under the UN might be for only those that can pay for it. As for democratic ideals, the Security Council made the world safe for monarchy, not democracy as was ideally envisioned by President Woodrow Wilson in 1917.

Third, and perhaps more disturbing for many developing states, was the passage of Security Council Resolution 688, establishing safe-haven zones for

Kurds in northern Iraq. This resolution links human rights violations in Iraq to international peace and security. In other words, it allows for "humanitarian" intervention, whereby the sovereignty of a state may be militarily overridden by the UN to correct for perceived human rights violations. Developing states are well aware that it is their sovereignty that will likely be overridden in such cases (Pease and Forsythe 1993). The UN is certainly not going to intervene in British affairs regarding Northern Ireland or in Spanish affairs regarding the Basque region. Furthermore, given that the military forces of member states are used instead of UN forces, any state not aligned with the United States or Europe will fear UN intervention (Alvarez 1995, 8). This humanitarian exception to Article 2(7) of the UN Charter may lead to intervention for economic and political reasons unrelated to human rights under the guise of humanitarian concerns. Not surprisingly, China abstained, while India, Cuba, and Yemen voted against Resolution 688.

Marxist theory also highlights those who stand to benefit the most from the UN action in the Gulf Crisis. The "follow the money" compass points squarely at the U.S. military–industrial complex and U.S. oil companies. Defense contractors received billions of dollars in domestic and international orders, and U.S. oil companies obtained new contracts from Kuwait and their newly liberated oil. An alleged assassination plot against former President H. W. Bush was uncovered by the Kuwaitis during a visit by Bush and former secretary of state James Baker, who were in Kuwait to negotiate lucrative contracts for a consortium of Texas oil refineries after they had left public office.

A Feminist Cut

Feminist theory highlights the gender bias of the UN Security Council and the consequences for women and children. The first glaring fact regarding UN collective security during the Gulf Crisis was the almost complete absence of female decision makers. The only woman in any significant decision-making capacity was Prime Minister Margaret Thatcher of Great Britain, and her own political party removed her in November of 1990. All the chief executives of the member states and their permanent representatives to the Security Council were male. The Secretary-General was male. Traditional, liberal feminists point out that women were virtually excluded from the decision-making process in Iraq, the United States, and the UN.

Neofeminists, who argue that biological differences between men and women account for differences in behavior, point out that male dominance conditions the policies of states and hierarchically structured IGOs, and women and children can suffer as a result. Feminists note that the policies adopted by the UN toward Iraq had a greater impact on women and children than they did on the Iraqi leadership and Iraqi soldiers. The UN economic embargo is a case in point. UN Security Council Resolution 661 imposes a complete economic embargo except for immediate humanitarian supplies. These economic sanctions impacted the most vulnerable in Iraqi society, women and children. Women often bear the brunt of the sanctions because they sacrifice their rations of food for the other members (usually male) of their families. The effect of economic sanctions, whether intended or not, dramatically raised the child mortality rate and caused severe malnutrition among women and children in Iraq (Ascherio et al. 1992). The United Nations Children's Fund (UNICEF 1999) found that 90,000 deaths yearly in Iraq were due to sanctions and 5,000 children *a month* were dying as a result of sanctions. Sanctions led to a breakdown of water supply and sanitation, inadequate nutrition, and nonexistent health care. The continued use of sanctions after the conflict prompted the head of UNICEF and the head of the "oil-for-food" program to resign from their offices.

Once the UN/U.S. war with Iraq in 1991 began, it was again the women and children who suffered. The war began with air and missile strikes on areas populated heavily with Iraqi civilians. UN/U.S. forces unleashed an impressive barrage of firepower from the safety of planes and ships hundreds of miles away. The men, the soldiers, and the war-makers on both sides were protected by the latest military hardware and technology, while the women and children were left exposed. The ground war that would pit man against man did not begin until several weeks later, after the civilian centers and infrastructures necessary to sustain human life, such as electricity, water, and sewage systems, had been destroyed. The Iraqi prisoners of war (POWs) received more protection and assistance from the International Committee for the Red Cross (ICRC) and UN than Iraqi women and children.

The priorities of the UN are masculine in that military force, violations of sovereignty, and territorial integrity are most important to UN members, which conditions their methods (Enloe 1993). The UN Security Council sought to pressure the Iraqi leadership by imposing sanctions that hurt those who could do nothing about Iraqi policy. However, assassinating or militarily removing Saddam Hussein at the time was impermissible. Charging him with war crimes would have set an unacceptable precedent. As a result, the leadership stayed the same, and the Iraqi women and children continued to suffer. The interests of the sovereign state and the rules that govern how states and men behave with each other are more important than the lives of women and children. Meanwhile, even though there were women soldiers in the U.S./UN Gulf forces, they were forced to keep a lower profile than their male counterparts so as not to offend their Saudi hosts.

Women comprised the principal opposition of the UN/U.S. 1991 war against Iraq and continued to oppose UN sanctions and military strikes. Women's groups are part and parcel of the peace movement that opposes all nuclear proliferation and militarism. Women participate in such all-female NGOs as Minnesota's Women Against Military Madness and the Aldermaston Women's Peace Camp (UK) as well as in such mixed NGOs as the War Resisters International. Women make up an international network of tens of thousands of peace advocates that extends from Australia to Turkey. Yet, their activities are marginalized by governments, the UN, and the media because of their more feminine orientation toward peace. They are characterized as naive, idealistic, or misguided individuals who have little understanding of the realities of international politics.

Steve Niva (1998) provides an interesting postmodern feminist interpretation of the 1991 Gulf Crisis as a "remasculation" of the United States. The United States has suffered from an identity crisis since the 1970s, having lost the Vietnam War, experienced a crippling oil crisis, and had its wishes repeatedly ignored within UN agencies. Presidents Reagan and Bush attempted to diminish the Vietnam Syndrome with minor military interventions in Grenada (1983) and Panama (1989), respectively. Hollywood did its part, too, with Sylvester Stallone and Arnold Schwarzenegger playing macho soldier roles, single-handedly defeating the Soviets, the Arabs, or both. Yet, the Vietnam Syndrome was not easily shaken. The Vietnam War and the resulting American decline in international and diplomatic affairs raised serious questions about U.S. capability and about its will to lead. In other words, it raised questions of U.S. manhood. The Gulf Crisis remasculated the United States because it was able to defeat Iraq, control Middle Eastern oil, and dominate the UN.

Feminist theory emphasizes women and gendered roles in the Gulf Crisis. The lens of gender focuses on the conspicuous absence of women from the UN decision-making process and their unique experience under UN policies. Feminists highlight the masculinity of the use of armed forces and of international politics during the Gulf War. The activities of women, operating in their traditional gender roles as pacifists and nurturers, are also highlighted.

A Constructivist Cut

The constructivist approach emphasizes the role of shared values and norms, as well as the perceptions of decision makers. The staff and rules and procedures of UN agencies were effective in helping states define their common interests during the Gulf Crisis. Participation in international organizations encourages decision makers to consider the interests of others when determining their own national interests (Lyons 1995). The Gulf Crisis also illustrates that more was at work than a mere congruence of state interests. Individual leaders also played an important role in making the collective security efforts possible. Both George H.W. Bush and Mikhail Gorbachev preferred multilateral negotiations and approaches to unilateral or bilateral ones. Several world leaders since have followed their precedent. Both Bill Clinton and Boris Yeltsin conducted the bulk of their foreign relations through the UN. European leaders such as John Major, François Mitterrand, and Helmut Kohl, accustomed to multilateralism with the European Union, also fostered the spirit of cooperation. Tony Blair and Jacques Chirac continued the precedent. When decision makers share common values, policies change.

International cooperation during the Gulf Crisis was not a fluke. It was possible because of the commonly held belief in the rule of law. Iraq's invasion and annexation of Kuwait violated not only international law but also long-standing social laws and norms. Iraq's behavior was so inappropriate that others in the international community wanted to cooperate with each other through the UN, even though the material "interests" of many were not threatened. No existing state has ceased to exist because of military conquest since World War II. In the postwar era, governments have come and gone through military force, and states have been dismembered; but no state has disappeared completely through external violence. Yet, Iraq was trying to accomplish just that. And Iraq's aggression was so naked that it was unacceptable, even to those who would otherwise be sympathetic to its position. To put this in the words of a constructivist, the shared intersubjective understanding of this particular international norm helped define the national interest and the preferences of member states.

Societies are increasingly tied together and interdependent. Subsequent Security Council actions in Somalia, Haiti, and the former Yugoslavia (Bosnia and Kosovo) demonstrate that international cooperation is possible even when "aggression" is difficult to define, when the costs of intervention are high, and when great-power material interests are not directly engaged. In fact, Security Council actions in Somalia, Haiti, and the former Yugoslavia have greatly expanded its purview because it has linked situations occurring wholly and materially within the domestic jurisdiction of a sovereign state to international peace and security. This is an example of the UN functioning as a norm creator and in moving states to understand security in human terms.

THE SECURITY COUNCIL AND IRAQ AFTER THE GULF WAR

After the Gulf War, Iraq continued to challenge the authority of the Security Council by denying access to UN arms inspectors and being generally uncooperative. The Security Council periodically responded with air strikes by British and American forces against military targets, but clearly, the coalition against Iraq had begun to splinter. In November of 1997, the crisis in the Gulf threatened to deteriorate into violence again as Iraq thwarted UN inspectors and demanded the removal of U.S. members of the inspection teams. The international response was quite mixed. In spite of evidence that Iraq was hiding weapons of mass destruction (WMD), few members of the international community wanted an enforcement action. The difference of opinion stems from differing worldviews about the political, economic, and social forces at work in the Gulf Crisis. Realist thought can easily be discerned. According to Thailand's *Daily News*, "To be fair, Iraq, as a sovereign nation, has as much a right as ten or so other mostly big nations who develop nuclear, chemical and biological weapons" (U.S. Information Agency 1997a, 12). Sri Lanka's *Sunday Times* questions whether UNSCOM is the tool of the United States: "The question that UN Secretary-General Kofi Annan cannot dodge is how quickly and effectively he can rescue the United Nations from the United States. . . . Countries like China, Russia, India, and Japan represent more plainly 'We, the people' more truly than the United States. Right now, however, the Sheriff in the White House, playing globocop in a unipolar world, has picked his posse" (U.S. Information Agency 1997a, 12). Revelations of intelligence sharing between UNSCOM and the CIA did little to assuage concerns about UNSCOM as an extension of the United States.

The liberal worldview was also represented in the world's media. According to Nigeria's *Guardian*, "Dialogue, diplomacy, and restraint have prevailed over the option of war offered by the friction in Baghdad. This is a celebration of the resolution of a potentially volatile situation and the triumph of the ideals of the UN" (U.S. Information Agency 1997a, 13). Germany's *Die Welt* stated, "Ending the delaying tactics with the UN inspectors would be the quickest way to end the sanctions. That this is not happening is almost proof enough of secret and dangerous arsenals in Baghdad and a reason to continue the inspections" (U.S. Information Agency 1997a, 12). Great Britain's *Guardian* claimed, "The choices that still have to be made . . . will help decide not only what kind of country Iraq, potentially an immensely powerful state, will be in the future, but what kind of place the Middle East will be, and the kind of world in which we are all going to live in the next century" (U.S. Information Agency 1997a, 7).

The Marxist worldview was also represented. According to Pakistan's *Nation*, "During the previous Gulf War, America and her allies had staged a gory drama, the parallel of which is hard to find in recent history. These so-called custodians of human values had let loose hell on the Iraqi people, the disastrous effects of which are still felt by the Iraqi people in the form of various sanctions imposed on them. As a result of this horrendous war, oil wealth and the entire Middle East region has virtually fallen in the hands of America and Arab countries have been virtually reduced to the status of surrogates" (U.S. Information Agency 1997a, 12–13). The feminist perspective is not largely represented in the world's media. The print media did cover the suffering of the Iraqi people and the way in which UN sanctions negatively affected the lives of women and children. Moreover, PBS and BBC documentaries detailing the devastating effects of sanctions generated wide international support for ending sanctions in Iraq. The international media's reaction to UN airstrikes and sanctions in Iraq shows that competing worldviews exist and affect the way the actions of international organizations are interpreted.

In 2001, the Iraqi situation continued to be a stalemate. UN inspectors had not been in Iraq since 1998, sanctions were still in place, and the United States and UK periodically carried out air strikes against Iraqi installations. The U.S. airstrikes against Iraq on February 16, 2001, angered many in the Muslim world. The Organization of Islamic Conference (OIC) condemned the raids and questioned their timing (*Washington Report on Middle East Affairs* 2001, 38). Then secretary-general of the OIC, Dr. Abdul-Wahid Belkziz of Morocco, stated that the United States had once again overstepped UN Security Council authority and poisoned the move toward Iraqi reconciliation with the UN. Moreover, the raids were unjustified and a violation of international law.

The September 11, 2001, attacks on the United States changed the international environment. The UN, through Security Council resolutions 1368 and 1373, moved quickly to support the United States by recognizing its right to self-defense from a nonstate actor and called upon member-states to cooperate in efforts to cut off financing to terror groups. U.S. military action in Afghanistan in 2002 had UN approval as it was an act of self-defense against the Al-Qaeda network, which was being harbored by the Taliban government. The United States had sought a diplomatic solution by asking the Taliban to turn over Osama bin Laden and other terrorists in the network and the Taliban declined. Therefore, it was left with little recourse other than military action. However, the overwhelming international consensus regarding the legitimacy and legality of the U.S. use of force in Afghanistan faded quickly as the United States and Great Britain then turned their attention to Iraq and its alleged WMD. The two countries, the principal enforcers of UN sanctions and punitive air strikes, saw Iraq as an unacceptable threat in the post–September 11 world. Both states sought to renew UN support for dealing with the decade-long problem of Iraq, this time in the context of the "war on terror." However, little credible evidence linked Iraq to September 11 in spite of U.S. rhetorical efforts to do so.

Whether this 2002–2003 crisis with Iraq is best understood as part of the U.S. war on terror or as an issue about its noncompliance with past Security Council resolutions is subject to debate (see, e.g., Simpson 2005). A safe argument is that the crisis involved both. The international coalition against Iraq in the 1990s had fractured, yet the terror attacks renewed a sense of urgency in the United States and Great Britain in preventing the proliferation of WMD. In November 2002, the two countries were able to obtain Security Council Resolution 1441 that recalled the past resolutions against Iraq, especially with regard to disarmament, and declared that Iraq's failure to comply would make it liable to material breach. Continued defiance would result in further material breach and "serious consequences." But the resolution did not include the "all means necessary" clause that diplomatically authorizes force. The wording of Resolution 1441 was deliberately vague, which provided political cover to all the parties and allowed the Iraq issue to move forward at the UN (Byers 2004).

The United States sought additional authorization from the Security Council after renewed inspections failed to root out WMD. The then secretary of state Colin Powell gave a dramatic presentation before the UN Security Council in February 2003 detailing Iraq's continued violations of Security Council sanctions. He provided evidence that Iraq was thwarting UN inspections by hiding equipment and denying inspectors the opportunity to interview Iraqi scientists. Powell also displayed intelligence indicating elaborate Iraqi chemical, biological, and nuclear weapons programs as well as ties to the Al-Qaeda terrorist network. Yet, the Security Council remained unpersuaded, and the United States abandoned the attempt of securing an additional resolution authorizing military force after threatened vetoes by France, Russia, and China. Moreover, it could not persuade a majority of the nonpermanent members to vote for the proposed resolution. In March 2003, the United States and an informal "coalition of the willing" invaded Iraq without explicit Security Council authorization. This coalition declared their actions were permissible based on previous Security Council resolutions and the UN Charter (Byers 2004; Taft 2005). At the same time, opponents of the invasion claimed the coalition had acted with no legal basis, a position that has since been supported by many legal analysts (see, e.g., Franck 2003; Hakke 2004; Simpson 2005).

The actions of the United States and the "coalition of the willing" generated a crisis at the UN that persists today. In 2003, Secretary-General Kofi Annan declared that the U.S.-led invasion of Iraq was illegal and in contravention of the UN Charter. The U.S. invasion and occupation of Iraq has not gone well, and the continued instability, characterized by suicide bombings, insurgent attacks, and sectarian violence, breeds international political discord. Moreover, no WMD were found, and much of the evidence presented by Secretary Powell before the Security Council has since been discredited. The benchmark political successes of the transition to formal Iraqi sovereignty, elections for the provisional government and the permanent government, and a referendum on the Iraqi constitution have been overshadowed by continuous insurgent and factional violence. The August and September 2003 terrorist attacks on UN headquarters in Iraq, killing scores of people, further strained U.S.–UN relations.

The damage done to the UN by the U.S.-led invasion of Iraq can be interpreted in a number of ways. Glennon (2003) stakes out the structural realist position. He argues that the "UN's rules governing the use of force, laid out in a charter and managed by the Security Council, had fallen victim to geopolitical forces too strong for a legalist institution to withstand" (Glennon 2003, 16). He points out that the United States sought UN approval but that it also warned that it would act alone if the UN failed to cooperate. The politics at work in the UN Security Council were old-fashioned power politics whereby great powers France, Russia, and China sought to restrain the superpower—a superpower intent on maintaining its preeminence. The inability of the Security Council to prevent the 2003 Iraq War was just the latest piece of evidence that the security mechanism of the UN is broken. Butler (1999, 19) points out that, for the most part, the Security Council has been "bypassed, defied and abused" during the 1990s. The crisis with Iraq simply brought this to the forefront. The underlying balance of power in the international system marginalized the Security Council in this case, just as it had done in the past.

The policies of President George W. Bush were liberal in their orientation in that the war was geared toward solving the problem of WMD in the hands of a rogue state and bringing democracy and markets to a very illiberal area of the world (Fukuyama 2006, 65–66). The tension within the liberal school of thought is whether the United States should have taken a militaristic posture to accomplish this liberal world order. The interventionist position represented by neoconservatives in the United States is pitted against those that argue that the United States should lead by example, not through military force. For neoconservatives, the weakness of international institutions is caused by illiberal states. Either these institutions need to be reformed or new ones have to be created that reflect and promote liberal values. As a presidential candidate, Senator John McCain proposed that the United States throw its resources and intellectual energy around creating a League of Democracies. Other liberals, particularly liberal institutionalists, were critical of the Bush administration for undermining existing international law and organizations (see, e.g., Jenkins 2003; Simpson 2005; Weiss et al. 2004, 95–97). The United States cannot promote the idea of the rule of law without agreeing to follow the law. Furthermore, democracy cannot be imposed. Democracy needs to be nurtured and promoted through reform policies and good governance.

From a Marxist view, U.S. policies toward Iraq represent its attempt at establishing an empire that is fundamentally economic in nature (Chomsky 2004; Ferguson 2004; Fotopoulos 2003; Tariq 2003). The September 11, 2001, attacks provided a pretext for the United States (and the transnational elite) to continue to use its overwhelming power to impose its vision on the rest of the world. The United States is not engaging in old-fashioned power politics, but rather in old-fashioned imperialism, which brought it into conflict with the material interests of China, Russia, and France in Iraq. These countries may share a common threat from radical Islam, yet they remain divided over the strategy and access to the energy resources in the region. As a result, the United States was unable to gain Security Council support for its imperial endeavor, and the UN was powerless to stop it. The UN could not even muster support within the General Assembly to challenge the United States. Many NGOs called upon the General Assembly to invoke the Uniting for Peace resolution, yet not one state was willing to risk the political and economic consequences of crossing the United States in the General Assembly. The U.S. decision to bar corporations from states that opposed the intervention from lucrative reconstruction contracts demonstrated the tension surrounding the material interests at stake in Iraq. The UN then provided tacit *ex post facto* approval of the U.S. intervention by establishing a presence in Iraq, which then made it a target of insurgent forces in Iraq. Radical Islam, which has co-opted the Marxist language of imperialism, focuses on the corruption of elites in Muslim states and capitalist oppression, and continues to challenge the liberal world order that allows capitalism to thrive.

Feminist NGOs have pointed out that the 2003 Iraq War has threatened the status of women in Iraq. They point out that under Saddam Hussein, women had more rights than women in other Muslim countries. Women had "the right to drive, to attend coeducational college classes, work outside of the home in offices with men and to inherit property, among other rights" (*Women's International Network News* 2003, 10). They have expressed concern that the deteriorating security situation in Iraq and the rise of religious fundamentalism in the Iraqi government will threaten women's rights. Women's groups have pushed for the inclusion of women in the formation of the interim Iraqi government and for the inclusion of women's rights in the new Iraqi constitution. Noelleen Heyzer, the executive director of the United Nations Development Fund for Women (UNIFEM), argued that "The perspectives of women offer the best promise of meaningful reconstruction and the development of a working effort" (*Women's International Network News* 2003, 10). Women's NGOs continue to push the United States and the UN to integrate women into the peacebuilding process in Afghanistan and Iraq and remain concerned that women and women's issues have taken a backseat because of the unstable security situation in both countries. Women groups also spearheaded the opposition to the appointment of John Bolton as the U.S. ambassador to the UN during the Bush administration. One such group, Citizens for Global Solutions, demonstrated in Washington and launched a Web site opposing Bolton (Bosco 2005). Domestic and international opposition to John Bolton, who once claimed that there "is no such thing as the United Nations," made Senate approval on the nomination unlikely, forcing President Bush to resort to a recess appointment to install him at the UN. Bolton was forced to leave his position after his recess appointment expired.

A constructivist interpretation of the Security Council meltdown centers on the perceptions and misperceptions of the individuals involved. Marfleet and Miller (2005, 355), responding to Glennon, argue that the leaders of France and the United States had "inaccurately gauged the preferences of the 'other' " and overestimated their ability to influence and control the situation. They conclude that "one explanation for the events leading up to the Iraq war is the human failing of hubris. It was the pathology of overconfidence, as much as the irresistible push of some ineffable force poised to smash the UN, that generated these inauspicious outcomes" (355). It is, after all, individuals who make key decisions, and they are subjected to the same human conditions that affect us all. Pride and overconfidence set into motion a disastrous series of events.

Part of the problem according to constructivists was that the United States was not abiding by two important international norms, namely, that states solve disputes multilaterally and should be reluctant to use force (Finnemore 2004). The U.S. invasion was illegitimate because the United States acted without explicit Security Council authorization and seemed too willing to use force without first exhausting other diplomatic options. The U.S. position, as represented by Bush administration officially, was framed in terms of American security, not international security (Mor 2007, 240). This poisoned the debate and the United States, rather than Iraq, was seen by other states as the principal threat to international peace.

SECURITY COUNCIL AND RELATED REFORMS

The criticisms of the UN and the Security Council have given rise to a variety of reform efforts. These reform efforts are important because they attempt to make the UN more credible as an inclusive global institution (see, e.g., Alger

1996; Bedjaoui 1994; Kennedy and Russett 1995). One major reform effort under consideration at the UN is to change the membership of the UN Security Council. In 1965, the UN Charter was amended to expand the Council from nine to fifteen members. The expansion was necessary because the overall size of the UN had increased by virtue of the decolonization process and the formation of new states (*UN Chronicle* 1997, 31). Many newly independent states, acutely aware of the consequences of war and other forms of international aggression, sought a greater voice in the decision-making process related to international security.

Expanding both the permanent and nonpermanent membership of the Security Council was under consideration in negotiations leading up to the 2005 World Summit. The contentious debate centered on which states should be given seats and whether expansion would make the Council even more unwieldy. The highly politicized environment at the UN in 2005 prevented any serious consideration of Security Council reform proposals. As Weiss and Crossette (2006, 4) state, the best that could be accomplished at the 2005 World Summit was a generic commitment to support Security Council reform and to adapt its working methods. States could not move beyond their entrenched position, and as a result, the Security Council continues to lack the credibility and the institutional capability to effectively address contemporary international security problems.

Contemporary international security problems involve several highly charged issues revolving around how to define and combat terrorism, the responsibility of states to protect populations against genocide, war crimes, ethnic cleansing and crimes against humanity, and the management of post-conflict reconstruction. These issues are embedded in geostrategic, economic, ethnic, and moral dimensions that make relative agreement, much less consensus, impossible. Because of divergent worldviews, one person's terrorist is another's freedom fighter and one person's humanitarian intervention is another's imperialism. The politics at the UN reflects this competition of values and determines in large part assessments about whether the UN is part of the problem or the solution. Hence, it is remarkable that at the 2005 World Summit, member states committed themselves to the principle of **responsibility to protect (R2P)**. In the 1990s, many at the UN began to rethink international security as meaning state security. The humanitarian crises of the 1990s (in the former Yugoslavia, the genocide in Rwanda, and the proliferation of "failed states") prompted a reconceptualization of security as "human security." The main threat to peace and security now emanates from conditions within states—political oppression, forced population movements, human rights violations, famine, disease, and economic deprivation. However, state sovereignty often stands in the way of meaningful multilateral action. The UN has sought to redefine state sovereignty as the R2P. If a state is unable or unwilling to protect its population, then that responsibility falls to the international community. Most observers recognize that this commitment at the 2005 Summit did not establish a right to humanitarian intervention as it requires that any collective action be taken through the Security Council. Given the

Security Council's record of reaching consensus, the chances of formal UN intervention is quite slim. Rather, R2P can be seen as a political catchword that can be interpreted in any number of ways (Stahn 2007). For example, China sees R2P as meaning that states have the responsibility to protect their sovereignty, and the UN can only intervene in situations involving failed states and, even then, action must be taken by the Security Council (Xue 2007, 89–91). This is vastly different from the view of many liberal states that Security Council authorization is not necessary for humanitarian intervention (Bellamy 2005; Matlary 2004).

One important accomplishment of the 2005 World Summit was the creation of a UN Peacebuilding Commission to strengthen the institution's capacity to help countries transition from war to peace. While the Security Council remains marginalized on most security issues, the UN does have experience and a decent record of reconstruction and rebuilding after war. The UN Peacebuilding Commission, backed by a support office and a standing fund, increases the UN capacity at helping societies recover from war. Established in 2006, its first initiatives center on long-term capacity building in Sierra Leone, Burundi, and Liberia.

Another important reform unrelated to the 2005 World Summit centers on curbing the abuse and sexual exploitation by UN troops and civilian personnel involved in UN peacekeeping missions. Embarrassing revelations of prostitution and pornography rings, child rape, and sex abuse involving members of peacekeeping missions in the Balkans, Congo, Liberia, and Ivory Coast have greatly tarnished the reputation of the UN. In the past, the UN tended to have a "boys will be boys" attitude and could do little other than to occasionally repatriate peacekeepers back to their countries. Any punishment was left up to that individual's state. The UN has strengthened the authority of the office of the Secretary-General to investigate any allegation of misconduct and to remove soldiers. The Secretary-General has instituted a "zero-tolerance" policy, which involves zero sexual contact between peacekeepers and the civilian population. Nevertheless, the slow pace of substantive change in attitudes at the UN has been criticized both internally at the UN and externally by organizations such as Refugee International (Hoge 2005, A5).

The "zero-tolerance" policy has been complemented by UN efforts to "engender" peacekeeping. Security Council Resolution 1325 (October 31, 2000) recommended that the Secretary-General find ways to integrate women into peacekeeping and police operations. This resolution has gone a long way in bringing women's ideas and skills to the peacekeeping table and recognizing how women uniquely contribute to and resolve violence (see, e.g., Hunt and Posa 2001; Olsson and Tryggestad 2001). According to Olsson (2001, 97–110), the UN successfully integrated women into the Namibian peacekeeping mission at all levels, which partly explains why there were so few cases of sexual harassment and exploitation. The altruism of UN peacekeeping missions is incongruent with the underlying masculinity associated with the military and related deployments, which contributes to an environment in which local women and children are vulnerable to exploitation and abuse (Whitworth

2004). The inclusion of women as peacekeepers and advisors is an important step in helping the UN tackle the problem of sex abuse because women are uniquely positioned to challenge traditional ways of doing business.

NUCLEAR PROLIFERATION

One of the principal threats to international peace and security, and perhaps to humanity, is the proliferation of WMD. The most potent of WMD are nuclear weapons that have the capacity to destroy entire cities, countries, and the world. The September 11 terror attacks generated renewed urgency to control these weapons to reduce the probability of their use. If a couple of extremists with box cutters and airline tickets could so dramatically disrupt world affairs, imagine the consequences if they had acquired nuclear weapons. And what if extremists were to gain control of a state that possesses nuclear weapons? The U.S. invasion of Iraq in 2003 was justified in part by the need to control the spread of WMD. The United States ultimately went to war without UN authorization; however, that should not obscure the important role international law and organizations have played in nuclear arms control and disarmament.

The nuclear nonproliferation regime began soon after the advent of nuclear weapons. In 1946, the UN General Assembly, with the encouragement of the United States, created the short-lived UN Atomic Energy Commission to confront with problems and dilemmas created by the discovery of nuclear energy. This commission is most noted for a plan put forth by one of its American commissioners, Bernard Baruch. The so-called Baruch Plan detailed ways the commission could control atomic energy, technology, and weapons. It called for UN control of nuclear technology and weapons and included an extensive UN role in the operation and inspection of nuclear facilities. The United States agreed to relinquish control of its small arsenal, but only after the plan had been fully implemented and inspection procedures institutionalized. The distrust between the United States and the Soviet Union eventually led to the demise of the plan and the UN Atomic Energy Commission. The Soviet Union viewed the commission and the Baruch Plan as U.S. propaganda ploys while the United States maneuvered behind the scenes to solidify its monopoly over nuclear energy and weapons. Certain opinion circles in the United States, wary of Soviet intentions and power, argued it was idealistic and foolish to follow through on the Baruch plan and vigorously lobbied against it on Capital Hill. Hence, this early attempt at nuclear nonproliferation never really got off the ground.

In 1949, the Soviet Union exploded its first atomic weapon and the United Kingdom followed suit in 1952. Not only did these states acquire the know-how to produce the weaponry but they also adapted the technology to make them more destructive. The U.S. bombs dropped on Hiroshima and Nagasaki during World War II were fission weapons where elements (Uranium-235 and plutonium) are split causing destructive explosion and radiation. In contrast, the more deadly, yet more complicated, fusion weapon involves forcing two atoms (usually from hydrogen) together causing the release of tremendous amounts of energy. While the United States was the first to develop fusion weapons, the Soviet Union exploded the largest hydrogen bomb in 1955 (Diehl and Moltz 2008, 9).

Controlling nuclear weapons is problematic because it involves a technology that can also produce an infinite amount of energy to meet the world's growing energy needs. With fossil fuels in limited supply and climate change emerging a grave environment threat, more and more countries are seeking alternative energy sources that are renewable and do not emit greenhouse gases. The potential of nuclear technology as an energy source was evident when U.S. President Dwight Eisenhower gave his famous "**Atoms for Peace**" speech before the UN General Assembly in 1953. President Eisenhower outlined a framework to promote the safe, peaceful, and secure uses of nuclear technology. Public officials acknowledged that the technological genie could not be put back into the bottle, so it became imperative to control and harness the technology for positive and productive purposes.

The Atoms for Peace speech provided the impetus for the creation of the IAEA in 1957 by eighty-one states. The three part mission of the IAEA includes nuclear verification and security; safety; and technology transfer. Technically, the IAEA is an independent agency in that it was established outside of the UN system through its own treaty. Nevertheless, the IAEA considers itself part of the UN family. It is located in Vienna, Austria and has a staff of over 2,000 people. The IAEA reports annually to the UN Security Council and the General Assembly. The early history of the IAEA was overshadowed by the Cold War arms race and proliferation continued. In 1960, France developed nuclear weapons and, in 1962, the United States and the Soviet Union came to the brink of nuclear war during the Cuban Missile Crisis. In 1964, China joined the nuclear club. At this point, five states had acquired nuclear weapons and the size of their nuclear arsenals was spiraling upward. Proliferation now had two dimensions. The first is **horizontal proliferation** defined as the increase in the number of states that have acquired nuclear weapons, and the second is **vertical proliferation** that refers to the growing size and sophistication of the nuclear weapon arsenals.

The horizontal and vertical proliferation of nuclear weapons was accelerated by the development of new kinds of delivery systems. As a practical matter, nuclear weapons have two basic parts: the warhead and the delivery system. During the early part of the Cold War, the principal delivery system for nuclear warheads was the airplane; however, with the development of ballistic missiles technology, defending against a nuclear attack became a great deal more difficult (if not impossible). Ballistic missiles can be based on land and at sea, aboard ships and submarines. The spiraling arms race was of major concern to both nuclear and non-nuclear states, yet efforts at nuclear arms control faced several persistent obstacles. The first obstacle comes from the "push" of new technology. Once a technology has been developed, it is very difficult for states not to use it because if they do not take advantage of the technology, another state will.

Also, if that technology gives a military advantage to one state, other states then seek to develop tactics and alternative technologies to counter that advantage. Technology-push fuels arms races. A second obstacle is the horizontal proliferation of nuclear weapons. The more actors at the negotiating table, the more difficult it becomes to find an arrangement that will please all the parties. A third obstacle is verification. Since nuclear weapons directly impact a state's security, ensuring that others will not cheat on their arms control obligations is high priority. Facing these obstacles, nuclear and non-nuclear states came together to craft the centerpiece to nuclear nonproliferation.

Nuclear NonProliferation Treaty (NPT)

The NPT came into force in 1970 and represents a comprehensive approach to the threat posed by the spread of nuclear weapons and nuclear-weapons technology. The NPT strikes a unique, if unequal, bargain between nuclear-weapon states and non-nuclear weapon states by recognizing that nuclear technology cannot be unlearned and that it can be used for both constructive and destructive purposes. As such, it obligates the nuclear-weapon states not to transfer nuclear weapon technology and materials to non-nuclear states. Non-nuclear weapon states agree not to seek or develop the weapons. At the same time, the NPT allows for the transfer of nuclear technology and materials for peaceful purposes as long as those transfers are transparent and monitored by the IAEA for safety and security. Recipient states are required to submit to IAEA monitoring and inspections to verify that the materials are not being used to develop nuclear weapons. By providing states with access to peaceful nuclear technology, the international community provides incentives for states not to divert their scarce resources toward the development of nuclear weapons. The treaty (Article VI) also obligates nuclear weapon states to end the nuclear arms race and to eventually disarm themselves of all nuclear weapons. Parties to the NPT recognize that the total disarmament is not likely in the near future but it remains the long-term goal of the regime. The duration of the original treaty was twenty-five years and in 1995, member states renewed the treaty indefinitely. Every five years, states hold a "review conference" to assess the status of the treaty and identify strategies for achieving NPT goals. For example, an important outcome of the 2000 review conference was the so-called "13 Steps," which outlined thirteen practical steps that a state could take to achieve the goal of nuclear disarmament. The 2005 review conference ended in discord, fueled in part by the U.S. invasion of Iraq and its inability to find WMD. The conference also wrestled with the extent that non-nuclear weapons states have an inalienable right to nuclear technology and know-how for peaceful purposes. An outcome of the 2010 review conference was to reaffirm a fifteen-year-old goal of establishing the Middle East as a nuclear weapons–free zone and called for a 2012 regional conference to achieve that aim.

Nuclear nonproliferation illustrates the nexus between international law and international organizations. In addition to being a multilateral treaty, the NPT is also a dispute resolution system that manages conflict over the use of nuclear technology among member states (Suleman 2008, 209). The NPT provides the legal framework for the regime and the IAEA is the monitoring body providing the parties with information regarding who is using nuclear technology and for what purposes (energy, medical, etc.). The IAEA also performs the valuable services of inspection and verification. The UN coordinates and, in some cases, enforces compliance with nonproliferation efforts. The 189 NPT member states recognize that the use of nuclear energy needs to be regulated and the regime represents what is possible with global governance without a global government. The NPT has worked remarkably well. At its inception, the NPT recognized a *de jure* nuclear club of five states (United States, Russia, United Kingdom, France, and China). Since then only five other states have acquired or developed nuclear weapons. Three of those states (India, Pakistan, and Israel) are not signatories to the NPT. South Africa developed weapons under the white, racist, apartheid regime when it was not party to the NPT. It became a signatory in 1991 and, with the transition to democratic rule, it fully disarmed in 1994 under the supervision of the IAEA. North Korea withdrew from the treaty in 2003 and exploded crude fission weapons in 2006 and 2009. Hence, the *de facto* nuclear club now stands at four—not a bad record for a technology that has been around for some sixty-five years. As for reversing the vertical proliferation of the nuclear weapons, the arsenals of nuclear weapon states have declined significantly—although these states still have a long way to go to reach the goal of total disarmament.

The nuclear nonproliferation regime, of course, faces many challenges. With 189 members, it is nearly universal; however, India, Pakistan, and Israel remain outside of the regime and North Korea's withdrawal threatens to destabilize the framework. Making the NPT universal is a necessary but elusive goal. Without universal membership, states may decide to seek weapons for deterrence. Also, states will be reluctant to begin the process of disarming if others retain their unverified arsenals. Another challenge is developing more robust inspection and verification protocols. The IAEA is very respectful of sovereignty and must rely on the cooperation of governments. Revelations of suspected illicit programs in Libya, Syria, and Iran as well as North Korea's program suggest that IAEA monitoring could be improved. A third challenge is promoting accountability and compliance. Non-NPT states face few consequences for remaining outside the regime. States that are party to the NPT, but are secretive, deceptive and uncooperative, know that sanctions, if any, will be difficult to implement. The IAEA has no enforcement capabilities and must rely on states and the UN for the political will to confront noncompliant states. Yet another challenge is the creation of a new *de facto* category of states under the NPT—states that are "**nuclear weapon capable.**" States like Japan, Germany, the Netherlands, and Brazil have the technical skill and materials to build a nuclear weapon. By taking the fuel for nuclear power plants and enriching it, it is relatively easy to make a weapon. "There are two main ways to turn civilian technology to military use. The first is to enrich uranium fuel from its usual level of 5 percent for reactors to the 90 percent needed for a bomb, a modest step that requires longer processing in centrifuges. The second is to take the spent reactor fuel and mine it for plutonium, the other main fuel for a bomb," (Broad and Sanger 2006). The challenge for the NPT regime is that non-nuclear weapon states can acquire the technology and know-how for peaceful purposes and the IAEA is there to help them safely use that technology. However, that technology and assistance also enhances the capability of states to also produce weapons, especially if states have substantial civilian nuclear energy programs. If Japan and Germany can be nuclear weapon capable, then why can't Egypt, Turkey, or Iran?

Nonproliferation and disarmament are important goals for the UN (Tannenwald 2004, 3–20). The UN plays a coordinating role in providing states with a forum for international negotiations. The NPT was negotiated and concluded under the auspices of the UN and the UN hosts the five-year review conference. The UN, along with the IAEA staff, provides the expertise in identifying and solving the complex problems related to implementing the treaty and strengthening its effectiveness. Perhaps more importantly, the UN Security Council can partner with the IAEA and apply pressure when there is sufficient political will. With Iraq, the UN Security Council created a very intrusive inspection regime. With North Korea and Iran, the Security Council authorized several rounds of sanctions. The danger posed by the spread of WMD in the wake of September 11, 2001 generated renewed interest in strengthening the nonproliferation regime; however, several events have rocked the NPT foundation. Not only did Pakistan test its first nuclear weapon in 1998 but it also revealed in 2004 that the father of the Pakistani bomb, Adul Qadeer Kahn, ran an elaborate proliferation ring that had been trading nuclear bomb materials and technology to Iran, Libya, and North Korea for decades (Hoagland 2004, A 23). North Korea, having withdrawn from the NPT in 2003, detonated a nuclear device in 2006, prompting a new round of international sanctions. In 2007, Israel conducted a military raid in the Syrian desert that destroyed what many experts believe to be a nuclear reactor provided by North Korea to Syria (Sanger and Mazzetti 2007). In 2009, North Korea tested another nuclear device and long- and intermediate-range ballistic missiles. Also, looming large is Iran and its suspected nuclear weapons program. In the following case study, the conflict surrounding Iran and its nuclear ambitions are analyzed in relationship to its rights and obligations under the NPT. The case study examines the behavior of the UN Security Council and the IAEA to show how international politics and international law affect the ongoing crisis.

CASE STUDY 2: IRAN[2]

In 1968, Iran signed the NPT and placed its ambitious nuclear program under the nonproliferation regime. Prior to 1968, Iran, under the leadership of the Shah, partnered with the United States under the Atoms for Peace program

---

[2]The chronology of events is drawn from *CBS News*, The BBC, Reuters, and the IAEA. See
http://www.cbsnews.com/elements/2007/02/22/in_depth_world/timeline2504696.shtml
http://www.iaea.org/NewsCenter/Focus/IaeaIran/iran_timeline.shtml#september02
http://news.bbc.co.uk/2/hi/middle_east/806268.stm
http://www.reuters.com/article/idUSTRE64I2O620100519.

and embarked on an extensive nuclear energy program. After 1968, Iran cooperated with the United States under the oversight of the IAEA to develop nuclear technology and facilities, but after the 1979 Islamic Revolution, its nuclear program was suspended because the ties between them were severed. In 1989, at the end of the Cold War, Iran restarted its program, this time working with Russia, China, and France for the peaceful utilization of nuclear technology. Although controversial in U.S. opinion circles, these cooperative initiatives were compliant with NPT and supervised by the IAEA. In 2002, Iran began construction on a nuclear reactor at the Bushehr power plant and confirmed uranium enrichment facilities at the Natanz plant and a heavy water facility in Arak. Iran did not originally notify the UN or the IAEA of these developments, but in 2003 Iran agreed to IAEA inspections. The developments were controversial because the techniques used to enrich uranium for use in power plants can also be used to make nuclear weapons. Later that year, IAEA head Mohamed El Baradei issued a report criticizing Iran for not being forthcoming regarding the extent of its nuclear activities when traces of weapons-grade uranium were found at the Natanz and Arak sites. Ministers from the EU called on Iran to become a party to an NPT protocol that gives IAEA inspectors the right to conduct more intrusive examinations of its facilities (Barringer 2003). Iran agreed to suspend its uranium enrichment activities and then signed the protocol. The IAEA later reports that no evidence was found to verify that Iran had actually suspended uranium enrichment; however, there was also no evidence that Iran was pursing nuclear weapons. The United States publicly disputed the latter finding.

In June 2004, IAEA criticized Iran for its lack of proactive and timely cooperation with inspectors and for preparing to launch a large-scale enrichment program. In September, the United States called on the UN Security Council for sanctions to pressure Iran to comply with IAEA inspection and verification requirements. Iran responded by announcing it was resuming large-scale uranium enrichment. In April 2005, Iran embarked on a uranium conversion project, which is a technological step that precedes enrichment. In May, the EU linked trade and other issues to an Iranian cessation of the conversion cycle. Iran responded by agreeing to suspend the conversion and enrichment until an agreement was worked out; however, in August, Mahmoud Amadinejad was elected president of Iran and he announced a resumption of the conversion process, which resulted in a suspension of talks by the EU. Amadinejad also addressed the UN General Assembly claiming that all states have an inalienable right to produce nuclear fuel, which by default, means they have a right to the materials and the "know-how" to enrich uranium.

Pivotal events occurred in 2006. In January, Iran broke IAEA seals at its facilities in Natanz, which resulted in the IAEA reporting Iran to the UN Security Council in February. In July, the UN Security Council threatened sanctions unless Iran suspended its nuclear program and in August the IAEA reported that Iran had continued with its enrichment and conversion activities. In December, the UN Security Council voted to impose sanctions on Iran for the first time. The sanctions were modest in that they only targeted trade in sensitive nuclear technology. Nevertheless, Iran retaliated by barring IAEA inspections in January 2007.

In February 2007, Russia suspended its cooperation with Iran in constructing a nuclear power plant and the IAEA reported that Iranian enrichment efforts had expanded rather than complying with the Security Council demand that it cease enrichment and conversion activities. Iran, undeterred, continued its nuclear research. In November, the IAEA reported that Iran continued to defy the Security Council. In December, U.S. intelligence officials concluded that Iran had ceased work on a nuclear weapon in 2003 although its enrichment activities would make Iran capable of developing a weapon sometime between 2010 and 2015. In February 2008, Iran successfully tested a ballistic missile as part of its space program, raising alarm about the potential dual purpose of delivering a warhead at long range. In March 2008, the UN Security Council tightened sanctions, banning trade in items that have both military and civilian purposes. At the same time the EU offered trade incentives if Iran would agree to suspend its enrichment activities. The EU set an informal August deadline for Iran to demonstrate its willingness to cooperate. In May, the IAEA reported that Iran was stonewalling and hiding its nuclear activities from inspectors. In July, Iran tested intermediate and long-range missiles, signaling that it was capable of retaliating if attacked. The informal August deadline passed and Iran tested a missile capable of launching a satellite into orbital space. In September, the Security Council passed a new resolution reaffirming its demands but imposed no new sanctions. In November 2008, Barack Obama was elected president of the United States and he offered Iran more dialog on its nuclear program.

In June 2009, after a controversial and disputed election, Ahmadinejad declared victory over the "green movement" and the Iranian government cracked down on the opposition. In September, Iran admitted to the IAEA that it had a secret nuclear facility near the holy city of Qom. This admission was seen as an attempt to blunt the impact of the U.S. revelation of the site. Iran then test fired several intermediate and long-range missiles. In October, the Security Council proposed that Iran send a significant portion of its low-enriched uranium abroad where it could be made into a special fuel that could then be used to make medical materials. Iran agreed and also allowed the IAEA to inspect the Qom facility. The IAEA also presented a draft plan to reduce Iran's stockpile of low-enriched uranium. In November, Iran rejected the plan and the IAEA passed a resolution condemning Iran for developing the Qom enrichment facility in secret. Iran responded by announcing plans to develop ten more nuclear facilities.

In January 2010, Iran formally rejected key components of the IAEA plan to send its uranium abroad, but then in February appeared to acquiesce, accepting the deal and then testing another missile capable of lifting a satellite into orbital space (and delivering a weapon). It also began enriching uranium at a higher 20 percent level at the Natanz facility. The IAEA issued a report suggesting that Iran was actively pursing nuclear weapons. In March, the United States, France, and

UK began negotiations with Russia and China about a new round of UN sanctions against Iran, but China and Russia expressed skepticism that sanctions would be effective. In April, the United States hosted a fifty-state summit on the threats posed by nuclear proliferation and terrorism. Prior to the start of the summit, the United States released its 2010 Nuclear Posture Review, where it pledged that it would not threaten or use nuclear weapons against states that are party and compliant with the NPT. The United States also renewed its commitment to disarmament and moved forward with Russia to reduce the size of their existing arsenals by a third. Iran responded by announcing the start of a new uranium enrichment plant. In May, the United States again pushed for a new round of sanctions in the Security Council and Brazil and Turkey, nonpermanent members, offered to mediate with Iran. As momentum grew among the five permanent members for a new round of tougher sanctions, Iran, Brazil, and Turkey announced a deal for Iran to suspend its uranium enrichment activities and to send its stockpile of low-enriched uranium to Turkey so that it could be processed into materials suitable for medical purposes. The permanent five (especially the United States, France, and the UK) expressed skepticism of this newest deal, and in June, the Security Council passed a resolution placing additional sanctions on the Iranian Revolutionary Guard and on banks and firms doing business with Iran in sensitive areas. Iran responded by suspending nuclear talks. How are we to understand the role of international law and international organization in the Iran nuclear crisis? Did the UN Security Council and the IAEA play a constructive role in mediating the dispute between Iran and the nuclear weapon states? What actors and processes are driving the crisis and what are the likely outcomes?

A Realist Cut

The Iran nuclear issue is a slowly developing crisis that reflects the ongoing struggle for power principally between the United States and Iran, but also involving key European states, Russia, China, and rising powers such as Brazil and Turkey. The NPT, the IAEA, and the Security Council are instruments used by these competing states to achieve their aims. "One must accept the stark reality that the [nonproliferation] regime is a reflection of the work of larger forces in the international system. The underlying successes and failures are functions of relations between the great powers, their strategic objectives, and their power equations"(Aboul-Enein 2010, 68). In this particular case, the United States wants to remain the dominant power in the Middle East and is using these legal and organizational mechanisms to counter the growing power of Iran. In 2002, George W. Bush included Iran in his "axis of evil" speech, targeting Iran as a growing threat to the United States. In 2003, after the initial military success of the invasion and occupation of Iraq, the United States appeared ascendant. With U.S. forces to the east in Afghanistan and the west in Iraq, Iran suspended its nuclear weapons program and acquiesced to IAEA inspections as an effort to forestall a possible U.S. attack. As the United States militarily bogged down in both Afghanistan and Iraq, Iran became more emboldened knowing that relations between the United States and the Security Council and IAEA had soured over the lead-up to the invasion of Iraq and the subsequent unraveling of the occupation.

Seizing on this opportunity, Iran's conservative government successfully exploited loopholes in the NPT and great-power competition (notably between the United States France, Russia, and China) to gain nuclear technology. Iran was also able to highlight the inequities and double standards of the NPT regime between nuclear weapon states and non-nuclear weapon states. Why was Iran singled out when the nuclear weapon states still maintain sizable arsenals and are upgrading those arsenals periodically? The NPT bargain was that non-nuclear weapon states would forgo weapons in exchange for nuclear technology for peaceful uses and for the weapon states to begin the process of disarmament with the goal of the eventual elimination of nuclear weapons. Iran has the right, as a sovereign state and as a signatory to the NPT, to acquire the materials and the "know-how" to master the nuclear fuel cycle. In a populist twist, Iran also argues that non-nuclear weapon states also have a right to maintain an independent fuel cycle (Afrasiabi and Kibaroglu 2005). This means that non-nuclear weapon states should not have to rely on others for uranium or its enrichment. This also means that even though many states may become "nuclear weapon capable," they still have a right to the technology. Finally, Iran was able to highlight that there were very few consequences for withdrawing and remaining outside of the NPT regime. India, Israel, and Pakistan maintain important military and economic ties with the *de jure* nuclear club and North Korea is diplomatically protected by China. Iran also knows that these states acquired the materials and technology from somewhere. The nuclear weapon states are obligated not to provide such technology under the NPT. In short, Iran has successfully shown the injustices of the NPT and has gained support for its position among non-nuclear weapon states, enhancing its soft power capabilities.

Many realists argue that the United States overplayed its hand in the Middle East, antagonizing Iran, in some mistaken, idealistic belief that it could transform Middle Eastern states into liberal democracies. The United States ought to recognize that it has similar interests with Iran in curbing the kind of Sunni extremism represented by Al-Qaeda and its affiliates. Iran and the United States do not have to like each other, but they share enough interests to cooperate in stabilizing the neighborhood. Instead, the United States placed Iran in an axis of evil, effectively targeting it for a future attack. If Iran wants to escape the fate of Iraq and Afghanistan, then it must develop an effective deterrent. For the United States, the balance of power in the Security Council has shifted away from the United States and its Western allies to Russia and China, who are willing to wield their veto to stop council actions that threaten their economic interests with Iran. After the Iraq intelligence fiasco where the existence of WMD was portrayed as a "slam dunk" by U.S. officials, other states are understandably skeptical of U.S claims of an illicit Iranian weapons program. Even though the IAEA provides an independent assessment of Iran's actions and capabilities, the IAEA has no enforcement capabilities and must rely on a cooperative Iran to conduct thorough inspections.

The NPT, the IAEA, and the Security Council are playing intervening roles in the conflict between the United States and Iran, with each state using the law and the organizations to further its own interests. For the United States, the NPT and the IAEA are low-cost ways to try to rein in Iran's nuclear ambitions, while at the same time building a public relations case that the United States had exhausted all diplomatic means should it decide to use military force. The probability that Security Council would authorize military action to prevent Iran from developing nuclear weapons is nearly zero. For most states, a nuclear-armed Iran is something they could live with and the cost of war with Iran, UN-authorized or not, is great. Iran could respond by militarily closing the straits of Hormuz, cutting off oil supplies from the Middle East. U.S. bases in Iraq and Afghanistan are vulnerable to Iranian missile strikes (Saikal 2006, 196–197). Iran could even retaliate by targeting Europe. Whether the United States (or Israel) resorts to military force will be determined by the costs and the benefits of a military strike, not its legality. Iran will likely continue to exploit the vagaries of the NPT and the operational protocols of the IAEA to obtain the technology and material necessary for developing nuclear weapons. If it becomes nuclear weapon capable, Iran will enhance its geostrategic position in the Middle East and retain the option of developing weapons in the future.

The NPT regime is unraveling because the interests and the bargaining power of states have changed. The regime has been under stress since the end of the Cold War and it will eventually collapse (Mearsheimer 1993; Sagan and Waltz 1995). With regards to Iran, the members of the nuclear club have put their immediate economic interests over nonproliferation and more non-nuclear weapon states are seeking to develop nuclear energy in the face of rising oil prices. The NPT must be adapted in a way to include states such as India, Pakistan, and Israel and to address noncompliance by current and former members (Iran, Syria, Myanmar [Burma], and North Korea). However, reaching an agreement to strengthen the NPT regime among so many diverse members is unlikely. If, or when, Iran develops nuclear weapons, the logic of deterrence theory holds that states must respond to new distribution of capabilities with their own deterrent capabilities and defensive systems (Brookes 2008). This action–reaction process will lead to a spread of nuclear weapons across the Middle East. For realists, if this alternative is not acceptable to states, then the great powers must act either alone or in concert to prevent it and to deter others for going down the same path as Iran. One strategy is that of "minilateralism" (Naim 2009, 136–135). This strategy involves bringing the smallest number of states together to solve problems. The fewer states at the table, the easier, it is to reach an agreement. Those states that have the most influence and power need to work together to dissuade Iran (or the United States) from its course of action. If that fails, war is a very distinct possibility considering the costs and the probability of success. Russia and the United States are best positioned to cooperate, at least in the short term, to stem future nuclear threats (Zarate 2009). Regardless of how one "games-out" the probable scenarios, the future of the NPT regime looks very bleak and war is a distinct possibility.

A Liberal Cut

Liberal institutionalists are similar to realists, except they point out that the norms embodied in the NPT and the actions of IAEA provide states with the framework and information necessary in order to make reasoned, rational choices. Most states share similar interests in preventing the proliferation of WMD and the regime can ease the structural pressure for states to acquire WMD. The IAEA can mitigate a state's concern that an adversary is developing nuclear weapons and the regime also imposes consequences (sanctions, diplomatic ostracism, etc.) on states that sign on to the NPT but then do not abide by their obligations and secretly pursue a weapons program. The combination of interests and norms show that international organizations and international law can help states overcome collective action problems and mitigate the systemic conditions that lead to arms races (Paul 2003). Although not perfect, the regime has lived long past its predicted demise because it has been useful for states to help stabilize and normalize their relations.

The nonproliferation regime also provides states with a dispute resolution mechanism that helps them work through conflict relating to a state's use of nuclear technology. "The system seeks to manage the competing desire of states to have access to peaceful nuclear technology and to provide national security" (Suleman 2008, 209). The regime institutionalizes norms and rules that guide and frame the actions of states. Liberal institutionalists argue that states comply with the NPT because the benefits of nuclear technology transfer and help with developing nuclear energy outweigh the benefits that might be obtained by acquiring nuclear weapons (Rost-Rublee 2009, 10–11). Cooperating states reap the benefits of increased foreign investment while offending states are isolated and struggle economically. Currently, the NPT suffers from indifference, but if states make the necessary investments, the regime again can check the nuclear weapon ambitions of states (Kitfield 2008, 28).

Even though some states have acquired or are actively seeking to acquire nuclear weapons, others have given them up. Ukraine and South Africa voluntarily gave up their nuclear weapons so they could become in good standing with the international community. In the 1990s, both states were transitioning to liberal democratic governments and part of that transition involved signing the NPT and disarming under the supervision of the IAEA. The fate of the weapons could have derailed the political reforms; however, by dismantling the arsenals both states were able to gain economic benefits and acceptance from the international community (Chafetz 1993). Libya publicly abandoned its WMD programs in 2004 and has since restored diplomatic relations with most states. The NPT regime provides stability and continuity to world affairs during uncertain and tumultuous times.

The Iranian case poses significant challenges to the nonproliferation regime because the interests of Iran are focused on sustaining the Islamic government and acquiring nuclear weapon capability rather than seeking to more fully integrate into the world economy and international community. Hence, Iran does not respond to the usual incentives. The nonproliferation regime must adapt to provide new rules and norms for changing times and situations. For example, one rule change is that states would no longer be permitted to develop their own means for enriching uranium (Broad and Sanger 2006). Rather, states needing enriched fuel for medical or energy purposes would have go to "fuel banks" where the transaction would be monitored and tracked by the IAEA. Export controls could be implemented through Nuclear Suppliers Group, an international organization of nuclear supplier countries that is committed to supporting nuclear nonproliferation and the IAEA. It would be more cost effective for states to simply import nuclear fuel (and submit to monitoring), rather going through the more costly processes of trying to master the fuel cycle. The nonproliferation regime, while imperfect, has controlled the spread of nuclear weapons while at the same time provided for the verifiable and transparent use of nuclear technology. The world is better off for it.

A Marxist Cut

The NPT regime is an example of how unequal treatment and double standards can be institutionalized and codified under international law. That law is then used by the strong to control the weak, inhibiting the progress of developing states. For Marxists, the NPT exists to ensure the dominant position of the great powers, allowing them to control access to nuclear technology and materials. It also creates a legal oligopoly of nuclear weapon states legitimizing their ability to destroy cities, countries, and civilizations. States that reject the existing world order or seek to alter it to include different values are targeted by the UN Security Council and the IAEA, which does the bidding of the nuclear powers. States such as Israel, India, and Pakistan escape serious political pressure or scrutiny. Non-NPT states that have acquired nuclear weapons are rewarded with extensive military and economic assistance, while states that have rejected capitalism and the liberal world order are isolated. It is not the threat of proliferation that is of concern, rather it is the spread of WMD to states that openly reject the status quo. Iran's interpretation of the NPT and its activities has a great deal of support among developing countries because of the organized hypocrisy of the nuclear weapon states.

The capitalist world economy promotes proliferation in a number of ways. First, the demand for nuclear energy goes up when the price of fossil fuels goes up. In order to obtain a sufficient amount of energy from nuclear power, states must have an extensive nuclear energy program that also gives them the potential to develop nuclear weapons. The extreme volatility of oil prices and the finite nature of oil supplies drive many states to pursue nuclear energy. Recent estimates suggest that more than forty states were **nuclear latent states** in that they have the industrial infrastructure, materials, and scientific expertise to produce nuclear weapons (Rost-Rublee 2008, 421). In other words, they are nuclear weapon capable. As the number of states that utilize nuclear energy grows, so will the number of states that can develop nuclear weapons. Only those that challenge the primacy of the nuclear weapon states will be singled-out for action. Iran is uniquely positioned as its actions can affect the price of oil, which affects the demand for nuclear energy for peaceful purposes.

Second, nuclear energy and nuclear weapons are also quite lucrative. In 2006, in contravention of forty years of nonproliferation policy, the United States and India signed a nuclear deal that will generate multibillion dollar contracts for U.S. firms seeking to sell nuclear reactors and other materials. The deal is also expected to generate additional business relating to additional military and economic cooperation. The deal effectively rewards India for remaining outside of the nonproliferation regime while firms in the nuclear industry profit. Nuclear nonproliferation and safeguards take a backseat to profits. Even in crisis situations, firms put the profits ahead of national interests (Jacobsen and Hofhansel 1984). This is one of the reasons many multinational firms continue to do business with Iran, even though their home countries are trying to reign in Iran's nuclear ambitions. In 2010, China announced a similar but significantly smaller deal with Pakistan, creating another precedent for ignoring the rules and rewarding a state with a track record of nuclear proliferation. Many companies and their home countries would be delighted to help Iran to develop its civil nuclear industry. The value of such nuclear deals does not take into the value of the nuclear black market where both state and nonstate actors may seek to acquire illicit nuclear materials. While accurate figure are difficult to come by, most estimates value it as a multibillion dollar enterprise. The profit motive once again trumps security.

On the disarmament side of the NPT equation, Marxists note that while some dismantling of arsenals has occurred, the nuclear weapons states continue to spend billions to upgrade those arsenals. Governments may insist that upgrades are necessary for insuring the credibility and reliability of their deterrence capabilities; however, domestic pressure from the military and the companies that produce and maintain nuclear weapons prompt governments to continue to spend enormous amounts on these destructive weapons. In 2010, President Obama negotiated an important arms reduction treaty with Russia, while at the same time announcing his intention to spend $80 billion over the next ten years to modernize the U.S. arsenal. Only a year before, a federal panel concluded that U.S. nuclear arms were sufficient to guarantee deterrence and that upgrades to the arsenal were not needed (Broad 2009). The money and jobs associated with the defense industry means that new generations of weapons will be created even when they are unnecessary and complicate U.S. nonproliferation efforts.

A Feminist Cut

The gender dimensions of the nuclear weapons highlight the superior–subordinate relationship between what is masculine and what is feminine. The drive to master the technology and acquire weapons of mass destruction represents a kind of status associated with being masculine. The "ideas and expectations about gender are woven through the professional and political discourses that shape all aspects of how weapons of mass destruction are considered, desired and addressed" (Cohn 2006, 1). The relationship between "maleness" and weapons is intertwined and the acquisition of the ultimate weapon—the nuclear warhead coupled with the most sophisticated means of delivery, ballistic and cruise missiles—represents the highest form of power and status. States that do not possess them suffer from "missile envy" (Caldicott 1984).

The narrow utility of WMD for war fighting suggests that possessing them has considerable symbolic value. Chemical and biological weapons have status as the "poor man's nuclear weapon." Acquiring nuclear weapons means attaining an elite status. Nuclear weapon states are politically the most masculine of states. Because of these weapons, these states are the most powerful and international relations revolve around their interests and needs. They retain large arsenals because of the "logic" of strategic deterrence. Their capability is also source of national pride. In 1998, India conducted three nuclear tests, much to the dismay of the international community. Tushar Gandhi, the great-grandson of Mohandas Gandhi, was "proud it was done in India and by Indians" and a leading Hindu politician, Balasaheb Thackeray, was thrilled, claiming "we have to prove that we are not eunuchs" (Burns 1998). The tests were important because they demonstrated that India was now an equal with the other nuclear powers. Similarly, Iran's quest for nuclear technology and perhaps weapons is Iran's way of asserting its autonomy and independence in the face of more powerful states, namely, the United States: "Seen as a sexualized point of view, the possession of weapons of mass destruction may be seen as the 'great equalizer' or 'great compensator,' a way of getting back at the global, omnipotent, 'alpha male' . . ." (Myrttinen 2003, 41). In other words, Iran is asserting its masculinity and demonstrating its unwillingness to be subordinate to the nuclear powers. Mastering the nuclear fuel cycle (and the having the ability to assemble nuclear weapons) is a source of national pride for Iran, regardless of who is president of the country. The Iranian nuclear program has broad support among men, women, and the many different factions of Iran's very pluralistic society because it represents national progress, sophistication, and strength.

The nuclear weapon states take great pride in their military capabilities and their ability to obliterate the enemy. Disarmament is a lofty, idealistic goal but in a masculine political environment both domestically and internationally, disarmament also means emasculation. International efforts to make the NPT truly universal must overcome to close association of nuclear weapons with masculinity if it hopes to bring the likes of India, Pakistan, Israel, and North Korea under the NPT framework. Dismantling nuclear weapons must be separated from the "manhood" of these states. The same holds for the nuclear weapon states.

Similarly, the nonproliferation regime rests on the international law represented by the NPT and the multilateral diplomacy centered around the IAEA and the Security Council. Unfortunately, for the United States, "consulting, negotiating, acknowledging interdependence and—worst of all—depending on others are activities that are culturally marked down as weak and lacking in masculinity" (Cohn 2006, 6). Similarly, IAEA inspections are trivialized as being too polite or ineffective or not aggressive enough. International law and organizations can compliment to work of states, but at the end of the day, many observers believe that it is military muscle of states and the willingness of states to use it that determines whether proliferation occurs or not. The consequences of war, especially if they involve the use of WMD, are considered in terms of disrupting the oil supply or the threat to troops in the field and other military assets, and not the civilian casualties or the environmental aftermath.

A Constructivist Cut

States, or their representatives, define their national interests and identity based on events, values, or perceptions. The nuclear nonproliferation regime is a story of changing interests and identities and the NPT and the IAEA have both reflected and affected that change. Alexander Wendt (1999) points out that the mere existence of nuclear weapons does not create a threatening environment, rather it is how certain actors view each other, or in constructivist jargon, the inter-subjective meaning of their relationship. The United States does not view the extensive arsenals of Israel or Great Britain as a threat, yet North Korea's possession of a few weapons and the potential of Iran's nuclear weapon capability constitute a gathering danger to U.S. security. The history and the values of the states cause them to define and interpret specific situations in relation to "the other." The interaction of actors over time can change their perceptions, attitudes, and interests. Japan and Germany were once mortal threats to the United States. Today, their mastery of nuclear technology does not threaten the United States. The IAEA, the NPT, and the UN have helped develop shared identities, values, and interests.

Specifically, the NPT has formalized the tradition of the nonuse of nuclear weapons (Paul 2009). Since Hiroshima and Nagasaki, nuclear weapons have not been used, even in situations where it would have been expedient and saved the lives of soldiers. The norm of the nonuse of nuclear weapons defines the limits of acceptable behavior and constrains the actions of states (Tannewald 2008). Arguably, the nonuse of nuclear weapons could be the result of low utility of such weapons for war fighting or because of the logic of deterrence; however, it is hard to imagine a modern scenario in which the use of nuclear weapons would be justified or legitimate. International law and organizations have institutionalized this norm and reinforced it through the nonproliferation regime.

NGOs also play a role in creating and diffusing nonproliferation norms. One NGO, in particular, has been active in this regard—The Nobel Foundation. It awards the Nobel Prizes for a variety of endeavors, including physics, chemistry, and peace. The Nobel Prizes were a bequeath from Albert Nobel to acknowledge human accomplishments and progress. In 2005, the IAEA and its leader Mohammad El Baradei were awarded the Nobel Peace Prize for "for their efforts to prevent nuclear energy from being used for military purposes and to ensure that nuclear energy for peaceful purposes is used in the safest possible way." By highlighting and publicly rewarding the work of the IAEA, nuclear nonproliferation was placed at the center of world politics. In 2009, the Nobel Prize for Peace was awarded to President Barack Obama in part because of his vision for a world free of nuclear weapons. The award represents an example one of the ways in which nonstate actors seek to influence world politics and key decision makers. Barack Obama had not even assumed the presidency when the award was announced and during his acceptance speech, he acknowledged the honor and the pressure the award created. NGOs influence the norms and the development of international law in both direct and indirect ways.

CONCLUSION

In this chapter, we have briefly outlined the UN's role in maintaining international peace and security, whether defined as state security or human security, by tracing the activities of the UN Security Council and highlighting the functions of the UN General Assembly and UN Secretary-General. We have seen that the UN and its organs do not exist in a vacuum; rather, they are influenced by a variety of actors, forces, and international dynamics. The security issue of nuclear proliferation is also explored in terms of the NPT and the role of the IAEA. The case studies of Iraq and Iran illustrate what the different theoretical approaches have to say about which actors and forces determine or explain the behavior of international organizations and what the consequences are to individuals, groups, and societies. Each theoretical lens enhances our understanding of international law and organizations and also the nature of global governance.

KEY TERMS

international
  security 111
security of states 111
human security 111
the Nuclear
  Nonproliferation
  Treaty (NPT) 112
the International Atomic
  Energy Agency
  (IAEA) 112
Article 2(4) of the UN
  Charter 112
the Security
  Council 113

absolute veto 113
collective security 114
consensus 115
commitment 115
organization 115
aggression 115
the General
  Assembly 116
Uniting for Peace
  resolution 116
the Secretary-
  General 117
peacekeeping 118

peace enforcement 119
peacebuilding 119
responsibility to protect
  (R2P) 138
Atoms for Peace 141
horizontal
  proliferation 141
vertical
  proliferation 141
nuclear weapon
  capable 143
nuclear latent
  states 151

SUGGESTED READINGS

Aoi, Chiyuki, Cedric de Coning, and Ramesh Shakur. 2007. *The Unintended Consequences of Peacekeeping Operations.* Tokyo: United Nations University Press.

Asmus, Ronald D. 2002. *Opening NATO's Door: How the Alliance Remade Itself for a New Era.* New York: Columbia University Press.

Bellamy, Alex, Paul Williams, and Stuart Griffin. 2004. *Understanding Peacekeeping.* Cambridge, UK: Polity Press.

Mieville, China. 2006. *Between Equal Rights: A Marxist Theory of International Law.* London: Haymarket Books.

Rupp, Richard E. 2006. *NATO after 9–11: An Alliance in Continuing Decline.* New York: Palgrave.

Weiss, Thomas. 2007. *Humanitarian Intervention: Ideas in Action.* Cambridge: Polity Press.

Trade

Oone of the oldest and most controversial features of international relations is trade—the seemingly simple act of exchanging goods and services between societies. On the one hand, international trade yields mutual benefits: It increases the diversity and quality of consumer goods and services, facilitates the diffusion of technology, provides jobs, and promotes efficiency. On the other hand, trade can also destroy national industries, displace workers, and threaten national culture and identity. Thus, international trade has been, and continues to be, a force that produces both cooperation and conflict between societies.

The controversies generated by trade make it one of the leading issues in contemporary international affairs. In this chapter, we look at some of those controversies, while reviewing the historical development of trade and the current rules governing international trading policies and practices. We examine the World Trade Organization (WTO) in terms of its organization and its role in handling contemporary trade issues. Then we investigate the landmark WTO case of the U.S. Clean Air Act in order to understand the influence of the WTO on increasingly interdependent societies. In the second case study, we explore how other international organizations, namely, multinational corporations (MNCs) and nongovernmental organizations (NGOs), approach the controversial issue of trade in genetically modified (GM) foods and organisms. The case studies illustrate how economic issues are also political issues and are better understood in the context of the political framework that gives them meaning and significance.

THE HISTORY OF INTERNATIONAL TRADE

Trade and trade issues predate the modern nation-state. The ancient and medieval worlds knew trade issues. Thucydides stressed the strategic importance of trading routes between the city-states of Sparta and Athens and the kingdom of Macedonia. Aristotle struggled with the contradictory effects of trade on ancient Greek society. The Roman Empire depended for its lifeblood on trade throughout the ancient world, from Britannia to conquered Greece and Egypt. And the Roman Catholic Church engaged in transnational exchanges around the world, dealing with a variety of cultures. The Crusades, for example, quickened the flow of goods from East to West and back.

The history of significant trade between nation-states began in the sixteenth century during what is called the mercantilist period. The monarchs of the emerging Western European states used trade as a tool for enhancing national wealth and power. States sought to achieve a "favorable" balance of trade whereby their trade surpluses (exports greater than imports) translated into growing national treasuries. The basic purpose of trade was to accumulate wealth. States engaged in "predatory" practices, seeking to establish monopolies in foreign markets and establishing colonies that could serve both as captive markets and as reservoirs of cheap resources and labor. States could enrich themselves by controlling their trading industries and stockpiling gold.

In the latter part of the eighteenth century and the early nineteenth century, the influential writings of Adam Smith (1723–1790) and David Ricardo (1772–1823) became popular among the emerging class of merchants and entrepreneurs. Smith argued for the government to take a laissez-faire approach to the economy, including international trade. Ricardo, through his theory of comparative advantage, argued that mercantilist trading practices actually hurt states because they promoted inefficient industries. International market forces, not monarchs or parliaments, should determine what industries a state should specialize in. A trade surplus cannot be maintained because it causes inflation at home, making domestically produced goods less attractive in foreign markets.

These liberal economic thinkers formed the ideological foundation for British hegemony and for the rules of nineteenth-century trade. Trade was characterized by multilateralism, low tariffs, and the limited use of quotas. After 1846, international trade expanded considerably with the repeal of the British Corn Laws, a unilateral reduction of agricultural tariffs. This action was reciprocated internationally, so that trade in both natural resources and manufactured products grew. Technological innovations and the industrial revolution increased the volume and the diversity of traded goods. That trade was not always voluntary, however. European states possessed colonies in Africa, India, Southeast Asia, and Latin America; and they had coerced trade agreements with other societies like China and Japan. While international trade brought wealth to many in Europe and the United States, it also brought violence and domination to others.

The expansion of trade continued until it was disrupted by World War I in 1914. World War I spurred aggressive economic competitiveness among nations that were not fighting each other. Governments, influenced by the ideas of Alexander Hamilton and Friedrich List, adopted nationalist policies to protect and expand the industrial sectors of their economies. Later, the Great Depression caused states to be even more protectionist as governments scrambled to shield their domestic industry from predatory trade. In 1930, for example, the United States enacted the Smoot–Hawley Act, which levied tariffs of more than 50 percent on imports, in response to the protectionist measures of other trading states. U.S. trading partners responded in kind, and international trade came to a virtual standstill. Then, after German and Japanese aggression brought about World War II, international trade remained distorted and limited.

In hindsight, U.S. officials, most of whom had a liberal worldview, argued that economic nationalism and the predatory "beggar thy neighbor" policies of the early twentieth century precipitated both world wars and the intervening depression. In other words, politics and the immediate needs of states had triumphed over economics and private individual initiatives. They also recognized that Roosevelt's New Deal programs had generated positive effects on the domestic economy and raised citizens' expectations. Thus, after World War II, the challenge for U.S. leadership in the international economy was a big one—how to establish a liberal international economic order in a world of nations ravaged by war and hampered by underdevelopment.

The United States met the postwar challenge by establishing the **Bretton Woods System**, named after the New Hampshire town where much of the postwar planning took place. The architects of the **Bretton Woods System**, most notably British economist **John Maynard Keynes** (1883–1946), sought to strike a balance between the interests of states and the need for international economic stability. Characterized as **the compromise of embedded liberalism**, the Bretton Woods System required governments to commit to liberal economic principles, with the recognition that states have legitimate economic interests, including full employment, low inflation, and steady economic growth (Ruggie 1982). To that end, states retain the right to regulate the domestic economy but must agree to participate in various forms of multilateral policy negotiation and coordination at the global level.

The Bretton Woods System was based on three pillars: economic development, monetary stability, and trade. The first two pillars were anchored by the World Bank and the International Monetary Fund (IMF), respectively (discussed in Chapter 7). The third pillar of Bretton Woods, trade, began with a series of negotiations that resulted in **the General Agreement on Tariffs and Trade (GATT)**. In 1946, the Economic and Social Council (ECOSOC) of the UN convened a conference to consider the nature of the postwar trading order. The GATT was designed to be an interim measure until the proposed **International Trade Organization (ITO)** got off the ground. However, the ITO Charter, which was hammered out during the 1948 UN Conference on Trade and Employment in Havana, was not ratified by the U.S. Senate. The requisite two-thirds majority could not be achieved, as both the left and the right criticized the lack of protection for U.S. workers and national industries. Many in the Senate also expressed concern about U.S. sovereignty because the United States did not have a veto over ITO decisions. The ITO treaty was withdrawn by Truman in 1950; thus the GATT became, by default, the post–World War II institutional framework for international trade.

The principal goal of GATT was to jump-start international trade through tariff reduction, a process guided by the principles of **reciprocity, nondiscrimination, and multilateralism.** These goals were accomplished through a series of "rounds" in which trade negotiators would seek a reduction in tariffs for one country, then apply it to others. The central tool in this process is the **most-favored-nation status (MFN)**. MFN means that member states must treat all fellow member states the same. If a state grants a trade concession to one member, it must provide that same concession to all members. The United States and other member states have used MFN under GATT to liberalize trade and also to encourage good behavior internationally.

GATT was an institution designed for market economies, so most communist countries took no part in GATT negotiations. The market economies succeeded in reducing tariffs on industrial and manufactured goods through a series of negotiations—notably, the Kennedy Round (1962–1967), the Tokyo Round (1973–1979), and the Uruguay Round (1986–1993). The latter GATT rounds involved talks on previously taboo areas. These areas included trade in agricultural products and trade in services such as banking and telecommunications.

In addition, new forms of trade protectionism, known as **nontariff barriers (NTBs),** had to be addressed. NTBs are more difficult to identify and harder to negotiate because they include such traditional state policy tools as taxes, subsidies, and regulation. Governments legislate and regulate for the "public good," and their actions can inhibit the free flow of goods—and now services—across national borders. By exercising traditional policy tools, states have created new, more sophisticated forms of protectionism.

NTBs can include **subsidies**, which may be direct or indirect. Governments can, for example, simply write checks, making payments directly to firms. Or they can hand out tax breaks or provide needed services, thus subsidizing firms indirectly. Whether direct or indirect, such subsidies afford firms protection from international competition. With governmental assistance, they do not have to compete on the same level as foreign firms. Consider Boeing, Inc. Boeing receives billions of dollars a year in defense contracts for its products—aircraft ranging from high-performance fighter jets to huge transport and freight planes. These defense contracts permit Boeing to develop aeronautical innovations paid for by taxpayer dollars, innovations that also have commercial applications for civilian aircraft. Thus, Boeing has a considerable advantage over foreign producers seeking to compete in the civilian aircraft market. Can we say, then, that defense contracts constitute a NTB to trade?

Another kind of NTB is the **voluntary export restriction (VER)**. VERs are bilaterally negotiated agreements whereby exporters agree to limit the number of goods they send to the other country. In the 1980s, for example, the Reagan administration pursued VERs with Japan to reduce the number of Japanese autos exported to the United States. Japanese officials have claimed that such restrictions were far from "voluntary" and that they were in fact but mirror images of the quotas that had been all but eliminated under the GATT. Japan agreed to the VERs, not on its own initiative but because U.S. officials threatened to limit Japanese access to U.S. markets.

Governmental regulation can also serve as NTBs. Governments can mandate that products meet certain safety and environmental standards, which can exclude foreign competition. Some states even have an industrial policy that utilizes governmental regulation and subsidies to give preferential treatment to certain industries, which helps them compete abroad. These firms do not have to worry about going out of business because they are part of a nation's long-term industrial plan. They can "dump" products, selling them below cost, and corner international markets. NTBs have been the source of considerable difficulty under GATT, in part because of its ad hoc procedures. Decided on a case-by-case basis, the process of determining whether a specific government action is an impermissible NTB or a legitimate state policy is highly politicized.

Latter-day rounds of GATT have demonstrated that contemporary trade negotiations have entered into a new phase of contentiousness. Traditionally, agricultural products and agricultural industries have been matters of national security: A state unable to feed itself is vulnerable to an enemy embargo. Moreover, in many countries, the family farm is a repository of cultural heritage and a symbol of national identity. And, in some states, like France and Japan, agricultural interests exert enormous domestic political pressure and are disproportionately represented in legislatures. For these reasons, agricultural industries have been protected through tariffs and are heavily subsidized.

Trade in financial, commercial, and technological services is also politically contentious. In many countries, important financial and commercial institutions such as banks, insurance companies, and utilities are either owned or extensively regulated by the state. Arguably, these services are so critical to the economic health and the physical well-being of societies that they cannot be trusted to foreign-owned providers. Disagreements regarding the liberalization of such services have paralyzed negotiations—so much so that it has been difficult even to place the issue on the agenda.

According to free-trade advocates, the protection of agricultural industries and services has made them inefficient and uncompetitive. In their view, many farms in the United States were so heavily subsidized that they ceased to be businesses and became welfare recipients. Accordingly, agricultural subsidies were cut extensively in the United States, and to a lesser degree in Europe, in the 1980s. The reduction of subsidies led to the demise of many family farms, and agricultural industries were compelled to reorganize after being exposed to market forces. This reorganization had extensive social and political consequences. Farmers staged protests across Europe, and EU subsidy reform slowed to a crawl. In the United States, music groups held concerts to raise money for Farm Aid, a nonprofit organization created to help struggling and displaced farmers. In spite of domestic support for small farmers in the United States, protective measures were reduced and many went out of business. Their place was taken by large corporate farms—agribusinesses that could efficiently produce large volume for domestic consumption and overseas markets.

THE WORLD TRADE ORGANIZATION (WTO)

The difficulties in liberalizing the agricultural and service sectors, together with the increasing use of NTBs, prompted GATT members to form the WTO. The GATT was considered to be inadequate for several reasons. First, the GATT was fundamentally a provisional international agreement. When it became clear that the ITO would never get off the ground, negotiators were forced to develop ad hoc procedures for settling disputes. This made the dispute process chaotic, complicated, and inconsistent. Second, the GATT's jurisdiction was quite limited. Technically, only tariffs and quotas on manufactured and industrial goods fell under the purview of GATT. However, with the globalization of production, the need for further liberalization and the removal of NTBs increased in urgency. Third, GATT as an organization had questionable legal status; it needed to become both more impartial and more authoritative to tackle the volatile issues of contemporary trade. Often deprecated as the "General Agreement of Talk and Talk," the GATT had no mechanisms for authoritatively and systematically resolving disputes. Thus, as the last order of business during the Uruguay Round, GATT members voted the WTO into existence.

On January 1, 1995, the WTO officially became operational. Headquartered in Geneva, Switzerland, the WTO consists of 153 members. It incorporates previous GATT agreements, but its mandate has been expanded to include agriculture, services, and intellectual property rights. The WTO also has the authority to review state policies affecting trade and to authorize sanctions against errant states. Funding for the WTO is based on each member's share of the total trade among WTO members.

The WTO has had some success. In the first year of its existence, the WTO was able to get its members to commit to liberalization talks on financial and telecommunications services. In 1997, sixty-eight states agreed to "wide-ranging liberalization measures" for basic telecommunications, while seventy states agreed to open their financial services sectors, thereby accounting for "95 percent of trade in banking, insurance, securities and financial information" (WTO 1999).

The WTO has also been exercising its authority to settle trade disputes, particularly as they relate to NTBs. This aspect was particularly controversial because the WTO is permitted to review the regulations and the tax codes of members to determine if their intent or overall effect is trade protection. This is troublesome for states, accustomed to the final say in policy within their own territories. The WTO attempts to balance state interests and the interest of free trade (represented by economists and trade experts) such that both can be represented and neither always assumes dominance over the other.

The WTO touts itself as a member-driven, consensus-based IGO.[1] That is, the WTO tries to reach decisions through consensus. When consensus is not possible, its voting procedures demand either a two-thirds or three-fourths majority rule, each state having one vote. The WTO is organized around four levels. At the top is **the Ministerial Conference,** which is attended by all member states. The Ministerial Conference must meet at least once every two years and is responsible for the long-term strategic planning of the organization. While the WTO encourages consensus, four situations are likely to trigger a vote of WTO members. First, a vote may be required for interpretation of existing multilateral trade agreements. Second, a vote may be necessary to waive an obligation assumed under trading agreements. Third, amendments to existing multilateral agreements require ministerial approval. Finally, the admission of new members to the organization must be approved by WTO members. Since its inception, no WTO decision or ruling has required a vote of the Ministerial Conference.

The day-to-day operations of the WTO are handled by the remaining tiers. Below the Ministerial Conference is **the General Council.** The General Council consists of overlapping bodies, including the **Dispute Settlement Body** and the **Trade Policy Review Body.** These very important organs oversee dispute settlement procedures and scrutinize members' trading practices. The third level of organizations consists of councils that oversee broad areas of trade. These include **the Goods Council, the Services Council,** and **the Trade-Related Aspects of Intellectual Property (TRIPS) Council.** The fourth level breaks down these areas even further into specific aspects, such as "access" or "technical barriers." All the members of the WTO belong to these organs; however, much of the work is done by the committees.

The WTO is supported by a small bureaucracy (500 people) called the Secretariat. The Secretariat leadership consists of the Secretary Director General, currently Pascal Lamy, and four Deputy Directors-General. The Secretariat is staffed by trade experts and economists who review the trade policy of members and provide the General Council with expertise, training, and technical support. The Secretariat, which provides the "expert panels" that adjudicate unresolved disputes, is part and parcel of the appeal process. The function of the Secretariat is to denationalize multilateral trade negotiations by providing neutral analyses. Its neutral competence is designed to take the politics out of trade.

---

[1]The description of the organization and decision-making procedures of the WTO is taken from its Web site www.wto.org.

Depoliticizing and denationalizing trade is a formidable task. Politics is about determining who gets what, when, how, and why. Trade involves the global distribution of resources and wealth, and governments are reluctant to allow markets or international organizations to divide "the global pie." States practice protectionism for many, interrelated reasons—reasons that may have little to do with efficiency or comparative advantage. They may, for instance, seek to protect certain industries or restrict trade in certain technologies for reasons of national security. Industries involved in producing military hardware or sophisticated war-fighting technologies are critical to a state's security.

States may also protect industries that hold the most promise for future economic growth and prosperity. In the 1980s, the United States extended trade protection to American computer chip manufacturers. Comparative advantage may have dictated the production of another product, say, potato chips; but U.S. firms were going to produce computer chips, whether or not it was efficient to do so. Computer chips were the industry of the future, and American firms were going to be part of that infant industry, regardless of its initial profitability.

Governments may also practice protectionism to give mature industries time to adjust to new competitors or evolving market realities. The Reagan administration made extensive use of VERs to limit the number of Japanese auto exports to the United States. Japanese automakers had garnered a significant share of the U.S. market, contributing to layoffs and unrest in the ranks of American labor, not to mention cries of "foul" among American managers and shareholders. This normally free-trade administration provided the mature U.S. automobile industry with the time to restructure and retool in order to become competitive domestically and internationally.

Democratic societies are likely to protect industries because the nature of their politics demands it. In pluralistic societies (such as the United States and Canada), interest-group pressure can establish protection for certain sectors and industries in an ad hoc fashion. But European states and Japan, each to varying degrees, tend to formulate some kind of industrial policy, which is a concerted plan to develop the economy and manage international trade. Industrial policy tends to favor certain groups over others in terms of subsidies and tax breaks. Critics of industrial policy claim that it promotes cronyism and the "good old boy" network. Defenders counter that pluralism, as it is practiced in the United States and Canada, amounts to much the same thing, except that it is protection to the highest bidder. Either way, the end effect is government protection of industries, which inhibits free trade. The tension between liberalization and protectionism permeates most trade issues.

MULTINATIONAL CORPORATIONS (MNCs)

MNCs are a potent force behind free trade. The reduction of tariffs, quotas, and NTBs is important to MNCs because it lowers the costs of production and allows them to distribute their goods and services globally. Multinational financial and telecommunications firms are very interested in the liberalization of services because they are poised to enter markets that were previously closed to them. Intellectual property rights, which range from movies, music, computer hardware, and computer software, to pharmaceuticals and genetics, are also important because MNCs have invested significant resources in their research and development. MNCs are concerned about the pirating of their products by competitors. If a technology or a technique or a product can be easily copied, MNCs stand to lose billions in profits. Without state enforcement of their intellectual property rights, MNCs are reluctant to make the initial investments in research and development.

MNCs have changed considerably since they first became an integral part of the trading scene. Early MNCs were largely European- or American-owned firms that were involved in extracting raw materials, including oil and ores. They were headquartered in advanced industrialized countries, and their subsidiaries were located in colonies and former colonies. The subsidiaries exported raw materials to the West, where they were turned into a variety of manufactured goods by both national and multinational firms. The manufactured goods were then exported to the developing world for sale. Developing states experienced chronically bad terms of trade because exports of relatively cheap raw materials could not balance out the far more expensive manufactured imports.

MNCs changed their foreign direct investment (FDI) strategy when they ventured into manufacturing outside their home countries. They were engaged in horizontal investment whereby they manufactured the same goods everywhere. This allowed them to bypass protectionism in host countries (Gilpin 1987, 254). Host countries gained the advantage of goods produced within their territory; however, their domestic industries were displaced and their infant industries were unable to compete with the more seasoned MNCs. Home countries, too, suffered disadvantages; manufacturing jobs were lost and industries waned as MNCs adjusted and expanded into new markets.

During the 1980s, MNCs shifted to a vertical investment strategy, in which outputs of some factories serve as inputs for others (Gilpin 1987, 255). The production process is broken down into its component parts and distributed around the world. The purchase of a manufactured product is now a global transaction, from concept to design and manufacture, and then to the showroom floor (or Internet site). For example, a multinational automobile company producing a car for U.S. markets might have the automobile designed in Germany, the electronics assembled in Korea, the brakes made in Mexico, and the tires made in Ohio. The product is then assembled in stages at different plants before it is turned out to market. Profits from the sale of that automobile are distributed to shareholders from around the world. In short, MNCs have developed global economies of scale and have become truly multinational in nature. While MNCs are still mainly headquartered in the West, they have shareholders globally. Their primary allegiance is to their shareholders, and not necessarily to the countries in which they are located.

Free trade, the WTO, and MNCs have many opponents. Free trade is not always seen as a universal good. It creates winners and losers, and the benefits of trade are often distributed in a grossly unequal manner. Entire groups within and between societies can be marginalized. The WTO may magnify and intensify the differences between winners and losers, with the winners coming out on top not by virtue of extraordinary market savvy or some revolutionary innovation, but because they are powerful enough to create the rules that inevitably favor their interests. Some opponents predict that the WTO and MNCs will dismantle the capitalist welfare state because it is too interventionist. Free traders want governments to protect their interests, regardless of what the people in democratic societies may want, all for the sake of efficiency and corporate profits.

The arguments of both the opponents and the proponents of the WTO and free trade are shaped by their worldviews, and each emphasizes different aspects of trade. In the following case study of the WTO and the U.S. Clean Air Act, we look at the first major case before the WTO to illustrate how the different perspectives interpret the roles and effectiveness of international organizations in addressing the conflicts associated with international trade.

CASE STUDY 3: THE U.S. CLEAN AIR ACT

In 1996, the first grievance was filed with the newly created WTO. This grievance, lodged by Brazil and Venezuela against the United States, claimed that certain provisions of the 1990 U.S. Clean Air Act discriminated against their gasoline exports to the United States. Under Environmental Protection Agency (EPA) regulations, gasoline companies must produce the same quality of gasoline that they produced in 1990 (Crow 1996, 37). The EPA pegged the amount of pollutants released into the atmosphere to 1990 levels in an effort to stabilize that amount. Accordingly, each company was assigned a different baseline level because each produced different kinds and quality of gasoline during the baseline year. Determining the 1990 baseline quality of domestic producers was relatively easy and readily verifiable; however, determining the baselines of gasoline imported from foreign sources was not. As a result, the EPA assigned foreign producers a special baseline—one that was the "average" of all the domestic producers in 1990.

In their complaint, Brazil and Venezuela argued that the EPA regulation discriminated against their exports and was an impermissible NTB to trade. They claimed that the environmental standards set for their companies were unfairly high and that their firms should receive the same treatment as U.S. domestic producers. In other words, the Brazilian and Venezuelan firms ought to have an individual, not an average, 1990 baseline. In response, the United States argued that its domestic producers would face unfair competition. The foreign imports would be cheaper because the imports were of a lesser quality, falling far below the U.S. average (Crow 1996, 21). The WTO convened a panel of experts to review the grievance and ruled, in January 1996, that the

EPA regulations did in fact discriminate against imported gasoline. The United States appealed the decision, but the ruling was upheld by the WTO appellate body in April 1996.

The Clean Air Act case was an important test of the WTO as a governance institution. The grievance filed by Brazil and Venezuela marked the first time WTO procedures were used to authoritatively resolve disputes, and it involved its most powerful member, the United States. As James Baccus, a U.S. representative to the WTO appellate body, said, "Without the U.S., the WTO would weaken and wither away. It would become a commercial 'League of Nations' incapable of enforcing the rules of trade. The emerging rule of law in world trade would be replaced by a ruinous reign of commercial chaos, confusion and collapse" (cited in Crow 1996, 37). The WTO told the strongest country in the world that one of its environmental regulations was an impermissible barrier to international trade and the United States abided by the WTO ruling. The EPA revised its rules to permit foreign producers to petition the EPA for individual baselines for gasoline exported to the United States.

What lessons are to be learned from this case? What issues and actors are important for understanding international trade? Did the WTO and the countries involved make the right decisions? How do their decisions affect individuals and groups within and between societies?

A Realist Cut

Traditional realists and economic nationalists see the WTO ruling as an unacceptable erosion of state sovereignty. They fear that the WTO will undermine governments, compromising their ability to regulate the domestic economy. The capacity of WTO officials to review government policies and declare them "impermissible" effectively means that the WTO has the final say regarding policy and regulation. Criticisms of the WTO as a threat to sovereign prerogatives also make good press for conservative politicians, but may not translate into any measurable loss of sovereignty. As Clayton Yeutter, the trade representative during the Reagan administration, said, "The sovereignty argument is pointless, for every trade agreement we've signed in the past 200 years has in some way infringed on our sovereignty" (cited in Crow 1996, 37).

Neorealists see in the WTO a useful tool, one the United States can use to achieve its immediate and long-term trading goals. Recall that neorealists and neomercantilists are all for free trade and markets when it suits national interests. Participation in markets is seen as the path to great-power status. Free trade or markets, however, should not prevail if the national security is threatened. An EPA regulation implementing the Clean Air Act is hardly a pressing national security interest of the United States. In fact, the EPA regulation itself compromised U.S. energy security because it limited the number of suppliers of petroleum products (Crow 1996, 21). While crude oil supplies are important for national security, so are reformulated gasoline sources. Increasing the number of suppliers, both domestic and foreign, has always been the goal of the United States. U.S. domestic firms were not seriously threatened by foreign competition, so no governmental protection was necessary (Buckley 1996, 70).

In deciding to abide by the WTO ruling, the United States made a shrewd political move. The WTO nullifies a law that sets environmental standards too high for domestic and foreign producers of gasoline alike. Meantime, the United States publicly sacrifices its sovereignty for the "collective good," thereby setting the precedent for WTO authority internationally. The United States gains additional suppliers of reformulated gasoline while simultaneously strengthening the organization it has long wanted to create. A robust WTO is necessary to root out and eliminate trade discrimination, the vast majority of which is against U.S. products and services (Buckley 1996, 70). Thus, the United States sacrifices little and gains a lot. National governments want organizations like the WTO to support their policies, share the blame for unpopular measures, and increase their access to markets and resources (Bayne 1997). The WTO decision in the Clean Air Act case fits the bill. Since this case, the WTO has often ruled in favor of the United States against some of its more intractable trading partners. For example, the United States received a favorable ruling against the EU in an important computer networking case (Sanger 1998, C1). The WTO will also be extremely useful to the United States in trade negotiations with Japan (Lincoln 1997). For neorealists, the issue turns less on sovereignty and more on security. The central question, then, is, how an international organization can facilitate the long-term economic and security goals of the United States? The United States can certainly ignore any WTO decision that genuinely threatens its security—and WTO officials know it. Therefore, they are not likely to issue any such decision.

A Liberal Cut

The WTO ruling in the Clean Air Act case demonstrates the constructive role that a liberal supranational institution can have on the settlement of trade disputes. The United States, having quarreled with Brazil and Venezuela about the legitimacy of the EPA regulations for several years, had achieved no breakthroughs in the ongoing negotiations. In 1994, the EPA had proposed new regulations that would have allowed foreign producers to petition the EPA for an individual baseline, provided supporting data were supplied (Crow 1996, 37). The U.S. Congress rejected this proposal, despite EPA claims that most foreign gasoline was likely to be on par with domestic gasoline. According to Jeffrey Schott of the Institute of International Economics, the "U.S. implicitly admitted the violation and attempted to negotiate a settlement with Venezuela" (cited in Crow 1996, 37). The WTO confirmed what many trade experts already knew—the regulation unfairly and unnecessarily discriminated against Venezuelan and Brazilian exports.

The Clean Air Act case was a technical, complicated trade issue, not the broad environmental issue portrayed in the media. The preamble of the WTO recognizes the importance of environmental protection and concerns. The WTO incorporates the GATT exception to discriminatory measures used to meet valid societal goals such as environmental protection. The panel of trade experts determined that the regulation was not crucial to environmental protection and served only to exclude imports. The continued existence of the regulation is more likely the result of congressional parochialism and bureaucratic inertia.

The WTO is concerned about the environment and has a committee that considers the impact of free trade on the environment. Trade protectionism can be quite sophisticated, often well hidden in politically popular policies. Unilateral environmental regulations are important and legitimate prerogatives of states; however, they may not be used to discriminate against foreign imports when no environmental benefit can be demonstrated. The principal goal of the WTO is to liberalize trade because free trade generates the resources necessary for environmental protection, leads to environmental technologies, and forces the efficient use of natural resources through competition (Nissen 1997). The link between wealth and high environmental standards has been clearly established: Wealthy societies can afford stringent environmental regulations. Trade liberalization encourages multilateral efforts to protect the environment, raising the environmental standards in the developing world.

For liberals, the Clean Air Act case was an NTB case—one that the WTO helped to denationalize and depoliticize by using scientific data and trade experts to distinguish between permissible state policy and illegal protectionism. Trade and environmental protection must be allowed to reach a global balance or equilibrium. The issues of trade and the environment encompass a multitude of groups with competing national and international interests.

A Marxist Cut

For Marxists, the Clean Air Act case demonstrates that environmental protection and free trade are rarely compatible. The WTO prefers businesses over people and threatens other laws designed to protect the environment and consumers (Khor 1996). Businesses, free markets, and free trade are privileged at the cost of consumers, workers, and the environment (Laarman 1996). Worse, the WTO has overridden the wishes of the American people: "Industry pounded the Clean Air Act at every stage of the lawmaking process: in congressional hearings, in congressional drafting of the legislation, in the EPA's protracted rule-making process, in threatened lawsuits. Venezuela was well represented too, by the elite Washington, D.C., law firm of Arnold and Porter" (*Multinational Monitor* 1996, 5). When those efforts failed, the WTO finished the assault.

Marxists assert that the domestic and foreign components of the oil industry are the chief beneficiaries of the WTO ruling—a notion confirmed by the industry's own leading journal: "[T]he EPA may find itself so distracted by the politics of foreign baselines that it loses its taste for even stricter regulation of U.S. gas" (Crow 1996, 21). Existing and future environmental regulations must, perforce, take a backseat to the expansion of trade. The WTO rejected the argument that the EPA regulation was designed to achieve the valid goal of limiting the amount of pollutants in the air. As a result, substandard gasoline may now be imported to the United States, while the EPA is deterred from raising gasoline standards.

The WTO decision is problematic for two reasons. First, the WTO emphasizes markets and trade as a solution to social and environmental problems and does not consider that they might be part of the problem. The cause of environmental problems lies in the use of natural resources to produce goods for ever-expanding markets. Lip service to "sustainable development" notwithstanding, the WTO Committee on Trade and the Environment is more concerned with the effect of environmental protection upon free trade than with the impact of trade upon the environment (Williams 1996). Within the WTO framework, there is no provision to coordinate multilateral environmental and trade negotiations. Thus, many multilateral environmental treaties can be either nullified by the WTO or marginalized in the wake of fast-track trade negotiations. Even liberals recognize that the WTO does not distinguish between national and international environmental protection measures and that WTO procedures must be amended to ensure environmental protection both nationally and internationally (Helm 1996; Hudnall 1996; Nissen 1997; Schoenbaum 1997; Steinberg 1997).

Second, the WTO is shrouded in secrecy (Weissman 1994). WTO hearings are closed to the public, and documents are classified. The public and NGOs have little input in the decision-making process. MNCs, on the other hand, are amply represented by their governments, whose officials participate in the WTO. These companies help to elect public officials in each country; furthermore, they happen to be the countries' largest employers. Also, MNCs fund research, raising concerns about a corporate bias in scientific studies on environmental effects. Many of the scientists conducting these studies have been employed by the very industries suspected of causing the alleged environmental damage (Castleman and Lemen 1998, 28). The "neutrality" of the WTO, putatively based in impartial science and economics, really advances the interests of international business at the expense of national industries, the environment, and labor.

The incompatibility of environmental protection and free trade is demonstrated by the "race to the bottom" phenomenon (Brecher and Costello 1994). Societies around the world are reducing labor and environmental protections in order to attract foreign direct investment and to keep firms from relocating abroad. The WTO's mission is to lower trade barriers to promote international competition. It also creates competition among governments to attract businesses to locate within their territory and to employ their citizens. Environmental and labor regulations are being

attacked both domestically and internationally. The result is an overall reduction in the protection of people globally. Since the WTO ruling in the Clean Air Act case, environmental regulations protecting dolphins and sea turtles have been ruled as impermissible barriers to trade (*New York Times* 1998, A18).

A Feminist Cut

Feminists argue that the central problem with the WTO is its assumption that trade liberalization and WTO policies have gender-neutral effects. Feminists maintain that trade liberalization has differential effects on women and men, particularly as it relates to their wages, employment, and social burden (Wide 1998). The lowering of wages and the displacement of workers affect women in the workplace and in the home. The lowering of trade barriers encourages firms to exploit cheap sources of labor, which, because of the wage differential, are mostly women in the developing world. Feminists also decry the absence of women in key policy-making positions within the WTO and the exclusion of women as subjects of study in trade analyses.

The Clean Air Act case exemplifies how the environment and other social causes are marginalized by the pursuit of free trade. While the nullification of one regulation does not have a direct effect on all women, it shows that WTO trivializes issues that tend to be important to women. If environmental regulations are vulnerable in the most advanced and industrialized economies, then environmental protection in less developed countries (LDCs) becomes even less likely. Women's experiences in the developing world are different from men's (and from Western women's) because they are directly tied to the environment for their survival. Environmental degradation lowers the quality of life for women and children.

The discourse attending the Clean Air Act case accents the masculine bias of the WTO's liberal orientation. Postmodern feminists point out that a superior–subordinate relationship obtains between the issues of free trade and the environment. Free trade is given priority "because liberal conceptions of progress have fostered a split between man and nature where nature is to be dominated" (Ashworth and Swatuk 1998, 87). Natural resources are to be exploited, and "science" and "development" will save the world from the consequences of environmental degradation. The treatment of trade and the environment as separate, technical issues is a very masculine way of understanding the world (Shiva 1989). By breaking down trade and environmental regulation into their smallest components, WTO experts have, in effect, "missed the forest for the trees." Every environmental regulation distorts trade in some manner.

A Constructivist Cut

The U.S. Clean Air Act, as the first case before the WTO, sets an important precedent about the values and the ideas promoted through the fledging organization. The case represents the first institutional effort at norm creation. The WTO sought to articulate norms that would properly balance the evolving national and environmental interests of states with the requisites of a global trading system. Values were not imposed, rather competing values and interests were articulated and balanced in a way that was acceptable to the parties involved. The WTO was part and parcel of the process by which states, in this case the United States, define their interests in relation to their trading partners. The U.S. interest was to abide by the WTO decision because the U.S. identity was that of a leader willing to "go first" and demonstrate to others the appropriate state behavior when faced with an undesired WTO ruling.

Constructivist analyses of the WTO are limited in part because the actors, both state and nonstate, are in the process of constructing a global trade regime. The extent to which certain values and norms are shared by the various actors is in question. Even at the regional level, disagreements abound about the extent of permissible government protectionism, and even about whether certain government subsidies or programs constitute protectionism. As such, the few constructivist analyses that do exist tend to focus on regime change or how certain values and norms are promoted within the WTO. For example, developing states were instrumental in helping the international community transition from GATT to the WTO (Ford 2003, 115–138). While other theories marginalize the role of developing states in creating the WTO, the constructivist approach better explains how the support of developing countries for a robust, rules-based trading system actually strengthened the norm of multilateralism. By seeing interests as being reflexively constructed, we can understand why developing states would support the WTO when it seemed to go against their material interests. Similarly, other theories misrepresent the WTO as a coercive organization forcing states to go against the national interest. Through the constructivist approach, the WTO can also be understood as a framework for human interaction and an elaboration of a system of rules that will lead to the legalization of behavior (Wolfe 2005, 339). This kind of "legal constructivism" traces the development of law and legal norms within the WTO.

Lang (2006) argues that John Gerald Ruggie's idea of "embedded liberalism" resulted from the evolution of the changing meaning of liberalism for different actors over time. The compromise of embedded liberalism is normative idea relating to how a global trade regime might be constructed around some government intervention as opposed to neoliberal normative underpinnings that are suspicious of state involvement through subsidies or regulation. By paying attention to ideational factors, we can see how norms are incorporated into institutional trade arrangements. The Clean Air Act case shows how environmental protection is an important and evolving state interest. Perhaps international organizations when guided by a "global ecological Keynesianism" can sustain both the environment and free trade (Murphy 1994).

CHALLENGES FOR THE WTO

The WTO faces an uncertain political and economic future as trade talks have stalled and the unprecedented financial crisis, which began in 2008 in the subprime mortgage market in the United States, quickly spread around the world in part because of the liberalization of the financial services that took place under the auspices of the WTO. In 1997, the WTO and its member states reached a historic financial agreement that would allow multi-national banks and insurance companies to operate globally and in many emerging markets. The initial international response to the WTO-sponsored agreement was mixed.

Liberal supporters applauded the agreement as a success for global governance. According to India's *Indian Express*:

> The financial services agreement is the third feather in the World Trade Organization's cap this year, after the information technology and telecoms agreements. Given the Asian crisis, any financial services pact is an achievement . . . Anti free trade voices have been particularly sharp in America of late. In the end, it was at once a true compromise. (U.S. Information Agency 1997d, 6)

This sentiment is shared by *The Australian*:

> As the Asian currencies have fallen to new lows in recent days, the World Trade Organization pact signals a welcome renewal of the region's commitment to freer and fairer trade . . . It reassures investors in Asia that the region's governments are serious about more transparency and certainty for overseas investors, while recognizing that policies which protect domestic industry at the expense of competition are likely to exacerbate their national economic problems. (U.S. Information Agency 1997d, 4)

Predictably, the Marxist worldview is not nearly as optimistic as the liberal worldview. According to Hong Kong's *South China Morning Post*:

> It is striking how the delight over last weekend's 102-nation pact to liberalize financial services has come from the Americans and Europeans. It is they who stand to benefit the most from the World Trade Organization accord to open up markets all over the world for powerful multinationals to dominate . . . U.S. Trade Representative Charlene Barshefsky could scarcely contain her jubilation, talking of it in terms of a trade deal rather than a genuine attempt at liberalization, and frankly admitting that it would provide tremendous opportunities for American firms. (U.S. Information Agency 1997d, 4)

The liberalization of financial services allows foreign firms unprecedented access to domestic banking and insurance industries. Such access can destabilize developing countries and threaten national firms. In 2008, this liberalization, coupled with limited oversight at the national and international level, means that a crisis in the once obscure subprime mortgage market in the United States almost brought down the entire global financial system.

The WTO has also come under fire from its own members over its priorities and procedures. In August 2000, a UN-appointed study team reported that the WTO was a "nightmare" for developing countries and should be brought under UN scrutiny (*Reuters* 2000, 13). The UN Subcommission on the Promotion and Protection of Human Rights concluded that rules are "grossly unfair and even prejudiced" and "reflect an agenda that serves only to promote the dominant corporatist interests" (*Earth Island Journal* 2001, 16). This UN report, along with other types of international criticism, has raised questions regarding the legitimacy and the promise of the WTO.

In October 2000, the smaller members called for a change in the WTO dispute system. Led by Japan, the smaller countries argued that "the U.S. and the EU are using the dispute settlement rules in ways that suit them and not abiding by the rules for everyone else" (Olsen 2000, 9). Under existing rules, the plaintiff party determines whether the defendant country is in compliance with the WTO ruling. This allows large states, with large economies, more leverage because the compliance decision can be used as a negotiating tool. If a state is found in violation of WTO rules, that complaining party is allowed to impose trade sanctions against the offending party. Those sanctions are supposed to be lifted when the complaining party is satisfied of compliance. In practice, this has allowed large economies, like the United States and the EU, to use a determination of compliance (regardless of whether or not the practice has actually stopped) to get concessions from the defendant state in any kind of negotiating situation. This means that the United States and EU, if they are in conflict, can reach a compliance agreement to satisfy each other but not actually comply with WTO rules. Because the economies are valuable to each other, they can use compliance as carrot or stick in their relations. Conversely, the smaller states lack the clout to force compliance from the larger economies. The larger economies simply acknowledge the WTO ruling and accept sanctions without actually complying. Put another way, the large economies know sanctions against them hurt the small states more, which reduces the bargaining power of small states. The Japanese-led coalition wants to change the rules so that the WTO determines whether or not a state is in compliance with WTO rules, and not the plaintiff state. To date, the United States and the EU have resisted this particular reform.

In November 2001, the **"Doha Round"** of WTO negotiations was launched in Doha, Qatar, with an initial target completion by the end of 2005. The meeting, in part, was held in the Middle Eastern country to distance WTO negotiations from the political protests that characterized and disrupted the 1999 WTO meetings in Seattle, Washington. Doha was not as readily accessible to protestors and the Qatar government was better able to restrict the activities of those protestors who managed to make their way to Doha. The agenda of the Doha round reflects past WTO priorities, with particular attention to TRIPS and the liberalization of the agricultural sector. China was also formally admitted to the WTO at the Doha meeting.

Doha round negotiations continued in 2003 in Cancun, Mexico. The Cancun meeting, again characterized by protests, albeit smaller than Seattle, collapsed abruptly due to the individual policies of states and a division between rich and poor states. According to Bhagwati (2004, 53–63), the United States, following a Bush administration pattern, threatened to bypass multilateral institutions, like the WTO, in favor of a coalition of states willing to liberalize trade and to enforce intellectual property rights. Developing states sought to link the reduction of trade barriers to agricultural products to agreements relating to TRIPS and further liberalization of financial services. Many developing countries oppose the continued subsidies to farmers in the advanced industrialized states.

Since Cancun, lower-level WTO negotiations have met with modest success. Sessions in Geneva (2004) yielded an agreement that would cut the export subsidies given to farmers in developed countries in exchange for better access to markets in developing countries. The Geneva success, however, was overshadowed by subsequent negotiations in Paris (2005) as France protested the subsidy cuts to its farmers and negotiations bogged down over technical issues. Negotiations moved to the Ministerial Level in Hong Kong in December 2005; however, the meeting resulted in a weak agreement to end agricultural export subsidies by 2013 and to continue to develop a set of comprehensive trade rules. The stalled global trade talks coincided with the major trading states, particularly the United States, China, and the EU, negotiating their own trade agreements with their principal trading partners, raising the specter of rival and competing trading blocs (Schifferes 2005). In 2008, Doha Round talks collapsed without an agreement. These talks failed in large part because of the looming financial crisis moved additional trade liberalization talks to the back burner. As the crisis unfolded, states resorted to old school protectionism (tariffs) and restricted stimulus (e.g., "Buy American" provision of the U.S. stimulus package) to shield their national economies from a potential depression. Even without the crisis, developing states, led by India and China, wanted to protect their farmers, many of whom are poor, from international competition, while the United States and other states demanded more access to their markets. The negotiations were complicated by a global spike of fuel and food prices that caused the parties to become further entrenched. The spike in food prices demonstrated to India and China that they needed to be able to feed themselves locally. To the United States and other food exporters, it meant the need for further liberalization to bring food prices down. As more farmland is devoted to bio-fuels, rather than food production, the probability of chronic food shortages across the developing world increases dramatically.

In the following case study, we examine the contentious trade issue of GM foods, which has complicated global efforts to liberalize the agricultural sector. What is GM food? Is GM food safe? Do states have the right to regulate the trade of GM foods and organisms? Is such regulation impermissible protectionism? What is the role of international organizations in this trade debate?

CASE STUDY 4: GENETICALLY MODIFIED FOODS AND ORGANISMS

Genetically modified foods and organisms are products that have had their DNA and other genetic materials manipulated by scientists. Unlike hybrid plants, which involve the joining of related plants and organisms, GM products have the desired gene from one organism—a bacterium, plant, or animal—implanted into the DNA of another organism (Maynard 2000). Consider a GM soybean. "A soy DNA is spliced with petunia DNA to produce a plant engineered to survive otherwise toxic doses of herbicide" (Maynard 2000). This would mean that weeds could easily be killed among the standing soybean crops. This process of genetic engineering is also called **"transgenesis"** or **"transgenetic"** manipulation. This process allows scientists to create disease- and insect-resistant crops or crops that are high in minerals or vitamins. This, in turn, leads to higher crop yields and less pesticide and herbicide use. The most common GM foods include corn, soybeans, potatoes, and tomatoes and their derivatives like corn flour or tomato sauce.

As a trade issue, GM products have several points of contention. The first point of contention focuses on the intellectual property rights of GM products. Can firms patent the tomato or potato once it has been genetically manipulated? This has significant implications because if GM foods and organisms become integrated within the food supply, MNCs could own the intellectual property of the food basics. At the same time, MNCs such as Monsanto and DuPont have invested vast resources into the development of GM products and want a return on their investment. A second point relates to the safety of GM products. Do these products pose a hazard to humans, plant, or animal life and the environment? Critics of GM products say safety tests have not been adequate to insure public health or environmental protection. Third, how should trade in GM products be regulated? Given the promise and the potential threat of GM foods, governments have had to navigate a political minefield to craft trade policies that balance domestic concerns with the requirements of a liberal trading order. Trade policies have been categorized as "Promotional," "Permissive," "Precautionary," or "Preventive" depending on the degree to which governments attract or deter GM products (Paarlberg 2001, 27).

GM products are a source of friction between the United States and EU and also between the United States and the developing countries. These countries disagree regarding the benefits and risks associated with GM foods, and these disagreements have manifested themselves in a full-fledged trade dispute. The WTO did not formally consider the issue until a case was filed by Thailand in 2000 (*Agra Europe* 2000b). In January 2000, 130 states met in Montreal to hammer out an agreement on biosafety rules, called the **Biosafety Protocol**. This treaty, which pitted the United States against everyone else, allows states to bar imports of GM seeds, microbes, animals, and crops that they deem may harm the environment (Pollack 2000, A1). Critics of the treaty claim it contains too many loopholes; however, it does recognize that GM products are distinct and need to be regulated separately from other products (Pollack 2000, A6). While the central aim of the treaty is to protect the environment from unintended consequences of genetic engineering, the United States has argued that such protection can also be used to discriminate against U.S. agricultural exports and MNCs. The controversy surrounding GM products has not gone away as the EU and other countries have continued to reject GM exports from the United States, even in spite of a 2006 WTO ruling that banning GM foods was impermissible under trade rules? How do we understand and make sense of this issue?

A Realist Cut

The issue of GM foods and organisms relates to national security in two interrelated ways. The first has to do with the safety of GM products. States must ensure the safety of GM foods for human consumption and for the environment. Governments should not rely on the assurances of MNCs, which supposedly have conducted exhaustive tests, or on international agreements for safety guarantees. International agreements by their very nature are watered-down compromises and not an adequate form of protection. The increase of "bio-threats" makes it incumbent upon governments to ensure food safety themselves. Second, the state must achieve food security. That is, the state must ensure that the country has enough food to sustain itself. If GM products can deliver on their promises, then countries, especially the poor ones that have chronic food shortages, should embrace the technology. Governments should avoid becoming dependent on foreign MNCs for the bulk of their food supply and should be willing to challenge patents and intellectual property rights. In other words, they should accept intellectual property rights on paper, but not actually enforce them. Their farmers and national industries should take full advantage of the new technology if it is proven safe.

The experience of European states serves as an example of how states put their national interest, in restricting GM foods and organisms, ahead of European unity and good trade relations with the United States. Their experience with "mad cow" disease, bacteria-contaminated meat, benzine in soft drinks, hoof-and-mouth disease, and dioxin in poultry, pork, and beef has called into question the efficacy of EU in assuring health and consumer protection. The screening of GM products for biosafety is almost always done at the national level (Paarlberg 2001, 23). In 1999, France banned a type of GM maize because a sufficient risk assessment had not been conducted (*Agra Europe* 1999). The EU has since issued a moratorium on approving GM organisms at the behest of EU governments until EU regulations are updated to satisfy public concerns. Until European governments have reviewed the safety of GM foods, they will only allow the import of those proven safe. Good relations with the United States depend on much more than the trade of a few GM seeds and crops. The recent terrorist attacks on the United States have put this particular trade issue on the back burner. While U.S. firms and farmers have lost nearly $1 billion in exports, the war on terrorism stalled a U.S. complaint to the WTO. According to Carol Forman, member of Bush's agricultural trade policy advisory committee, "We have every reason to get along with the European Union right now. They are our biggest supporters in a life-and-death struggle" (Lambrecht 2001, A8). States need to make calculated decisions based on their national interest and their bargaining position at the time. Conversely, Europe's opposition to the U.S. war with Iraq perhaps paved the way to a formal WTO complaint in 2003.

Similarly, many developing countries have resisted GM products by refusing to buy GM seeds and planting them. Countries like Kenya, India, and Brazil have very precautionist policies because of the safety concerns; however, their dependence on food assistance from donor countries like the United States leaves little choice in terms of what to accept in humanitarian aid. The EU, siding with many developing countries, asked the UN World Food Program (WFP) to buy only non-GM products for distribution of food aid. In an official statement, Europe said, "it is the legitimate right of developing countries' governments to fix their own level of protection and to take the decision they deem appropriate to prevent unintentional dissemination of GM seeds" (Bosch 2003, 1798). China, on the other hand, has embraced GM technology and is engaged in large-scale planting. Such technologies promise to compensate for the food and water shortages within China. U.S. firms, however, remain concerned about their intellectual property and seek WTO and national enforcement of their rights.

A Liberal Cut

GM foods and organisms represent a technological innovation that could revolutionize food production on a global scale and better the lives of millions of people. In addition to higher crop yields and less use of pesticides and herbicides, GM foods hold a great deal of promise, which includes frost-tolerant sugarcane, rice engineered with vitamin A to prevent blindness in the people of developing countries, milk with reduced lactose for lactose-intolerant people, nuts and other products that do not cause allergies, cereals with enhanced fiber content, oil with increased essential fatty acids, and fruit with increased vitamin and mineral content (Maynard 2000, 22). Such innovations are important if we are to feed nearly 9.1 billion people, the Earth's expected population in 2050.

Genetic modification techniques also have nonfood applications. GM crops can be used to produce modified oils, chemicals for the pharmaceutical industry, and biodegradable plastics (Halford 2001). Human testing has already begun on edible plant vaccines against diarrhea, E. coli, and Hepatitis B, which could be extremely beneficial to countries that do not have access to clean syringes and needles (Halford 2001).

Neoclassical liberals argue that the "hysteria" surrounding GM food is unfounded (Borlag 2003). Firms that specialize in GM foods and organisms have strong incentives not to bring to market products that are harmful. Companies like DuPont and Monsanto spend millions of dollars on research and development to ensure the safety of their products. It would be irrational for them to place products on the market that could harm their customers, destroy their reputation, and anger their shareholders. If the self-interest of MNCs is not enough, these firms must also jump through governmental hoops to prove their products are safe. In the United States, GM food and organisms are tested according to U.S. Department of Agriculture (USDA) and the EPA guidelines. One of the most prestigious organizations, the National Research Council, has systematically analyzed the data and found that environmental concerns, such as whether GM crops spliced with a pesticidal trait might impact nontarget species, are real. However, the impact is likely to be smaller than the impact of using chemical pesticides, the traditional way of protecting crops (*Journal of Environmental Health* 2000). European and EU complaints regarding GM crops and their subsequent restriction amounts to protectionism, which will make their farmers even more inefficient than they already are. Europe, leading the developing countries, is using national passions and unfounded fears regarding safety to discriminate against higher-quality products. They may protect farmers in the short term, but the consequence is the stunting of Europe's GM industries, which will make them even more uncompetitive in the long term (*The Economist* 1998b).

Other liberals do not see the controversy surrounding GM food and organisms as necessarily a bad thing. NGOs, women's groups, MNCs, and the scientific community have put forth their views in the free market place of ideas, which has led to the development of knowledge regarding GM food and organisms. Almost all of the scientific evidence suggests that GM food is safe; however, these groups have brought to the forefront potential problems, such as new allergies and unintended environmental consequences. It has contributed to the growing partnerships between otherwise adversarial groups. For example, the top economic advisor to DuPont is Paul Gilding, the former head of Greenpeace (Friedman 1999, A31). In 2000, more than fifty MNCs have joined a UN environmental pact that obligates them to take steps toward improving the environment. The UN has suggested that GM foods be available to poor countries to alleviate poverty and malnutrition as the benefits outweigh the risks (Schrope 2001, 109). The competition of interests between all the involved parties can lead to an equilibrium of interest in which all needs are addressed.

NGOs have lobbied governments and IGOs extensively to at least give consumers a choice of whether to consume GM foods and organisms. The bulk of these lobbying efforts have been geared toward labeling of GM products. These efforts have been more successful outside the United States because current U.S. regulations do not distinguish between GM food and other types of food. Firms are concerned that the public is misinformed about the risks and the benefits of GM foods and organisms and that labeling the foods would make them unsellable. This is supported by the EU market research agency, Eurobarometer, when it found that ill-informed skepticism was fueling the public's aversion to GM food (*Agra Europe*, April 28, 2000a). The better approach is to provide the public with as much information as possible without implementing unnecessary regulations. This can be accomplished through international cooperation. The EU and the UN have agreed to set up an international biosafety information exchange center with a Web site open to the public (*European Report* 2000, 504). "The center will collect legislative, legal, and scientific data on genetically modified organisms (GMO) and how they are marketed and compile a list of the GMOs that are authorized or banned in each country. It will be run by independent experts, research scientists, lawyers, representatives of industrial concerns and nongovernmental organizations" (*European Report* 2000, 504). International organizations can bring a variety of resources—diplomatic, technical, and financial—to bear on problems to the satisfaction of most of the interested parties.

A Marxist Cut

The controversy surrounding GM food and organisms illustrates the power of MNCs to manipulate scientific studies, government agencies, and international organizations. First, many of the scientific studies of GM food have been funded by the MNCs themselves. Monsanto, DuPont, and Cargill have spent millions of dollars researching the safety of their products and, not surprisingly, have found that their products are safe. Scientists and researchers are well aware of which "scientific" results lead to more funding and research grants. Serious questions remain about the adequacy of the testing, the validity of the conclusions, and therefore the safety of GM products (Callahan 2000; Greenpeace 1999; Klotter 2001; Warwick 2000). Government agencies do not provide an effective check. Government agencies such as the USDA, the FDA, and the EPA implement regulations that favor and are tailored to the needs of business. These firms have contributed millions of dollars to elect officials who will serve their interests. These officials in return pass laws that favor the GM firms. Agencies in the United States proceed on the premise that products are safe until proven hazardous. Risk tests are only done on GM foods that have a history of causing allergies or illness (Pires-O'Brien 2000). If government agencies are effective at restricting these GM products of questionable safety, then MNCs can turn to international organizations. The EU is already moving to force its members to lift its ban on GM products, and the UN is advocating the use of GM foods in developing countries. It is only a matter of time before the WTO weighs in on the issues, and it is a sure bet that it will deem the safety regulations of member states as an impermissible NTB to trade. MNCs are able to coopt personnel of governments, IGOs, and many NGOs.

One of the more troubling aspects of GM foods and organisms is the insistence of MNCs and their home governments on the acquisition and enforcement of intellectual property rights. This amounts to the privatization of nature, as MNCs tinker with the genetic makeup of plants and animals and then claim ownership of the genetic material. Increasingly, every aspect of life right down to the DNA is reduced to private property. Resources belonging to everyone are few as MNCs are insisting that governments and the WTO grant and enforce their property rights. This amounts to the "highjacking of the global food supply" and "biopiracy" (Shiva 1997, 1999).

The liberal promise of GM food as a means of alleviating world hunger and malnutrition is also problematic. Currently, there is enough food to meet the nutritional needs of every man, woman, and child on the planet. The dire Malthusian predictions of population growth outpacing food production have not come true because of innovations in agriculture. Yet, today millions of people die from starvation because they do not have access to food. Today, millions of tons of food spoil because the market is oversaturated. The market distributes food resources only to those that can afford to buy them. The supply of food is not why people are starving, it is the way food is distributed. None of the MNCs that produce GM food has ever suggested that food prices might actually decline so that they might be affordable to the world's poor. In fact, the agricultural industry is one of the world's most subsidized industries because, if left to market forces, food prices would collapse. MNCs that produce GM foods and organisms only seek to revolutionize agricultural production to favor their techniques and products; however, they provide no real discernable benefits to the world's population.

MNCs also create a corporate dependence. These firms purchase seed companies and co-ops that sell seeds to local farmers. Farmers are bound by the intellectual property rights of the MNC, which means they cannot engage in the time-honored practice of taking the seeds from a harvested crop for the following planting seasons (Grogan and Long 2000, 42). MNCs cannot monitor every farmer from Nicaragua to Nigeria, so they have used GM techniques to create sterile seeds. Termed "terminator" technology, biotech MNCs have developed the ability to engineer sterility into the second-generation seeds, which could affect the livelihoods of the 1.4 billion people who rely on farm-saved seeds (Paarlberg 2001, 99–100; Warwick 2000, 50–51). Farmers would be forced to buy new seeds every year. Another strategy of MNCs is to surround the farmer with interlocking technologies, which forces the farmer to buy products from the firm. A firm that sells disease-resistant GM seeds may also sell a compatible herbicide. Or they may sell an "upgrade" such as a chemical that may improve yields or processability. Unless the rights of farmers are protected or the GM technology is regulated, MNCs could control the world's food production. This amounts to "biocolonialism."

A Feminist Cut

The gender dimensions of the issue of GM foods and organisms are interrelated and threefold. First, it is through NGOs that women have had the greatest voice regarding their concerns about GM products. NGOs such as the Canadian-based Rural Advancement Foundation International or the National Federation of Women's Institutes have been vocal and active opponents of GM technology and have pressured governments to take their concerns seriously. Women, through NGOs, have mobilized to take on the

MNCs and their home governments and have been successful in enacting restrictive policies, especially in Europe and India. Other NGOs that have large female participation include the Campaign, Greenpeace, RAGE, Mothers for Natural Law, and the Bioengineering Action Network.

Second, women have been the principal opposition to GM foods. Public opinion polls in the United States and Europe show that women are far more skeptical than men regarding the safety of GM foods. In one ABC television poll, 62 percent of women thought GM foods were unsafe compared with 40 percent of men (Langer 2001). More importantly, 65 percent of women said they are less likely to buy GM products, while men, only 49 percent (Langer 2001). What accounts for this gender gap? Women's traditional gender roles involve feeding the family unit. This entails subsistence farming in many areas of the developing world, and, in the developed countries, women are the primary shoppers. It has been women's groups domestically and internationally that have demanded the right of replicate seeds and the labeling of GM food and organisms. Women seek to have choice about what they feed to their families and are willing to pay more for unaltered food (*Pulse* 2000). Women are also more likely to oppose GM food on ethical grounds. Women tend to be more uncomfortable with tinkering with nature and are more wary of the unknown and unforeseen effects of the genetic modification of plants and animals.

Third, the discourse of the debate regarding GM foods emanating from MNCs, governments, and IGOs is quite gendered. Critics of GM foods and organisms are dismissed as hysterical, irrational, and antiscience. Opponents of the labeling of GM foods claim that the public is uninformed regarding the benefits and hazards of GM foods, and labeling will hurt sales and serve no safety purpose. After all, the AMA and the FDA have found that there was "no scientific justification for special labeling of GM foods" (Langer 2001). Examined through a postmodern feminist lens, this translates into saying that women are uninformed and irrational regarding GM foods, so it is up to the FDA and other organizations to protect women from themselves. In other words, women, who do the shopping, are not to be trusted with making consumer choices regarding food. Similarly, any government or IGO that questions the safety or the usefulness of GM foods is feminized as silly and irrational. International organizations, like many NGOs or UN agencies, that highlight the intrusion of culture, power, dominance, or wealth on the practice of science are trivialized and marginalized. In short, hidden gender assumptions are at play in the contentious issue of GM foods and organisms.

A Constructivist Cut

Constructivists highlight the importance of national identity in understanding the controversies surrounding the trade of GM foods and organisms. For example, France's identity is reflexively shaped by its opposition to what it deems as American cultural imperialism. France's position on GM foods is not based on scientific arguments per se, but rather on the result of U.S. pressure on France and the EU to accept GM imports (Willging 2008, 199). Moreover, French national identity is epicurean, as a society that defines what good food is and how good food should be produced, prepared, and served. To be French means to enjoy the social relations of fine food production, preparation, and dining. GM food is distinctly American and thereby associated with McDonalds, and the large, tasteless proportions that have led to the epidemic of obesity in the United States. Any corporation or international organization that seeks to resolve the conflict of GM foods needs to take into account national identity, especially in cultures that organize themselves around food.

The constructivist approach is also useful in understanding whose ideas matter and why. Constructivists have demonstrated that NGOs have been quite influential is interpreting what intellectual property rights mean in the WTO, especially in relation to HIV/AIDS medicines (see, e.g., Sell and Prakash 2004). Business and NGOs articulate different normative arguments as to why intellectual property rights should be enforced or not. By building networks and invoking different values and identities, actors can construct a trade regime in GM food and organisms, recognizing that the regime is in transition. Trade in GM foods will change as actors, interests, and identities change. In the face of rising food prices, issues related to food "security" and "piracy" will shape the trade dimensions of GM food and organisms and the extent to which trade is allowed and intellectual property rights enforced. Social learning about the positive and negative aspects of GM foods will also play a role.

KEY TERMS

Bretton Woods System 159
John Maynard Keynes 159
the compromise of embedded liberalism 159
the General Agreement on Tariffs and Trade (GATT) 159
International Trade Organization (ITO) 159
reciprocity, nondiscrimination, and multilateralism 160
most-favored-nation status (MFN) 160

nontariff barriers (NTBs) 160
subsidies 160
voluntary export restriction (VER) 160
governmental regulation 161
the World Trade Organization (WTO) 162
the Ministerial Conference 163
the General Council 163
Dispute Settlement Body 163

Trade Policy Review Body 163
the Goods Council 163
the Services Council 163
the Trade-Related Aspects of Intellectual Property (TRIPS) Council 163
Doha Round 174
genetically modified foods and organisms 176
transgenesis or transgenetic 176
Biosafety Protocol 176

SUGGESTED READINGS

Barton, John H., Judith L. Goldstein, Timothy E. Josling, and Richard H. Steinberg. 2008. *The Evolution of the Trade Regime: Politics, Law and Economics of the GATT to the WTO*. Princeton, NJ: Princeton University Press.

Davis, Christina L. 2003. *Food Fights over Free Trade: How International Institutions Promote Agricultural Trade Liberalization*. Princeton, NJ: Princeton University Press.

Peet, Richard. 2009. Unholy Trinity: *The IMF, World Bank and the WTO*. London: Zed Books.

Ricardo, David. 1965. *The Principles of Political Economy and Taxation*. London: Dent; New York: Dutton.

Ruggie, John Gerald. 1982. International Regimes, Transactions, and Change: Embedded Liberalism in the Post–Cold War Economic Order. *International Organization* 36 (Special Issue): 379–415.

Development

Development represents one of the principal challenges of twenty-first-century international relations. Chronic poverty, malnutrition, and disease characterize most of the developing world and are creeping into segments of the developed world. Economic stagnation and rampant inflation cripple economies, causing high levels of debt, unemployment, and underemployment. The economic disparities between rich and poor continue to widen at an accelerated pace. The disparities between rich and poor are contributory causes of war both within and between nations. In the view of many, development is the best strategy for avoiding violent conflict and averting political upheaval in the future. Unfortunately, no consensus exists as to the causes of poverty or the meaning of development. As a result, development issues remain controversial in international forums.

In this chapter, we examine controversies surrounding the issue of development and the international organizations which are involved in development and the alleviation of poverty. The financial crises of the 1990s (with emphasis on the Mexican peso crisis and the Indonesian economic meltdown) serve as the first case study to illustrate how development issues are directly related to international economic stability. The financial crises of the 1990s provide important historical background and perspective for understanding the global financial crisis that began in 2008. The second case study focuses on the **Millennium Development Goals (MDGs)** and the role of international organizations in promoting and meeting these goals. The case studies show how differing worldviews and approaches inform and expand our understanding of the complexities of international development.

WHAT IS DEVELOPMENT?

Development has many different meanings. For some people, development means macroeconomic growth and the accumulation of wealth. For others, development means improving the human condition. These conceptions are not necessarily mutually exclusive, but they arise from competing worldviews that often contest the causes of, and therefore the solutions to, poverty and underdevelopment. Thomas (1998) characterizes the development debate as a struggle between the **"orthodox"** and the **"critical."** The orthodox approach largely follows the mainstream tradition, interpreting development in the Western, liberal manner. Measured quantitatively with economic statistics, development means increases in gross domestic product (GDP) per capita over time and rising levels of industrialization (Sen 1996). It involves the transition of traditional societies, which are agrarian and subsistence-based, into modern societies founded on wage labor, cash, and consumerism (Rostow 1971). Markets are the preferred solution to poverty and underdevelopment because they have proven to be the most efficient way to promote economic growth, diversification, industrialization, and production. Markets also efficiently distribute resources and generate significant levels of wealth. The quality of life for the poor improves as the economy expands.

In the orthodox view, chronic underdevelopment and poverty are most often the results of irrational state policies and regulations. States that practice extensive protectionism or seek to develop export industries in which they have no comparative advantage encourage inefficient industries. Such industries are doomed to fail because they cannot compete once they are exposed to international competition. The state cannot protect domestic industries indefinitely. Economic development occurs when states integrate into a global economy based on free trade, specialization, and an international division of labor (Gilpin 1987, 266). Governments that interfere with the price mechanism or seek to bureaucratically "plan" economic development sacrifice efficiency, growth, and wealth for good intentions that cannot be realized. The central difference between neoliberals and Keynesian liberals is the extent to which the government is involved in markets, and when the government is involved, the extent to which its policies benefit the supply (business) side or the demand (workers and consumers) side of the equation.

The obstacles to development in the orthodox sense include population growth, corruption, and excessive government spending. The poorest developing states have high population growth rates, which undermine their economies' sustainability. Corruption compounds the problem. Venal government officials steal millions in foreign assistance for personal gain while forcing MNCs to pay millions in kickbacks and bribes, thus deterring foreign investment. Excessive government spending to subsidize transportation, energy, or prices of manufactured goods creates huge government deficits and massive debt. Many developing states are mired in a cycle of poverty and debt that undermines long-term, stable, sustained economic growth. Development can be accomplished only by introducing significant market reforms and reducing state intervention in the market.

The *critical* approach asserts that the orthodox conception of development is ethnocentric and inadequate at measuring the quality of life. Consider the orthodox indicators of development—GDP per capita and levels of industrialization—which take only market exchanges into account. They do not measure barter transactions nor do they take into account such forms of unpaid labor as the work of women in the home or children on the farm. GDP per capita ignores informal sectors of the economy not subject to market forces. Western conceptions of development include only the growth and the expansion of the market. They assume that the expansion of the market translates into a higher standard of living for individuals; however, the "trickle-down" effect has been difficult to substantiate.

The critical approach brings a different, more flexible conception of development to its analyses. Development, to critical theorists, is the ability of people to meet their material and nonmaterial needs through their own efforts (Thomas 1998, 453). This allows different societies to set their own standards for progress and frees them from meeting the Western standard, a standard that judges all societies by the extent to which they resemble the West. Development is measured by different criteria—the fulfillment of basic human needs, the condition of the natural environment, and the extent to which the marginalized are politically empowered (Thomas 1998, 453). These criteria measure the quality of life. GDP and levels of industrialization ignore many quality-of-life issues important in the developing world. They do not measure the extent to which people have access to adequate nutrition or sanitation nor do they measure the differences between the rich and poor within developing societies. GDP statistics do not show that the gap between the rich and the poor continues to widen. GDP statistics can be misleading. For example, the value of a forest is not included in GDP calculations until it is cut down and sold as lumber. GDP does, however, include the value of medical services for treating cancer caused by pollution and chemical contamination. Given the disparities between the rich and the poor in terms of income and quality of life, GDP figures reflect the enrichment of elites in developing countries, but they are silent on the costs to the vast majority of citizens. The orthodox measures are useful only to Western economists trained to understand the world in terms of abstract mathematical models—models they believe to be universal despite their irrelevance to reality in the developing world.

The orthodox approach to development also ignores the colonial history of many developing countries and the patterns of exploitation by former colonial powers. The historical experience of Africa, Asia, and Latin America is significantly different from that of Europe and the United States. According to Frank (1979), underdevelopment of the periphery is a consequence of expanding capitalism. Capitalism in the West flourished because the West had captive resources, labor, and markets. The periphery continues to be exploited through neocolonialism. Developing countries are relegated to subordinate positions in the international division of labor. The developing world continues to provide inexpensive raw materials and labor to the global economy. This subordinate position leads to chronic balance-of-payments difficulties as developing states import expensive manufactured goods. Wealth flows from the periphery into the core.

The critical approach to development focuses on the relative gains between and within societies. In other words, they maintain that the distribution of benefits is important for understanding development. Critical theorists question the orthodox view that everyone benefits from free trade. In periphery societies, millions of people are displaced by governments seeking to develop export industries in specific raw materials. Land that once fed families is now used to produce cash crops to be sold in world markets. Only the elites, who sell cash crops, benefit from exports, while the vast majority of the population becomes poorer. Coca-Cola and Adidas sweatpants may now be available at the lowest possible cost, but adequate housing, health care, and educational opportunities are scarce. Regardless of which view of development you embrace, the development picture of many countries is bleak. One billion of the world's population lives on less than $1 a day, and more than 3 billion of the world's 6.2 billion people live on $2 a day. The ability of developing countries to increase their GDP and enable their citizens to meet their basic human needs is impaired by the massive debt they have acquired in the last fifty years.

DEBT

Between the orthodox and critical views, development issues are extremely contentious; however, the two approaches do have some common ground. Both agree that the principal obstacle to development is **external debt**. External debt is money that is owed to foreigners and repayable in foreign currency. The external debt of the developing world is estimated to be more than $700 billion, and the servicing of that debt accounts for more than 20 percent of their exports. How did the poorest nations acquire such a large debt? And what are the best ways to handle that debt without compromising economic growth? It is here that the orthodox and critical views part ways: They differ on the origins of debt and hence on strategies for solving the debt crisis.

The orthodox view of development tends to focus on the endogenous, or internal, causes of Third World debt. Excessive government spending and domestic consumer demands led to the explosion of external debt. Governments provided social welfare, health, and educational programs even though they did not have the tax base to support such programs. Third World governments borrowed from abroad instead. They also borrowed money to subsidize the prices of energy and domestic manufactured goods—goods their citizens could ill afford. In addition, Third World governments spent excessively on their militaries. Seeking to modernize their militaries, they spent billions of borrowed dollars to acquire the latest, most sophisticated military hardware. To compound the problem, pervasive government corruption meant that billions of dollars were stolen by the very officials who were supposed to guide the development of their own countries. Many development loans were channeled to inefficient businesses—businesses that had little chance of succeeding in competitive international markets. In sum, developing states simply borrowed more than they could afford, mismanaged a large portion of it, spent a lot of it frivolously, and lived well beyond their means.

Critical approaches to development emphasize the exogenous, or systemic, causes of Third World debt. Critical theorists argue that the debt of developing states was the result of exogenous factors beyond the control of government officials. Third World external debt began to accumulate when neoliberal economists at the IMF and the World Bank advised developing states to borrow the capital they needed to achieve economic takeoff. However, the international economy was prone to chronic instability during the 1970s, making it extremely difficult for states to plan economic growth. Developing states were forced to borrow heavily from both Western governments and private Western banks, not for economic ventures, but just to survive. Furthermore, much of the bilateral "development" assistance from the West came in the form of "military credit," whereby developing countries received loans solely for the purchase of military hardware. In effect, such loans served as indirect subsidies to Western defense industries, but failed to strengthen Third World economies.

Other systemic causes were also at work. Third World debt first ballooned after Arab members of the Organization of Petroleum Exporting Countries (OPEC) placed an embargo against the United States because of U.S. support of Israel during the 1973–1974 Arab–Israeli conflict. The price of oil quadrupled, and the effects of the sharp price rise were felt worldwide. Non-oil-producing states were forced to borrow heavily from private and public sources in order to meet their legitimate energy needs. Whereas the West experienced economic stagnation and inflation, developing states suffered more acutely because their economies were not as diversified. Their exports dropped precipitately as no one was buying raw materials for manufacturing. Their fragile economic base was compromised even further when another round of oil price rises in 1978–1979 led to the virtual collapse of their export markets.

During this period, private international banks encountered significant pressure to lend as "petrodollars" began to pour into their accounts. Bankers, eager to put together attractive loan packages to Third World governments, negotiated low but adjustable interest rates. Unfortunately, these loan packages lost their attractiveness as U.S. interest rates rose into double digits, approaching 20 percent by 1979. As a result, developing states were forced to borrow even more at those higher rates just to pay the interest on previous loans. They also had to export more in order to earn the foreign currency to make loan payments. Commodities markets became flooded, lowering prices and then driving them down further. The situation was exacerbated by a full-fledged economic recession in the United States during the early 1980s. The resulting global economic contraction forced the leading Third World debtors, such as Mexico and Brazil, to seek relief from the spiral of external debt service. In order to deal with the crisis, private creditors formed the **London Club** and the state creditors formed the **Paris Club** to coordinate their responses to debt renegotiations. The mounting debt contributed to the financial crises of the 1990s (discussed in the following section) and remains one of the principle obstacles to development today. Currently, the world's poorest countries owe well over $1 trillion.

The orthodox and critical views of development and debt management are reflected in the international organizations involved in promoting economic development. Public international financial institutions like the World Bank, the IMF, and the regional development banks take a traditional, orthodox approach to international development, as does the WTO. MNCs are also quite orthodox in their outlook. UN bodies directly involved with poverty alleviation and development, such as the UN Conference on Trade and Development (UNCTAD), the UN Industrial Development Organization (UNIDO), and the UN Development Program (UNDP), are more critical in their orientation. Many NGOs, such as Oxfam, Third World Network, Consumers International, and the Asia Indigenous Women's Network, have also adopted a more critical view of development and advocate alternative development strategies. In the following section, we survey a few of the IGOs central to development—the World Bank, the IMF, UNCTAD, and UNDP—in terms of their organizational structures, their roles, and their development approaches.

THE WORLD BANK

The **World Bank** consists of two development institutions, the **International Bank for Reconstruction and Development (IBRD)** and the **International Development Association (IDA)**. The IBRD was created as the development "pillar" under the Bretton Woods system. It is an independent agency within the UN system and is responsible for UN multilateral lending. Originally, the IBRD focused its lending almost exclusively on the reconstruction of Europe. It did not start lending extensively to the developing world until the late 1950s. Multilateral public lending was designed to supplement private loans in order to jump-start both domestic and foreign investment in Europe and later the Third World. With productive investment, capital would flow to the areas where it is most needed and where the returns on investments are greater.

The IBRD remains the conservative base of the World Bank Group; it makes traditional loans, although at somewhat lower interest rates than those of commercial banks. The IBRD lends almost exclusively to governments and makes its lending decisions on the basis of a weighted voting scheme that reflects the proportion of member states' contributions, making the IBRD essentially shareholder-owned. Its resources come from states and from capital markets through private borrowing. Its lending policies are determined by the board of governors. Over time, the IBRD has vacillated, shifting from a conservative lending institution to a development agency (Mikesell 1972). The IBRD has sought to alleviate Third World poverty by making loans to governments for projects that contribute to a state's earning and productive capacities (Sanford 1988).

The IDA was created in 1960 to serve the investment needs of the poorest Third World nations. Many developing states are so mired in poverty and burdened by debt that, even under the best of circumstances, they could never meet the conservative lending criteria of the IBRD. Thus, the IDA provides "soft" loans—loans whose repayment periods are extensive, ranging from thirty to fifty years, and whose interest rates are very low, ranging between

1 and 3 percent. Some loans may be interest-free, in which case the countries are usually assessed a small administrative fee. In order to qualify for IDA loans, countries must meet income guidelines, measured by GDP per capita. These guidelines are adjusted periodically. In 2008, countries could qualify for IDA loans if their national income was less than $1095 per capita. The IDA provides development loans to the poorest of poor in order to generate economic growth in areas otherwise marginalized in the global economy.

The World Bank is served by several affiliates. In 1956, the first affiliate, **the International Finance Corporation (IFC)**, was created to encourage private investment in developing states (Bennett 1995, 313). The IFC provides "seed money" to attract investment capital from a variety of domestic and foreign sources. The IFC also makes loans to and direct equity investments in private companies to stimulate private enterprise and private investment (Riggs and Plano 1994, 288). In 1989, the IFC established the International Securities Group (ISG) to advise companies from the Third World on how to issue stocks, for example, and on how to get listed on the major stock exchanges (Riggs and Plano 1994, 188). By attracting domestic and foreign investors to the Third World industries and companies, developing countries can accumulate the "critical mass" necessary for sustained economic growth and development. The IFC works to build the private sector in developing countries.

In 1966, another affiliate, **International Center for Settlement of Investments Disputes (ISCSID)**, was established as part of a treaty to help states and individuals settle disputes regarding foreign investment by MNCs through mediation and arbitration. Parties to the treaty agree to submit investment disputes to the ISCSID for resolution. Over time, most foreign investment agreements between MNCs and states include a provision to submit disputes to the ISCSID and it is now the principal forum for resolving such disputes.

In 1988, the **Multilateral Investment Guarantee Agency (MIGA)** was created. Although MIGA's goal are similar to that of its affiliate counterparts—encourage domestic and foreign investment in developing economies—it is not a lending agency. Rather, MIGA insures private investment against loss. Specifically, it insures against losses that result from political risk, such as war, civil strife, or expropriation (Riggs and Plano 1994, 289). Thus, MIGA helps private investors spread the risk of investing in politically and economically unstable areas. The guarantee of investments encourages private investors to take a look at otherwise shaky ventures.

The World Bank's Articles of Agreement commit the bank to economic and political neutrality. The World Bank and its affiliates are supposed to make loan determinations on the basis of sound principles of international finance, not a state's political or economic orientation. According to Article 4(10) of the Articles of Agreement,

> The Bank and its officers shall not interfere in the political affairs of any member; nor shall they be influenced in their decisions by the political character of the member or members concerned. Only economic considerations

shall be relevant to their decision, and these considerations shall be weighed impartially in order to achieve the purposes stated in Article I.

In spite of this commitment to political and economic neutrality, the World Bank has been politicized. It serves the political interests of its donors (Ascher 1990, 115–140). The United States, which is the largest contributor to the World Bank, has used its voting share to block loans to politically undesirable states and reward allies. The Bank engaged in significant lending to repressive regimes in the Philippines, Argentina, and Haiti, enabling these regimes to continue their abusive practices. The Bank is also accused of engaging in destabilizing "nonlending." In Chile, for example, it cut off loans to the newly elected Allende government (Brown 1992; Swedburg 1986). Donor efforts to manipulate the Bank's lending policies have drawn international criticism from both orthodox and critical circles.

The World Bank consists of 184 member states, which are, in essence, shareholders in the bank. It is headed by a Board of Governors, one governor for each member state. The Board of Governors, which meets at least once a year, provides the long-term strategy for the Bank. Decisions are based on a weighted voting system where the weight is roughly proportional to the member's share of Bank contributions (which is based on its share of capital and trade). A Board of Directors runs the day-to-day operations of the Bank. It consists of twenty-four directors, who are elected by the Board of Governors. Each director wields the vote of the country that elects him or her. The Board of Directors elects the president of the World Bank, who represents the Bank politically and provides leadership and direction.

The World Bank is administered by a bureaucracy that often strives to distance itself from political control. Under the leadership of former World Bank president Robert McNamara, the World Bank developed considerable autonomy by creating a complex project review process and by boosting the volume of Bank lending. The project review process emphasizes perfection in project proposals. Proposals are "ultra-sophisticated—large in scale, elaborate in design, and highly technical" (Ascher 1990, 127). The executive directors, through whom donor states exercise direct influence, are basically presented with polished, finished proposals, which they almost always approve. The World Bank staff helps countries prioritize economic plans and prepare project proposals. The staff is able to exert influence by manipulating what goes before the directors. "The very sophistication of the models on which they [the projects] are based limits the opportunities for criticism, especially from the directors, thus promoting the Bank's autonomy" (Ascher 1990, 127).

The World Bank has also been able to increase the volume of its lending through two measures. First, the World Bank has successfully encouraged contributions from other states, including the oil producers. Second, the Bank has successfully raised money through international capital markets. The increase in the volume of Bank lending has diluted the voting share of some of the larger donors. Periodic adjustments in the voting formula are made because of the shifts in contribution levels. World Bank lending is rarely done in isolation. It is part of a vast array of co-sponsored projects and programs. Most of the World Bank's loans are used in conjunction or are coordinated with the regional development banks or UN agencies. The World Bank's principal partner in development assistance is the third pillar of the Bretton Woods system, **the International Monetary Fund (IMF)**. The World Bank and the IMF distribute the lion's share of the available multilateral development assistance.

THE INTERNATIONAL MONETARY FUND (IMF)

The IMF was also created at the 1944 Bretton Woods conference and was charged with providing for a stable international monetary order. To that end, the IMF coordinates international currency exchange, the balance of international payments, and national accounts (Goldstein 1996, 363). Money is a crucial lynchpin to any economy. It facilitates the efficient exchange of goods and services. However, a stable monetary order is difficult to construct and maintain. A stable monetary order rests on three important factors: liquidity, adjustment, and confidence (Gilpin 1987). Liquidity refers to the amount of currency needed to conduct transactions. Adjustment refers to the mechanism through which national accounts are settled. Confidence refers to a widely held subjective belief that the currency is, and will continue to be, worth what the government or traders says it is worth.

Originally, the IMF under the Bretton Woods system provided for a stable monetary order by making the U.S. dollar the key currency, and then tying the dollar to a fixed value of gold. This created a system of "fixed" exchange rates. One ounce of gold was equivalent to $35. The currencies of the world were then fixed to the dollar. Liquidity was provided by U.S. deficit spending at home and abroad. International markets were flooded with U.S. dollars, which were used to exchange currencies. Adjustment in national accounts was done internally by the IMF and the central banks. When states joined the IMF, their central banks deposited with the IMF a certain amount of their currency and a certain amount of gold and dollars. (Today, countries deposit a certain amount of hard currency.) States could then use these reserves or borrow from the IMF to settle their national accounts. Recall that a state's financial position is related in large part to its balance of trade in goods and services and direct foreign investment. The IMF settled the differences in balance-of-payments accounts through changes in hard currency reserves. Confidence was provided by U.S. gold reserves.

The Bretton Woods monetary system was based on the idea of "embedded liberalism." Under embedded liberalism, states have a great deal of autonomy with respect to their currency and national accounts. States were permitted, with IMF approval, to readjust their currency exchange rates to help with long-term balance-of-payments difficulties. States could also borrow money from the IMF to meet their short-term balance-of-payments deficits. In other words, the IMF is the central bank of the world's central banks. The IMF did much to stabilize the international monetary system during the reconstruction of Europe and Japan.

This pillar of the Bretton Woods system collapsed in 1971 when the United States unilaterally delinked the dollar from gold. The U.S. dollar had become extremely overvalued owing to the deficit spending the U.S. government used to finance the Cold War, the Vietnam War, and the Great Society programs. Delinked from gold, the dollar was devalued by more than 10 percent, and then the value of the dollar was determined by the market, creating a system of floating exchange rates. Consequently, the values of the core currencies were exposed to market forces in a "managed float." That is, the values of major currencies are determined by market-driven flexible exchange rates, but governments can intervene to stabilize key currencies experiencing volatility. The IMF now serves as the forum for intergovernmental consultation regarding the management of market-determined exchange rates.

In structure, the IMF is very much like the World Bank having a Board of Governors and a Board of Directors, over which a managing director presides. Voting is weighted, based on each member's quota. It is administered by a professional bureaucracy that scrutinizes loan applications based on conservative lending principles. Since the collapse of the monetary pillar of Bretton Woods, the IMF has become increasingly involved with Third World development and the transition of the former Eastern Bloc and Soviet successor states from command to market economies. The currencies of these countries are exceptionally unstable, and the IMF and World Bank have worked together to create comprehensive aid packages designed to provide immediate stability and to stimulate economic growth and long-term development. In many respects, the IMF has become the **"lender of last resort,"** giving loans to otherwise insolvent governments.

In the late 1980s, the lending practices of the IMF and the World Bank shifted considerably in response to the debt crisis and the chronic instability of economies in the developing world. In the mid-1980s, the debt crisis had become so acute that several of the world's largest debtors—Mexico, Brazil, and Argentina—threatened to default on many of their loans. The "normal" capital flows were reversed, with the South sending more capital to the North. The IMF and World Bank, together with private lending institutions, thus engaged in a series of debt restructuring initiatives (even, in some cases, debt forgiveness) in order to stabilize currencies and economies.

IMF and World Bank loans to developing countries, termed **"structural adjustment loans,"** come with strings attached. They are conditioned on the recipient state's implementing conventional (orthodox) market reforms (Danaher 1994, 3), such as the following:

selling state enterprises to the private sector;
raising producer prices for agricultural goods;
devaluing local currencies to their world market value;
reducing government deficits;
encouraging free trade;
attracting foreign capital.

These reforms, which are designed to introduce market forces into the economies of developing states, reflect the orthodox view of development. The orthodox view of development parallels liberalism as a worldview in that both see the market as the solution to underdevelopment while ascribing to state intervention and protectionism a causal or exacerbatory role in underdevelopment. Given that trade, development, and currency stability are intertwined, market reforms become essential. Unless these market reforms are made, the IMF and World Bank are, in the orthodox view, "just throwing good money after bad." However, structural adjustment loans, and their attendant strings, are controversial because they drastically reduce the role of the government in managing or regulating the economy.

THE UN CONFERENCE ON TRADE AND DEVELOPMENT (UNCTAD)

Critical responses to orthodox approaches have found a voice in UNCTAD. Created in 1964 by a General Assembly resolution, UNCTAD serves under the auspices of the ECOSOC. UNCTAD emerged as a forum for developing states dissatisfied with their terms of trade, their growing poverty, and Western restrictions on commodities. Ironically, the first UNCTAD was organized by seventy-seven less-developed nations, known as the Group of 77 or G-77, to pressure the developed countries into further trade liberalization, particularly with respect to commodities and agricultural exports. Led by Raul Prebisch, the former head of the Economic Commission on Latin America (ECLA), UNCTAD 1 (the first plenary meeting) argued that reducing tariffs on manufactured products served the interests of the North while ignoring those of the South, because developing states' exports (raw materials and commodities) remained subject to steep tariffs. Furthermore, the prices of commodity products were very unstable, and any sustained growth in the South would require stable commodity prices. UNCTAD pointed out that the international division of labor relegated the developing states to the relatively unprofitable production of raw materials. As a result, wealth flowed from the South to the North. To counter the net flow of capital to the North, UNCTAD called on the developed states to transfer at least 1 percent of their GNP to developing countries in the form of multilateral development assistance.

The demands of developing states fell largely on deaf ears. The developed countries, especially the G-7, were strongly opposed to any measures that involved the authoritative, rather than the market, distribution of resources (Krasner 1985). But the Group of 77, a title that now refers to more than 125 developing countries, was able to institutionalize UNCTAD by making it a permanent UN body that reports directly to the General Assembly. The G-77 exercised its majority in the General Assembly to give UNCTAD a larger voice in international trade issues. Located in Geneva, Switzerland, UNCTAD is served by a small Secretariat. The Trade and Development Board meets annually to address the issues of developing states in global trade. UNCTAD is funded through the voluntary contributions of member states, and all members of the UN may belong to UNCTAD. Needless to say, contributions from developed nations have been quite small.

UNCTAD holds plenary meetings every four years. The early meetings reemphasized the developing world's view that their position in the international division of labor, a position that was coerced and imposed by the North, is the cause of their underdevelopment. In the 1970s, the conflict between North and South manifested itself in an effort on the part of Third World states to establish a **"new international economic order" (NIEO)**. Third World states sought to authoritatively raise the prices of raw materials and agricultural products. Emboldened by the success of OPEC, many Third World countries attempted to form commodity cartels to "artificially" raise the price of commodities on open markets. These efforts met with little success because most commodities, unlike oil, have a large number of producers and are easily substituted or stockpiled. Agreements among producers are difficult to reach, making the commodity vulnerable to "cartel-busting" strategies.

The NIEO called for Third World states to have more say in the IMF and the World Bank, asking, for example, that they be granted additional **Special Drawing Rights (SDRs)**. SDRs, which the IMF created after the United States delinked the dollar from gold, resemble a world currency; they are based on the average of all the major currencies to replace the dollar-gold standard. Special access to SDRs would permit developing states to correct for trade imbalances and balance-of-payments difficulties without having to induce a recession through austerity measures. Developing states did not want to rely on the IMF's weighted voting system, which the developed states controlled, in order to get stabilization loans. In 1974, the G-77 successfully used its majority in the General Assembly to pass the Charter of Economic Rights and Duties of States (UNGA Resolution 3281), which called for equal participation in international financial institutions and a more equitable distribution of wealth. The NIEO also called for a Generalized System of Preferences (GSP) whereby developing states could export to other developing states duty-free. This amounted to developed states' granting most-favored-nation status to developing states without requiring the usual norm of reciprocity. This strategy would allow developing states to improve their balance of trade without threatening fledging industries.

UNCTAD's influence in shaping development issues waned a great deal with the collapse of the Soviet Union. The end of the Cold War and the transition of the former Eastern Bloc and Soviet successor states into market democracies meant the end of an ideological alternative to capitalism. During the Cold War, developing states were in a better bargaining position because they could play West against East. The United States and its allies were generous with military and development assistance as part of their joint efforts to contain communism in the Third World. Absent the communist threat, the developed world has little reason to listen to the concerns of the developing world. Furthermore, the transition of the former communist states means that more states are seeking a slice of the global development pie. Given finite resources and lacking a viable economic alternative, developing states are forced to play by the rules created by the advanced industrialized states.

UNCTAD maintains that developing states are caught in a perpetual cycle of poverty and underdevelopment because of their disadvantaged position in the international division of labor. Their export income is derived from low-profit primary products, rendering them vulnerable to economic expansions and contractions in the global economy. Global economic recession induced by the U.S. recession in the 1980s hit developing states extremely hard, deepening their already serious debt. During the 1980s and early 1990s, the UN shifted its focus from development activities to relief as violent conflict and economic collapse led to large humanitarian crises. Cracks began to appear within the developing world as their economic situations continued to worsen. Some states sought reconciliation with the North, while others advocated "delinking" from the international economy. UNCTAD was also politically opposed by the developed states as they cut their voluntary contributions to UNCTAD, opting to fund the UNDP instead.

UNCTAD has taken a less confrontational approach to promoting development but still tends to blame the North for malnutrition, underdevelopment, and poverty in the South. UNCTAD 9 (1996), which was held in Midrand, South Africa, placed special emphasis on poverty as the principal threat to international stability. In the opening address, the then South African president Nelson Mandela stated that "Without relief of the poverty which pervades much of the world, our democracy and human rights will for many be a formality, and always in jeopardy" (UNCTAD 9, 1996). The tone of UNCTAD 9 was more conciliatory, calling for "greater international cooperation" in addressing globalization and marginalization. UNCTAD 10 (2000) held in Bangkok, Thailand, addressed the issue of social justice in a globalized world. UNCTAD sought to expand the discussion of globalization beyond the unification of markets to the idea of shared knowledge for security and development. Most members of UNCTAD, however, remained pessimistic about the prospects for alleviating poverty in the developing world under the existing world system.

UNCTAD 11 (2004) and 12 (2008), in Sao Paulo, Brazil, and Accra, Ghana, respectively, focused on the opportunities and challenges presented by globalization to the development agendas of member states. The theme of these conferences was to provide coherence for national development policies with the processes of globalization. UNCTAD's efforts at the end of 2008 addressed the deteriorating condition of many developing states in the face of the worldwide financial crisis. UNCTAD called for more regulation of global financial markets and highlighted that developing countries would suffer even greater harm if the world fell into a recession. As the global economy contracts, overseas development assistance (ODA) from wealthy states tends to decline and earnings from exports fall.

THE UN DEVELOPMENT PROGRAM (UNDP)

The UNDP was created in 1965, when the General Assembly merged two UN development programs: the Expanded Program of Technical Assistance (EPTA) and the Special United Nations Fund for Economic Development (SUNFED). UNDP is funded through voluntary contributions of members. It coordinates development projects with other UN specialized agencies and the World Bank and the IMF. UNDP emphasizes technology transfers and aids developing states with technical development assistance. UNDP operations are more palatable to the developed states because they do not stray far from the orthodox view of development and liberal approaches to achieving economic growth. Yet, even the UNDP has criticized orthodox development efforts, especially structural adjustment loans.

UNDP coordinates projects with the UN Children's Fund (UNICEF), the World Food Program (WFP), the World Health Organization (WHO), and many NGOs such as World Vision and Oxfam. These groups are "on the ground" and thus are witnesses to the human suffering and the social consequences of structural adjustment. The UN development bureaucracy advocates a bottom-up approach to development rather than a top-down approach. In this sense, they lean toward the more critical view of development: They see development as the ability to meet basic human needs—clean water, good sanitation, and adequate housing and foodstuffs—rather than a simple increase in a nation's GDP per capita. A local, bottom-up approach to development improves the lives of more people than do the macrolending policies of the IMF or the World Bank.

The idea that development means not just economic development but also "human" development is promoted by the UNDP. Beginning in 1990, the UNDP launched the *Human Development Report (HDR)* with the purpose of putting people first in the development process. In these annual reports, UNDP links development to human security by exploring different dimension and perspectives. For example, in 1998 the HDR examined global consumption patterns which showed how maldistributed goods and services are. In 2008, the HDR focused on the challenges and threat of global warming to development and human security. This report complements its 1994 report analyzing the requisites of "sustainable development," a concept discussed in the next chapter. In 2009, the relationship between human migration and human development was explored and in 2010 the HDR celebrated 20 years of presenting useful and provocative views of development.

The orthodox and critical views of development correspond with the theories used in this text. Liberals adhere to orthodox views regarding development and hence advocate market-oriented prescriptions. Realists tend to see development in an orthodox light, but oppose liberal prescriptions, particularly those that remove the state from key sectors of the economy or if market forces threaten the security of the state. Orthodox approaches can undermine state power and that is unacceptable for many nationalists in the developing world.

Developing states have fought brutal nationalist wars against colonial powers and have experienced great-power intervention. Third World states are wary of political, economic, and social initiatives that impinge on their sovereign prerogatives. Hence, many developing countries combine realism with Marxist views of exploitation. Many developing countries see liberal strategies as protecting the rich at the expense of the poor. Liberal approaches tend to blame the state or individuals and do not consider the global context and the international division of labor that fosters underdevelopment. Marxists argue that absent a change in the capitalist mode of production, developing states should shield themselves from market forces as periodic crises in markets cause global instability. Governments should promote domestic industries and grassroots efforts to allow people to help themselves. Most feminists, save for liberal feminists, also have a critical view of development because orthodox views ignore the differential impacts of economic development programs on women. The constructivist approach allows us to understand how the idea of "development" has changed over time and how international organizations have helped define states' developmental interests. In the next case study of the financial crises of the 1990s, we intertwine the orthodox and critical views of development with the analyses generated by realism, liberalism, Marxism, feminism, and constructivism in order to understand the origins of the crises and to evaluate international efforts to manage the crises.

CASE STUDY 5: FINANCIAL CRISES OF THE NINETIES

During the 1990s, the international community witnessed a series of financial crises across the developing world which devastated the lives of hundreds of millions of people. The first crisis occurred in Mexico in 1994, and the contagion spread to neighboring countries in 1995. In 1997, the Asian crisis wreaked havoc on Thailand, South Korea, and Indonesia. Russia and Brazil followed in 1998, Equator in 1999, and Argentina in 2000. The crises were particularly dire for Mexico and Indonesia, and their experiences serve as the foundation of the case study.

Mexico

On December 19, 1994, the Mexican government unilaterally devalued the Mexican peso. The Mexican government argued that the peso, which was pegged to the U.S. dollar at a fixed exchange rate, was overvalued, stifling economic growth. Mexico's exports had become more expensive in foreign markets, while foreign imports remained quite affordable in Mexican markets. The trade deficit, particularly with the United States, was undermining domestic expansion. But when the Mexican government devalued the peso by 20 percent to curb excessive imports, it did so without consulting either business or labor (Lustig 1995, 46).

The peso devaluation caused a panic in Mexican financial sectors as skittish foreign investors abruptly withdrew from Mexican markets. The run on Mexico's foreign currency reserves forced the government to allow the peso to float freely against the dollar. The peso float had the unfortunate consequence of spurring speculation, causing an additional decline in the peso's value and the loss of $8 billion in foreign currency (Ramirez 1996, 129). The panic then spread to neighboring markets in Latin America. While these markets and their currencies were not particularly overvalued, foreign investors retreated to traditionally safer markets. The value of the U.S. dollar also declined dramatically against other hard currencies.

To keep the Mexican government from going bankrupt, the United States, Japan, and Europe, together with the IMF and the World Bank, put together a $50 billion stabilization package. And, in accordance with past practice, that stabilization package came with strings attached. First, the United States, which contributed $20 billion to the recovery effort, insisted on almost immediate repayment. The U.S. Congress was reluctant to bail out Mexico, so President Clinton was forced to dip into Federal Reserve funds normally used to protect the dollar against speculative runs. The United States demanded that revenues from PEMEX, Mexico's state-owned oil company, be directly deposited into the Federal Reserve. PEMEX is one of the largest earners of foreign currency for Mexico.

The IMF also required the usual structural adjustments. According to Ramirez (1996), the IMF package involved austerity measures that included a 10 percent cut in all government expenditures, an immediate 35 percent increase in petroleum prices, an immediate 20 percent increase in electricity prices, a value-added tax of 10–15 percent, and a sharp reduction on the availability of money and credit. The IMF claimed that these measures would reduce Mexican consumption and increase savings, which in turn would restore investor confidence in the Mexican market. The total stabilization package induced an economic recession for about a year, after which economic growth rebounded (*The Economist* 1998a, 8).

Indonesia

Indonesia has a population of 212 million people, making it the fourth most populous country in the world. It is a sprawling archipelago consisting of 13,500 islands, and its main industries are oil, gas, and tropical timber. It is considered one of the more dynamic and promising economies in Southeast Asia and has experienced impressive economic growth in the past thirty years. Dubbed as the "Asian tiger" and as "the East Asian miracle," Indonesia served as a model of economic development. However, in 1997, the value of many of the key Southeast Asian currencies fell to record lows. Beginning with the devaluation of the Thai baht, the Indonesian rupiah also fell in value. In order to prop up the rupiah, Indonesia borrowed $33 billion in short-term foreign loans and closed sixteen insolvent banks. In July 1997, Thailand requested IMF assistance to help arrest the fall of its currency and meet its balance-of-payments responsibilities. As the Thai baht began to lose its value, investors in all the major Southeast Asian economies began selling their assets, causing the currencies to fall even further. Instead of borrowing more money to keep the rupiah at its fixed rate, Indonesia let the rupiah float. The rupiah fell a dramatic 70 percent (*BBC News* 1999).

In January 1998, the United States and the IMF launched a joint aid package of $43 billion for Indonesia. The United States and the IMF hoped to stave off a regional crisis like the one that affected much of Latin America after the fall of the Mexican peso. Indonesian President Suharto, who had been in power for over thirty years, agreed to the IMF conditions on economic reform. This involved tax reforms, restructuring of the banking system through recapitalization, loan collection, anticorruption legislation, removal of price controls, government deficit reduction, and the privatization of state-owned businesses. In March 1998, President Suharto was elected (through his usual dubious means) to his seventh five-year term as president. Violent antigovernment protests erupted as price increases went into effect as part of Indonesia's agreement with the IMF to remove price controls and subsidies. Protesters and political opponents of Suharto called for his resignation, and violence broke out on the streets of Jakarta, Indonesia's capital. In May 1998, Suharto resigned and was replaced by Vice President Habibie. Habibie pledged to hold elections in 1999; however, the violent protests continued.

In June 1999, Indonesia held its first free election in forty-four years, and Megawati Sukarnoputri's party won a plurality vote (the most votes but not a majority) in parliament. As in most parliamentary systems, the legislature is responsible for electing the executive, which means if no party gets a majority of the seats in the parliament, then a coalition must be formed in order for the president (also called prime minister in some countries) to be elected. Sukarnoputri is the daughter of former president Sakarno, who was unceremoniously removed from office (with the blessing of the United States) in 1965. At the same time, the crisis in East Timor, a decades-old ethnic conflict on one of Indonesia's 13,500 islands, came to a peak as East Timor sought its independence. The simmering East Timor conflict has claimed more than 100,000 lives over the years, and the economic crisis provided the East Timorese separatists with the opportunity to secede. Furthermore, the islands of Java, Bali, and Sumatra were also experiencing separatist unrest. By September 1999, it appeared that Indonesia might disintegrate as a political unit.

In a surprise move, the Indonesian Parliament elected Adurrahman Wahid over Sukarnoputri in October of 1999. Hailed as "a champion of tolerance, inclusion and self-respect," Wahid began to implement the reforms required by the IMF, albeit in a slow and ad hoc manner (Bresnan 2000). The reforms were met with opposition by Indonesian elites as well as by mass protests. The domestic economic situation failed to improve, and the Indonesian government began to balk at further reforms, fearing more unrest (*Xinhua News Agency* 2000). The IMF withheld installments of the $43 billion package until it could gain compliance from Indonesia (*United Press International* 2001). By 2001, Wahid's popularity began to drop, and the pace of reforms slowed to a halt. This set the stage for a political crisis that would lead to the eventual impeachment of Wahid and the election of Sukarnoputri during the summer of 2001. After the election of Sukarnoputri, the IMF released a $400 million installment.

What factors precipitated the Mexican and Indonesian financial crises? Did international organizations help or hurt these situations? Who stands to benefit and who stands to lose from World Bank and IMF intervention? Whose interests did these organizations serve? Realist, liberal, Marxist, and feminist theory generate different answers to these questions, highlighting different development issues and dynamics. The constructivist approach illustrates how these organizations engaged in monetary norm diffusion and how the organizations adapted to new and challenging financial crises.

A Realist Cut

The variants of realism differ slightly regarding the wisdom of the Mexican bailout. Traditional realists see the Mexican peso crisis as a classic example of why the market should ultimately serve the state and why interdependence is not necessarily a good thing for sovereign states. In 1994, just a year before the peso crisis, the United States, Canada, and Mexico formed the North American Free Trade Agreement (NAFTA), which created a common market among the three members, reducing many remaining tariffs and other barriers to trade. The ultimate goal of NAFTA is to establish a free trade area covering the entire Western Hemisphere. Many nationalists in the United States, Canada, and Mexico adamantly oppose NAFTA because the agreement reduces state autonomy, erodes national borders, and undermines national industries. Furthermore, NAFTA makes it easier to transmit economic and political ills from one member to another. The peso crisis illustrates this point. The peso crisis weakened both the Canadian and the U.S. dollars. The United States had no choice but to bail out its ailing neighbor because U.S. leaders had unwisely tied its fate to an economically and politically unstable Mexico.

Neorealists see expanding markets as a potential source of wealth and power, but insist that states cannot be ruled by them. Markets and individuals do not necessarily behave rationally; rather, markets and investors often react on the basis of rumor and unwarranted panic. Most observers see the peso crisis in just such a light (Roett 1997; Wiarda 1995). It was this kind of behavior—an irrational response—that nearly brought down the Mexican state and threatened the U.S. economy. The market must serve the interests of the state, not the other way around. States must be concerned about the long-term health of the country, not the immediate short-term interests of skittish foreign investors that want governments to subsidize their risks.

A realist analysis of Mexico's position criticizes the liberal choices made by the Mexican government over the years (Vasquez 1997). Mexico's economic woes are the result of its attempts to follow a liberal model of economic development. This model fosters asymmetrical interdependence relationships with the United States, giving the United States undue influence over Mexican affairs. The peso crisis is just another phase in the long history of Mexican chronic instability, which is caused by its proximity to the United States and its effort to develop along the same path.

The peso crisis is directly related to the debt crisis that traps Mexico in a vicious cycle of interest payments on loans so large that repayment is inconceivable. According to the IMF and the World Bank, Mexico must increase its exports in order to earn foreign currency, which it needs to pay its external debt. However, much of Mexico's external debt is the direct result of U.S. political choices in the Middle East in 1973. The IMF and the World Bank perpetuate the cycle of dependence by providing structural adjustment loans. Yet, structural adjustments have not been proven to provide long-term economic stability and growth (Kudlow 1994, 46). The United States used Mexico's debt and the peso crisis to secure access to Mexican oil and Mexican markets through the IMF. The IMF imposes unfair costs on the Mexican people. According to Mexico's nationalist *Excelsior*, "The reduction of public spending and the financial and monetary contraction will eventually lead to a collapse of the productive sector, which will accelerate the already alarming levels of unemployment . . . The adjustments . . . push the nation to the brink of social tolerance" (U.S. Information Agency 1995b, 2). The pain of structural adjustment should be borne by American investors and not the Mexican people.

Realists also criticize the choices made by the U.S. government. The U.S. government's decision to liberalize the financial sector and deregulate U.S. banking has put the entire American financial system in peril. The lending practices of banks were such that many banks made loans for which they never expected repayment (Isaak 1995, 185). Knowing that states do not go out of business, banks figured they could lend money without risk and were quite loose with their financing. Gambling on sovereign borrowing, they thought they could not lose because they would continue to earn interest over an indefinite loan period, making money even if they lost the principal.

Mexico was clearly taking advantage of this situation. Following the advice of the Cambridge School of Economics, Mexico borrowed as much money as the West would lend (Isaak 1995, 186). The Cambridge advisors, who were of a leftist bent, argued that Mexico could increase its leverage with the United States if it became heavily indebted to U.S. banks. "As economist John Maynard Keynes observed, if you owe your bank a hundred pounds, you have a problem; but if you owe your bank a million pounds, the bank has a problem" (Isaak 1995, 186). The devaluation of the peso and the resulting peso crisis forced the United States to bail out Mexico because it would have caused the financial collapse of several U.S. banking and investment institutions. The U.S. government and the IMF are indirectly insuring U.S. investment in Mexico by enabling investors to make speculative ventures with very little risk.

Indonesia.   The story of Indonesia, on the other hand, illustrates the primacy of politics over abstract economic principles. The spectacular growth experienced by Indonesia was the result of state policies that promoted key industries and enhanced the strategic significance of the expansive archipelago. The United States has been integrally involved in Indonesia since the 1965 violent overthrow of President Sukarno, a communist-nationalist. The U.S. war in Vietnam, as well as other conflicts in Southeast Asia, made Indonesia central to Cold War Southeast Asian politics. After the *coup* against Sukarno, his replacement, President Suharto (by most accounts an authoritarian dictator), developed key national industries (oil and gas) using the foreign assistance provided by the West. The Western powers wanted to create a bulwark against communism in this troubled area. The resulting economic growth led to increased foreign direct investment which spurred the industrialization and urbanization. The Suharto government provided an attractive environment for foreign investment—a growing consumer market, tax incentives, and liberal banking policies. More important, labor unrest was easily quelled by the repressive arm of the Suharto dictatorship. The state made Indonesia an "Asian tiger," not an unrestrained market. It successfully parlayed its strategic geographic position and its natural resources to become a dominant power in the region. It harnessed market forces to serve and enrich the state, all with the blessing of the IMF and the United States. The Cold War significance of Indonesia cannot be underestimated. Billions of development assistance dollars poured into Indonesia because the Western powers saw Indonesia as the key to stability in Southeast Asia even after the disastrous policies of the 1970s. Using their voting power within the IMF and the World Bank, the West endowed Indonesia with the financial resources to establish industries that favored the economic development and the oil interests of the industrialized countries.

The Southeast Asian crisis did not originate in Indonesia, but in Thailand. The Indonesian government made a fundamental mistake when responding to the shockwaves. Indonesia did not impose capital controls when investors began selling their Indonesian assets. It was the free flow of capital (money in search of a good return) that sank the Indonesian economy (Kristof 1998, 6). Investors pulled their money out of Indonesia for no good reason other than that they panicked. India and Malaysia imposed strict capital controls and were able to ride out the economic storm. By preventing investors from getting out, the panic subsided and capital stayed invested in their economies. UNCTAD has backed the right of countries to adopt emergency capital controls to prevent panic selling; however, the IMF was opposed. Regardless of what external agencies say, governments must take matters into their own hands to prevent economic crisis. The IMF's remedy of floating exchange rights only made the situation worse. The austerity programs angered the population and eventually forced Suharto from office. According to former IMF director Michel Camdessus, "We created the conditions that obliged President Suharto to leave his job" (Hanke 2000, 84). The IMF created considerable human suffering in the course of trying to accomplish a political goal (Hanke 2000, 84).

A Liberal Cut

The extreme libertarian position on the IMF/World Bank bailout of the Mexican peso mirrors the realist position, except that libertarians object on economic rather than political grounds. The IMF and the World Bank are interventionists in the market. IMF/World Bank bailouts underwrite investors and bond holders. The IMF is not a defender of free markets. Rather, it socializes personal investment risks (Hawke 1995, 110). The IMF/World Bank packages disrupt the relationship between reward and risk and hence encourage foolish investment. The market should determine which businesses and banks succeed and fail. Instead, Third World bureaucrats mismanage the economy by creating an artificial financial environment to attract foreign investments (Herbener 1995). If multinational banks and investment firms make bad decisions, they should pay the consequences, as should their individual shareholders—the ones who raked in big double-digit returns in the first place.

A less extreme liberal position sees the IMF and the World Bank as instrumental in averting economic crises. The peso crisis posed significant risks to the world financial system because it threatened the stability of the dollar and emerging markets. According to the *Excelsior*, "The anticipated credit will deactivate a dangerous if not major time bomb: It will prevent Mexico from declaring a debt moratorium, which could have sparked a great global financial crisis, in which the first to drop dead of bankruptcy would be the emerging markets" (U.S. Information Agency 1995b, 2). The IMF should not bail out every country that mismanages its economy (*The Economist* 1995b). However, as the lender of last resort, it can stabilize economies and encourage market reforms. The IMF and the World Bank can help monitor capital flows in emerging markets and improve on early warning.

In 1993, IMF officials told Mexico that the peso was overvalued and was creating a trade imbalance large enough to threaten long-term economic health (Kudlow 1994). But the Mexican government did not want to raise interest rates (to induce savings) or devalue the peso, as both would be politically unpopular at home: Mexican businesses would find it difficult to afford loans, and Mexican citizens would find foreign goods suddenly out of reach. Political considerations outweighed sound economic policies. Poor political choices ultimately undermined economic confidence in an economy with a lot of promise. Structural adjustment was necessary to put the economy back on track. The IMF and World Bank loans also prevented contagion, or the so-called tequila effect. During the initial stages of the peso crises, other Latin American markets also experienced investor panic. The aid packages went a long way toward providing investor confidence and controlling the panic spillover into other emerging markets. The IMF and the World Bank promote interstate cooperation to help societies manage the ill effects of interdependence.

Recall that liberal institutionalists argue that international organizations help states overcome collective action problems. Through the creation of international regimes, economic growth and prosperity in an anarchic world can be achieved. The growth in global finance has been made possible only through concerted efforts of states, facilitated by their respective central banks and the IMF (Kapstein 1996). This global finance regime gives states the central responsibility for the supervision of banks, which enables governments to manage financial crises like the Mexican peso crisis. Former president Bill Clinton has commended the G-7 (the seven wealthiest nations) and the IMF for their instrumental role in addressing the Mexican crisis. The advanced industrialized countries agreed at the 1995 Halifax conference to establish an early warning system that called for early and full disclosure of monetary and financial information, and for tougher reporting standards. This will allow markets to "react more quickly and nations will be pressed to implement sound policies in a timely manner" (U.S. Department of State Dispatch 1995, 4). This cooperation would not be possible without the institutional cooperation and independence of the central banks and the IMF.

Finally, liberals defend NAFTA, arguing that the peso crisis occurred in spite of, not because of, NAFTA. NAFTA, they claim, levels the playing field. Tariffs between the United States and Mexico were at an all-time low when NAFTA was finally approved. The NAFTA agreement simply recognizes and regularizes the market that already exists between Mexico, the United States, and Canada. Had NAFTA been defeated in 1993, the peso would have collapsed, whereupon immigration to the United States would have increased dramatically (Wright 1995). NAFTA helped defuse the peso crisis because it ensured an engaged United States with an interest in its third-largest export market. NAFTA and the IMF offer the best defense against the crony capitalism that leads to political corruption of the market.

Indonesia shows that state-led economic growth is unsustainable in the long run and contributes to crony capitalism. Unless market forces are eventually allowed to discipline key sectors of the economy and force efficiency, industries will be unable to compete in the global market. The so-called "third way" between capitalism and socialism involved government planning and the formulation of industrial policy. Government officials would use tax, credit, and trade policies to encourage industrial development in key sectors, to ensure a greater equality of income distribution, and make investments in education and research and development. This strong state role in the market created the illusion of prosperity in Asia, but in fact has led to corruption and economic collapse.

Many neoclassical liberals argued that the IMF should not soften the blow to the Asian economies or for foreign investors (Bartlett et al. 1998). According to these liberals, the IMF created a "moral hazard." Investors poured money into overinvested industries and Western bankers made hundreds of billions of dollars in risky loans with the knowledge that they would be bailed out if things got tough. "In this case, the pattern of rushing in emergency aid to soften economic crises actually encouraged the making of bad loans that helped set up the crisis" (Bartlett et al. 1998, 64). The IMF should let the market discipline participants rather than mete out the discipline themselves through structural adjustment loans. The IMF is useful if it stays within its narrow mandate, promotes the flexible exchange rates, and helps with short-term balance-of-payments difficulties. (Blinder 1999). The IMF intervention should not be so dramatic as to interfere with the internal workings of the market. IMF interventionist policies have "privatized profits and socialized losses" (Longman and Ahmad 1998, 37).

Liberal institutionalists argue that the IMF was the only institution that could help avert an economic crisis that affects the lives of billions of people. The IMF can restore investor confidence and economic growth even if the by-product is that some creditors will be protected from the full consequences of their poor economic choices (Longman and Ahmad 1998). The IMF, the World Bank, and NGOs can help promote sustainable development by promoting better governance in the developing world. Good governance involves political accountability, freedom of association and participation, a sound judicial system, bureaucratic accountability, and market reforms (Landell-Mills and Serageldin 1991). International organizations can provide incentives and technical knowledge that foster pluralism.

Liberal institutionalists acknowledge that structural adjustment is painful, but necessary. The reason the economic crisis in Indonesia deepened after IMF intervention is that reforms were inadequately implemented (Mussa and Hacche 1998). The IMF has helped reform monetary and fiscal policy and put the Asian economies back on track. The IMF and World Bank have also recognized that Indonesia and the other Asian countries were not solely at fault. The nature of the system itself is prone to panic and speculation, and the IMF and World Bank can help smooth out the sharp edges. The IMF and World Bank, through their policy-based loans, are the best mechanisms for handling economic crises and instituting market-based reforms. They also help governments make good economic choices. Austerity programs are necessary for societies that have been living well beyond their means.

A Marxist Cut

Marxists understand the Mexican peso crisis through class analyses. Traditional Marxists see the peso crisis as the result of the chronic instability of capitalism and residual colonialism. The wealthy business class seeks to pass the cost of instability onto the working class through the coercion of the state and international organizations. The IMF and World Bank are agents of capitalism, although Marxists differ as to whose specific interests they serve. Those that take a state-centric approach see the World Bank and the IMF as agents of the core states, which exploit the resources and the labor of the periphery and the semiperiphery. The debt crisis of the 1980s was largely the result of money being foisted upon periphery/semiperiphery states by core banks with the approval of core countries (see, e.g., Gilpin 1987, 323). Yet, the creditor nations, which are the largest shareholders in the IMF and the World Bank, would not accept any responsibility for the debt crisis and insisted on full repayment (Kahler 1985; *The Economist* 1991).

The creditor nations and the IMF have decided to take a case-by-case approach to debt relief rather than a comprehensive approach. This strategy has allowed the debt crisis to fester, allowing otherwise insolvent banks to continue to exploit developing countries. The IMF and the World Bank, which are supposed to be politically and economically neutral, make it a condition of their financial support that debtors should continue to service their bank debt. This strengthens the bargaining position of core banks: "The IMF and the Bank, it seems, used both their muscle and their money to rescue banks from embarrassment; living standards and the prospects for growth in the debtor countries appeared to rank low among their priorities. This interpretation undoubtedly exaggerates the institutions' freedom to act. But it has a disturbing core of truth—as many insiders would privately admit" (*The Economist* 1991, S23).

It is not surprising, then, that the IMF would bail out private investors from the United States when the peso crashed. The United States used its influence in the IMF to ensure that the investments of U.S. capitalists were protected at the expense of taxpayers, the bulk of whom are of the working class. According to India's *Telegraph*, "The peso rescue package . . . exposed Mexico to the most criminal neo-colonial plunder by U.S. business. . . . The dictates of the new world order and the IMF–World Bank–WTO are pauperizing the masses more and more" (U.S. Information Agency 1995b, 8).

Traditional Marxist analyses highlight the effects of IMF and World Bank conditionality on the working class. The structural adjustment programs produce a very grim reality for most Mexicans—reduced wages, reduced social services, increased energy prices, and higher prices for consumer goods (Heredia and Purcell 1996, 274). Most Mexicans have their wages and savings in pesos, while their elites maintain their fortunes in hard currencies safely deposited and insured in multinational banks. The austerity programs implemented in the 1980s for debt relief did not help the Mexican economy. While these programs were in effect, the standard of living of most Mexicans fell, and the disparity between rich and poor widened. "Since 1982, privatization and deregulation have contributed to a steep concentration of income and wealth. In what analysts term a 'trickle up' process, there has been in Mexico a massive transfer of resources from the salaried population to the owners of capital and from public to (a few) private hands" (Heredia and Purcell 1996, 282–283). Poverty and underdevelopment simply have not diminished, even with government cutbacks, NAFTA, and increased privatization. Poverty has actually worsened, and social justice remains nonexistent. The working and the middle classes have borne the brunt of structural adjustment and will pay the costs of the peso crisis. "The international rules of the game give labor and capital asymmetrical treatment. Whereas capital can always find a safe-haven country, labor cannot freely enter other countries" (Lustig 1995, 85).

The peso crisis served to further impoverish Mexican workers. Their wages bought only a fraction of what they used to buy. On the other hand, Mexican-based exporters and the owners of maquiladoras benefited because of reduced wages and increased exports to the United States (Koechlin 1995). With fewer jobs and higher interest rates, workers in Mexico had difficulties meeting their basic human needs. A Chase-Manhattan memo expressed concern that President Zedillo might respond to mass demonstrations by "yielding to worker demands which [would] further aggravate the economic situation" (cited in Cockburn and Silverstein 1995, 66). Chase-Manhattan was interested in stability and investor confidence, which meant that the interests of workers had to be suppressed. The use of wage repression policies as an international debt mechanism is a common feature of structural adjustment and contributes significantly to worker poverty (Adelman and Taylor 1989).

U.S. workers also bore the costs of the Mexican bailout. U.S. taxpayers subsidized the peso and Mexican debt, bailing out the Wall Street speculators who had far more money and resources. The U.S. government and the IMF did not criticize capitalists for their risky investments. Instead, investment houses were rescued by the people who can least afford it. And while the workers were saving capitalists from their own "risks," U.S. corporations increased investments in Mexico. After the devaluation of the peso, the United States maintained a trade deficit with Mexico, largely because U.S. multinationals were displacing U.S. exports. The result was a net loss of jobs for the United States.

The IMF and World Bank bailout of the Mexican peso benefited foreign investors who stood to lose fortunes. The U.S. government and the IMF had to bail out investors because transnational capital interests have successfully tied their fates to that of the subordinate classes, particularly in the West. If the big multinational banks like Chase-Manhattan go under, it could bring down the entire U.S. financial system. Millions of people would lose their investments, and the global economy would likely collapse. Yet, the collapse of the global economy would be largely insignificant for billions of people. Their daily, marginalized lives of poverty and subsistence will continue whether the stock prices of multinational corporations rise or fall. Regarding the lessons of the peso crisis, India's *Telegraph* opined, "Western observers and their agents in India are trying hard to propagate the virtues of liberalization, globalization, and market system under the hegemony of international imperialist capital . . . The realization of progress for the masses and the country demands a total break with the IMF–World Bank–WTO regimes and the MNCs and the FIIs" (U.S. Information Agency 1995b, 8).

With Indonesia, Marxists agreed with neoclassical liberals in that bailout of Indonesia by the IMF amounts to "socialism for the rich" (Longman and Ahmad 1998, 37). They only differed in explaining why the wealthy benefit. Neoclassical liberals believe that the market is naturally unbiased and only becomes distorted by politics, whereas, for Marxists, the market is inherently biased and political and favors the interests of the dominant class. IMF bailouts are just another example of how the working class subsidizes the global bourgeoisie. Like the Mexican peso crisis, it is the working-class people in both the advanced industrialized and the developing countries that end up paying the bills, as it is through their income and payroll taxes that their governments either contribute funds to or pay back the IMF. President Suharto and his family were not the only ones who were enriched through the kleptocratic period. Economic policies favored the former Dutch colonial administrators, Dutch MNCs, as well as their neo-imperialist successors, U.S. MNCs.

The IMF has also "strongly encouraged" Indonesia to attract foreign direct investment and to privatize government-owned industries. This amounts to allowing the same foreign banks and MNCs that made the initial bad investments to buy up lucrative sectors of the economy. This pattern has been seen in Mexico, South Korea, and Thailand (*Multinational Monitor* 1998). The banks and investment firms in Japan, Europe, and the United

States are bailed out because the loans the IMF makes to developing countries in crisis are used to pay these foreign creditors. With the structural adjustment loans to liberalize the economy, these same creditors are then presented with a buying opportunity, snapping up assets at bargain-basement prices (*Multinational Monitor* 2000). These privatized factories and service operations have had their labor forces dramatically slashed, and labor laws are "reformed" to give the new owners power to fire workers and hire them back at dramatically lower wages. Workers see their incomes slashed, while austerity leads to rising food and fuel prices. Labor in Indonesia has been unable to organize because their original leadership was eradicated during the 1965 civil war, during which more than 1 million people were killed in anticommunist purges. Suharto's secret police "managed" any additional labor threats. As a result, the voice of labor was muted during the most recent crisis, and the political and social instability claimed the lives of thousands of people (Kansas 1998). And in a dialectic twist, the IMF policies that are designed to save capitalism have stoked Islamic fundamentalism and ethnic conflict, which could mean capitalism's demise in Indonesia.

Indonesia also did not implement the one policy that could perhaps have eased its crisis—capital controls. Both Suharto and Wahid considered various forms of capital control, but the plans were rejected by the IMF. The IMF, and its doctrinaire position favoring the unfettered flow, pressured Indonesia to abandon capital control efforts. According to IMF managing director Horst Koehler, "the introduction of capital control would hinder a sustained and a broad economic recovery. What is needed to strengthen confidence in the rupiah, that is quite clear, is a steady and feasible implementation of the economic program" (*Xinhua News Agency* June 5, 2000). The costs of implementing this economic program are paid for by the working poor, while the free flow of capital benefits only one group—transnational capitalists looking to maximize their return by any means necessary.

A Feminist Cut

The feminist theoretical approach has a lot to say about IMF and World Bank policies and their effects on women. In addition to decrying the lack of women in the decision-making process, feminists claim that IMF and World Bank policies amount to balancing budgets on the backs of women (Cunningham and Reed 1995). The Mexican austerity program has a more significant impact on women. Mexican women are the first to lose their jobs, and those who do not lose their jobs have seen their wages cut. While men also experience these effects, women make less than men. Moreover, women are also engaged in child rearing. Economically, women and children are disproportionately affected by structural adjustment. Socially, women and children also suffer. Rates of domestic violence are higher during economic hard times as men take out their frustrations on their families.

Mexican austerity has caused food and energy prices to rise dramatically. Many women are responsible for providing food for themselves and their families, and higher prices make stretching the devalued peso even more difficult. Women are usually the ones who have to work harder, and they are more likely to suffer nutritionally. The reduction of government spending in the areas of health, welfare, and education directly affects the status and the social development of women in Mexico (Buchmann 1996). Children, particularly young girls, also suffer from the lack of educational and health spending. Limited family resources tend to be devoted to the males at the expense of female family members (*WIN News* 1995). Concern about the immiserization of women and children as a result of IMF and World Bank conditionality has led UNICEF to call for "adjustment with a human face."

The IMF and the World Bank sponsor projects that promote export industries because of the need to earn foreign currency. Most developing states have export industries in commodities or cash crops, which means that governments must appropriate land that was once used for subsistence farming. Unfortunately for women, who are principally involved in barter or informal trade, their livelihoods are directly threatened as they are forced off the land to make room for cash crops and export industries, which are controlled by men and which further solidifies men's dominant position over women.

The IMF and the World Bank dispute any direct link between their structural adjustment programs and the impoverization of women and children. They argue that market reforms will empower women to take greater control over their lives. Citing their liberal economic models, these officials claim it is irrational for firms and governments to discriminate against women. Women must be allowed equal opportunity to education, jobs, and credit. Markets will raise the status of women because they will break down traditional patriarchal institutions that keep women down. Women integrated into the global economy can improve their social and economic status. Liberal feminists tend to agree with the IMF and the World Bank but also recognize that economic opportunities continue to be denied to women in market economies.

Many socialist feminists counter that it is precisely this liberal quasi-feminist approach that diminishes the status of women. In fact, the inclusion of women in the development process has led to the global feminization of poverty (Khoury 1994; Simmons 1992). Women are now working double the time, engaging in both paid and unpaid labor. Women's wages remain at 60–70 percent of men's wages. The problem with many liberal economic analyses of the effects of structural adjustment lies in their assumption that macroeconomic policies are gender-neutral. This assumption, while simplifying analyses, could not be further from the truth. According to a Women in Development (WID) report from Europe, "Macroeconomic policies are biased in favour of men, for they do not take into consideration the sexual division of labour, nor the time and the energy that go into caring for children and a household—activities carried out primarily by women, even in the most 'advanced' societies" (cited in *WIN News* 1995, 32).

Liberal economic theory as a tool ignores the economic contributions of women; as a result, it yields unsatisfactory results regardless of who uses it, male or female. The WID office of the World Bank is charged with ensuring that women are included in the development process. However, WID does not challenge the capitalist route to development or the gender bias of liberalism (Goebel and Epprecht 1995). Rather, it sees the problem as something internal to societies that markets can solve. WID is ethnocentric in that it promotes the West's liberal, feminist model of development while ignoring the cultural and ethnic experiences of Third World women. These experiences are dismissed as "traditional" and arguably oppressive to women. The market will incrementally incorporate traditional and informal sectors of societies, liberating women. In reality, however, this view reduces women to "resources" and wrongly implies that women in the advanced industrialized countries are progressing to positions of equality (Simmons 1992).

The IMF and the World Bank emphasize the development and the enhancement of export industries, resulting in the formation of export processing zones (EPZs). This requires "flexible labor" policies, which deregulate labor by explicitly marginalizing unions and allowing companies to bypass government-sanctioned collective bargaining. This attracts foreign investment and spurs economic growth. Many argue that IMF and World Bank structural adjustment loans and NAFTA have led to the development of maquiladoras in Mexico. Maquiladoras are factories located along the Mexico–U.S. border. "These factories can import duty-free parts, semi-finished goods and other items from the U.S. These are then finished or assembled by lower-wage Mexican workers and freely re-exported to the U.S. market" (Balaam and Veseth 1996, 70).

Maquiladorization of Mexico also means that labor is becoming feminized. According to Guy Standing of the International Labor Organization, "The types of work, labor relations, income and insecurity associated with 'women's work' have been spreading, resulting not only in the notable rise of female labor force participation but in a fall in men's employment as well as a transformation—or feminization—of many jobs traditionally held by men" (1996, 405). The emergence of maquiladoras has been accompanied by increasing numbers of women in manufacturing jobs that were previously held by men. Many of these factories, characterized as "sweatshops," exploit female labor in Mexico, which is 30–40 percent cheaper than male labor in Mexico and 70–80 percent cheaper than labor in the United States. The entry of women into the workforce has increased the supply of labor and reduced labor's bargaining power. In spite of the rhetoric of empowerment and cooperative partnerships, IMF and World Bank policies place egregious burdens on women. And, as with other international organizations, women are virtually excluded from the upper echelons of decision making within the IMF and the World Bank.

In Indonesia, IMF-imposed government austerity meant that the government spent less on food and fuel subsidies, education, health care, and social welfare. As a result, women bore the brunt of austerity as they were responsible for food, fuel, education, and health care. In Indonesia, women were disproportionately illiterate, in poor health, and inadequately nourished (*WIN News* 1999). The effects of IMF structural adjustment on Indonesian women were similar to those experienced by Mexican women. The structural adjustment loans led to social unrest that manifests itself as an increase in rape and domestic violence. Some men, powerless against their government and the IMF, vent their frustrations on the weak and vulnerable. The development of export industries meant the permanent displacement of rural women who engaged in subsistence farming. Women who were able to find factory work faced the sweatshop conditions of long hours and low pay. They received lower wages than men and were often hired as day laborers instead of full-time permanent employees. Many were subjected to sexual harassment.

In spite of the WID office of the World Bank, the experience of women under structural adjustment was ignored by the IMF and the World Bank. After nearly twenty years of feminist critiques, these institutions continued to disregard the impact of their policies on women. Additional feminist criticism of the IMF is considered repetitive (nagging—as postmodern feminists might highlight). Liberal feminism, that tends to agree with the IMF, still cannot explain the lack of enforcement of women's rights in developing countries. In Indonesia, women are constitutionally guaranteed the same rights, obligations, and opportunities as men; however, the government does nothing to enforce those rights. The disparity between the rights that are guaranteed in law and those that exist in fact seems to be of no concern to the IMF and the World Bank. With all their emphases on "good governance," not one IMF or World Bank loan has been withheld because of the (mis)treatment of women.

Feminists also encountered difficulty trying to organize women in Indonesia because feminism was associated with the United States. "In Indonesia, writings that question the implementation of human rights often reveal the fear that securing human rights means adopting liberalism, making people individualistic, egoistic and, thus disrupting the spirit of togetherness and solidarity" (Budianta 2000). In Indonesia, liberalism is associated with a notion of Western women that many Indonesians find offensive. Motherhood, subservience, and chastity are considered sacred in Indonesia, and Western notions of feminism are seen as a form of imperialism. The tension created by the collision of Western-styled capitalism with traditional Muslim culture further marginalized women. Women who seek equal rights or participation in the Western sense are considered unpatriotic and are reminded of their feminine duties to the community and family (Sunindyo 1998).

Women's NGOs continued to document women's human rights abuses and brought them to the attention of the international community. The anti-IMF riots in Jakarta were widely reported in the international media; however, the frequency of rape was missing from press analysis. NGOs and the Indonesian government-sponsored National Human Rights Commission pointed out that while the IMF unrest involved the killing of protesters and the destruction of property, it also involved the systematic rape of ethnic Chinese women and girls. The actual numbers of reported rapes range from 85 to 168; however, many NGOs report that the number was a lot higher (*WIN News* 1999). What is not in dispute is that these Chinese women and girls were targeted in an organized and coordinated manner over a three-day period. The IMF and the World Bank policies have a masculine bias and can have otherwise unnoticed side effects.

A Constructivist Cut

Constructivism has been slow to make inroads into the study of international political economy (Kollman 2008). As such, constructivist approaches to the financial crises of the 1990s center, imprecisely, on the agent–structure debate, the evolution of the "liberalization" discourse, social learning, and organizational change within the IMF and the World Bank. While no constructivist analyses focus specifically on the Mexican and Indonesian crises, the constructivist approach does provide a bridge between theories by showing how certain values and norms can dominate the development of discourse at different times. For example, the debates between and among liberals and between Marxists are debates about the agent–structure problem. To what extent is the system (in this case capitalism or a particular regulatory framework) responsible for the crises and to what extent are the choices of decision makers and other actors such as individuals, consumers, banks, and MNCs responsible? The answer, for constructivists, is both. Normative values are embedded in the theories that are used to analyze the crises. Neoliberals, for example, value personal responsibility and rationality which highlight poor choices or irrational behavior when problems arise. Marxists on the other hand value equality and therefore focus on who benefits and who bears the costs of a particular economic system or policy.

We also need to recognize that humans created capitalism and the norms associated with the system. Actors have different identities and values that are shaped by social norms of the system. In the case of Mexico, its development identity is defined in large part by its relationship to its prosperous and powerful neighbor. It gained status by joining NAFTA as a partner with the United States and Canada. Joining NAFTA meant embracing the neoliberal value system which places more emphases on market-based solutions to national problems, rather than state-driven solution. A fixed exchange rate for the peso was incompatible with value system and was the root of the crisis. Capitalism and liberal values have changed in part because of crises such as these and because states, international organizations, and their decision makers are reacting to different circumstances and the perceived lessons learned. While some constructivists argue that we still need to consider structure (Cooper et al. 2008), the norms and identities of individuals and institutions matter as well (Nielson et al. 2006).

The liberalization discourse has undergone significant transformations over time. For example, when Keynesian economics was a guiding theory from the 1950–1980, the IMF and the World Bank emphasized state management of the economy and even promoted the idea of state ownership of key national industries. In the 1980s, the neoliberal ideas of Hayek (i.e., privatization, deregulation, and free markets) came into vogue, and the IMF and the World Bank lending reflected those values. However, the IMF and the World Bank are not simply imposing a "one size fits all" ideology on developing states. They are interacting with states and other actors responding to events (and understanding those events through their own culture and identity). According to Leiteritz (2005, 1), it was the internal organizational culture of the IMF that was responsible for developing and implementing policies that emphasized the liberalization of international capital movements. However, the IMF was unable to institutionalize the norm of capital account liberalization at the global level because of the Asian financial crisis. The members of the IMF Board of Executives had different and contested interpretations as to the causes of the crisis. Therefore, they disagreed as to whether states should be able to use capital controls in a crisis (Leiteritz 2005). The Asian crisis affected the extent to which the liberalization of international capital movements was embraced by actors in the international community. The IMF changed as a result of social interactions with other actors during the Asian crisis.

Change at the World Bank and the IMF also results from "norm entrepreneurs" who can shape organizational structures and institutional identity (Nielson et al. 2006; Park 2005). Women, who were once overlooked within the development process, are now at the center of World Bank development efforts. Gender equity is seen fundamental for pursuing development whether in the orthodox or critical sense. The experiences of women under structural adjustment programs for Mexico and Indonesia have been documented, and policies have been modified. In 2001, the World Bank adopted a mainstreaming gender and development policy to make the bank more responsive to the needs of women in client countries. The World Bank is involved in more than 80 projects that are designed to reduce gender disparities in development and which contribute to the economic empowerment of women (see www.worldbank.org/gender). Both the IMF and the World Bank have come to accept that raising the status of women translates into greater economic growth. As we will see in the following section and in the next chapter, the values of gender equality and sustainable development have been embraced and internalized by both the IMF and the World Bank.

The Global Financial Crisis (2008–). The global financial crisis has brought the experience of financial and currency instability to the advanced industrialized countries. The causes of the crisis are contested but it is safe to say that the U.S. housing bubble, fueled, in part, by subprime lending by banks and other financial institutions, burst, triggering a global lending freeze (Shiller 2008). The contagion was global because financial institutions, governments, and retirement funds around the world bought exotic financial instruments and derivatives (which included subprime mortgages) and then also purchased insurance on those instruments to minimize their risk. As these instruments began to fail, insurance companies did not have the resources to cover the losses, nearly causing a total collapse of the global financial system. As the world's largest financial MNCs teetered on the brink of collapse, governments scrambled to respond. The scale of the crisis meant that states, along with their central banks and the IMF, had to coordinate their responses—a difficult task since they had different world views regarding causes of the crisis. For many

European governments with their neo-Keynesian liberal perspective, the cause of the crisis was lax regulation on the part of the U.S. government, which gave financial MNCs a free hand. Without proper rules, the financial institutions engaged in incredibly risky behavior using financial instruments many did not understand (such as credit default swaps). The Glass–Steagall Act, passed during the Great Depression to separate commercial banking from investment banking, had been repealed, which allowed financial MNCs to make investments with money they did not have. Insurance firms were not required to have assets on hand to cover the policies they sold to investors. As the subprime market began to fail, it caused a cascade of failures with other financial instruments and the insurance policies designed to hedge against uncertainty, threatening the entire financial system. The appropriate government response for most European governments then would be to bailout the firms (or nationalize them) and then re-regulate them to curb their excessive risk taking and to ensure that no firm could become "too-big-to-fail." Given the globalization of finance in the 1990s, states would need to create a new globally regulated financial order, many dubbed "Bretton Woods II." The United States and the United Kingdom, wary of extensive regulation, opted for government intervention (bailouts, loan guarantees, stimulus, and increasing the monetary supply) but resisted comprehensive reform. For Marxists, the global financial crisis is the quintessential example of the financial booms and busts associated with capitalism because transnational bourgeoisie once again took excessive risks, knowing they would be bailed out. Because of their political clout, they are able to write rules that favor their interests whereby their profits are privatized while their risks are borne by everyone. For feminists, financial MNCs are dominated by men, who fancy themselves as "masters of the universe." Their excessive risk taking is a combination of high levels of testosterone and a desire to outcompete their male counterparts. MNCs, along with the World Bank and the IMF, tend to see this behavior as normal and actually good because it brings economic growth and profits. Yet, they resist the idea that financial crisis may have biological roots.

The ensuing "Great Recession" illustrates many aspects of our theoretical approaches. The debate as to whether and how governments should respond is complicated by the need to respond collectively to the global crisis. International negotiations expanded from the G-8 to the G-20 (The 20 largest economies); however, agreement was elusive. This crisis has had a profound effect on populations in the advanced industrialized countries, with the situation in Iceland and Greece being the most acute. As the availability of loans dried up, the economy at all levels began to contract, causing a wave of layoffs, foreclosures, and bankruptcies. Governments and businesses found it difficult to obtain loans. Not surprisingly, the industrialized economies argued that stimulus and deficit spending are necessary to ride out the crisis, while developing states noted the double standards shown by the West and the IMF. When the developing world experienced financial crises, the West and the IMF imposed severe austerity on them, forcing them to make painful structural adjustments in their economies as a condition of emergency loans. Developing states were forced to cut government spending and benefits and their people were forced to endure high levels of unemployment and declining wages. Now that "the shoe was on the other foot," the IMF and Western governments refused to follow their own prescriptions.

As a constructivist might argue, a central aspect of the current crisis is a crisis in confidence. Individuals, governments, IGOs, and MNCs no longer have confidence in the financial system and in the value of their assets or money. Confidence is subjective, and as the rules and norms undergirding the global financial system collapsed, so did confidence. Without that shared understanding, the world cannot have a global financial system. The formidable task ahead for the international community is to build a new framework with as much shared understanding and buy-in from constituencies as possible. It is unclear if the international community can succeed.

CASE STUDY 6: MILLENNIUM DEVELOPMENT GOALS

Multilateral approaches to the issue of development involve activities that extend beyond the IMF and the World Bank. At the 2000 World Summit, the members of the UN set ambitious development goals that require extensive international cooperation among all UN members and agencies. The **MDGs** blend both orthodox and critical approaches to development and employ a more people-centered approach to development. The interrelated goals are ambitious. The first goal is to eradicate extreme poverty by halving the proportion of people living on less than $1 a day and who suffer from hunger by 2015. Success in reaching MDG 1 is conditioned on the success of MDG 2, which is to provide universal primary education to both boys and girls. MDG 3 is to promote gender equality for women, which involves giving girls and women equal access to education at all levels. MDGs 4 and 5 center on reducing, by two-thirds, the child mortality rate and improving maternal health care, respectively. The first five goals need to be pursued simultaneously along with efforts to combat AIDS and other infectious diseases—MDG 6. AIDS, malaria, and tuberculosis are debilitating preventable diseases that have a direct impact on the quality of life for millions of people. Prevention requires education and the improved status of women. MDGs 7 and 8 focus on sustainable development and building a global partnership for development. Each goal is accompanied by concrete measurable targets.

The ambitious goals set at the Millennium Summit reflect the UN's concern for meeting the basic human needs of the world's population by 2015. Economic development must go hand-in-hand with human development in order for either to be successful. While a great deal of consensus exists that these goals are both necessary and, with proper attention, attainable, divisions remain on the appropriate strategies. The 2005 World Summit illustrated some of the disagreements surrounding how best to achieve the MDGs. Initially, the United States sought to remove any mention of the MDGs from the agenda in part because the MDGs involve international and governmental intervention in the world economy; however, international protest caused it to back down. President George W. Bush included the MDGs in his speech to the General Assembly but provided few specifics as to the role of the United States. Progress toward specific targets has been slow; however, the largest creditor nations did agree to forgive approximately $20 billion of debt owed by the poorest nations in October 2005, demonstrating their commitment to removing one of the principal obstacles to development.

Progress toward meeting the MDGs by 2015 has not been altogether promising. The UN Human Development Report (2005, 18) states the following:

- The MDG target for reducing child mortality will be missed with the margin equivalent to more than 4.4 million avoidable deaths in 2015. Over the next ten years, the cumulative gap between the target and the current trends adds more than 41 million children who will die before their fifth birthday from the most readily curable disease—poverty. This is an outcome that is difficult to square with the Millennium Declaration's pledge to protect the world's children.
- The gap between the MDG target for halving poverty and the projected outcomes is equivalent to an additional 380 million people in developing countries living on less than $1 a day by 2015.
- The MDG target of universal primary education will be missed with 47 million children in developing countries still out of school in 2015.

The MDG initiative has met with some success in large part because of the progress of China in terms of poverty alleviation, primary education, and gender equality. Its double digit economic growth and increases in international trade have improved the lives of millions of Chinese and have had a significant impact on MDG statistics. However, sub-Saharan Africa and parts of South Asia have actually gotten worse.

In 2008, rising fuel and food prices exacerbated the living and working conditions of the poor around the world. With the accompanying inflation, those living in poverty and extreme poverty faced difficulty meeting subsistence nutritional needs. The global financial crisis has meant that wealthy states are less generous in their ODA. Since 2005, ODA has declined and, with the financial instability in the advanced industrialized countries threatening to take down the global financial system, increases in ODA are not likely. The global financial crisis is unprecedented on several levels, and the turmoil is reshaping the nature of financial regulation and international development. Under President Obama, the United States has embraced the MDGs as the principal vehicle for its multilateral approach to alleviating poverty and promoting development. According to the 2010 U.S. MDG strategy report (http://www.usaid.gov/our_work/mdg/), the United States proposes pursing four imperatives: leverage innovation; invest in sustainability; track development outcomes; and enhance the principle and practice of mutual accountability. Will the MDGs as a multilateral strategy be successful in reducing poverty and promoting development? How do we explain the emergence of the MDGs and analyze international efforts to meet these goals?

A Realist Cut

As an international initiative, the MDG strategy is well-intentioned but insignificant. Its insignificance is measured by the extent that states, which comprise the international community, are willing to devote their scarce resources. While the absolute cost of meeting all of the MDGs remains in dispute, this international community has largely agreed that if the richest countries in the world would devote 0.7 percent of their gross national income, then the international community could eliminate extreme poverty globally. That is, the world's richest states need only devote $0.70 of every $100.00 they earn to development in order to lift the rest of the world out of extreme poverty. To date, only a few countries such as Norway, Sweden, Luxembourg, Denmark, and the Netherlands have met this benchmark. That so few states are willing to commit what seems to be such an insignificant amount demonstrates that alleviating extreme poverty around the world is not a particularly high priority for these states.

The United States has routinely opposed formal requirements that require states to contribute a fixed amount of money to ODA. The United States objected to including the 0.7 percent benchmark in the **Monterrey Consensus**, which resulted from the 2002 International Conference of Financing and Development held in Monterrey, Mexico. The conference was called to determine how to harness the financial resources necessary to meet the MDGs. The UN could only "recommend" that states increase their ODA to the 0.7 percent level. Is the United States stingy and uncaring? No. The United States opposes international initiatives that authoritatively redistribute wealth on ideological grounds and practical grounds. Wealth is better redistributed through market mechanisms, not national and international governmental agencies (especially when those agents are corrupt, incompetent, or both). A state could throw $1 trillion at the problem, and it still would not solve the problem. The United States needs to devote its scarce resources to enhancing its security and its own nation-building and poverty alleviation.

Redistributing wealth ultimately means redistributing power. While 70 cents for every $100 earned seems like such a small figure, it does add up. For example, in 2006 the national income for Norway was approximately $240 billion and the national income for the United States was approximately $13 trillion. If each were to contribute 0.7 percent of their income to ODA, Norway would give approximately $1.68 billion and the United States would give approximately $91 billion. Overtime, that is a significant transfer of wealth, and the wealthy do not remain wealthy long if they give away their money. The United States routinely devotes 0.23 percent of its national income to ODA (approximately $29 billion), much more in absolute terms than Norway. While Norway may be more generous in terms of its willingness to devote more of its national income to ODA, the U.S. "generosity" has a greater impact.

From a realist perspective, international aid actually does more harm than good (Easterly 2006). UN efforts at developing and attempting to fulfill the MDGs are laudable, but such grand plans usually fail. International institutions are inefficient and too removed to effectively administer a grand plan. Infusion of resources leads to corruption and mismanagement at the UN and for aid recipient states. States seeking to assist others in meeting the MDGs would do well to devote aid bilaterally to insure proper management. For example, the United States, in 2002, established the Millennium Challenge Account (MCA), which is overseen by a government corporation called the Millennium Challenge Corporation (MCC). This initiative allows states that meet certain conditions of economic liberalization and good governance to apply for development aid. While few of the poorest countries are eligible, those that take steps to help themselves can receive assistance. For those poorest countries, especially those mired in civil war and other violent conflict, the only alternative may be intervention (Collier 2007). The UN, NATO, and/or the EU do not have the capacity or the political will necessary for a successful intervention. Only a powerful state is capable of intervention, and states are not going to intervene unless they have a compelling national interest to do so. Few are willing to spend their treasure and blood for purely altruistic or humanitarian reasons.

The success story in development is China; however, China's progress is not due to the UN or any other global initiative. Rather, China harnessed market forces to develop the country, while retaining its socialist government. It was the Chinese state that took it upon itself to improve the lives of its citizens. It violated human rights domestically and associated and engaged with brutal regimes in Africa to ensure access to raw materials and African markets. Yet, if there has been any progress to meeting the MDGs, it is because China has improved the lives for so many of its people. At the same time, these very African states are regressing.

A Liberal Cut

From a liberal perspective, markets and the empowerment of individuals, both male and female, with civil and political rights will enable them to reduce poverty, hunger, and disease. The central difference between neoliberals and Keynesian liberals is the extent to which national and international agencies are involved. For most liberals, the MDGs are attainable with the appropriate level of funding and the right economic policies. By drawing upon the ideas and resources of civil society, the international community can meet the basic human needs of the world's population. Neoliberals stress that the governments of the poorest states must be reformed if international efforts to meet the MDGs are to be successful. Corrupt governments and their ill-conceived policies have contributed to the extreme poverty experienced by their citizens. Part of the Monterrey

Consensus involves good governance reforms in exchange for increased ODA. If states have failed or governments remain corrupt, then the international community can do very little to implement policies that are designed to achieve the MDGs.

Neoliberals also highlight the role of the private sector in implementing MDG strategy. **The Global Compact,** an initiative of former secretary-general Kofi Annan, is designed to be a liaison between intergovernmental organizations and national and multinational business. Over 4,300 businesses have joined the Compact and have become partners in the MDG strategy. The principal theme of the Global Compact is **corporate social responsibility (CSR)**, and it recognizes that the business community has an important role in alleviating poverty. Economic growth is part of the MDG strategy and is part of the developmental footprint (Newell and Frynas 2007, 669). Other NGOs that comprise civil society are also pivotal not only in implementing MDG policies but also in formulating them. Perhaps the most influential is the Gates Foundation, which is devoted to improving global health. Founded by Bill Gates, the former Microsoft CEO, and his wife, Melinda Gates, this organization has mobilized considerable resources and talent to combat preventable diseases throughout much of the world. For neoliberals, the private sector has the most potential for marshalling the resources necessary for meeting the MDGs. The role of the private sector was reaffirmed at the 2008 World Economic Forum in Davos, Switzerland.

Former neoliberals, such as Nobel Prize–winning economist Jeffery Sachs (2005), argue that while market forces are powerful, they are insufficient for reducing poverty in countries that are geographically challenged or suffer from poor infrastructure. Such countries tend to have populations that suffer from debilitating diseases and have little or no access to health care or medicine. Sachs and others have argued that if wealthy countries increase their ODA to a combined $150 billion, the international community could easily meet the MDGs. This money could be for disease prevention (antimalaria bed nets), the treatment of disease (AIDS drugs), and improving the access of the poor to the Internet (cell phones and computers). It could also be used to build infrastructure such as roads, bridges, schools, water sanitation, and electrical grids. Some liberals, such as Paul Collier (2007), argue that the "bottom billion" people living in the poorest countries are slipping deeper into poverty. The MDGs may need to be refined to focus more on these individuals, 70 percent of whom live in Africa. In most cases, extreme poverty and disease are caused by civil war and other forms of violent conflict that have been going on for decades. The cycle of violence creates perpetual poverty and misery for the civilian population. In some cases, foreign intervention may be necessary, as in the case of Sierra Leone, in order to disrupt the cycle of violence. The international community can also negotiate treaties that put pressure on dictators and their bankers (since their deposits are in Western banks). Sometimes, political and military intervention is necessary to help societies escape the poverty trap.

A Marxist Cut

The need for the MDGs illustrates the failure of capitalism and markets to fairly create and distribute wealth. Extreme poverty is the consequence of capitalism, and it cannot be eliminated through more capitalism. While MNCs pay lip service to the MDGs, their participation in the Global Compact is more public relations than substantive action. MNCs still seek policies that allow them to exploit raw materials, labor, and markets. Socialist China is one of the few success stories in part because the state is strong enough to regulate MNCs and its 1.3 billion-person market. China's experience cannot be replicated because other developing states do not have power to stand up to the advanced industrialized countries and the IMF and the World Bank.

One of the targets of MDG 1 is to halve the number of people who suffer from hunger. Reaching this goal is complicated because of the dramatic rise in food prices in 2008. The rise in food prices has many causes, such as the diversion of food crops to biofuels which are poured into gas guzzling cars in the United States. This leads to increased hunger in the developing world. Marxists also stress that IMF and World Bank policies eroded state investment in agriculture and state support for local farmers (Freese 2008, 11). By forcing trade liberalization of developing states, while doing little to discourage subsidies to farmers in wealthy countries, farmers in the developing world cannot compete and the population becomes dependent on the subsidized agriculture surpluses imported from advanced industrialized countries. MNCs are cynically using the MDGs to promote genetically modified food and biotechnology even when neither has much potential to alleviate poverty and hunger (Freese 2008, 10).

Absent a collapse of capitalism, Marxists argue the socialist policies that redistribute wealth and resources are the only way to meet the MDGs. Given that few states are particularly generous to noncitizens, the future of the so-called "bottom billion" is bleak indeed. The global financial crisis only exacerbates an already dire situation. The rich capitalist states will be dealing with hunger, poverty, and disease among their own populations and are not going to be concerned about people in distant lands. Sadly, scarce financial resources will be used to bail out multinational banks and large corporations rather than improve the lives of ordinary people. The socialist policies implemented by governments in capitalist states amount to socialism for the rich.

A Feminist Cut

Feminists applaud the MDGs for their gender focus. The UN recognizes that women and girls tend to be the most marginalized in society and are the least likely to benefit from globalization and markets. The first step is to eliminate the gender disparity in primary education. China has made the most progress, while Sub-Saharan Africa and South Asia appear to be moving in the wrong direction. The fundamental problem in these areas is that cultural and religious traditions prevent women from being educated. As a result, these women are almost guaranteed to be excluded from decision making at the national, regional, and local levels. Nor are they likely to hold jobs outside of the agricultural sector and those that do find employment are easily exploited. Culture and religion remain formidable barriers to taking this basic, yet crucial, step to empowering women. Since gender discrimination embedded in culture and religion does not warrant sanction or intervention by the international community, progress to improve the status of women will remain painfully slow. Changing harmful cultural and religious traditions from outside invites charges of cultural imperialism and persecution. Such efforts encounter stiff resistance, not the least of all from the women that such efforts are designed to help.

Promoting change from within, however, is more promising. For example, several countries in southern Africa have implemented quota systems in their national legislatures, reserving seats solely for women. Countries such as Rwanda and Uganda have over 25 percent of women occupying parliamentary seats. Of course, such "empowerment" of women does not necessarily translate into improved status for women, but it does raise the profile of women in government. In 2006, Ellen Johnson Sirleaf was elected president of war-torn Liberia, making her the first female leader in Africa. Her campaign slogan was "All the men have failed Liberia . . . Let's try a woman this time." Since her election, enrollment in primary education increased from 44 to 80 percent, with girls comprising the majority of new enrollees (Kelly 2008). While many challenges lay ahead for Liberia, President Sirleaf had made important progress for meeting the MDGs and the international community has invested significant resources in rebuilding the country. Incremental progress in investments in the education of girls may one day yield important dividends for the quality of life in Liberia.

The education of women and girls in poverty-stricken societies also means improvements in women's and maternal health. For example, women with four years of primary education were able to correctly understand instructions for the administering of rehydration salts, while those with secondary education could understand the environmental causes of diarrhea (Kabeer 2005, 16). Women with some education are better able to look out for their own well-being and are better able to protect themselves and their families from disease. While feminists applaud the emphasis on gender for meeting the MDGs, they decry the poor financing and the slow progress in prodding patriarchal governments to change by the UN and the international financial institutions IFIs.

A Constructivist Cut

Constructivist theory shows how international organizations create norms and play an important coordinating role in poverty relief operations and in improving health. It was the UN that created the MDGs and developed a system-wide strategy for achieving them. Throughout the 1990s, a series of development conferences were held by the UN which brought together states, NGOs, MNCs and other actors in order to pursue and define the value of development. The definition and pursuit of this value involves different actors, with different identities (identities which are fluid because of relational dimensions between parties). The UN as an institution also has its own notion of what development is. "Development" as a concept may be contested, but it does not mean that the different conceptions cannot all be pursued simultaneously by different actors. What is remarkable is that the UN has been able to construct a relatively consensual strategy for alleviating extreme poverty and improving the lives of a billion people in impoverished areas of the world.

The MDG strategy revolves around the Millennium Project, the Millennium Campaign, and the Millennium Reports (MDGRs). The Millennium Project was commissioned in 2002 by then secretary-general Kofi Annan to develop action steps for achieving the MDGs. The Project, headed by Jeffery Sachs, sought to promote scholarly research efforts to tap new ideas for achieving the MDGs and for prioritizing operations. The project's main objective was to embed the MDGs in world development activities. This meant attempting to maneuver development institutions such as the IMF and the World Bank to consider MDG strategy in their lending. While there is still a long way to go, recent studies suggest that the IMF now plays an important catalyst role for ODA earmarked for the MDGs (Bird and Rowland 2007, 856). The project presented its recommendation in 2005 and retained an advisory role until 2006. The project was the first step in the UN's operational process.

The Millennium Campaign is geared toward raising global awareness and building global support for the MDGs. This means advising states as to how to develop policies to meet MDGs and then to actually implement those policies. While largely a public relations endeavor, the campaign has successfully placed the MDGs on the agenda of states, MNCs, and in the minds of ordinary peoples.

The MDGRs represent country report cards. These self-assessment tools help states think about the MDGs and to critically evaluate how their government policies assist (or hurt) progress toward the MDGs. Over 140 states have filed MDGRs, and the UN also does its own independent assessment. While the news is not always positive, the MDGRs challenge states to improve their policies and their records.

At the end of the day, the MDG initiative may be unsuccessful. But it has, at least for the time being, focused the attention of a variety of actors, with a variety of identities and values, on pursuing a strategy that would benefit the most marginalized. The world is what we make it, and for this period, a constellation of actors brought their ideas and resources to bear on a global problem that ultimately affects us all. Even in the face of the 2008 global financial meltdown, the MDGs have not been forgotten, and the warnings for those outside of the mainstream have been vindicated to a certain extent. The process of global learning and global change is not pretty, but it does provide historical reference and if necessary a tutorial on "lessons learned."

CONCLUSION

The issue of development combines issues of colonialism, trade, financial stability, and gender. The case studies illustrate how the different theoretical approaches view the central issues of development and the role of the UN, the IMF, the World Bank, and NGOs in the development process. Variations of the theories either advocate or challenge the orthodox and critical views of development. For example, traditional realists, liberals, and liberal feminists tend to have orthodox views of development. However, neorealists recognize that the uneven economic playing field enables great powers to exploit developing states through increased economic leverage. Marxists and some feminists argue that sustainable economic development, either in the orthodox or critical sense, is simply not possible under pure capitalist market conditions. Constructivism bridges the difference between theories and provides explanations as to how international organizations can help develop relatively common identities and values.

KEY TERMS

Millennium Development
Goals (MDGs)   185
development   185
orthodox
development   186
critical development   186
external debt   188
London Club   189
Paris Club   189
World Bank   190
International Bank for
Reconstruction and
Development
(IBRD)   190
International
Development
Association
(IDA)   190

the International Finance
Corporation
(IFC)   191
International Center for
Settlement of
Investments Disputes
(ISCSID)   191
Multilateral Investment
Guarantee Agency
(MIGA)   191
the International
Monetary Fund
(IMF)   193
lender of last resort   194
structural adjustment
loans   194

The UN Conference on
Trade and
Development
(UNCTAD)   195
new international
economic order
(NIEO)   196
Special Drawing Rights
(SDRs)   196
Monterrey
Consensus   219
the Global
Compact   221
corporate social
responsibility
(CSR)   221

SUGGESTED READINGS

Collier, Paul. 2007. *The Bottom Billion*. Oxford: Oxford University Press.

Easterly, William. 2006. *The White Man's Burden: Why the West's Efforts Have Done So Much Ill and So Little Good*. New York: Penguin Press.

Khoury, Inge. 1994. The World Bank and the Feminization of Poverty. pp. 121–123 in *Fifty Years Is Enough: The Case Against the World Bank and the International Monetary Fund*, ed. Kevin Danaher. Boston, MA: South End Press.

Sachs, Jeffery. 2005. *The End of Poverty*. New York: Penguin Press.

Sen, Amartya. 1996. Development: Which Way Now?. pp. 1–28 in *The Political Economy of Development and Underdevelopment*. 6th ed., ed. Kenneth P. Jameson and Charles K. Wilber–. New York: McGraw-Hill.

Shiller, Robert. 2008. *The Subprime Solution: How Today's Financial Crisis Happened and What to Do About It*. Princeton, NJ: Princeton University Press.

The Environment

The natural environment is composed of air, land, and water resources. From these resources, human life and biodiversity are sustained. The idea that the environment ought to be protected seems obvious, but how to manage the earth's global resources is as contentious an issue as development. The environment directly relates to development and to the operation of the global economy. Natural elements provide food, energy, and the raw materials necessary to support the world's population, which is estimated to be approximately 6.8 billion people. The protection of global resources is controversial because economic activity involves the exploitation of natural resources to produce goods and services. How are societies to balance the growing resource needs of industrial societies with the natural environment? How do societies promote development and continue to support their people in the manner they have grown accustomed without destroying their natural habitat? In this chapter, we examine international efforts to protect the environment and to manage global resources. We look first at collective action problems associated with environmental protection, then at the structure of IGOs involved in managing land and sea resources. Our case studies cover international efforts to combat climate change and **the International Whaling Commission (IWC)** and its efforts to protect the whales.

THE TRAGEDY OF THE COMMONS

The difficulties in protecting the environment are often illustrated with the "**tragedy of the commons**" parable, first articulated by Garrett Hardin (1968). This parable shows how many individuals, each acting rationally, can destroy the very resources that sustain them all. Consider a village in which all sheep owners are entitled to use the commons (a collectively owned pasture) to graze their sheep. Each owner has an economic incentive to use the commons, grazing as many sheep as possible, because the commons is "free": Using it lowers the cost of raising the sheep, thereby increasing profit at the market. And higher profits mean each owner can raise even more sheep. But as each owner adds more grazing sheep to the commons, the commons itself deteriorates. The grass, once so lush, disappears; the topsoil, denuded of roots, turns to mud in the rain; and the muddy ground washes away. Overexploited, the commons is destroyed, and with it, the community itself—a tragedy.

It seems logical, then, that community members should work together to protect the commons on which their livelihood depends. To do so, they can pursue two alternative strategies. First, they can create an authoritative body to regulate the commons. This body would determine how many sheep each person may graze, monitor the condition of the commons, and make sure that the commons is replenished. This strategy can be successful only if the interest of the authoritative body lies in preserving the commons and not in protecting the interests of the powerful sheep owners. After all, it must decide communal questions: What is a fair number of sheep for each person? What regulations are necessary? And what kinds of regulations would unduly interfere with commerce? The trouble is, even when the authoritative body is absolutely authoritative, owning both sheep and commons, the protection of the commons is not guaranteed. Consider, for example, the former communist governments in Eastern Europe and the Soviet successor states. These governments—authoritative bodies—owned both the means of production and the natural resources. Yet, these governments chose to focus on industrialization at the expense of the environment.

The second strategy is to privatize the commons, assigning property rights to individuals. With this strategy, individuals have incentives to care for their own property. Overgrazing your own land would be irrational, meaning that it would go against your individual self-interest. Your interest lies in preserving your land in the best possible condition, given your grazing needs. This strategy also has complications. In the first place, assigning property rights is an inherently political process. Who gets what and how much? And what is the rationing mechanism? Are only the rich entitled to buy and use the commons? Furthermore, an authoritative body is still needed—a body capable of assigning those property rights and enforcing them.

The tragedy of the commons allows us to understand how global "commons" are fast becoming depleted and why global actors, in seeking to use and protect the environment, are encountering difficulties. Consider fishing in international waters. International waters, which are not owned by any country, comprise a "collective good." Each fishing boat operating in international waters has incentive to catch as much fish as it possibly can. However, there are many such boats, all fishing the same water, all depleting the same stock of fish; collectively, they are threatening the industry itself. Each boat individually reaps the profits yielded by a larger catch of fish, but no boat bears the whole cost of its activity. The costs of overfishing are externalized, meaning that the costs are borne not by the industry or owners but by society as a whole.

Avoiding the tragedy of the ocean commons means dealing with the same plague of problems attending the protection of our hypothetical pasture. In fact, protecting the ocean's resources is even more difficult because multiple actors are involved. Governments, MNCs, IGOs, and NGOs have different interests and capabilities. Landlocked states and seafaring states compete for a share of the ocean resources. National and local fishing companies compete with MNCs. Other issues include determining where state sovereignty ends and the global commons begins. Debates rage on the best strategies for managing the ocean resources: Many governments and MNCs seek privatization of the ocean commons, while many IGOs and NGOs seek more authoritative regulation of the environment.

Intuitively, privatization of the environment seems impossible, particularly as it relates to the oceans and the atmosphere. How can individuals privately own the air or the water? You can't partition the atmosphere, outlawing breathing in private space, nor can you divide up all the fish, making them stay in privately owned sections of the ocean. Water might be privatized by creating zones; however, pollution knows no bounds, as past incidents of oil spills have demonstrated. Privatization of "difficult to divide" natural resources usually takes the form of licenses—a license to fish or a license to pollute. That is, firms buy the rights to use the resources of the atmosphere or the ocean. As we'll see later in this chapter, pollution rights are a key feature of international efforts to counter global climate change. For our current purposes, however, we simply recognize that both strategies—regulation and privatization—involve some kind of authoritative body either to create environmental regulations or to assign and enforce property rights with regard to using natural resources. And both strategies are controversial because neither has been particularly effective at protecting the environment.

One of the principal challenges to environmental protection is that of balancing the capitalist mode of production, which involves the use and mass consumption of natural resources, with such values as preserving biodiversity and ensuring clean air, land, and water. The market cannot easily determine the price of these values; moreover, environmental protection can hurt profits and undermine industries and jobs. Environmental problems are part and parcel of economic development, so that the attending issues and controversies are intertwined. The concept of **sustainable development** is therefore an important one—it is used to describe efforts to maintain stable economic growth without undermining the environment and permanently depleting resources.

The theories of international relations differ as to how to achieve sustainable development; some even question whether such a balance between the environment and economic development is even possible. Much of the environmental degradation today is attributable to the development in just seven or eight advanced industrialized states. These states, particularly the United States, consume the vast majority of the world's resources and account for a significant portion of the world's waste. Can the planet sustain this kind of development without experiencing a tragedy of the commons on a global scale? And can other countries, such as China, India, Russia, and Brazil, have the same consumption habits as the West? The answers to these questions depend on your theoretical lens. Realists are pessimistic about international cooperation in protecting the environment, arguing that states must do what they can to protect themselves and minimize external environmental threats. International competition for natural resources and raw materials will increase as more and more states develop. States must be able to get the resources they need, through the exercise of power if necessary. Liberals see the market as a means for promoting efficient use of raw materials. They argue that the market will force firms and individuals to use their resources wisely; otherwise they will be uncompetitive in the global economy. Environmental costs—externalities that are not included in the price of goods—should be managed by international environmental regimes. Marxists see environmental protection as incompatible with capitalism. Environmental protection fetters international and domestic commercial activities and undermines profits. Environmental protection will always take a backseat to the interests of capitalists seeking to maximize profits and quarterly returns. Firms and individuals will take an "exploit and move on" approach to the environment until some entity with the power decides to stop them. Feminists tend to see current environmental protection as futile because most protection strategies are masculine in nature. This means that most strategies are informed by the idea that humans are somehow separated from their environment. The environment is something that man can control, conquer, and dominate. It is masculinist to think that science and scientific understanding will always solve environmental problems that arise from environmental exploitation. The constructivist approach illustrates how the international environmental regime and associated norms have been created and how those norms are diffused throughout the system.

ENVIRONMENTAL PROBLEMS

Most environmental problems revolve around pollution and resource depletion. Some problems can be corrected. Others cannot. Some kinds of pollutants can be treated, restoring land or water. But radioactive wastes and chemical pollutants in sufficient concentration can also permanently kill a body of water or render areas of land uninhabitable. Some resources are renewable, like fresh water and trees, while other resources, such as oil and coal, are not.

Five interrelated environmental problems have been of contemporary international concern—**deforestation, desertification, biodiversity, ozone depletion,** and **climate change.** Deforestation involves the clearing of forests for economic and social reasons. The most obvious reason for cutting trees down is for timber. Timber is processed into the lumber that builds houses, furniture, and the like. Another reason is to provide additional farmland for crops or grazing. Yet another reason is to provide additional living space for growing populations. These reasons are not trivial. The survival of millions of people depends on subsistence farming, which involves "slash and burn" techniques.

But the consequences of deforestation are dire. They involve soil erosion and loss of habitat for plant and animal species. More important, deforestation means the loss of the major producers of oxygen—trees. Trees are the principal mechanisms for recycling carbon dioxide into oxygen. Deforestation raises the level of carbon dioxide in the air, rendering it less breathable to animal life, and contributes to the warming of the atmosphere. The tropical rain forests in Latin America, Africa, and Asia are crucial to the ecological balance of the planet because they recycle 90 percent of the earth's carbon dioxide.

Desertification is closely related to deforestation because the removal of trees makes the topsoil unstable and robs it of the necessary nutrients that sustain vegetation. Normal rainfall patterns are disrupted, and the land becomes a desert—barren and uninhabitable. Desertification has posed a serious problem in Africa, where (normal) periodic droughts have been exacerbated to the extent that entire populations are now at risk. Desertification has created millions of environmental refugees, provoking unprecedented levels of starvation. Desertification is directly related to food security and has been linked closely with famines in Ethiopia, Somalia, and Sudan.

Biodiversity refers to the number and variety of plant and animal species. Biodiversity is considered important because local, regional, and global ecosystems depend on different species for continued existence. "Key species" are lynchpin plants and animals that are necessary for sustaining the food chain. Plankton, which is a tiny microorganism found in salt and fresh water, is just such a species. The extinction of plankton could collapse a food chain that includes salmon and trout, whales and dolphins, and seals and bears. In biodiversity, more is better and protecting the "more" is better still. Thus, it is better to try to preserve biological complexity, in all its varieties, than to risk the unknown consequences of losing a species about which humans know very little. Biodiversity is tied to deforestation and desertification because the destruction of ecosystems destroys the habitat of plant and animal species. Efforts to preserve biodiversity include trying to protect species from extinction even if they have not been identified as a key species. Endangered species like the spotted owl or the humpback whale deserve to be protected for reasons that extend beyond their current economic value or the short-term costs of their protection. Long-term rewards might be indeterminable now, but the uncertainty of the costs of their loss is unbearable in an increasingly wealthy world.

Ozone depletion is the deterioration of the ozone layer caused by the release of chlorofluorocarbons (CFCs). CFCs are used extensively as propellants; they are common in refrigerating units and in aerosol preparations such as antiperspirants and hair sprays. The ozone layer is an important component of the earth's atmosphere because it provides the principal shield between the earth's surface and the sun. It protects, for example, against the harmful effects of ultraviolet (UV) light. Exposure to excessive UV can cause certain kinds of cancers and genetic mutations. Ozone depletion has been documented by a variety of international sources studying expanding atmospheric holes. While such holes are principally located over the South Pole, they have also been found in Africa, Australia, and New Zealand. From the appearance of three-legged frogs to the disappearance of entire species, many ill effects have been attributed to a combination of deforestation, desertification, and ozone depletion.

Climate change refers to the gradual increase of the earth's overall temperature. Many attribute the rising temperature to the burning of fossil fuels and the buildup of greenhouse gases (carbon dioxide, CFCs, and methane) in the earth's atmosphere. The causes and consequences of climate change for the environment and human life are disputed by scientists, economists, governments, IGOs, and NGOs. Scientists disagree as to how much the world's temperature will increase; estimates range anywhere from three to twelve degrees. They disagree as to whether the process of climate change can be reversed. Some even disagree as to whether climate change is even a bad thing for the planet. Moreover, international efforts to address climate change are complicated by competing worldviews, the North–South conflict, and the continuing primacy of state sovereignty in world politics.

International efforts to protect the environment and manage the earth's natural resources have led to a proliferation of international environmental organizations, which include IGOs, MNCs, NGOs, and regimes. In the following sections, we'll outline some of those international organizations and look at the UN-sponsored conferences that are central to the interrelated environmental issues of deforestation, desertification, biodiversity, ozone depletion, and climate change.

THE STOCKHOLM CONFERENCE (1972)

The first comprehensive international conference addressing the environment was the UN Conference on the Human Environment, held in Stockholm, Sweden. **The Stockholm Conference** produced 26 principles and 109 recommendations regarding human settlements, natural resource management, pollution, educational and social aspects of the environment, development, and international organizations (Bennett 1995, 335; Greene 1998, 317). The Stockholm Conference is perhaps best remembered for advocating the creation of the **United Nations Environmental Program (UNEP)**, for establishing transnational monitoring networks, and for institutionalizing the principle of the Common Heritage of Mankind.

The UNEP was created shortly after the Stockholm Conference by the General Assembly and is overseen by the Economic and Social Council (ECOSOC). It is administered by a small Secretariat, which organizes and promotes interagency cooperation within the UN system. The UNEP also helps coordinate the monitoring of environmental problems by UN agencies and NGOs. The UNEP is funded by the Environmental Fund, which is made up of voluntary contributions. The UNEP possesses no supranational authority and therefore must rely on the cooperation of states, UN agencies, and NGOs for fostering environmental protection.

The UNEP is central to the global monitoring of environmental conditions. This network consists of monitoring stations with links among UN offices, state agencies, and NGOs. In addition to measuring pollution and documenting the status of natural resources, this monitoring network collects data regarding potential environmental threats. Environmental NGOs play a pivotal role in helping to define environmental problems and identifying issues and strategies. NGOs also provide expertise and credible analysis of environmental conditions to governments at the local and national levels and to IGOs.

The Common Heritage of Mankind is an important principle that attempts to define the global commons. The principle seeks to clarify the extent to which specific areas belong to all the countries on the planet. These are places whose resources everyone may exploit and all have the right to use—international waters, the deep seabed, and orbital space. The Common Heritage of Mankind is fundamental. It identifies, defines, and protects the global commons. It promotes the idea that everyone should reap the benefits of the global commons, not just those with means to utilize them. As a result, the North–South conflict and development issues are inextricably intertwined with the principle of the Common Heritage of Mankind. This is illustrated clearly by the efforts to manage the ocean resources.

THE UN CONFERENCE ON THE LAW OF THE SEA (UNCLOS)

The United Nations Conference on the Law of the Sea (UNCLOS) reflects the limited international understanding of rights to and protection of the oceans and their resources. UNCLOS builds upon the first modern law-of-the-sea conference, which was held in 1958. This conference attempted to reconcile two principles—state sovereignty and freedom of the high seas. Many coastal states claimed absolute sovereignty over large areas of the oceans, a claim that conflicted with the historic principle of the free navigation of the high seas. Widespread disagreements existed (and still exist) among states as to where the state's territorial jurisdiction ends and international waters begin. What is the best way to measure and define national claims of sovereignty? The 1958 conference attempted to resolve this dispute by measuring the depth as well as the breadth of the territorial sea. Traditionally, the territorial sea was defined as an area extending three nautical miles from the shore, over which states exercised exclusive and complete jurisdiction. This three-mile marker was rooted in nineteenth-century precedent, being the average range of cannon-fire. Coastal states also claimed that sovereignty extended to the edge of the continental shelf, where the ocean floor drops off into the deep seabed.

States, however, have sought to extend their sovereignty further, claiming jurisdictions of 200 beyond-shore miles, regardless of where the continental shelf ends. So more disagreements arose: Is this sovereignty absolute? Does it extend to resources or is it limited to navigation? These disagreements were particularly acute because the 200-mile zones often overlapped. Moreover, they would allow island states to extend their territory and their sovereignty considerably. The 1958 law-of-the-sea convention addressed these concerns, but was unable to resolve them among the negotiating parties.

After several failed rounds of negotiations in the 1960s, international efforts to regulate the oceans were revived in 1973, in part because of the momentum generated by the Stockholm Conference. The UNCLOS (1973–1982) extended the territorial sea to twelve miles, where states may regulate shipping. As shipping has important environmental and security implications for nations, coastal states have the right to impose shipping regulations. UNCLOS also established a 200-mile exclusive economic zone, granting coastal states the rights to all the fishing and mineral resources within that area. We can see in the 200-mile zone an effort to privatize the commons. States have been unwilling to yield the necessary sovereignty to create a supranational body to regulate the commons. But by privatizing the commons, coastal states get the rewards and pay the costs of controlling large areas of the oceans. Theoretically, these states will behave rationally—they will protect the oceans and their resources because it's in their immediate and long-term self-interest to do so.

The UNCLOS was controversial because it ceded significant resources to coastal states, many of which are exceptionally wealthy. Many poorer and land-locked states protested the conference provisions because the public good was greatly reduced. Coastal states could exclude others from the 200-mile zone, keeping the less advantaged from exploring the deep seabed that extends beyond the zone. The conference created the International Sea Bed Authority to monitor deep-sea exploration, but it is still unclear as to whether and how deep-sea resources will be distributed. Those who capitalize on the global commons, which now lies beyond the 200-mile zone, are supposed to share the wealth with the international community. Yet, those having the capability to exploit the deep seabed are reluctant to commit the resources for exploration if their profit margins are significantly narrowed. To complicate matters even further, some coastal states want to extend their jurisdictions even further, well beyond the 200-mile exclusive economic zone. The United States did not sign onto UNCLOS until 1994 after extracting significant concessions that many see as undermining the entire treaty. The U.S. Senate still has not ratified the treaty. Today, the Arctic is at the center of controversy as melting sea ice has led to a "resource rush" of sorts. Eight states with Arctic coastlines have rights under the treaty to the natural resources of the Arctic. In 2007, Russian submarines planted a Russian flag on the Arctic deep seabed and, in 2008, Canada announced its intention to build two bases near the Arctic circle. These actions represent attempts to demonstrate sovereignty of the vast resources of the Arctic.

EFFORTS TO PROTECT BIODIVERSITY

Several unilateral, bilateral, and multilateral initiatives to protect biodiversity and natural habitat have drawn attention to the peril of sea and land mammals as well as birds. Although these efforts have met with varying degrees of success, they have all sought to save habitat and species from spoilage and economic exploitation. The following international treaties have been established to preserve habitat and protect biodiversity (Greene 1998, 316–317):

- 1971 Ramsar Convention (conserves wetlands—the natural habitat of waterfowl);
- 1972 Convention on Trade in Endangered Species;
- 1972 London Dumping Convention (restricts the disposal of chemical and nuclear wastes at sea);
- MARPOL Convention (curbs oil pollution).

In addition, IGOs, such as the IWC, have also been established to protect certain endangered species. Most efforts to protect biodiversity occur at the national level because states exercise direct jurisdiction over habitat. For example, the U.S. Endangered Species Act protects domestic species like the eagle, the spotted owl, and timber wolves, while the U.S. Marine Mammal Protection Act extends protection to sea mammals outside national jurisdiction by restricting trade with countries that harvest dolphins or whales. For the most part, habitat protection falls to states through domestic legislation.

The Rio Conference (discussed in detail later in this chapter) led to the Convention on Biological Diversity, which was signed by 155 states. The legal framework of the treaty acknowledges the sovereign rights of states to resources within their territorial jurisdiction, but commits states to the protection of species, ecosystems, and habitats. The treaty also establishes rules for the use of genetic resources derived from plants and animals. Unsurprisingly, the North–South divide made negotiating this treaty difficult: "Developing countries were concerned that an international treaty might put unwanted limitations on the use of their natural resources, including forests . . . Developed nations, on the other hand, wanted continued access to the plant and animal life in developing nations" (Press 1992). Money issues represented another impediment. Developing countries wanted the richer countries to pay for their conservation. The protection of fish, animals, birds, and plants together with their habitats is an expensive endeavor, requiring a significant commitment of financial resources—resources that developing states simply cannot spare. Developing states also want to share in the wealth generated from pharmaceuticals and the genetic engineering of plant and animal life originating in their countries. The treaty recognizes that wealthy nations have a responsibility to help fund conservation internationally; however, monetary contributions are, for the most part, voluntary and remain small.

THE VIENNA CONVENTION OF THE PROTECTION OF THE OZONE AND THE MONTREAL PROTOCOL

Ozone depletion threatens biodiversity and poses a health hazard to humans. The Vienna Convention (1985) and the Montreal Protocol (1987) laid the basis for significantly reducing the amount of CFCs that can be released into the atmosphere and established a schedule for their eventual elimination (Benedict 1991). The Montreal Protocol also creates a trust fund, known as the Multilateral Fund, which helps developing states acquire substitutes for CFCs and other ozone-depleting substances. The Vienna Convention and the Montreal Protocol, which have been revised on several occasions, have been widely hailed as important environmental protection successes because they bridged the gap between North and South through compromise and consensus. Most scientists were able to agree as to the causes and consequences of ozone depletion. The principal depleting agents are relatively easy to identify, and the agents have comparable, nonharmful substitutes.

The successes of the Vienna Convention and the Montreal Protocol have set an encouraging precedent for international environmental cooperation; however, implementation of the agreements has encountered domestic roadblocks in the United States. Several CFC-producing firms have filed suit in federal court, claiming that certain aspects of the treaty violate due process. Some have asked Congress to exempt CFCs that are used in inhalers for asthma. But in spite of such problems, the Vienna Convention and the Montreal Protocol show that compromise and consensus can be achieved without resorting to "the lowest common denominator" approach that has plagued other international negotiations to protect the environment. Currently, 191 states are party to the Montreal Protocol, and according to the U.S. Environmental Protection Agency, the ozone layer is repairing itself.

THE RIO CONFERENCE

The UN Conference on the Environment and Development (1992) held in Rio de Janeiro, Brazil, simultaneously and systematically addressed the interrelated environmental issues of desertification, biodiversity, climate change, and deforestation. **The Rio Conference**, also known as the **Earth Summit**, was attended by representatives of more than 150 states, while several hundred NGOs participated in a parallel conference. Among the attendees were more than hundred heads of state, signaling the emergence of economic development and protection of the environment as priorities for the international community.

The Rio Conference adopted the theme of "sustainable development." First articulated in 1987 by the World Commission on Environment and Development (also known as the Brundtland Commission), sustainable development is economic development that "meets the needs of the present without compromising the ability of future generations to meet their own needs" (World Commission on Environment and Development 1987, 43). Sustainable development recognizes that the kind of economic development that has occurred in the advanced industrialized countries cannot be replicated in the Third World without grave environmental consequences. The Brundtland Commission assigned significant responsibility for environmental degradation to the advanced industrialized countries and raised important equity issues between North and South. It also considered the rights of future generations. The Rio Conference adopted the Brundtland recommendations, adding new dimensions to environmental protection and socioeconomic development.

The Rio Conference was the culmination of years of preparatory work in drafting agreements known as **framework conventions** (Greene 1998, 330)—international agreements that establish basic aims and principles but impose no binding obligations on states. During the Rio Conference, three principal framework conventions were adopted: the Convention on Climate Change, the Convention on Biological Diversity, and the Convention to Combat Desertification. Unfortunately, a framework convention on deforestation failed. International negotiations could generate no consensus regarding principles, norms, aims, or procedures for arresting deforestation. This setback notwithstanding, framework conventions are useful. They provide the first steps in systematically addressing interrelated and interdependent environmental problems.

The parties to framework conventions commit themselves to following up their agreements with legally binding treaties. Parties agree to cooperate on setting broad goals and to cultivate concrete strategies for achieving more narrow and specific objectives. The framework conventions provided the basis for negotiations of the Conventions on Biological Diversity and Desertification. More than 130 nations met in 1997 in Kyoto, Japan, to tangibly implement the United Nations Framework Convention on Climate Change (UNFCCC). The UNFCCC called on the industrialized states to cap their emissions to 1990 levels, but the parties could not agree on a timetable. The UNFCCC also established mechanisms for monitoring climate change and commits the advanced industrialized states to partially fund emission-control measures in the developing world (Stevens et al. 1992, 11). The Kyoto Conference, which was designed to give the international agreement on climate change treaty status, sought to achieve emission stabilization and reduction goals. The conference also addressed the always-controversial issue of financing, which is discussed at length in our case study on climate change.

The Rio Conference also adopted Agenda 21, which is an 800-page program for promoting sustainable development in the twenty-first century. Agenda 21 is divided into four sections. The first section deals with issues relating to social and economic development. It addresses poverty, consumption patterns, population, human settlements, and policy making as they affect the prospects of achieving sustainable development. The second section focuses on the conservation and management of resources for development. Specifically, this section addresses protection of the atmosphere and land and ocean resources. It outlines strategies for combating deforestation, desertification, and drought. It also addresses the use of toxic chemicals and the disposal of hazardous and radioactive wastes. The third section explores ways to strengthen the role of major sociodemographic groups such as women, youth, indigenous peoples, NGOs, workers, unions, farmers, business, industry, and scientists. The fourth section deals with ways and means of implementation of Agenda 21. This section examines financial resources, the transfer of environmentally sound technology, and promoting environmental awareness.

Agenda 21 consists of forty chapters that outline a very ambitious and forward-looking program for environmental protection and economic development. It also calls for the creation of the **Commission on Sustainable Development (CSD)** to help implement and monitor Agenda 21 initiatives. Created in December 1992, the CSD is a fifty-three-member functional commission of the ECOSOC. More than a thousand NGOs are accredited to participate in the Commission's work. The CSD is charged with promoting visibility of sustainable development in UN activities and for improving the coordination of environmental and development programs among UN agencies and within and between states.

Progress has been slow at the national level as many countries, including the United States, encountered domestic trouble in passing the appropriate national legislation. Many of the agreements worked out and signed during the Rio convention established basic aims but did not formally bind or commit states. The CSD, seeking to keep the Rio momentum going, put forth a comprehensive document entitled "Programme for the Further Implementation of Agenda 21" (UN Commission on Sustainable Development 1998) to encourage states to continue pursuing meaningful sustainable development policies.

Agenda 21 also addresses the financing of environmental protection and sustainable economic development. It calls for the **Global Environmental Facility (GEF)** to help finance sustainable development efforts. The GEF, which became operational in 1991, was created to facilitate concessionary financing for the Third World to assist in managing the greenhouse effect, the loss of biodiversity, and ocean pollution (*Finance and Development* 1991). The GEF is jointly operated by the World Bank and the United Nations Development and Environmental Fund (UNDEP). Its initial start-up $1.5 billion was provided by the advanced industrialized world. As the GEF Web site states, since its inception, the GEF has provided $6.2 billion in grants and generated more than $20 billion in cofinancing with other development organizations.

The Rio Conference was a success in that it brought most of the world's nations together to address myriad environmental and socioeconomic developmental problems. The conference brought together NGOs and IGOs, representing states, women's groups, business, industry, labor unions, scientists, and indigenous peoples. The Rio Conference highlights the increasing importance of NGOs in international governance. Thousands of NGOs are involved with influencing international environmental issues. These NGOs defy any defining characteristics. They can be religious, secular, for-profit, nonprofit, private, or public. NGOs influence environmental governance by defining or redefining environmental issues, lobbying governments, proposing draft texts of conventions, lobbying international agencies, and monitoring the development and implementation of international agreements (Porter and Brown 1991, 54). These nonstate actors have carved out a central place for themselves in the formation of national and international environmental policies.

Are international efforts to protect the environment sufficient? Are they equitable? What is the best way to balance environmental protection with economic development in a global economy—an economy largely based on natural resource extraction and consumption? The complexities of environmental controversies are illustrated next in the case study on climate change. This case highlights the deep differences between rich and poor nations and deep-seated divisions over the causes and consequences of climate change. It demonstrates how competing worldviews make international consensus-building difficult and how different groups within and between societies seek to pass the costs of climate change on to others and even on to future generations.

CASE STUDY 7: CLIMATE CHANGE

Climate change refers to the progressive increase of the temperature of the earth's atmosphere attributable to the buildup of greenhouse gases (carbon dioxide, CFCs, and methane) that are trapped in the atmosphere. According to the Intergovernmental Panel on Climate Change (IPCC),

> [H]uman activities—such as the burning of coal to run industries and gasoline to fuel automobiles—are warming up the global climate. Left unchecked, the "enhanced greenhouse effect" is expected to alter the earth's climate and adversely affect human health, ecosystems, farming, forestry, water levels, and human development. (*World Bank News* 1997, 6)

Climate change is further exacerbated by indiscriminant land clearing, the lack of reforestation, and the expanding market for tropical timbers.

Climate change became a focal point of international environmental protection in the late 1980s as more and more scientists began to warn that climate change was real and had both immediate and long-term consequences. Rising sea levels threaten coastal and island states and their human settlements. Weather extremes, such as floods and drought, threaten hundreds of millions of lives, destroy habitat and crops, and can lead to the destruction of temperate and tropical rain forests. Increased economic development and rapid population growth ensure that global emissions of carbon dioxide will increase; meanwhile, the square acreage of forest, particularly the tropical rain forests, will decrease as the need for living space, fuel, and raw materials becomes greater. Without the forests, carbon dioxide levels will rise, increasing global temperatures.

In November 1989, sixty-eight countries met in the Netherlands to address the climate change issue. Three strategies were given consideration. First, all states should commit to stabilizing or reducing carbon dioxide emissions by a certain date in the future. Second, only the advanced industrialized countries should stabilize or reduce their greenhouse gas emissions. These countries should also pay for new technologies to help the developing world cultivate more efficient industries and energy-consumption patterns. This strategy was advocated by many Third World nations, particularly India and China, who argued that Third World states were not responsible for current climate change trends. Rather, climate change was the result of the North's industrialization process and the U.S. love affair with the automobile. Developing countries need new industries to alleviate poverty and promote economic development, which translates into an increase in energy use. Curbing greenhouse gas emissions in the Third World would put undue burdens on their economies, stifling economic growth and limiting consumption. It also makes the Third World pay the externalized costs of the economic development of the West. The third strategy, advocated by the United States, the former Soviet Union, and Japan, was to conduct more research and try to reach a scientific consensus before committing to any specific reduction or stabilization plan. These three strategies, or variations thereof, have been debated, albeit acrimoniously, at the preparatory climate change conferences in Geneva, at the Rio Conference, and at the Kyoto Conference in 1997.

The causes and the consequences of climate change are contested. Several observers question whether enough evidence exists to conclude that climate change is, in fact, a real environmental condition. Long-term temperature records are incomplete, and documentation is inadequate. After all, in the 1970s, environmentalists and meteorologists warned, not of warming, but of a coming ice age. Others acknowledge that climate change exists but disagree as to its causes or its effects. Many argue that warmer temperatures are an acceptable price to pay for our current standard of living and technological advancement. A few even argue that countries in the Northern hemisphere, like Russia and Canada, could benefit from climate change.

Several facts, however, are not in dispute. People in the industrialized countries account for less than 25 percent of the world's population, but generate the majority of the heat-trapping gases. Even though the advanced industrialized countries account for the lion's share of emissions, in terms of economic output, they are far more efficient users of fossil fuels than are developing countries. Economic output refers to the metric tons of greenhouse gases emitted per million dollars of gross domestic product generated. Using this measure, China, India, Russia, and the rest of the developing world have far more "dirty industries" and are less efficient. Thus, their pollution rates are higher, given what is produced and consumed.

The Kyoto Conference was held in December 1997 to build upon the **UN Framework Convention for Climate Change** (UNFCCC), which was an outcome of the Rio Conference. The initial agreement was hammered out after 11 days of turbulent debate. **The Kyoto Protocol** included three major features. First, the 159 parties to the Protocol agreed to reduce worldwide emissions of greenhouse gases by 5.2 percent below 1990 levels by the year 2012 (*Online Newshour* 1997). All the parties were permitted to set their own reduction targets to achieve this goal. The EU, the United States, and Japan agreed to reduce their emissions by 8, 7, and 6 percent below 1990 levels, respectively. Second, only the advanced industrialized states were required to meet their agreed-upon target. The Kyoto Protocol required the thirty-eight developed states to reduce their greenhouse gas emissions, as they tend to be the largest emitters. The developing countries were only required to set voluntary limits. Third, the Kyoto Protocol allowed for the trading of emission permits. That is, developed countries could buy the right to emit greenhouse gases from countries in the developing world. This would help all nations to achieve their collective goal: Worldwide greenhouse gas emissions could dip overall, while Third World industries could afford to develop greater efficiencies—efficiencies that would benefit both the developing and the developed world.

In March 2001, the Bush administration announced that the United States would reject the Kyoto Protocol. The Bush administration stated that the treaty would hurt the U.S. economy and would not succeed because developing countries were exempt from binding emission cuts. The U.S. withdrawal from the treaty dealt a significant blow to further multilateral negotiations. Having the largest greenhouse gas emitter on the sidelines caused other important industrialized states to reconsider their efforts (Revkin 2001, A8). Nevertheless, the international community led by the EU continued to negotiate curbs on greenhouse gas emissions. In November 2001, binding rules for the Kyoto Protocol were developed. Termed the "Marrakech rules" after the city in Morocco where they were negotiated, the 165 nations agreed to the following points (*Associated Press* 2001, A15):

- Industrialized countries are to cut or limit greenhouse gas emissions by an average of 5.2 percent from 1990 levels by 2012.
- Countries may offset requirements or earn credit by properly managing carbon sinks (forests and farmlands that absorb carbon dioxide).
- Emissions trading using permits to buy and sell the right to pollute.
- Countries that do not meet their target emissions will face mandatory punishment.
- In order for the treaty to take force, it must be ratified by fifty-five countries responsible for 55 percent of the greenhouse gas emissions.

The Marrakech rules were the culmination of difficult negotiations between the competing interests of nation-states, and represent the desire of the vast majority of nations to address climate change. The United States chose to "free ride," which damaged the Kyoto process. With the United States on the sidelines, nearly all of the advanced industrialized countries had to ratify the treaty in order to reach the requisite 55 percent of the worldwide greenhouse gas emissions. Still, the Marrakech rules represented an important milestone in industrial history (Revkin 2001, A8). The Bush administration maintained that the United States was committed to solving the problems of climate change, but in its own way and at its own pace (Revkin 2001, A8).

In 2004, Russia formally approved the Kyoto Protocol, which brought the treaty into force. In 2005, the UN hosted a conference in Montreal in order to finalize strategies for implementing Kyoto. The United States participated in nonbinding talks in Montreal but continued to formally reject the protocol. The Montreal Conference met with modest success in that parties to Kyoto agreed to extend their commitments to reducing greenhouse gas emissions beyond 2012, when Kyoto expires. Developing states resisted binding reductions for their emissions but were willing to continue to implement Kyoto. The consensus among parties to the treaty was to continue to combat climate change with the hopes that a change in administration in the United States would result in bringing the remaining industrialized states on board. Then, the international community could turn to negotiating more binding reductions for developing countries.

In 2007, efforts to curb climate change were reinvigorated when Kevin Rudd was elected as Australia's Prime Minister. Australia was the only other industrialized state that had not committed to Kyoto besides the United States. With Australia on board, the 2007 UN Conference in Bali, Indonesia, focused more squarely on how to combat climate change after 2012. The conference resulted in the **Bali Road Map**. The road map sets a climate change agenda (items included technology transfers and deforestation) as well as a deadline to have a binding treaty ready by 2009 which would replace Kyoto in 2012. The 2008 election of Barack Obama renewed international optimism for engaged U.S. leadership in combating global climate change. The **Copenhagen Conference**, also referred to as **COP 15** because it was the 15th meeting/conference of the parties to the UNFCCC, was convened in December 2009 to negotiate the post-Kyoto binding treaty. The outcomes of the COP 15 were disappointing not only because the binding treaty did not materialize but also because the gap between the North and South regarding fairness and the need for mitigate emissions could not be bridged. The United States fully and actively participated in the negotiations; however, the best that was achieved was an agreement by states to try to achieve a binding treaty before December 2010. In August 2010, Secretary-General Ban expressed doubt that an agreement can be reached before that deadline. Will international efforts result in effective public international law? Will international efforts be successful at reducing greenhouse gas emissions? Who stands to gain and who stands to lose from this process?

A Realist Cut

Environmental issues such as biodiversity, desertification, and climate change occupy the realm of low politics for most realists. These issues take a backseat to geostrategic and military concerns because environmental threats are distant and convoluted while environmental protection is costly. More important, the rewards of environmental protection are uncertain at best. States in the international system need to be kept apprised of potential environmental threats, but they should not sacrifice more important and more immediate interests such as a strong, healthy, and diversified economy.

Climate change is the kind of environmental issue that bumps against traditional notions of national interests. If climate change is the result of the human way of life, then humans will need to change the way they live. But, they are not likely to change without a very good reason, and bad weather in other parts of the world usually isn't a good enough reason. In general, realists argue that "free riding" on any climate change agreement would be quite easy and highly likely. While many, if not most, states are willing to cooperate in curbing greenhouse emissions, other states—free riders—can reap the rewards of a reversal of climate change without paying the price. Free-riding states can then devote their resources to increasing their economic or military strength at the expense of the environment and the collective efforts of states to reduce greenhouse gas emissions. Free-riding states can even nullify the efforts to check climate change. The end result is quite similar to the Prisoners' Dilemma (Chapter 3). If everyone cooperates, the efforts to curb climate change are likely to be effective, producing the best outcome for everyone on the planet. Unfortunately, incentives to defect are great. If one large emitter, like the United States or China, defects—or if a group of states defects—the efforts of the rest are for naught. So each state would be better off not cooperating, because chances are high someone is going to defect.

Which states are likely to be free riders? That depends on whether you're a realist from the developed world or a realist from the developing world. Realists in the North argue that any international agreement on climate change that does not include binding target reductions on countries like China, India, Mexico, and Brazil is pointless (Zengerle 1998, 10–11). Developing states now account for more than 50 percent of greenhouse gas emissions by 2010 and China has surpassed the United States as the world's largest emitter. Thus, developing states are, in effect, free riding because they are permitted to increase their emissions, while the developed world must fundamentally change its way of life. The U.S. Chamber of Commerce argued that the Kyoto Protocol would cost the average American family of four some $30,000 to meet the U.S. commitment (U.S. Chamber of Commerce 1998). The advanced industrialized states would have been downright foolish to agree to such costly (and substantive) changes in lifestyle with no assurances of success in reducing greenhouse gas emissions from the developing world. Thirteen members of OPEC actively oppose binding reductions for developing states and are supported by the G-77 (Barnett 2008, 1). Their oil interests are far more important than cooperating on climate change. Without binding reductions for developing states, reversing climate change will be impossible. At the 2009 Copenhagen Conference, developing states resisted binding emissions and the *de facto* leader of the G-77, China, deliberately snubbed the advanced industrialized states by sending a relatively low-level official to the "heads of state" meeting to negotiate with Barack Obama and German leader Angela Merkel (Lynas 2010, 24). It insisted on watering down strong provisions relating temperature targets and long-term targets for global emission reductions For many observers, China's obstructionist behavior was indicative of a new geopolitical reality, where its interests were driving negotiations (Giddens 2010). China "is assuming the mantle of a superpower, and it's not pretty" (Lynas 2010, 24). In an almost identical fashion to the earlier U.S. positions on climate change, China acknowledges climate change and it is aggressively pursuing green strategies on its own terms (Ying 2010, 28–29).

Realists from the developing world take another view. They argue that climate change is the fault of the advanced industrialized states, whose great power status is directly related to their long history of greenhouse gas emissions. The developed states currently produce the lion's share of emissions and will produce approximately half of them in 2010. Yet, the advanced industrialized states want to distribute the costs of climate change onto developing countries, costs they can ill afford. According to the editorial opinion in Brazil's *Folha de Sao Paulo* on December 8, 1997,

> The position of the developed countries is also comfortable. Once nature is devastated, these nations, the United States in particular, want to divide the destruction's costs worldwide. . . . But the developed countries are the major emitters of polluting gas. The United States, leading the ranking polluters, is the one that defends the slower rate for the reduction of burning of fossil fuel that produces the greenhouse effect. (U.S. Information Agency 1997b, 12)

The motives of states, particularly the powerful ones, factor into international negotiations. According to Gu Qi in China's *Jiefan Ribao*, Kyoto negotiations can be explained in a variety of ways. "One explanation for U.S. behavior is that its national interests are more important than global interests. . . . For its own economic interests, the United States is unwilling to accept restrictions, and is guilty of using various delaying tactics" (U.S. Information Agency 1997b, 3). At the same time, the United States saw the European proposal of reducing greenhouse gas emissions to 15 percent below 1990 levels as unrealistic. The Europeans knew full well that such a plan would not be considered seriously; however, the plan did allow the Europeans to take the moral high ground and engender support among developing nations. The COP 15 negotiations demonstrated that developing states retained a lingering distrust of the United States. Given U.S. past behavior, developing states were simply not going to commit to doing more than the United States. The U.S. position in Copenhagen was that "it could only commit to internationally what was in the draft legislation before the House of Representatives and the Senate in the US, which meant a very modest reduction compared to 1990 and limited international oversight" (Doelle 2010, 92).

Realists from both developed and developing states rail against the loss of state sovereignty implied by international climate change law. According to U.S. Senator Chuck Hagel (R-NE), "This is the United Nations, for the first time ever . . . having the power to dictate to a nation, to the United States, how much energy it can use, what kind of energy it can use . . . Meteorologists can't even tell you from forty-eight hours to forty-eight hours what kind of weather we're going to have. In Kyoto, they were talking about one-hundred-year weather patterns" (cited in Zengerle 1998, 10–11). During Kyoto negotiations, one of the central debates was whether climate change was actually occurring. During Copenhagen negotiations, all 193 states acknowledged it was occurring, although a sizable number questioned whether human activity during the last 100 years was actually causing the climate to change. Undoubtedly, realists in developing states are equally concerned about yielding state prerogatives to international organizations given the unknowns and the likelihood of free riding.

For realists, states that cooperate with binding international efforts to check climate change and reduce carbon dioxide emissions face job losses, skyrocketing energy prices, and high taxes on its citizens. All of these are unacceptable costs for an environmental issue that offers uncertain rewards, if any. The incentives for others to free ride could even mean that states that actively cooperate may face a relative decline of economic and military capability. The best that states can do, absent a higher authority, is to tend to their own economic and security needs and respond to environmental threats as they arise. The U.S. approach has been to develop a framework at home for reducing greenhouse gas emissions and then try to encourage others to follow its lead (Purvis 2004, 175). Given U.S. power (and domestic success in reducing emissions), perhaps it would be better for others to abandon the UN-based Kyoto process and adopt a U.S.-based regime that includes some Kyoto initiatives instead (Hovi and Skodvin 2008, 129–130). This approach is known as Kyoto-Lite. The disappointing outcome of COP 15 shows that regardless of who is running states, cooperation in confronting climate change is difficult, if not impossible, to accomplish.

A Liberal Cut

The liberal views of climate change break down into two positions: the neoclassical economic perspective and the neoliberal institutionalist perspective. The neoclassical economic perspective is the position originally advocated by the United States at the Kyoto Conference—zero reduction of greenhouse gas emissions, but a cap on emissions. Each state is then assigned a "right" to emit, based on its economic output. Recall that economic output refers to metric tons of greenhouse gases emitted per million dollars of gross domestic product generated. Embedded in this proposal is the right of states to buy and sell emission permits that would force economically expanding states to buy the right to emit greenhouse gases from other states. According to Britain's *Daily Telegraph* (December 10, 1997), "the U.S. proposal is based on its own successful domestic experience with tradable permits for sulphur emissions. This kind of market solution boosts efficiency and puts a ceiling on overall emissions."

The neoclassical perspective relies heavily on the idea that the best way to protect the global commons is to privatize it. Giving states the right to pollute gives them, in effect, property rights in the atmosphere, whereby both the environment and economic development can be sustained. The U.S. proposal sought to establish an effective equilibrium between the demands of economic development and environmental protection as it relates to climate change by bringing market forces to bear upon both interests. One of the central problems of development is the externality of many environmental costs. But if firms are forced to pay as they pollute, they will come closer to bearing the true costs of economic development—and the prices of goods and services produced will reflect those costs. Assigned rights to pollute, coupled with the right to buy and sell pollution permits, governments have incentives to encourage energy-efficient behaviors on the part of firms and individuals. And the more efficient states become, the more rights they can sell to less efficient states (or industries at the national level). At the same time, no artificial impediments are placed on economic growth, and flexibility is built into the greenhouse gas-reducing scheme.

One way that states can encourage energy-efficient behaviors for firms is to institute an investment tax credit for those utilizing energy-efficient technologies, both in existing and future sectors. According to Murray Weidenbaum (1992), investment tax credits have two positive effects. First, investment tax credits stimulate economic growth rates, and the increased economic output generates the resources to address environmental issues. Second, tax credits encourage the replacement of old, inefficient, pollution-generating capital equipment. The investment tax credit is thus a tangible, but nonintrusive, way for governments to use market forces to achieve both macroeconomic and macroenvironmental goals.

Neoclassical liberals are wary of environmental regulations that curb market forces or stress the role of the state. They argue that state control over industries and extensive regulation of the environment will not produce desirable environmental and economic results. As proof, they cite the former Eastern Bloc and Soviet successor states, where both the environment and industry suffered severe, and possibly irreparable, harm when market forces were eliminated through excessive bureaucratic regulation. The Soviet Union—a managed economy—left a legacy of "ecocide," the result of its efforts to become an agricultural and industrial giant (Sneider 1992, 10–11). The old Soviet territory, once rich in natural resources, is now massively contaminated by industrial pollution, pesticides, chemical fertilizers, and nuclear waste. Thus, states should have a limited role, lest bureaucratic inefficiencies undermine both the economy and the environment.

The liberal institutional approach specifies a much more prominent role for governments and international organizations. Rather than merely assigning and monitoring property rights, then letting markets govern the rest, the institutionalists maintain that national governments and international organizations are essential to international environmental governance absent a world government. The international environmental regime consists of states, IGOs, nonprofit NGOs, businesses, and the scientific community. These different actors represent both congruent and competing interests—interests that must be addressed openly and systematically in international forums. While all interests may not be equitably addressed and bargaining power may vary, the balance of all these interests will approximate an international public good. This dynamic brings about a consensus among a variety of groups and leads to the formation of knowledge-based groups known as epistemic communities.

The liberal institutionalist perspective has centralized and decentralized variants. The centralized approach reflects the arguments associated with the advocates of some kind of world government. The centralized approach is based on the idea that governments should agree to a "set of actions calibrated to achieve the desired reduction in emissions" (Cooper 1998, 72). The best way for governments to achieve a reduction in greenhouse gas emission is to tax the offending activity. This so-called carbon tax would be monitored by the IMF, which could report to the body that implements the climate change treaty. While the international community is a long, long way from an international tax, many advocated a central role for international organizations. This centralized view was never seriously considered at Kyoto, as the United States, a virtual veto state, strenuously pursued the neoclassical view. After Kyoto, liberal institutionalists argued that the United States could be compelled to join the Kyoto process by linking international trade agreements to international efforts to combat climate change (Stiglitz 2006). The WTO could be instrumental in this regard. By restricting imports from non-Kyoto participating countries, parties to Kyoto could induce Kyoto compliance. With the failure of COP 15 to produce a binding treaty to replace Kyoto, neoclassical liberals warn that such a strategy could lead to a trade war. With the global financial crisis, states need to resist the urge to use climate change to justify protectionist policies.

The decentralized view of international governance as it relates to climate change considers the local, municipal, subnational, national, regional, and international activities of all the different actors affected by climate change. It acknowledges a complex web of actors, each pursuing different goals and aims. However, unlike the neoclassical approach, it would not unleash unfettered market forces on firms and individuals to reduce greenhouse gas emission. Rather, it would marshal ideas. That is, divergent interests would compete in an international marketplace of ideas—an open atmosphere in which a variety of interests and arguments can be heard. This process, in turn, would further the advancement of knowledge. Competing interests within and between states, within and between industries, within and between NGOs, and within and between scientific communities, clash in this intellectual market. Such a clash will force a rethinking and redefining of previously held positions, prompting more rigorous debate.

The knowledge process, while arduous, can achieve global environmental protection without undermining individual, local, or national interests. The Kyoto Protocol, which builds upon the UN FCC, is far from perfect. But perfection was never the goal. International environmental protection will never be easy in an international arena where politics are influenced heavily by competitive nation-states. As stated in an editorial by *The Guardian* (December 11, 1997),

> We have seen the same old divisions setting developed nations against the developing with the same last-minute concessions and late night fudges. The result, assuming it can be pinned down and ratified, is acknowledged on all sides to be only a tentative stab attacking a problem already soaring out of control. All concerned, including environmental lobbyists, say that a defective accord is better than none. Wearily, we must accept the logic of this argument. (U.S. Information Agency 1997b, 8)

Pragmatism and process are the best routes to solutions that address competing concerns. These competing concerns are reflected in the World Bank's assessment of Kyoto and its own role in building the capacity and the economic resources of states to ensure economic development and environmental protection. To this end, the World Bank is working to mainstream renewable energy policies, to integrate climate change externalities, and to identify climate-friendly options in the World Bank Group Portfolio (*World Bank News* 1997). The World Bank strongly supports the compromise at Kyoto, which exempts developing states from mandatory greenhouse gas reduction targets. The World Bank, building upon neoclassical economic analysis, views economic development as necessary in order to create the wealth required to adequately address climate change. From international to local levels, economic development and environmental protection are pursued incrementally to the mutual benefit of individuals, firms, nations, and the world.

Liberals of all stripes recognize that Copenhagen was at best a disappointment and at worst, a disaster for international efforts to combat climate change. But optimists point out that while the UN-centered process is badly damaged, multilevel governance is possible. By aggregating all the policies of state and nonstate actors at the local, national, and regional levels, climate change is being addressed and accounts for much of the progress that has been made (Dimitrov 2010, 18).

In sum, the distinguishing features of any liberal view of environmental protection are the prominent roles of markets (political and/or economic) and the behavior of nonstate actors, particularly firms and NGOs. Environmental NGOs have created an expansive network of agencies that monitor environmental problems and lobby governments and IGOs for rules and regulations that protect the environment. Firms are also important because they are the ones generating wealth, and environmental regulation affects their interests. Governments are also involved in that they respond to domestic constituencies and enforce property rights (in this case, the right to pollute). Any environmental regime that addresses climate change must have the cooperation of states to enforce international rules and norms.

A Marxist Cut

Marxists point out that international efforts to protect the environment reveal widening differences between the rich and the poor. These differences relate to the causes of environmental degradation, the best strategies for environmental protection, and the determination of who should bear the burden of combating climate change (Linner and Jacob 2005). Like realists from the developing world, many Marxists see climate change as a consequence of the economic development of the North. However, Marxists emphasize that it is the economic development of the advanced industrialized countries that has caused the current crisis in climate change. The capitalist mode of production, with its emphasis on private property, wage labor, and markets, has undermined the natural environment. Hence, the Marxist lens focuses on capitalism and the mass consumer societies of the North as the principal culprit. Northern societies benefited from the unrestricted use of their own resources and access to resources in colonies in the South. They cleared millions of square kilometers of forest without any regard to the environmental consequences. The global capitalist economy is based on the consumption of fossil fuels by industries and consumers. To many Marxists, the UN emphasis on "sustainable development" is just a euphemism for sustaining the privileges of the dominant capitalist states or classes (Seabrook 1993). Radio commentary on *Westdeutscher Rundfunk* of Cologne stated that the U.S. position at the Kyoto Conference reflected its privileged status: "This is a climate policy according to the decisions of the lord of the manor" (U.S. Information Agency 1997b, 10).

The negotiations of the Kyoto Protocol represent the continuing dominance of neoclassical liberal economic thought. Gramscian Marxists point out that market solutions are near dogma at the IMF and the World Bank. Even decidedly liberal observers have recognized that these multilateral financial institutions and the regional development banks have yet to internalize "sustainable development" in evaluating loan applications and in their general lending practices (Porter and Brown 1991, 47–49). These international organizations stand in the way of significant environmental protection. To many Marxist-inspired observers, the recent emphasis of multilateral financial institutions on environmental protection is more "rhetoric" than "reality" (Foster 1993; Rich 1993). They continue to fund industry at the expense of the environment, and they limit the participation of NGOs in development and environmental projects (*Earth Island Journal* 1992, 20). The now infamous "Summers's Memo," written by former World Bank official Lawrence Summers (who is now the director of the National Economic Council in the Obama Administration), recommended that developing states should relax or discourage environmental regulations to lure dirty industries from developed states (Rauber 1992). While this recommendation makes perfect sense from a neoclassical standpoint, it bodes ill for the environment and climate change.

The Kyoto Protocol was a victory for capitalism and international businesses because it accomplished very little, which is precisely what industries wanted. Industries that are able to externalize their pollution costs are able to achieve higher rates of profits for their owners and shareholders. Industries are only concerned about their quarterly reports and prospects for growth. The furthest thought from the minds of most CEOs is the temperature of the earth's atmosphere and the environmental consequences one hundred years from now. The oil and automobile industries' displeasure with environmental regulation translated into direct and decisive influence on the U.S. position at Kyoto. According to an editorial in Japan's *Mainichi* on December 9, 1997, "About 50 U.S. senators and members of Congress as well as petroleum and auto officials are assembled at the conference site to keep close watch on Washington's insistence on a 'zero percent' reduction to the last. Isn't this the imposition of an environmental 'Pax Americana' on the rest of the world?" (U.S. Information Agency 1997b, 2). To many observers of the Kyoto negotiations, the U.S. position was untenable. As Italy's *La Repubblica* stated, "The United States . . . . will not accept meaningful changes in its ways of production and consumption" (U.S. Information Agency 1997b, 9). Denmark's *Information* editorialized, "The United States won a victory for the global market economy at the historic meeting in Kyoto. A precedent has been created where the most dangerous greenhouse gases will become trading commodities. The climate will not be the winner" (U.S. Information Agency 1997b, 10).

The Copenhagen conference failed in large part because of the inability of the West to recognize that capitalism is part of the problem. Although the United States was fully engaged in the COP 15 negotiations and President Obama attended the head of state meeting, the United States could offer very little because its government was captive to capitalist interests. The House and Senate, whose members are beholden to corporate campaign money, wouldn't even consider, much less pass, modest climate change legislation. This legislation could have demonstrated to the rest of the world that the United States was taking concrete steps to combat climate change and was willing to lead through example. Instead, members of Congress caved to corporate interests. Ironically, Republicans, who once advocated vigorously for "cap and trade" as a market-based strategy for reducing greenhouse gas emissions, now opposed it because corporations would have to "buy" the right to pollute. Corporations, on the other hand, wanted to be *given* the right to pollute because being forced to buy the rights amounts to a backdoor tax.

Marxists see environmental degradation as a contradiction of capitalism. The level of economic development of the capitalist core has come at the expense of the environment and the developing world. As the *Brundtland Report* states, future economic development cannot take place without grave consequences to the environment, which is why Kyoto is as much a conference on international equity, social justice, and economic ideology as it is about climate change. *Le Pays*, Burkina Faso's principal newspaper, declared,

> A tip of the hat to the Group of 77 that from now on wants to break from the triumphant capitalism, the all-powerful gospel of competition in the name of which the United States behaves, not only as the universal principal polluter, but also as transforming our countries into tubs for toxic wastes. It is true that the poor countries are the first victims of the destruction of the environment, the devastation of resources, the accumulation of noise pollution, the over-consumption of the rich, the economic system based on monopolizing profit, and the arrogance of civilization experts. (U.S. Information Agency 1997b, 9)

The conferences that followed Kyoto generated a lot of talk but little action. Ironically, one of the largest, attended by more representatives of states, IGOs, NGOs, and MNCs than previous conferences, was the COP 13 December 2007 meeting in the tropical resort of Bali, Indonesia. The location, timing, and estimated carbon footprint of the hundreds of private and jumbo jets necessary to deliver delegates raised serious questions about the international commitment to climate change. The conference was widely criticized as winter vacation for the transnational elite who were largely oblivious to the amount of greenhouse gas emissions the conference generated. In Copenhagen, the convergence of environmental and antiglobal capitalist activists (fueled by the 2008 global financial crisis) led the UN and the Danish government to effectively disenfranchise civil society from the negotiations (Fisher 2010, 14–15). NGOs had their credentials revoked or were not even permitted to register.

A Feminist Cut

The Rio Conference brought many women's issues to the forefront of the international agenda. The roles of women in sustainable development are argued to be central to the success of Agenda 21. One role of women is that of "environmental managers" (Cohen 1994). Women, especially those who live in the developing world with traditional and subsistence economies, are users and conservers of their immediate environment. They are "the major food producers and marketers, water and fuel wood gatherers, and overseers of domestic sanitation and waste disposal" (Cohen 1994, 8). Women are also the reproducers of the human population. Population growth translates into more energy consumers and the need for additional living space, both of which contribute significantly to climate change.

Many see rapid population growth as undermining the environment and the local and national economies (*Finance and Development* 1991). Women obviously play a critical role in promoting stable population growth because they can influence family size. Environmentalists, population advocates, and feminists all agree that improving the status of women globally is the most important means for controlling population growth. They argue that women must be allowed more control over their lives. Women must be politically and economically enfranchised, and they must have access to birth control and other reproductive services.

Yet, cultural and religious impediments remain, as does outright sexism. These features are prevalent both in the developed and the developing world. Many feminists are wary of government population policies because they have led to forced abortion and sterilization at one extreme (China and India) and the criminalization of birth control and forced childbearing on the other (Ireland). Feminists argue that population policies that are implemented without specific and guaranteed protection of the individual rights of women are catastrophic for women. They argue that a bottom-up approach that allows women control over their bodies and their lives will enable effective family planning and stable population growth. Only then will population pressures on the world's reserves of food, water, and other natural resources be alleviated.

While population growth is directly related to global consumption patterns, women are also important consumers of energy and gatherers of wood fuel. Taxes that attempt to restrict energy consumption put additional burdens on women. Climate change and international efforts to curb its effects have both positive and negative effects for women. On the positive side, women in developing countries are permitted to continue their energy consumption without formal restrictions. On the negative side, women will bear the brunt of substantial cutbacks in greenhouse gas emissions in the future. The irony of climate change is that its natural effects may impact men and women without discrimination. However, masculine solutions to the problems associated with climate change will likely pass the cost on to the most vulnerable in the international community. Feminists argue that a more local, horizontal, cooperative approach toward climate change is likely to be more effective than any global approach.

Ecofeminists have sought to redefine women's roles in environmental protection beyond the "women as environmental managers" (Peterson and Runyan 1993, 145). This includes demanding full participation by women in the formulation of policy at all government levels and redefining development that recognizes women's work, bartering, and informal sectors of the economy. Development must also be reconceptualized to include environmental costs and the costs of environmental restoration. Feminists also argue that the North–South divide that permeates much of international politics also affects feminist unity regarding climate change. Feminists have found themselves divided between liberal feminists and socialist feminists because of their theoretical differences. Socialist feminists criticize the consumption patterns in the West and the market-oriented strategies for addressing climate change. They see the market as a cause of climate change, not a solution. Feminists point out that in opinion polls around the world, women place the environment and climate change as a high priority for the international community.

The Copenhagen conference, in spite of feminist critiques, still approached the problem of global climate change as a technical, scientific issue. Negotiations focused on the science that predicts the environmental consequences of a 1.5 degree global average temperature increase versus a 2 degree increase. There were complicated economic models that determined the supported and unsupported "nationally appropriate mitigation actions" (NAMAs). What was missing from the discussions was the gender inequalities associated with climate change. Since women tend to occupy the ranks of the poor, they are more likely to suffer the worst effects of climate change such a flooding, drought, and violent weather (Sasvari 2010, 15). They are also more likely to become environmental refugees. Gender inequalities affect how people experience climate change and women must be engaged so that NAMAs do not fall disproportionally on the backs of women. On a positive note, 30 percent of COP 15 delegates were women.

A Constructivist Cut

The constructivist approach illustrates how the global climate change regime was created, norms and values developed and disseminated, and interests defined and redefined. For example, the social construction of the Netherlands' identity and its role in constructing climate change help explain the rise of climate change as an international issue (Pettenger 2007, 51–74). The identity of the Netherlands is that of environmental leader, on the frontier battling rising sea levels. Rising sea levels are a material fact; however, climate change is, in part, an idea constructed by individuals in the Netherlands seeking to explain rising sea levels. Over time, climate change has become "real" because it was socially constructed by a variety of actors.

Relatedly, constructivists explore how the identities of actors are formed and how some identities are privileged over others. In the case of climate change, actors include individuals, states, and international organizations. Identities are shaped and framed by the interaction with other actors under the structure of the Framework Convention for Climate Change, which helped actors develop shared definitions and common understandings of the processes and dynamics of climate change. The scientific method, itself a social construction, is seen by many as the preferable way to empirically indicate climate change. Knowledge is power and scientific knowledge, however imperfect, has drawn many to agree that the climate change is "real" and has material consequences for human beings.

The process of climate change becoming "real" was not progressive or linear. Countries like the Netherlands and international organizations like the UN sought to construct a discourse that would communicate to other actors the idea and material consequences of climate change. Countries like the United States and international organizations such as MNCs challenged that discourse and offered an alternative discourse of skepticism. The self-identity of the media, particularly the American media, is that of unbiased and fair reporters of the news. As such, the news media presented the "is climate change real?" debate to see if there were equal voices and scientific studies on both sides. Climate change remained contested for at least a decade as a result. Now, climate change is acknowledged to be real, but skeptics question whether humans are responsible (Avdeeva 2010). E-mails from prominent climate change scientists were leaked before the Copenhagen conference that seemed to indicate that the scientists where trying to exclude evidence that challenges the Intergovernmental Panel on Climate Change unequivocal finding that humans were changing the climate (Eilperin 2009). Conservative and libertarian NGOs used the pirated e-mails to fuel opposition to international efforts to curb global warming by creating a counter-narrative that petty, single minded scientists and UN bureaucrats were driving the process and were not to be trusted.

Norm creation is also a central focus of the climate change regime. One such norm is that of universal participation (Hoffmann 2005). The value that all states "should" participate in addressing climate change was embedded in the UN FCC, and the decision of the United States not to participate formally in Kyoto created international discord with other states. The rejection of the United States of this particular norm put pressure on the United States to change its position and also contributed to the emerging identity of the EU as the leader of the coordinated global efforts to address climate change. When the United States rejoined formal efforts in Copenhagen, a competition for leadership between the United States and the EU resulted, not because of material factors, but because of their intersubjective identities of who is the "leader." China used Copenhagen to establish that its interests were equal to those of the United States and the EU. Another norm of the international climate change regime is that of "equity." That is, in terms of the cost of combating climate change, who should bear the burden? Initially, the cost should be borne by the advanced industrialized countries. However, the climate change architecture (structure) that emerged from the Kyoto process was that the costs "should reflect the differing contributions of each country (and its members) to present and future climate change as measured by their current and historical greenhouse emissions" (Page 2007, 9). The Copenhagen conference was seen as important because if it had been successful, the climate change–related costs for poor countries would have been formalized (Moellendorf 2009, 247). The meaning of the equity norm is changing to accommodate changing identities and interests. At the same time, constructivists concede that the North and South may never converge because the actors have very particularistic notions of fairness (Parks and Timmons 2010).

CASE STUDY 8: WHALING

The IWC was created by the International Convention for the Regulation of Whaling (ICRW) in 1946. The ICRW recognized that the story of whaling was one of overfishing that had led to a dangerous depletion of whale stocks. At the same time, it acknowledged that whaling is an important industry for some countries and an important source of food for many indigenous peoples. The IWC created by Article III of the ICRW was designed to promote the interests of whaling states by preserving whaling stocks. Specifically, the IWC is responsible for the proper conservation of whale stocks and the orderly development of the whaling industry.

The IWC currently has eighty-eight members, with each state having one vote. Membership is open to any state wishing to sign on to the ICRW. IWC decisions are made on the basis of a simple majority except that a two-thirds majority is required when determining the following:

- protected and unprotected species;
- open and closed seasons;
- open and closed waters, including the designation of sanctuary areas;
- size limits for each species;
- time, methods, and intensity of whaling (including the maximum catch of whales to be taken in any one season);
- types and specification of gear and apparatus and appliance that may be used.

The IWC meets annually, is supported by a small Secretariat, and is represented by the Secretary-General. The work of the IWC is divided between three committees: the Scientific, Technical, and Finance and Administration. This division of labor within the IWC allows each committee to specialize and develop expertise in their areas. For example, the Technical committee deals with Aboriginal Subsistence Whaling and researches the patterns of whale consumption by aboriginal peoples like the Inuit in Alaska. In general, the IWC is charged with protecting endangered species, designating whale sanctuaries, setting quotas on whale kills, specifying hunting seasons, and regulating the capture of female whales with suckling calves. Moreover, the IWC is responsible for measuring and maintaining whale stocks, as well as conducting scientific research.

The IWC is an example of an international organization being created in order to avoid the tragedy of the commons. In this case, the IWC is supposed to protect whaling stocks and the livelihoods of whaling states. After World War II, when food supplies were low, the United States encouraged Japanese whaling to stave off famine. Whale hunting and whale products are integral parts of Russian, Icelandic, and Norwegian heritage. However, industrialization and technological innovations led to the mass killing and processing of whales, nearly to the point of extinction. The fourteen founding members of the IWC were countries that had sizable whaling industry and/or interests, and their goal was to protect the resource that sustained them all. Yet, the whale population had continued to decline. In spite of over forty years of IWC management, the whale population was decimated as whaling states exceeded their quotas and industrial pollution poisoned their habitat. Since the IWC is principally a scientific body and not an enforcement agency, it could only warn of impending disaster. Like many other IGOs, the IWC relies on the voluntary cooperation of member states.

By the 1970s, its membership had expanded to include more than thirty members, many of whom opposed whaling on moral and ethical grounds. In 1982, the IWC issued a fifteen-year moratorium on all commercial whaling, while permitting whaling for indigenous groups and scientific research. This was accomplished by setting the quota for commercial whaling at zero. The former Soviet Union, Japan, Iceland, and Norway opposed the moratorium, which went into effect in 1986, but only Norway formally objected to the moratorium. Japan was granted an exemption to kill whales for scientific purposes. In 1994, the IWC placed an indefinite moratorium on commercial whaling over the formal objections of Japan and Norway. Article V, Section 3, of the ICRW allows objections from members to IWC rules, which means the regulations adopted by the IWC are not binding on the objecting state. Hence, Norway and Japan are not bound by the moratorium and have continued whaling.

At the 2001 meeting, IWC members discussed two major issues—the revised management scheme and additional whale sanctuaries. The revised management scheme would lift the moratorium on commercial whaling and assign Norway and Japan whale-kill quotas. The creation of whale sanctuaries in the South Pacific and the South Atlantic was also at issue. When the IWC designates a certain area of the ocean a sanctuary, most types of whaling in that area are prohibited. The meeting of the IWC pitted pro-whaling states against conservationist states and ended in deadlock. The creation of the two new whale sanctuaries was blocked, as conservationists could not get the requisite two-thirds majority. The moratorium remained in place; however, IWC rules allow exemptions for objecting states. Hence, the whaling activities of objecting states are largely unregulated. In 2004, the IWC consisted of fifty-seven members, and the number of pro-whaling states increased from nine to twenty-one members (Revkin 2004, D4). Whaling states such as Japan have continued to recruit small developing states to obtain the necessary votes to overturn the IWC moratorium on commercial whaling. The small Caribbean island of Dominica was accused of selling its vote to overturn the moratorium at the IWC meeting in South Korea in 2005. Conservationist states alleged that Japan had agreed to finance two multimillion dollar fishing complexes in exchange for Dominica's support (*Sun-Sentinel* 2005, 12a). Dominica officials denied such a deal and stated that its vote was for the sustainable use of a resource. The moratorium was not overturned at this meeting; however, it remained a goal for whaling states. In 2008, the IWC again could not bridge the impasse between whaling and antiwhaling states. Japan and Iceland continue to whale, drawing protests from environmental groups and conservationist. In 2010, at the annual conference held in Morocco, the whaling states once again tried to overturn the moratorium on commercial whaling. Several states, including the United States and Switzerland, proposed lifting the moratorium and replacing it with a tightly controlled culling of nonendangered whale species. These states asked whaling states to agree not to hunt in the Southern oceans, in effect, acceding to the wishes of Australia and New Zealand, which oppose all forms of whaling (Jolly 2010). The Morocco talks collapsed without agreement because the requisite three-fourths majority could not be reached. Several questions are raised about the efficacy of the IWC. Is the IWC an effective institution of international governance? Whose interests does the IWC serve? What influences IWC decisions? What is the future of the IWC?

A Realist Cut

Issues such as whaling and efforts to "save the whales" occupy the realm of low politics. The depletion and extinction of animal resources are nothing new as they are often the unfortunate consequences of human interaction with other species. However, the case of IWC does present several lessons regarding sovereignty over natural resources and the role of bargaining power in influencing the decisions made by international organizations. The creation of the IWC was part of the post–World War II flurry of institution-building under U.S. hegemony. The goal was for the whaling states to manage whale stocks and thereby preserve their national heritage and identity. States have sovereignty over their natural resources and may utilize them as they see fit. By signing on to the ICRW, whaling states agreed to monitor and take steps to preserve whale stocks; however, they did not agree to put themselves out of business. As membership in the IWC expanded, it became clear that these new members, along with the United States, were interested in protecting "whale stocks" by eliminating the whaling industry altogether. Led by the United States, members such as Australia, New Zealand, the Netherlands, France, Germany, and the United Kingdom used the bargaining power within the IWC to establish the moratorium. These conservationist states, influenced by their own domestic environmental movements, saw the killing of whales as an immoral act. To these states, whales are majestic creatures deserving of special protection, and they used the IWC to achieve that goal. Whaling states were forced to either issue formal objections with the IWC or withdraw from it (as Iceland did). Norway simply exercised its sovereign right to object under the ICRW and has continued to whale in its own waters (Chadwick 2001). Japan was forced to bow to U.S. pressure and accept the moratorium in 1984, but was able to negotiate the "scientific research" loophole that would allow it to keep hunting whales. Within the IWC structure, the wealthy, more powerful states were able to influence the organization to achieve its environmental goals.

Whaling states have a choice between two strategies in securing their national interests with regard to whaling. First, they can seek to change the current balance of power within the IWC. Japan and Norway have been able to enlist the support of many small, developing states to create an obstructionist bloc. With eight or nine developing states, the whaling states can prevent the two-thirds vote necessary for regulations affecting their interests. Japan has specifically tied increases in development assistance to several Caribbean countries in order to gain their favorable votes within the IWC (*BBC News* 2000). Not surprisingly, this bloc of states was able to vote down the formation of additional whale sanctuaries at the 2001 meeting. They were also able to block efforts to more closely regulate "scientific" whaling. The pro-whaling faction is likely to get stronger if Iceland rejoins the IWC. Also not surprising then, Iceland's petition to rejoin the IWC was rejected by the conservationist states at the 2001 meeting. The 2010 Morocco conference was marred by more allegations of Japanese vote buying. *The Sunday Times of London* (June 13, 2010) filmed officials from pro-whaling states claiming that they voted because of Japanese foreign aid. These officials also admitted that they received cash payments to cover their travel and entertainment expenses. The entertainment included visits from call-girls. Japan is simply using its influence to obtain an outcome it desires from the IWC.

Second, whaling states could abandon the IWC altogether. Unless the moratorium on commercial whaling is lifted, the industry and the communities sustained by them could face extinction. The High North Alliance, a pro-whaling group with members from Canada, the Faroe Islands, Greenland, Iceland, and Norway, has lobbied their governments to withdraw from the IWC. Whaling states are looking toward the North Atlantic Marine Mammal Commission (NAMMCO) as a new vehicle of international cooperation. The NAMMCO seeks to reinstate commercial whaling and further the interests of whaling states (*BBC News* 2000). Whaling states still have incentives to stay with the IWC. First, "scientific whaling" is just as good as commercial whaling. All whaling states need to do is conduct a few tests and then process their scientific subjects for commercial use. It might mean some legal maneuvering around the Convention of Trade in Endangered Species, but it could be done. Second, states that have violated the moratorium on whaling face only international condemnation, but no real economic or political consequences. Until the conservationists are willing to put some teeth into the moratorium, whaling states have good reasons not to completely abandon the IWC. After all, the conservationist states are not going to risk their economic and political relationships with Japan, Norway, or Iceland over some whales. Without some kind of binding agreement, Japan and other whaling states can effectively hunt at will since the IWC has no enforcement power.

A Liberal Cut

Absent a higher authority in international relations, the IWC is the best alternative, balancing the needs of environmentalists, the whales, the whaling industry, whaling states, and conservationist states. Liberal interpretations of the IWC have several variants. One stresses the role of science. The IWC is based on a scientific foundation that seeks to preserve whale stock by learning about their migratory and birthing patterns. The problem with the IWC is that it is politically driven and has ignored the scientific findings of its professional and competent staff. From its inception until the 1970s, the IWC ignored its scientific analyses and predictions and presided "over the mass destruction of one great whale population after another" (Aron 2000). Today, the voice of science is again being ignored, "this time to prevent the taking of whales, regardless of their population abundance" (Aron 2000). Science does not take any moral position on whether it is right or wrong to hunt whales. Science provides decision makers with the facts about whale populations, migration, and reproduction (Schweder 2000). It is up to political actors to use the information in a manner that is mutually agreed upon. If whaling as an industry is to be permitted, there are several species, like the minke and sperm whales, which have sufficient populations for culling.

The neoclassical liberal argument suggests that one way to protect the whales and whaling industry is to assign hunting rights; however, this only works if the interests of both the whales and the industry are considered. If the industry is condemned and the interests of conservationists are privileged, then whaling states have no incentive to cooperate. Property rights and markets can balance competing interests, protect endangered whale species, and sustain an ocean resource. Consumers that object to whaling for moral or ethical reasons are free not to buy goods and services from whaling states.

The neoliberal institutionalists acknowledge that a significant loophole exists within the current regime which allows whaling states to hunt. Only effective regulation that is monitored closely by the IWC will insure that whale populations are effectively protected. Since the moratorium has been put in place, the whaling states have harvested more than 30,000 whales for "scientific purposes." The dispute between Australia and Japan regarding whale hunting in the Southern Ocean is now before the International Court of Justice. Australia claims that Japan has breached its obligations under International Convention for the Regulation of Whaling and must cease hunting. Although the case is in its early stages, institutionalists highlight that international law and organizations can help states resolve their disputes such that their other important relationships are not harmed.

A Marxist Cut

The plight of the whales and those who have taken up their cause illustrates the spectacular failure of the liberal promise of markets, science, technology, and shared values in solving, or even effectively managing, international problems. The market for whale products is not a niche, but a large one that is culturally based in northeast Asia and their extended relatives in Northern Europe and North America. If markets were allowed to decide the fate of the whales, then the days of whales are numbered. Does the rational self-interest of the whaling industry include the preservation of the resource that sustains them all? No, the whaling industry will hunt until every whale is "harvested." Their interests are immediate and short term—how much they kill and how much they can earn bringing the kill in. Through the process of subcontracting of whale services from hunting to processing to marketing, responsibility for the destruction of the whales is diffused. Whether the whales become extinct in five, ten, or fifty years is irrelevant to whalers. IWC has only provided the illusion of whale protection.

Scientific inquiry does little to help the situation. Every side in the dispute is able to marshal numerous scientific studies to support their position and dispute any findings from opposing viewpoints. The so-called unbiased science becomes so muddled that no one can agree as to whether scientific findings are valid, and all sides accuse each other of manipulating science to serve their own ends. Scientific uncertainty is used to politicize issues before the IWC. Japan has used "scientific whaling" to serve its commercial whaling interests, and while countries have called this commercial whaling in disguise, who is to say that countries that have a tradition of consuming whale meat and products are not interested in preserving this resource through scientific research? Whaling communities suspect the science that finds that whale meat may be unfit to eat. In 1999, after testing samples of whale meat in Japanese restaurants, American and Japanese scientists found that half of the meat held concentrations of heavy metals, dioxins, and Polychlorinated biphenyls (PCBs). This finding can easily be seen as a scare tactic to try to get consumers to abandon whale meat. Similarly, scientific studies of the Inuit have found that they have been contaminated with PCBs and pesticides from eating whale meat (Edwards 1998).

Technology has been of little use, unless one considers technology of mass killing a positive contribution. The IWC has, throughout its history, tried to promote the most efficient and humane way of killing whales. This translates into many dead whales, killed in an industrial yet humane manner. Has this technology been used to promote the fertility and the proliferation of whales? Has technology been used to track and document the activity of whaling ships and poachers? The vast majority of the research and development under the IWC is devoted to the "humane" killing of whales.

The idea of "shared values" of the "international community" is also absurd. The conservationist states oppose whaling because their culture finds it abhorrent and offensive, and they are trying to impose their cultural values on others (*New Scientist* 2001). Yet, these same countries have no problem with mass killing of cows, chickens, pigs, or kangaroos even though other cultures find those practices inhumane, offensive, or profane. Certain values cannot be distributed by the "marketplace of ideas" as it results in the lowest common denominator approach. That, in turn, means the demise of the whales—an outcome that both whalers and conservationists would like to avoid.

A Feminist Cut

A significant contribution of the feminist perspective is the question: Where are the women? Whaling has been and continues to be a manly pursuit. The whaling industry is controlled exclusively by men. It is men who captain the whaling ships and hunt the whales. Women are conspicuously absent at most levels of decision making within the industry or the IWC. Female scientists have conducted a few studies for the IWC; however, their influence is diluted because of the debate regarding scientific uncertainty relating to whale populations. Whaling is a masculine endeavor, lionized in fiction and folklore. This, in turn, perpetuates the hunting of whales.

The market for whale products is extensive and includes more than just whale for human consumption. However, the niche market of whale meat in the trendy, upscale sushi bar and restaurants in Japan is the domain of Japanese men (*Time International* 2001). Whale is considered a rare treat to be shared with male colleagues, like a fine scotch or handrolled Cuban cigars in the United States. Whale meat is also believed to cure impotence and enhance sexual prowess and virility. In fact, the continued trade of many types of endangered species is spurred by the belief that by consuming certain body parts, male sexual performance is enhanced. At the very least, the male's gender role as hunter contributes to the need to hunt animals in the wild and that has led the whales to the verge of extinction. In this sense, the feminist perspective problematizes the masculine when trying to explain the inability of the international community to prevent the decimation of the whale population.

This is not to say that women do not consume whale; however, they do so in large numbers only as members of indigenous peoples. And whale consumption has not been kind to their children. A study of the peoples of the Faroe Islands, north of Scotland, has showed brain and liver damage higher than normal in children whose mothers had eaten whale meat (Chadwick 2001). Studies have also shown that breast-feeding Inuit mothers can damage the health of their babies, as their milk contains ten times more chlordane than that of mothers in southern Canada (Edwards 1998).

Women have been active in antiwhaling NGOs such as Greenpeace and Save the Whales. They also have been at the forefront of conservation efforts and have taken whaling states to task in international and national fora. New Zealand Prime Minister Helen Clark has publicly insisted that Japan explain its vote-buying in the IWC (Department of Conservation 2001a). She also publicly denounced Norway when it announced that it would lift its ban on whale exports. New Zealand Conservation Minister Sandra Lee led the 2001 campaign to establish a whale sanctuary in the South Pacific (Department of Conservation 2001b). Women's voices are among the more strident and determined in banning whaling and establishing a new industry for the whales—whale watching.

A Constructivist Cut

Constructivism highlights the protection of whales and development of shared values regarding the consumption of whale products. Without the IWC moratorium on commercial whaling, the whale population could have been decimated and several types of whales could have become extinct. The moratorium was the first step to the preservation of the whales as a species. The values of the international community have evolved to include an almost complete consensus against whaling as an industry. The community has been willing to accept limited whaling on the part of indigenous peoples so that they can retain their independence and identity. However, the international community is almost universally opposed to whaling for commercial purposes and mass consumption. The market for whale products is small and borne out of nationalism and tradition. This niche market does not give whaling states the right to ignore their international obligations, engage in vote-buying, and slaughter whales. The IWC may not have the teeth to enforce the moratorium on commercial whaling; however, coupled with international efforts to protect biodiversity and prohibit trade in endangered species, it can expose deviant states. The whaling "regime" informs consumers about the practices of Japan, Norway, Russia, and Iceland and allows them to make educated choices regarding their consumer choices.

The story of the whales cannot be told without attention to normative considerations (Stoett 2005, 151). The conflicts in the IWC center on competing values and norms, not material interests. Over time, the antiwhaling norm was embraced globally, almost universally. International norms evolved from exploiting nature to protecting nature, and the normative shift conditions the relationships between states. The norm that endangered species ought to be protected grew out of tangible efforts on the part of states, through conference diplomacy and international organization (Epstein 2006). Whales are important symbols of global protection efforts. Japan's rejection of the antiwhaling norm is due to cultural and political structures that block the acceptance of the norm domestically (Hirata 2004, 177). In spite of Japan's rejection, Japan did cut short its whale-hunting schedule in 2008 because it found itself outside the "society of states" because of its whaling activities. Japan's view of self and identity internationally is that of a full and upstanding member of the international community. The international criticism and poor media coverage challenged that identity and caused a change in behavior.

CONCLUSION

Environmental problems like deforestation, desertification, climate change, and biodiversity are intractable and inseparable from the issues of equity and development. The theoretical frameworks of realism, liberalism, Marxism, and feminism approach equity and environmental protection quite differently. How these problems are to be managed will be debated, tabled, and readdressed in the decades to come. Each approach raises valid and legitimate points about the values that ought to be pursued with regard to climate change and whaling. Each approach seeks to order priorities according to their preferences and precepts. The challenge for environmental protection is how to determine which values will prevail and which arguments warrant substantive review. These are the roles and the politics of international organizations in the realm of environmental protection. The constructivist approach details and describes this process.

KEY TERMS

The International Whaling Commission (IWC)   227
tragedy of the commons   227
sustainable development   229
deforestation   230
desertification   230
biodiversity   230
ozone depletion   230
climate change   230
the Stockholm Conference   232
United Nations Environmental Program (UNEP)   232

the Common Heritage of Mankind   233
The UN Conference on the Law of the Sea (UNCLOS)   233
the Vienna Convention   235
the Montreal Protocol   235
the Rio Conference   236
Earth Summit   236
framework conventions   237
Commission on Sustainable Development (CSD)   238

Global Environmental Facility (GEF)   238
Climate Change   239
United Nations Framework Convention for Climate Change   240
Kyoto Protocol   240
Bali Road Map   242
Copenhagen Conference (COP 15)   242

SUGGESTED READINGS

Betsill, Michelle M., and Elisabeth Corell, eds. 2008. *NGO Diplomacy: The Influence of Nongovernmental Organization in International Environmental Negotiations.* Cambridge, MA: MIT Press.

Epstein, Charlotte. 2006. The Making of Global Environmental Norms: Endangered Species Protection. *Global Environmental Politics* 6 (May): 32–54.

Hirata, Keiko. 2004. Beached Whales: Examining Japan's Rejection of an International Norm. *Social Science Japan Journal* 7 (August): 177–197.

Hovi, Jon, and Tora Skodvin. 2008. Which Way to U.S. Climate Cooperation? Issue Linkage versus U.S.-Based Agreement. *Review of Policy Research* 25 (March): 129–148.

World Commission on Environment and Development. 1987. *Our Common Future.* New York: Oxford University Press.

Human Rights and Humanitarian Issues

International organizations play crucial roles relating to human rights and humanitarian issues. IGOs like the UN, EU, and the Arab League promote human rights and deliver emergency assistance to societies in crisis. NGOs (often functioning as subcontractors) work with IGOs to provide food aid and health, education, and legal services. Human crises are intertwined with political violence, poverty, environment degradation, and gross violations of human rights. In this chapter, we examine three issues—refugee protection, human rights, and international criminal law. We will look at the international law and international organizations that directly frame these issues, and we will see how they shape the contemporary international political landscape. The case studies investigate the UN response to the 1994 Rwandan genocide and the development of international criminal law and courts to hold individuals who commit genocide, war crimes, and crimes against humanity accountable for their actions.

REFUGEES

One of the more destabilizing events threatening international peace and security is the mass movement of people across international boundaries. World War II forced millions of Europeans and Africans from their homes. The 1948 Arab–Israeli War displaced almost the entire population of Palestine. The Cold War and the rise of Soviet-styled regimes caused many to flee communist oppression. The decolonization process generated tens of millions of additional refugees in Africa and Southeast Asia in the 1960s and 1970s. In the 1980s, the civil unrest in Central America and Haiti caused many to flee their homeland. During the 1990s, the Balkan crisis and the breakdown of civil order in many African countries once again put millions on the move. The twenty-five-year Afghanistan crisis has sent millions of Afghans into neighboring countries and abroad. Currently, more than twenty million persons are in "refugee-like" situations. Refugee movements create unimaginable hardship on individuals fleeing crisis and can destabilize neighboring countries as millions of people stream across borders seeking asylum, safety, or just food and water.

The international community has done much to protect "stateless" persons and to provide assistance. The UN responded to many of the post–World War II refugee movements by creating the **United Nations High Commissioner for Refugees (UNHCR)** in 1950. The UNHCR is charged with coordinating multilateral aid and seeking "durable solutions" to the plight of refugees. It attempts to establish a permanent settlement for each refugee situation and responds with emergency relief and care. More important, the UNHCR facilitates international cooperation among UN members, a task that is not easily accomplished because its scope and mandate extend well beyond the legal obligations of states.

The legal obligation of states is set out in the **1951 Convention Relating to the Status of Refugees and the 1967 Protocol.** Article I of the Convention defines a refugee as someone who has a

well-founded fear of being persecuted for reasons of race, religion, nationality, membership to a particular social group or political opinion, is outside the country of his nationality and is unable or, owing to such fear, is unwilling to avail himself of the protection of that country; or, who, not having a nationality and being outside the country of his habitual residence as a result of such events, is unable or, owing to such fear, is unwilling to return to it.

States that are party to the Convention have a legal obligation not to return refugees, or those seeking such status, back to a situation of persecution. This principle of "no return" is called *nonrefoulement,* and it is through this principle that refugees are ultimately protected. The process of obtaining legal refugee status involves a series of administrative steps. First, the individual enters the territory of the state and applies for asylum. The right to grant asylum is a sovereign prerogative of states. If asylum is granted, the individual is registered with the UNHCR and is considered a legal or *de jure refugee.* Arrangements are then made to find a more permanent or "durable" solution through one of three mechanisms—**voluntary repatriation, resettlement, or assimilation.** Voluntary repatriation is often impossible as the conditions in the refugee's country of origin are not likely to have changed in the short term. Resettlement in third countries usually depends on the ties between the individual and the third country, such as whether the individual has family in the third country. Assimilation, therefore, is the usual course of action. The refugee is usually given an opportunity, after a certain period of time, to apply for citizenship.

On the surface, the definition of a refugee seems sufficiently broad to include a wide range of persecution. However, the definition refers to *individual* persecution. Excluded are those who flee because of foreign occupation, generalized violence, civil war, civil disorder, and civil unrest. Also excluded are victims of extreme poverty or natural disaster. People who flee these conditions do not qualify because these conditions affect the general population as a whole. Asylum seekers must prove that they are individual targets of persecution. Many countries interpret "well-founded fear" as meaning the individual is more likely than not to face persecution upon return. In this sense, the definition of a refugee is quite narrow and the burden of proof quite high.

To complicate matters further, the mandate of the UNHCR has expanded to include more than just assisting and protecting *de jure* refugees. Unrest in Asia and the colonization process in Africa resulted in large-scale disorder and violence, producing large numbers of people resembling refugees, yet not qualifying under the narrow definition of the 1951 Convention. In 1957, the General Assembly authorized the UNHCR to use its good offices to assist those in Hong Kong regardless of the controversy surrounding their exact status (Gordenker 1987, 39–48). This allowed the UNHCR to use funds donated by governments to assist Chinese asylum seekers even though they did not meet the statutory requirements of the Convention. The UNHCR's mandate was expanded further as a result of its involvement during and after the Algerian revolt against France. The brutal counterguerrilla campaign by France sent tens of thousands of Algerians across the border into Tunisia and Morocco. The UNHCR moved to assist the Algerians, and the General Assembly later approved the UNHCR's actions. The UNHCR was also called into action in Cyprus after the 1972 *coup d'etat*, and invasion by Turkey caused large-scale internal displacements. Under the good office umbrella, the mandate of UNHCR expanded to include those who flee foreign occupation, civil war, and generalized violence, as well as **internally displaced persons (IDPs)** who are unable to flee. International law prescribes a rather narrow definition of a refugee and levies a legal obligation on states not to return refugees to situations of persecution. However, the scope of the UNHCR mandate extends far beyond the conventional framework. This discrepancy is at the heart of the current dilemma concerning the protection of *de jure* refugees and those who are likewise assisted by the UNHCR, *de facto* **refugees**. The role of the UNHCR has evolved to address "refugee-like situations", while the legal framework formalizing state obligations has not.

The UNHCR spends anywhere from $400 million to $1 billion annually, depending on refugee situations and the generosity of UN members. The UNHCR budget is voluntary, and contributions largely come from the United States, Japan, Germany, and other industrialized countries. The UNHCR budget is used to assist *de jure* and *de facto* refugees in developing countries that are unable to foot the bill alone. The UNHCR also works closely with other UN agencies assisting in refugee situations. The **World Food Program (WFP)** was established in 1963 to serve as the central UN agency for the distribution of food aid within the UN system. The agency has the dual role of providing emergency food aid in crisis situations and supporting economic and social development. The WFP provides for the basic food needs of refugees worldwide. The WFP responds with emergency food aid when population movements suddenly occur and works with the UNHCR on self-sufficiency projects.

The UNHCR also works closely with the **World Health Organization (WHO)**. WHO is the primary agency responsible for the health needs of refugees. WHO provides vaccinations for polio, measles, chicken pox, and other infectious diseases. Programs also include pre- and postnatal care for refugee women, as well as infant care. WHO provides instruction regarding AIDS and cancer prevention. Finally, WHO responds to outbreaks of malaria, cholera, and typhoid fever, which can occur in densely populated refugee camps.

The activities of the UNHCR and other UN agencies are complicated because refugee crises are rooted in international and civil war and the breakdown of public order. These tensions are exacerbated by environmental conditions such as drought or flooding, which results in famine and disease. Since very few meet the *de jure* definition of a refugee, UN agencies deal almost exclusively with *de facto* refugees and are often caught between warring parties, all of whom are willing to use humanitarian assistance to refugees as a form of leverage or even a weapon of war. UN personnel and property have become targets of violence. Durable solutions to these crises involve more than just responding with humanitarian assistance as the situation disintegrates into chaos. It involves early warning mechanisms and state-building after the crisis. International peace and security are inextricably linked to respect for human rights and human security.

Like the environment, human rights have taken center stage in international politics in recent years. Human rights violations and refugee crises in Chechnya, Iraq, Bosnia, Somalia, Kosovo, Rwanda, Congo, Burundi, and Sudan have generated a great deal of international concern and, in some cases, even intervention. Historically, the relationship between the government and its citizens has been an internal matter, falling well within the sovereign domain of states. However, beginning in 1945 and accelerating since 1970, human rights have become increasingly internationalized (Forsythe 1991a). Human rights are now legitimate values to be pursued through international politics. Chapter I, Article 1(3), of the UN Charter explicitly identifies promotion of human rights as a central concern of the UN. One purpose of the UN is "to achieve international cooperation in solving international problems of an economic, social, cultural, humanitarian character, and in promoting and encouraging respect for human rights and for fundamental freedoms for all without distinction to race, sex, language or religion." Chapter IX, Articles 55 and 56 of the UN Charter, restates the UN's responsibility for encouraging universal respect for human rights and levies a legal duty on states to cooperate in both the promotion and the protection of human rights. Beginning with the UN Charter, a proliferation of international human rights agreements has detailed civil, political, economic, social, and cultural rights. Human rights commissions and monitoring systems have been developed to implement these accords. Other treaties pertaining to genocide, racial discrimination, the rights of women, torture, and collective bargaining have also been negotiated. Like the environment, human rights generate significant controversy. No one is "against" human rights or the environment; however, people often disagree regarding the definition, implementation, and protection of human rights. Human rights are contentious because they challenge the principle of sovereignty and may even invite international intervention.

MAJOR HUMAN RIGHTS AGREEMENTS

In addition to the UN Charter, several international agreements pertaining to human rights have been reached. In 1948, the Universal Declaration of Human Rights was passed by the UN General Assembly without a dissenting vote, although South Africa, the USSR, and several Eastern Bloc states abstained from the resolution. The Universal Declaration of Human Rights lists thirty basic principles that are considered fundamental to human dignity. The Universal Declaration of Human Rights is not legally binding on states; however, it serves as an authoritative guide to interpretation of the UN Charter and represents the sense of the international community (Brownlie 1994, 21). It spells out **political and civil rights**, including the rights to life, liberty, personal security, and political participation. It also addresses **economic and social rights**, such as the right to work, to form unions, and to a standard of living adequate for health and well-being. In addition to these individual human rights, the Universal Declaration contains **collective rights,** such as the right to self-determination and development. The drafters of the resolution intended to follow up the Universal Declaration with a binding treaty or covenant that would have imposed specific duties and obligations on states (Donnelly 1993, 10).

The Universal Declaration of Human Rights explicitly links respect for human rights with international peace. According to the preamble, the foundation of freedom, justice, and peace in the world is the recognition of the dignity and equality of all human beings and their inalienable rights. Human rights are essential for promoting friendly relations between states and respect between individuals. In many respects, the Universal Declaration of Human Rights is revolutionary because it challenges state sovereignty and represents a higher moral authority.

Transforming rhetoric into reality has proven difficult. The binding international law that was supposed to follow the Universal Declaration of Human Rights was impeded by Cold War tensions and the attendant quarrels over social and economic rights versus political and civil rights (Donnelly 1993, 7–10; Forsythe 1991a, 121–127; Pollis and Schwab 1979, 1–18). The human rights debate was and is complex. It centers on three political arguments rooted in the historic East–West conflict, the continuing North–South conflict, and the ongoing debate between universalism and cultural relativism (Vincent 1988). The West, led by the United States, has emphasized civil and political rights over economic and social rights. The West used civil and political human rights to criticize the Soviet Union and to justify Cold War policies. The Soviet Union criticized racial discrimination in the United States and accentuated economic and social rights—rights to which the United States has paid little attention.

Developing states sought to actualize cultural and collective rights in addition to many economic rights. The North–South conflict, which focuses on the disparities between rich and poor in the international community, highlighted the inconsistencies in U.S. and European foreign policies. On the one hand, the West criticized the East for systematically denying civil and political rights, yet supported brutal colonial regimes, then authoritarian governments, as bulwarks against communism. The North systematically ignored the basic needs of people in the developing world and has denied that any "right to development" exists.

In the debate over universality versus cultural relativism, the question is fundamental: Are human rights universal—applicable to all—or must they be understood in the light of culture? Proponents of the cultural relativist approach argue that human rights, as conceptualized by the UN, are eurocentric. That is, the notions of political, civil, economic, social, and cultural rights found in Western European political and economic thought ignore non-Western approaches to human rights. Even economic rights, which are more closely associated with Marxism, are Western in origin. The philosophic and religious traditions of the Middle East, the Indian subcontinent, China, and Southeast Asia are ignored or marginalized by the human rights discourses. The inherent biases of human rights laws demand a relative approach to their implementation, lest the West impose its culture on the rest of the world.

The lag between the Universal Declaration and a more binding international law was the result of the very real political divisions within the UN. Two treaties were negotiated to set international standards and to implement human rights—the **International Covenant on Economic, Social and Cultural Rights** and the **International Covenant on Civil and Political Rights**. These treaties were opened for signatures in 1966 after nearly twenty years of heated, contentious debate. The International Covenant on Economic, Social and Cultural Rights recognizes and details the several important economic rights: the right to work, the right to fair remuneration, the right to safe working conditions, the right to form and join unions, and the right to strike. Special protection is also extended to working mothers before and after childbirth. This covenant also includes social rights such as the right to food, housing, and education. Cultural rights include the right to participate in the cultural life of a society and the right to benefit from scientific progress. The International Covenant on Civil and Political Rights recognizes the right to life, liberty, freedom of movement, equality under the law, and the presumption of innocence. It details the rights of association as well as the freedom of religion and conscience. It lists the right to free elections, universal suffrage, and the right to have access to public service. More than half of the member states have since become parties to both of the International Covenants.

The slow process of creating formal, legal obligations for human rights is a direct result of deep-seated disagreements about the definition and implementation of human rights. The lists of human rights are extensive and ambitious, and different states have different preferences about which rights ought to be actively pursued. East–West and North–South factions emerged.

The United States wanted civil and political rights to take precedence over economic and social rights. Rooted in liberal ideology, the U.S. argument centered on the idea that if individuals are armed with civil and political rights, they can actualize for themselves their economic and social rights. American suspicions of intrusive government, particularly in the marketplace, have focused U.S. human rights efforts on promoting civil and political rights. Only after these rights are guaranteed can individuals pursue a family, a home, or an education. The former socialist countries and many developing countries have argued that economic and social rights are necessary in order for individuals to participate in the political and civil life of the community. The state appropriately has a role in securing minimum standards of living, even if it means intervention in the economy. Non-Western societies expressed concern about Western conceptions of individual and gender equality. The promotion, protection, and implementation of human rights became an exceptionally politicized process in the highly charged environment of the Cold War. States were very slow to sign on to the international covenants; the treaties did not receive the requisite ratifications until 1976.

In spite of the political controversies surrounding human rights, the proliferation of international human rights agreements has continued. Some of the more notable agreements are the Declaration on the Granting of Independence to Colonial Countries and Peoples (1960), the Convention on the Prevention and Punishment of the Crime of Genocide (1948), the Convention Against Torture and Other Cruel, Inhuman, or Degrading Treatment or Punishment (1984), and the Convention on the Rights of the Child (1989). In 1993, the Vienna Declaration and Programme of Action for Human Rights resulted from the World Conference on Human Rights. The Vienna Declaration emphasized the universality of human rights and stressed that the right to development, the rights of women, and the rights of indigenous peoples need particular attention. In 2007, the General Assembly adopted the Declaration on the Rights of Indigenous People, which specifies rights to culture, language, and identity. The continuing proliferation of values and norms has led to a proliferation of actors involved in implementing and monitoring international agreements on human rights.

UN AGENCIES AND HUMAN RIGHTS

Several UN bodies and agencies are integrally involved in promoting and protecting human rights. The **Human Rights Council** is now the central UN body, replacing the defunct UN **Commission on Human Rights.** The Commission on Human Rights, which reported to the ECOSOC, was created shortly after the inception of the UN itself. This Commission drafted the 1948 Universal Declaration of Human Rights and actively worked to institutionalize the International Covenants. It consisted of fifty-three states and functioned to promote human rights, albeit in a nonconfrontational manner. Throughout its history, the Commission approached human rights protection by highlighting themes such as arbitrary detentions, torture, and the rights of children. Complementing the thematic approach, the Commission also addressed the specific human rights situation in states such as Cuba, Sudan, Afghanistan, and Zaire (now the Congo). The East–West and North–South conflicts meant that the Commission was always a highly politicized body. In the early twenty-first century, however, the Commission became even more politicized as states with very poor human rights records (such as Libya, Zimbabwe, Cuba, and Saudi Arabia) were elected from their respective regions, not to promote or protect internationally recognized human rights but to shield themselves and other rights-abusing countries from international criticism. The United States, on the other hand, which had always served on the Commission, did not get elected in 2001.

At the 2005 UN World Summit, member states agreed to abolish the discredited Commission and to create the Human Rights Council, which the General Assembly made a reality in March 2006. The Human Rights Council is a forty-seven-member body elected by the General Assembly. To ensure global representation, each region is allocated a certain number of seats. The developed nations are allotted seven seats, Eastern Europe has six, Latin America and the Caribbean have eight, Asia has thirteen, and Africa has thirteen seats. The creation of the Human Rights Council was not without controversy. The United States wanted elections to the Council to require a two-thirds majority to ensure that known violators of human rights were not able to obtain seats. The General Assembly, however, decided upon a simple-majority basis for elections. Elections were held in May 2006; however, the United States did not stand for election because it was concerned that the council would continue the practice of having gross violators of human rights as members. Some observers have argued that the United States was also concerned that it would not get the necessary majority of votes from the General Assembly to win a seat, further embarrassing the Bush administration (Wadhams 2006). According to Kenneth Roth, executive director of Human Rights Watch, "It's unfortunate that the Bush administration's disturbing human rights record means that the United States is today hardly a shoo-in for election to the council" (Hoge 2006b, A6). Unfortunately, the Council is still populated with notorious human rights abusers. Saudi Arabia, China, Pakistan, and Cuba were chosen in the first election. Moreover, the Council, in its first year, determined that only Israel deserved to be criticized, while Sudan, Myanmar, and Zimbabwe escaped formal international scrutiny. During the second year, the Council criticized Israel fifteen times and Myanmar once. The Council's disproportionate focus on Israel, while ignoring other states that routinely violate human rights, drew a rare rebuke from the otherwise reserved Secretary-General Ban Ki-Moon (Hoge 2007). In spite of its rather mixed record, the new Human Rights Council is expected to continue the work of the Human Rights Commission, which includes the institutionalization of the human rights covenants.

The Covenants themselves establish procedures and monitoring bodies to supervise their implementation. The Covenant on Civil and Political Rights creates the Committee on Human Rights to review state reports on their human rights records and to report to the ECOSOC and the General Assembly. The Committee may investigate individual complaints from citizens of states that have consented to this kind of oversight. This right of individual petition exists in very few countries. The Committee spends most of its time reviewing the implementation of the Covenant on Civil and Political Rights without any real authority to challenge signatories with weak human rights records.

The Covenant on Economic, Social and Cultural Rights gives the ECOSOC the authority to oversee its implementation. The ECOSOC originally created the Committee on Government Experts to review state reports, but this body was unable to effect a serious commitment to social, economic, and cultural rights. In 1985, the ECOSOC replaced the Committee on Government Experts with the Committee on Individual Experts. This new committee has been instrumental in establishing national guidelines for signatories regarding standards for adequate food, shelter, health care, and other rights (Weiss et al. 1994, 139). In addition to reviewing state reports, the Committee on Individual Experts also receives reports from NGOs and IGOs.

The 1993 Vienna Declaration and Programme for Human Rights called for the creation of the **United Nations High Commissioner for Human Rights (UNHCHR)**. The General Assembly obliged by creating the office, which became fully functional in 1994. This office was given responsibility to diplomatically promote and protect human rights, to provide advisory and technical assistance to states, and to coordinate UN education and public information programs. The UNHCHR is also charged with playing an active role in removing obstacles to the full realization of human rights and preventing the continuation of human rights violations. The UNHCHR can engage states in a dialog in order to secure respect for human rights; however, the High Commissioner can do little to force states to observe internationally recognized human rights. The vague language of the UNHCHR mandate falls far short of empowering the High Commissioner to confront the grave human rights situations. The Organization of Islamic Conference (OIC) followed the Vienna Conference by issuing **the Cairo Declaration**. The Islamic world used the Cairo Declaration to serve as the basis of the Islamic world's interpretations of human rights. The Islamic world views human rights as being defined by Allah and the Shari'a, or Islamic law. It posits different rights for women and men and highlights colonialism and racism as grave violations of human rights (*UNESCO Courier* 1994).

The Vienna Declaration and Programme of Action also raised the issue of women's rights as human rights. The international community has long looked the other way as women have been systematically denied their basic human rights. The Vienna Declaration reaffirmed that the rights of women and girls formed an inalienable and indivisible part of internationally recognized human rights. The **UN Conference on Women in Beijing (1996)** reaffirmed women's rights as human rights, but stressed that the status of women's rights was not significantly improving vis-à-vis the rights of men. The very fact that such an imbalance exists between men's "human" rights and women's "human" rights suggests that rights are, in large part, culturally determined.

The **International Labor Organization (ILO)** was established in 1919 as an autonomous agency of the League of Nations. This independent yet cooperative relationship was maintained with the creation of the UN in 1945. The ILO consists of three bodies: the International Labor Conference (a plenary body), the Governing Body (an executive committee), and the International Labor Office (the bureaucratic arm). The ILO's central purpose is to set international labor standards and to improve the rights of workers globally. In the post–World War II era, the ILO sponsored the following treaties relating to social, economic, and cultural human rights: the Freedom of Association and Protection of the Right to Organize Convention (1948); Right to Organize and Collective Bargaining Convention (1949); Equal Remuneration Convention (1951); Convention Concerning the Abolition of Forced Labor (1957); Discrimination Convention (1958); Equality of Treatment Convention (1962); Social Policy Convention (1962); Employment Policy Convention (1964); and the Convention Concerning Indigenous and Tribal Peoples in Independent Countries (1989). The ILO is the principal body in promoting economic, social, and cultural rights in a political arena that has emphasized civil and political rights, even at the expense of other human rights.

REGIONAL HUMAN RIGHTS ACCORDS AND AGENCIES

Regional accords also recognize, promote, and protect internationally recognized human rights. The European human rights regime is the most advanced and institutionalized of the regional arrangements. This regime is organized around the European Convention on Human Rights (1953). This convention contains several protocols that outline many, if not most, of the rights contained in the Universal Declaration of Human Rights, including civil and political rights as well as economic, social, and cultural rights. The convention also creates the European Commission on Human Rights, which functions as an ombudsman for individual complaints. The European Commission investigates petitions and seeks to negotiate an acceptable resolution for the parties involved. If such a resolution cannot be reached, the petition can go to the European Court of Human Rights, which consists of one judge from each of the members of the Council of Europe. One of the ironies of human rights protection is that areas that have the most comprehensive institutional arrangements are also areas that have good human rights records in the first place. As a result, very few cases have been brought before the European Commission, and even fewer have been brought before the European Court.

The Inter-American human rights regime is quite similar to its European counterpart in terms of organization. This regime, anchored by the Organization for American States (OAS), is based on three parts: the Inter-American Convention on Human Rights, the Inter-American Commission on Human Rights, and the Inter-American Court of Human Rights. The Inter-American Convention principally focuses on promoting and protecting civil and political rights, although the Convention devotes Article 26 to detailing social and economic rights. The Commission and the Court have the authority to investigate and adjudicate human rights claims. Unfortunately for human rights activists, this authority exists only in legal theory. In practice, these organizations have been ignored or bypassed by member states. The legal framework exists; but, because of the poor human rights records of many members, states have lacked the political will to make the law more effective.

NGOs AND HUMAN RIGHTS

A proliferation of human rights NGOs has accompanied the proliferation of human rights agreements and monitoring agencies. NGOs have come to play important roles in identifying and investigating human rights violations. They are also influential in pressuring governments and IGOs to meet their international obligations to promote and protect human rights. Several NGOs are particularly noteworthy. The first is the **International Committee for the Red Cross (ICRC)**. The ICRC's mission is to aid the victims of war, mainly civilians and prisoners of war. The ICRC is not directly linked to a human rights treaty, although its mandate does extend to human rights during war. The ICRC has "observer status" at the UN, the only NGO to be an official member. The ICRC heads a world federation of national Red Cross and Red Crescent units that are active in delivering humanitarian assistance in national emergencies.

Technically, the mission and legal status of the ICRC arise from the Geneva Conventions relating to international war. While the ICRC status in internal conflicts is unclear at best, the ICRC has played a role in the delivery of humanitarian assistance in many internal conflicts, including those in Ethiopia, Sudan, Bosnia, and Chechnya. The ICRC stresses that human rights remain human rights, even during war and violent conflict. Governments, military units, and civilians have the responsibility to meet their international obligations under international law and other humanitarian rules. The ICRC commands a great deal of international respect for its neutral competence and impartiality. The ICRC is independent of governments and international organizations and prides itself on championing the needs of victims of armed conflict and internal violence.

The ICRC generally takes a "**quiet diplomacy**" approach to promoting and protecting human rights during war. This especially holds true in its interaction with the United States and its detention policies associated with the "war on terror" and its facility at Guantanamo Bay, Cuba. The ICRC has visited the known overseas detention sites, and it is quietly pressuring the United States to allow it to visit clandestine sites, reportedly in Eastern Europe. Other NGOs rely on publicity and domestic and international political pressure to remind governments of their international obligations, the so-called "name and shame" approach. Amnesty International is such an organization.[1] Started in 1961, Amnesty International today has more than a million members, nearly 5,000 local chapters, in more than a hundred countries. Its mission consists of four focal points: to free all prisoners of conscience; to ensure fair and prompt trials of political prisoners; to abolish the death penalty, torture, and other cruel forms of punishment; and to end extrajudicial executions and disappearances.

Amnesty International pursues several strategies. First, it engages in worldwide campaigns that involve lobbying governments and international organizations, reporting on human rights issues, and educating officials regarding human rights abuses. These publicity efforts raise awareness of human rights and expose violations. Second, it assists individuals who are prisoners of conscience or have been detained without trial, providing legal assistance and social support. Third, it maintains an Urgent Action network for individuals who are in immediate danger of torture and execution. Government officials and media outlets are flooded with appeals and protests on behalf of those at risk. Fourth, Amnesty International sustains a specialized network of medical and legal professionals, as well as specialists in women's, children's, and workers' rights.

Human Rights Watch is another NGO that investigates and publicizes human rights violations. These activists have extensive networks that monitor the status of human rights and also attempt to hold nonstate actors responsible for their abuse. These nonstate actors include national and multinational corporations, guerrilla groups, and crime organizations such as drug cartels. Human Rights Watch also engages in special initiatives such as academic freedom, domestic violence, and prison conditions. It compiles annual reports on the human rights records of states; its reputation is such that its reports are used in congressional or parliamentary hearings and by executive and ministerial agencies. Human Rights Watch is also willing to take on unpopular causes against powerful states. In 1998, they were one of the few groups willing to take on the United States and the way the U.S. states disenfranchise voters. In Florida, people are denied the right to vote because they have a criminal record. This has led to the disenfranchisement of one in every three African American males in Florida (Davies 1998, 1A). According to a national study, 3.9 million Americans have lost the right to vote because of their criminal records, which includes 13 percent of the male population (Davies 1998, 1A).

Doctors Without Borders (Médecins Sans Frontieres) is an NGO whose 2,000-plus volunteers come from more than forty-five nations (Doctors Without Borders 1998). Established in 1971, it has offices in nineteen countries and operations in more than seventy countries. Doctors Without Borders is committed to providing medical relief to populations in crisis regardless of

---

[1] The discussion and description of Amnesty International is drawn from its Web site www.amnesty.org

ideology or national origin. Like the ICRC, Amnesty International, and Human Rights Watch, Doctors Without Borders is independent of governments and IGOs and is committed to impartiality. Doctors Without Borders attempts to work with the consent of parties involved but has, on occasion, delivered medical assistance without the approval of military or civilian authorities.

NGOs play central roles in the protection of internationally recognized human rights. Their people on the ground investigate alleged human rights abuses and provide legal representation to prisoners of conscience. NGOs also organize at the grassroots level to apply domestic political pressure to respect human rights and to get more individuals actively involved in the implementation of all human rights including economic, social, and cultural rights. They also consult with UN human rights agencies.

In spite of the proliferation of human rights accords, agencies, and NGOs, gross violations of human rights continue to occur on a large scale. Instances of mass killings, deliberate starvation, ethnic cleansing, systematic rape, summary execution, and genocide are still far too common. Economic, social, and cultural rights are routinely denied in the developing world and are under attack in the developed countries. Forced labor, child labor, and below-subsistence wages are commonplace in many areas, and the ability of workers to unionize has been compromised. The gross violations of human rights have generated renewed international interest in alternative ways to ensure respect for human rights.

HUMANITARIAN INTERVENTION

Traditionally, recognition, promotion, and protection of human rights have involved the use of diplomacy and political pressure to persuade and challenge states to improve their human rights records. Since the end of the Cold War, however, international enforcement of human rights has emerged as a controversial feature in international politics. UN humanitarian actions in Iraq (on behalf of Iraqi Kurds), Somalia, and Bosnia renewed interest in the notion of "humanitarian intervention." Broadly speaking, humanitarian intervention refers to "dictatorial interference" in the internal affairs of a sovereign state to secure and enforce human rights. Dictatorial interference can include both nonforcible and forcible measures. The former includes such measures as economic sanctions, withholding of aid, and the funding of opposition parties (Damrosch 1989). The latter refers to the use of military units within the territorial jurisdiction of a target state without the government's consent.

The controversy surrounding humanitarian intervention revolves around a central question: When is it permissible for international organizations to override state sovereignty to protect internationally recognized human rights? The broad definition of intervention as "dictatorial interference" makes it difficult to draw a distinction between impermissible intervention and permissible political activities because it includes both forcible and nonforcible measures. Recall that Article 2(7) of the UN Charter contains the companion principle of sovereignty, the principle of nonintervention. The UN is enjoined from intervening in the domestic jurisdiction of member states, and no member is required to submit such matters to the UN for settlement. In 1965, the UN General Assembly attempted to clarify what nonintervention meant with Resolution 2131:

> No State has the right to intervene, directly or indirectly, for any reason whatever in the internal or external affairs of any other state. Consequently, armed intervention and all other forms of interference or attempted threats against the personality of the State or against its political, economic, or cultural elements are condemned.
>
> No State may use or encourage the use of economic, political, or any other type of measure to coerce another state in order to obtain from it the subordination of the exercise of its sovereign rights, or to secure from it advantages of any kind. Also no state shall organize, assist, foment, finance, invite or tolerate subversive terrorist or armed activities directed towards the violent overthrow of the regime of any other state or interfere in the civil strife in another state. (UN General Assembly, Doc A/6014, December 21, 1965)

This same interpretation of nonintervention was included in another General Assembly resolution, Resolution 2625, titled the Declaration on Principles of International Law Concerning Friendly Relations and Cooperation Among States (1970). Article 2(7) and UN General Assembly Resolutions 2131 and 2625 contain the usual exception that nothing in these sections shall be construed as affecting UN Charter provisions relating to the maintenance of international peace and security.

Unfortunately, these provisions do little to define what precisely constitutes dictatorial interference. International politics involves trying to get actors to do things they might otherwise not do. This means applying political pressure and providing negative, as well as positive, inducements. Under the General Assembly construction of intervention, however, economic sanctions and political lobbying are impermissible. Developing states are concerned that human rights will be used to deny them development loans. The World Bank cut off assistance to Malawi and restricted loans to Kenya because of their human rights violations in 1992 (Riding 1992, A6). World Bank loans to China were scaled back in 1989 after the government's crackdown on a prodemocracy demonstration in Tiananmen Square (*American Banker* 1990, 18; Mann and Pine 1990, A1). Developing states argue that the World Bank is politicizing development loans, in contravention of the World Bank Charter, which commits the institution to political neutrality.

There is some question of jurisdiction with respect to human rights. According to China's former premier Li Peng, for example, "The issue of human rights falls within the sovereignty of each country. A country's human rights situation should not be judged in total disregard of its history and national conditions. . . . China . . . is opposed to interference in the internal affairs of other countries using the human rights issue as an excuse"

(*New York Times* 1992). Most developing states are sympathetic to this position. It is, after all, their sovereignty that is at stake: The UN has neither the will nor the capability to override the sovereignty of powerful states. UN intervention is possible only against the weaker members—members that lack the political protection of a permanent member of the Security Council. Powerful states may ignore their allies' human rights violations while seeking to punish political foes for committing the same violations. Developing countries, worried about this double standard, also stress another: While violations of civil and political rights tend to prompt UN intervention, violations of economic and social rights do not. The World Bank and the IMF freely demand structural adjustments in return for their loans—adjustments that interfere with the economic and social rights of their citizens.

Countering this view of human rights and intervention is the argument that human rights are proper international subject matters, despite the many disagreements over definition and implementation (Forsythe 1991b). Many states have become formal legal parties to human rights treaties, thereby internationalizing human rights. As the Permanent Court of International Justice stated in Nationalities Decrees in Tunis and Morocco (1923), "The question of whether a certain matter is or is not solely within the jurisdiction of a state is an essentially relative question; it depends on the development of international relations." Human rights are just as much an international concern as slavery and colonialism are. Both slavery and colonialism were once internal affairs, but no longer; neither is permissible state behavior, under any circumstances (Szasz 1983, 345). States and the UN have every right and the responsibility to oppose states engaging in slavery or colonialism. This logically extends to genocide and crimes against humanity.

The record of multilateral humanitarian intervention is rather sketchy. In 1966 and 1968, the UN Security Council authorized mandatory economic sanctions against Rhodesia (now Zimbabwe), after the white minority government declared independence from the United Kingdom and implemented minority rule. Recall that Chapter VII, Article 39, of the UN Charter states that the Security Council can "determine the existence of any threat to the peace, breach of the peace, or act of aggression and shall make recommendations or decide what measures shall be taken . . . to maintain or restore international peace and security." Security Council decisions are legally binding and member states of the UN have a duty to "accept and carry out" these decisions. Security Council resolutions regarding Rhodesia, particularly the 1968 decision, identify the human rights situation as a threat to peace (Van Dyke 1970). If the Security Council links human rights violations to international peace and security, then both forcible and nonforcible measures are legally permissible.

The Rhodesia case is a "fuzzy" precedent for nonforcible intervention because Rhodesia was not a recognized sovereign state and the Security Council resolutions did not clarify the precise legal basis for its authoritative review. South Africa represents a similar case. In 1977, the Security Council mandated an arms embargo against South Africa, which was then ruled by a white minority government and practiced apartheid, a policy that enforced a comprehensive segregation of races. The resolution never articulated what triggered its authoritative action aside from "the situation in South Africa" (S/RES/418, 1977).

Forcible intervention raises different questions regarding multilateral actions. Mandating economic sanctions or an arms embargo is one thing; using military force and other forms of violence is quite another. The first clearly identifiable, forcible UN intervention occurred during the Persian Gulf Crisis. After the cessation of hostilities between UN and Iraqi forces, the Iraqi government began a brutal campaign to suppress rebelling Kurds in northern Iraq and Shi'ite Muslims in southern Iraq. In 1991, the Security Council explicitly linked human rights violations occurring materially within a sovereign state to international peace and security in Resolution 688. The UN subsequently sent military units into northern Iraq without the consent of the Iraqi government to create a safe-haven zone for the Iraqi Kurds.

Iraq represents a unique case because it was part of a collective security action involving traditional security issues and concerns. A vanquished Iraq had little choice but to accept the UN action in northern Iraq. Even so, Resolution 688 was far from unanimous. China and India abstained from the vote on the resolution. Cuba, Zimbabwe, and Yemen voted against the resolution, claiming it was an unacceptable disregard for state sovereignty. In spite of Iraq's pariah status, developing states were sensitive to the precedent that denigrates traditional sovereign rights.

Many developing states are concerned that alleged human rights violations will be used as an excuse to mask other motives. Unilateral uses of force are almost always condemned because they represent clear violations of Article 2(4), which prohibits the threat or use of force in international relations. International organizations may sanction the use of force purportedly to correct human rights, but that does not necessarily justify the intervention or make it permissible. The Organization of Eastern Caribbean States sanctioned the U.S. intervention in Grenada to protect the lives of American medical students and restore civil and political rights. Yet, many in the international community and the General Assembly condemned the action. As long as international organizations must rely on the armed forces of member states to carry out resolutions, they will be vulnerable to the charge that they are motivated by the interests of powerful member states, not by concern for the rights and welfare of persons at risk.

As a result of the North–South divide on the issue of humanitarian intervention, the international community is forced to address human rights situations on a case-by-case basis. The breakdown of civil order in Somalia put a large segment of the population at immediate risk of starvation and disease. In 1992, the UN Security Council deemed the situation in Somalia a threat to international peace and security and authorized "all means necessary" to deliver humanitarian assistance. The Security Council also stated that anyone interfering in the delivery of humanitarian assistance could be guilty of a war crime, which was a direct warning to the warring rival factions. The UN action in Somalia was a success in providing immediate assistance, but it did little to create a political environment that could sustain peace. The UN was virtually chased out of Somalia, raising questions about the efficacy of using force to protect human rights. Is it possible to use force and maintain a neutral position within the existing domestic political arena?

The humanitarian crisis in Somalia triggered UN authoritative action, while others went relatively unnoticed. Grave human rights situations in Burundi, Mozambique, North Korea, Afghanistan, and Sudan did not prompt multilateral intervention, even though these crises were, at the very least, as dire as the Somali crisis. No clear pattern has emerged as to what kinds of human rights, and on what scale, might trigger authoritative review. During the Cold War, the political paralysis of the Security Council prevented any serious review of situations in Cambodia, Guatemala, El Salvador, Chile, and Ethiopia. After the Cold War, humanitarian action occurred in Iraq, Somalia, and the former Yugoslavia (Bosnia and Kosovo). The genocide in Rwanda serves as our next case study because it shows the difficulties in building an international coalition to confront gross violations of human rights. Rwanda also jump-started international efforts to create a new norm to prevent future genocides and other gross violations of human rights, called the **Responsibility to Protect (R2P)**, which is discussed at the end of this chapter.

CASE STUDY 9: RWANDA[2]

In April 1994, the tiny country of Rwanda took a disastrous turn toward genocide that would claim more than 800,000 lives in a mere 100 days. The victims were members of the Tutsi minority and moderate Hutus who were murdered with machetes and small arms in just a few weeks. The perpetrators of the genocide were roaming gangs of the ethnic majority Hutus consisting mostly of men; however, large numbers of women and children also took part in the carnage.

The genocidal killing began on April 6 after the airplane carrying Rwanda's Hutu president Juvenal Habyarimana and Burundi president Cyprien Ntaryamira was shot down by a surface-to-air missile on its approach into the Rwandan capital, Kigali. The two leaders had been attending a peace conference for the Great Lakes Region of Central Africa. This region has experienced wide-scale political unrest and violence, most of which stemmed from the ethnic conflict between Tutsis and Hutus. In 1993, the UN Security Council created and deployed a small, lightly armed peacekeeping force called the UN Assistance Mission for Rwanda (UNAMIR). UNAMIR's mandate was to help implement the cease-fire between the Hutu government and Tutsi rebels as part of the Arusha Peace Agreement. UNAMIR's 2,500 blue helmets consisted of troops from Belgium, Ghana, and Pakistan. Within hours after the downing of President Habyarimana's plane, the Rwandan presidential guard began hunting down the Tutsi and Hutu opponents of the president and killing them. On April 7, Rwanda's first female prime minister Agathe Uwilingiyimana (and

---

[2]The chronology of the events in Rwanda was compiled by Reuters and distributed by Tribunal Watch ubvm.cc.buffalo.edu.

Habyarimana critic) was raped and murdered. The ten Belgian peacekeepers assigned to protect her were tortured, brutalized, and killed.

The Hutu militia, known as the interhamwe, began the mass murder of the Tutsi minority. Rwandan radio incited the violence by directing killers to where Tutsis were hiding and filling the airwaves with hateful propaganda. More moderate leaders were murdered, as UN peacekeepers stepped aside. Thousands of Tutsis, fleeing the machetes, went to UN camps for protection. The Tutsi rebel force, known as the Rwanda Patriotic Front (RPF), launched an offensive to try to seize power and stop the killing. Several Western countries sent special forces to Rwanda; however, their mission was to evacuate foreign nationals out of Rwanda. The Tutsi employees of the Western embassies were not evacuated even though they faced certain death. On April 22, the UN secretary-general recommended that the UN Security Council either beef up and heavily arm UNAMIR or withdraw the peacekeepers from harm's way. The Security Council voted to reduce UNAMIR to a token presence of 270 people. As the UN withdrew from Rwanda, Hutu extremists overran the camps and slaughtered the inhabitants.

By July, Kigali fell to the RPF and over 1 million Hutus fled to neighboring countries. A new coalition government was formed with Tutsis prominently represented. The genocide was effectively ended. In November, the UN Security Council announced the creation of an international criminal tribunal to try the Rwanda "war" criminals. In November 1996, the UNAMIR mission was officially concluded. What factors precipitated the crisis? What factors influenced the behavior of the UN? What role did the UN play in the crisis?

A Realist Cut

The end of the Cold War effectively signaled the demise of the great powers' engagement of the Great Lakes Region and their interest in Africa in general. During the Cold War, the outcomes of political and ethnic conflicts in the region were of strategic importance to the superpowers in their ideological and territorial battle. The United States, European states, and the former Soviet Union meddled in African wars of independence, each trying to influence events in their favor. The end of the Cold War greatly diminished the strategic importance of Africa, and African states were left to themselves to solve their political and ethnic conflicts that had been inflamed and exacerbated by years of Cold War tensions. In short, by 1994 the great powers had no compelling national interests in Rwanda.

Unfortunately for the Rwandans massacred in the genocide, the UN's first post–Cold War foray into Africa was a disaster for U.S. armed forces. The U.S.-led UN intervention into Somalia in 1992 was to deliver humanitarian food and medical aid to the millions of Somalis at risk. Once that mission was accomplished, U.S. forces began the difficult task of state-building by trying to create a coalition government among hostile warlords. U.S. forces had to track down renegade warlords and attempt to disarm exceptionally well-armed militias. Nineteen U.S. "peacekeepers" were brutally killed, and their bodies were dragged through the streets of Mogadishu, the capital of Somalia. Because of Somalia, the U.S. policy was not to intervene in Rwanda and, therefore, the UN did not intervene (Forsythe 2000, 15). U.S. State Department officials were instructed not to use the word "genocide" even though it was clear to officials that the genocide was occurring (*Frontline* 1999). Rwanda even had a nonpermanent seat on the Security Council, but no one asked the Rwandan representative to explain what was happening or even to assure Security Council members that the activities merely amounted to a "breach of the peace." Neither the United States nor the UN would use the word "genocide" because genocide demands a response and the United States was committed to nonintervention (Lewis 2001, A5).

Where were the Europeans, the Belgians in particular? Belgium's historical and political ties to Rwanda suggest that perhaps they might have done something. The Belgian government, however, was reeling from the death of its peacekeepers. The Belgian government went on an extensive lobbying campaign to pull the UNAMIR force out of Rwanda. The Belgians did not want to lose face by pulling only their troops out so they lobbied Security Council members behind the scenes to pull out the entire peacekeeping force (*Frontline* 1999). They found a very sympathetic ear from the United States, who was still licking its Somalian wounds. The Hutus knew from the lessons of Somalia that "if you kill a few," they will leave and that is exactly what happened. After all, the conflict between the Tutsis and Hutus was not the fight of the Americans, the French, or the Belgians. Therefore, it was not the fight of the UN. Why should these countries risk the lives of their soldiers where they have no compelling national interest worth dying for? France was supportive of the Hutu government and continued to provide money and arms. The Tutsis made a monumental mistake by hoping the UN would prevent their slaughter. It was the RPF and its mere 4,000 troops that halted the genocide, and they did so with relative ease. The UN peacekeepers were better armed and trained than the RPF, yet they did nothing to halt the killings.

A Liberal Cut

The Rwandan genocide is a story of good intentions, missed opportunities, and institutional weaknesses that resulted in UN paralysis. And the echo of the Jewish Holocaust remains as in the words of Edmund Burke, "All it takes for evil to triumph is for good people to do nothing." The UN involvement in Rwanda and the Great Lakes Region was motivated by a desire for a lasting peace and humanitarian concern for those living in the area. UN agencies and UNAMIR were there to help promote social and political stability and to build confidence between the ethnic groups (Waters 2001, 5–16). The UNHCR, the WFP, the WHO, and UNICEF operate extensive programs designed to help Rwanda, not to hurt it. International organizations play positive and constructive roles in mitigating ethnic conflict; however, they are caught between traditional norms of sovereignty and demands for humanitarian intervention which inevitably involves taking sides (Esman and Telhami 1995). Peacekeeping missions and international agencies have limited mandates and resources and must proceed with the consent of the parties involved.

The descent into genocide happened very quickly and was precipitated by an event that no one could predict (the downing of President Habyarimana's plane). The initial shock and disbelief as to what was happening paralyzed UN officials on the ground. The perpetrators of the Rwandan genocide had proven themselves particularly vicious and committed and were willing to murder anyone standing in their way. UN personnel were also victimized and brutalized. The UN had to protect its people or pull them out of harm's way. Tragically for the Rwandans, the UN had no choice but to pull them out as its members were unwilling to militarily confront the Hutu extremists.

The UN did miss a few opportunities that might have averted the catastrophe or at least mitigated it. First, the UN could have authorized the seizure of weapon stockpiles to keep them out of the hands of Hutu extremists. However, given the murkiness of what was happening on the ground and the dangers of the mission, it was difficult for UN decision makers in New York to authorize a risky mission that could cost the lives of hundreds of peacekeepers and lead to a further deterioration of the situation. Given conflicting reports and a lack of political will for expanded peacekeeping, UN decision makers made a judgment call, albeit a bad one. A second missed opportunity on the part of the UN was failing to call the genocide, "genocide." The reluctance of UN officials to use the term allowed members to drag their feet and avoid taking action. By falling back on protocol and norms of diplomacy, the UN did not speak up against the slaughter.

According to an independent report commissioned by the Security Council (SC/6842 April 14, 2000), the failure to stop or prevent the genocide in Rwanda was a failure of the UN system as a whole. "The fundamental failure was the lack of resources and political commitment devoted to developments in Rwanda and the United Nations presence there. There was a persistent lack of political will by member states to act, or to act assertively enough, which affected the Secretariat's response, the Security Council's decision making and the difficulties in getting troops for the United Nations Assistance Mission for Rwanda" (UNAMIR). Genocide and other horrors are likely to continue until UN members find the political will and the resources for preventive action. UN missions into troubled areas need to have clear rules of engagement and must have a mandate to disarm belligerents, by force if necessary, and to raid arms caches. Just because the UN failed Rwanda does not mean it is evil and must be scrapped. The UN and its members must learn hard lessons, make the necessary changes, and try not to let this kind of horror happen again.

A Marxist Cut

The ethnic conflict between Hutus and Tutsis in the Great Lakes Region defies national boundaries. This ethnic conflict has manifested itself in wide-scale violence in Uganda, Congo (Zaire), Burundi, and Tanzania as well as Rwanda.

Ethnic hatreds might date back centuries; however, they are often used by colonizing powers to maintain political control over a country's resources and labor. Rwanda was a Belgian colony from 1918 to 1962. The Belgian government favored the Tutsi minority and created a Tutsi aristocracy to help them rule over the Hutu majority. This aristocracy was based on the racial superiority of taller, leaner Tutsis, and the notion of superiority was nurtured and fostered by Belgium (*Frontline* 1999). The Tutsis received preferential treatment in education and employment, and many were welcomed in white colonial circles. The discriminatory treatment and marginalization of the Hutus under Belgian rule barely raised an eyebrow on the UN Trusteeship Council. Recall from Chapter 2 that the Trusteeship Council was responsible for overseeing the decolonization process. Yet its members were the colonial powers, which was the equivalent of having the fox guard the chicken coop.

In 1959, Tutsi king Charles Mutara Rudghiwa died, creating a power struggle within Rwanda. Hutus and Tutsis clashed violently for more than two years until Hutus finally took power in 1961 and declared their independence in 1962. Rwanda became a member of the UN on September 18, 1962. With the Hutus in power, the Tutsi minority, once the elite of Rwandan society (next to the white colonialists, of course), were now persecuted. In 1963, a failed Tutsi invasion from Burundi (also a former Belgian colony and ruled by the Tutsi minority) resulted in the deaths of thousands more. Many Tutsis fled to neighboring countries or to Belgium. In 1972, a Tutsi minority government in Burundi massacred tens of thousands of Hutus in order to retain its political control. The Rwandan Hutu government responded in kind and expelled more Tutsis. It is against this colonial heritage and rocky independence that the Rwandan genocide is to be understood.

The "racialization" of the Hutu–Tutsi difference took place under colonialism and is at the root of the 1994 genocide (Mamdani 2001, 76–102). The feudal system created under Belgian rule led to almost complete dependence of the Hutu majority on the Tutsi minority. Hutus were kept extremely poor and uneducated, creating an inferiority complex. The Tutsi lords collaborated with their colonial benefactors in extracting most of the precious metals from Rwanda. Tutsis benefited greatly from Belgian rule in that they were rewarded financially and politically. Very little in the way of development took place under Belgian "trusteeship," and Rwanda has been and remains among the poorest of the poor. The ethnic tensions exacerbated by Belgian colonial rule and mistreatment laid the groundwork for the desperately impoverished Hutus to commit genocide.

The UN and its aid agencies are suspect in that they are seen as part of the problem, not the solution. Belgium still has limited economic ties to Rwanda and is the largest donor of foreign aid. That gives Belgium considerable leverage. Belgians compromised the leadership of the peacekeeping force. The good intentions of the UN have caused nothing but disaster for Rwanda. The independent report commissioned by the Security Council recognizes the very limited credibility of the UN among the Rwandans. The UN apology for not halting the genocide is hollow and meaningless, for the conditions that gave rise to the genocide remain. Only after the 2001 genocide trial of four Rwandans in Belgium were questions raised about the former colonial power's responsibility for the atrocities (*BBC News* 2001).

A Feminist Cut

According to liberal feminism, women are just as capable of brutality and violence as are men. And the Rwandan genocide supports this assertion. The role of Hutu women in the genocide is not widely publicized. Women, who were civil servants, teachers, nurses, and nuns were directly and indirectly responsible for the mass murder of Tutsis (Summerfield 1996, 1816). While some women participated directly in the killings, most women were involved with inciting the violence. "Some acted as cheerleaders, ululating the killers into action, and stripped the dead and the barely living of their jewelry, money, and clothes. They betrayed their own neighbors, friends and relatives to the militia" (Summerfield 1996, 1816). Many women who took part in the genocide were also staffers for international aid agencies. A few months before the genocide, these women were helping the UN and NGOs deliver humanitarian assistance to Rwanda's impoverished.

Women in leadership positions also joined in the genocide. Two Roman Catholic nuns were convicted of genocide in Belgium for providing petrol and leading militants to where Tutsis were hiding. Two women ministers in the Hutu government also actively promoted genocide. One of the women, Pauline Nyiramushuko, the minister for Women and the Family, visited refugee camps and supervised the murder of Tutsi men (Summerfield 1996, 1816). After the genocide, she found work with a UN aid agency, helping the victims until she was charged, along with six others, with genocide by the International Criminal Tribunal for Rwanda (ICTR), a body created by the UN after the genocide to try the perpetrators.

Rape was another important feature of the Rwandan genocide. Over 250,000 women were raped and, as is common with rigidly patriarchal societies, they and their children are now shunned by society (Royte 1997, 37). These women did not receive counseling or health care. Many were infected with HIV, the virus that causes AIDS. This amounts to a slow-motion genocide against Tutsi women. Once again the UN appears paralyzed, claiming a lack of resources and will, and the West, which turned a blind eye to the slaughter, is unwilling to donate the drugs that might add many quality years to their lives. If the UN was really sorry for their inaction, they could at least help mitigate the consequences of their inaction on the living victims.

The unexamined gender relations of Rwandan society also contributed to the violence. The rapes of the Tutsi women were particularly violent and brutal, as the Hutu men saw them as too proud and somehow above them (*Win News* 1998, 34). The subordination, or feminization, of Hutu males to Tutsis, especially Tutsi women, led them to treat their rape victims in an exceptionally horrific manner. Women's groups have asserted that the UN has failed to punish the rapists or extend help to their victims (*Win News* 1998, 34).

Essentialist feminism highlights the close connection between sex and violence. The fact that men could find it within themselves to commit systematic rape in the midst of machetes and body parts indicates that part of the problem of violence might stem from the essential nature of men. Rwanda is not an isolated incident. Men have historically used rape as a weapon to demoralize their male opponents by raping their mothers, wives, and daughters. However, physical arousal is required to commit rape. If violence triggers a sexual arousal in men, then international organizations need to take this into account if they are going to address systematic rape in the future. If the rape cannot be prevented, then at least programs should be in place to help the victims come to terms with their ordeal and help them pick up the pieces of their lives. The UN has done little to help the raped women of Rwanda, and it has been able to blame its inaction on the culture of patriarchal African society that shuns even discussion of women's "dishonor."

A Constructivist Cut

The constructivist approach shows how ethnicity is socially constructed and can be used by actors to foster political objectives and marginalize political opposition. In the case of Rwanda, "ethnicity" was constructed by Belgian colonizers so that it was able to rule the entire country by pitting an artificially constructed Tutsi minority against the artificially constructed Hutu majority. What was once a minor distinction between different social statuses was transformed by the Belgians into the idea of a master race (Tutsi) and slave race (Hutu) whereby the Tutsi were the "chosen" people of god destined to rule absolutely over the Hutus (Gourevitch 1998; Joireman 2003, 35–53). This constructed "ethnicity" was used as an instrument to divide the Rwandans and was reinforced through the Belgian-imposed educational and political institutions. It was the principal source of conflict that gave rise to a series of horrific crimes throughout Rwanda's postcolonial history as "Hutus" took power when the Belgians withdrew and ultimately fueled the 1994 genocide. If international organizations want to help Rwanda move beyond the genocide, they need to work to develop strategies to de-ethnicize the population and build a national rather than an ethnic identity among the people. Ethnicity is created by humans and it can be changed by humans.

In terms of the international community's response to the genocide, the constructivist approach illustrates how the social interactions of different kinds of international actors affect an actor's perceptions and expectations. For example, the international media portrayed the conflict as a tribal conflict, a very typical African conflict (Barnett 2002, 49). This allowed many key decision makers to dismiss the conflict as an Africa-thing dating back centuries. The biases and stereotypes that shape identity and understandings of others also affect decision making. International organizations are not immune. The UN has its own culture and norms that affect the way it perceives and responds to events. The norms that dominated the UN at the time of Rwandan genocide were neutrality, impartiality, and diplomacy (Barnett 2003, 179).

These norms were elevated above all other considerations, and as such the UN presented the killings to the Security Council in neutral way, that is, the deaths were part of an ongoing civil war. This allowed member states to more easily dismiss the genocide as an internal affair of Rwanda. The rules and norms of diplomacy involve not using strong words such as "genocide" (Joireman 2003, 54–71). At the UN Security Council, the norm is not to publicly dress down a fellow member, so the representative of Rwanda and the actions of the Rwandan government were not questioned. The silence was also reinforced by the Security Council wanting to appear impartial.

The norms and ethos of the UN Department of Peacekeeping also affected the way the UN responded to the crisis. When UNAMIR reported that it had evidence that Hutu extremists were planning to systematically kill Tutsis and the UNAMIR commander wanted to seize weapons caches, the primary concern was that UNAMIR could overstep its authority, not that Hutu extremists were about to slaughter Tutsis (Barnett 2002, 154–174). The international normative environment also shaped the interests and priorities of the Department of Peacekeeping (Paris 2003, 441). After the disastrous UN peacekeeping mission in Somalia, the international mood was against robust peacekeeping. The UN wanted to have a successful mission to rebuild confidence, and Rwanda seemed like an easy mission. The seizure of the weapons could have led to armed conflict between UN peacekeepers and Hutu militias, a risk the UN was not willing to take. The intersubjective understanding between the UN and the international normative structure led UN officials to reject sound proposals and strategies (Paris 2003, 441–473).

Postscript

The aftermath of the Rwandan genocide suggests that the international community has much to learn about responding to humanitarian crises. Only after the RPF had invaded Rwanda did the genocide stop, and it was then that the UN decided to intervene—to prevent a "genocide in reverse." Fearing reprisal killings by the invading Tutsi army, the UN Security Council passed Resolution 929 authorizing Operation Turquoise—a French intervention force to stabilize the situation. While French motives and interests continue to be debated, Operation Turquoise had the effect of allowing those who perpetrated the genocide in Rwanda to escape into neighboring countries. French forces were deployed between fleeing Hutus (including Hutu extremists and their families) and the RPF. As the Hutus, numbering over a million people, fled into neighboring countries, the UN was faced with responding to the resulting humanitarian crisis that results from such mass movements—starvation, disease, and violence. In Goma, Zaire, alone, a cholera epidemic claimed the lives of some 50,000 Rwandan refugees.

The UNHCR responded by establishing massive refugee camps especially in the Zaire (Congo) to provide safe havens and, working with various UN agencies and NGOs, set out to meet the basic human needs of the refugees. While the UN and NGOs were able to save the lives of many innocent civilians, they were unable to prevent the "militarization" of the camps (Terry 2002, 155–215). Since the Hutu extremists were able to blend in with the civilian population, they were able to reorganize in the camps, conduct cross-border attacks on Tutsis in Rwanda, and then return to the safe haven of the camps. Two NGOs, Doctors Without Borders and the International Rescue Committee, decided to withdraw from the camps rather than be complicit in the use of the camps as military sanctuary for those bent on genocide. The UNHCR did not withdraw, maintaining that the responsibility to disarm the camps lay with the Security Council. The new Tutsi-led Rwandan government warned the UN that if the cross-border attacks did not end, they would close the camps militarily. Rwandan troops eventually did invade and forcibly close many of the camps and returned the refugees to Rwanda. The troops did not withdraw and set the stage for what has been termed the "African World War" involving the armed forces of seven countries, where more than 3 million people died as a direct result of the violence and indirectly as a result of disease and starvation. In 2010, a preliminary UN report detailing the results of an investigation of the war (which formally ended in 2003) suggested that the Tutsi-led Rwandan government committed atrocities and possibly genocide against Hutu civilians in the Congo (Gettleman and Kron 2010). The outrage from Rwanda was swift as it threatened to withdraw from the UN peacekeeping mission in Darfur.

In 2008, another humanitarian crisis emerged as fighting erupted again in the Congo between Congolese government forces (composed of many Hutu extremists from Rwanda) and Congolese rebels (supported by the Tutsi-led Rwandan government). More than 250,000 refugees and IDPs were caught between the warring parties and were forced to flee. The UN peacekeeping mission, the United Nations Organization Mission in the Democratic Republic of Congo (MONUC), was caught off guard and did little to protect civilians. The commander of the 17,000-person peacekeeping operation, one of the UN's largest, abruptly resigned, and the UN once again seemed indecisive. Many of the refugees responded by attacking peacekeepers and aid workers for their failure to protect them. The legacy of the 1994 Rwandan genocide is still felt today in the deteriorating humanitarian crisis in the Congo.

On the human rights and accountability front, the UN Security Council created the ICTR, located in Arusha, Tanzania. The tribunal has been beset with procedural and substantive problems that have resulted in only a few convictions. The Tutsi-led Rwandan government refused to cooperate with the UN court because the court's jurisdiction also included the prosecution of Tutsis accused of war crimes, the court was located outside of Rwanda, and death penalty was not possible for those who organized and carried out the genocide. Given the concerns and shortcomings of the ICTR, Rwanda decided to proceed with a local, rather than global, form of justice, which has become known as the "gacaca trials." "Gacaca" means green space, or grassy area, in Rwandan. The gacaca trials are organized around the idea that there were different levels of accountability for the genocide. Those who organized, planned, and executed the Rwandan genocide would be tried at the international (for those who had fled Rwanda) and the national levels (for those who had not fled and for whom the death penalty applied). Yet, the genocide involved all sorts of crimes involving rape, assault, theft, and other lesser crimes. For Rwanda, the legal dilemma was how to hold those accountable for all the dimensions of the genocide without further overwhelming its fragile legal system. The gacaca represents a local form of justice where the members of the local community, most of whom are women, try these lesser crimes and determine the appropriate punishment, which ranges from time served to some kind of reparation. The death penalty is not an option in gacaca.

The gacaca trials have been criticized by international human rights organizations such as Amnesty International and Human Rights Watch because of the lack of procedural protections for defendants and the lack of progress in reducing the backlog of those charged with crimes during the genocide. Of particular concern is the requirement that defendants confess to crimes in order to receive reduced punishment, which could result in false confessions to charges that were brought on solely by the say-so of others. Moreover, the international community, as part of its overall democratization efforts, has tied some international aid to democratization in Rwanda. Unfortunately, given the demographic makeup of Rwanda, this would mean the return of Hutus to power, a situation unimaginable to the Tutsi minority. While Rwanda has a gender-quota system that brings women into its limited democratic institutions, it has not been as successful in including Hutus, who still account for approximately 89 percent of the population. As such, the aftermath of the Rwandan genocide remains a volatile and evolving situation where the victims of genocide are often at odds with the international community that failed to protect them and that is now pushing them into pursuing policies that in theory are good but in practice are likely to put them at risk.

INTERNATIONAL CRIMINAL LAW

The human atrocities of the 1990s prompted the international community to create a series of international criminal courts to prosecute those accused of the most egregious kinds of human rights violations: genocide, war crimes, and crimes against humanity. In a strict legal sense, there is a distinction between **international human rights law (IHRL)** and **international humanitarian law (IHL).** IHRL refers to the relationship between individuals and their governments and includes the civil, political, economic, social, and cultural rights spelled out in the relevant covenants discussed earlier in this chapter. Prohibitions against slavery, apartheid, and genocide also fall under the rubric of IHRL. IHL refers to the laws of war and armed conflict. According to the International Committee of the Red Cross (www.icrc.org), IHL seeks, for humanitarian reasons, to limit effects of armed conflict, particularly for those who are not, or no longer, engaging in hostilities. It also governs the weapons and tactics that can be used in armed conflict. (Scott 2010, 243–246). The ICRC correctly points out that IHRL and IHL are complementary, overlapping bodies of law, especially with the evolution of modern warfare and vague distinction between domestic and international affairs.

International criminal law (ICL) generally refers to the courts that have been created by the UN and the international community to prosecute those who commit serious violations of IHRL or IHL. These courts have detailed statutes specifying the crimes that fall within their jurisdiction and the applicable international (and in some cases national) law. These courts, through case law, have also contributed to the development of ICL especially as it relates to modes of liability and affirmative defenses. International criminal law is complex because it involves several kinds of criminal acts—the slave trade, piracy, hijacking, peacetime hostage-taking, terrorism, genocide, torture, apartheid, the waging of war, aggression, crimes against humanity, and war crimes (Van Glahn 1992, 323–363). The crimes committed in Rwanda and the former Yugoslavia caused the international community to revisit the idea of using international courts to hold individuals accountable. The International Criminal Tribunal for Rwanda (ICTR) and the International Criminal Tribunal for the former Yugoslavia (ICTY) (the subject of our case study later in this chapter) were created as ad hoc courts, meaning they were created for a limited time frame and their jurisdiction was limited to their respective geographic areas. Hence, the quest for international justice emerged in earnest for the first time since the Nuremburg Trials after World War II.

The **International Criminal Tribunal for the former Yugoslavia** was selected as our case study because it is more institutionalized and, arguably, has had more "success" than its Rwandan counterpart in conducting trials and obtaining convictions. It has also contributed to the development of international criminal case law and influenced the creation of the permanent **International Criminal Court (ICC) in** 1998. The ICC opened for business in 2002 when the Rome Statute, the constitutive treaty for the court, was ratified by the requisite sixty states. After a slow start and without U.S. support, the ICC has since began investigations and issued indictments for crimes committed in the Democratic Republic of Congo, Uganda, the Central African Republic, Kenya, and Sudan. The ICC was created because the international community no longer wanted to tolerate a culture of impunity and the ad hoc courts were not sufficient to confront and change that culture. While the ICC has not yet secured a conviction, it represents an important milestone in international criminal justice. The ICTR and ICTY have also influenced so-called hybrid courts such as the **Special Court for Sierra Leone** (2002), **Special Tribunal for Lebanon** (2006), and **Extraordinary Chambers in the Courts of Cambodia** (2006). As we will see later, justice that appears to be imposed by outsiders challenges sovereignty and can lack legitimacy. Hybrid courts blend the domestic law of the state with international law and procedures to prosecute cases. Hybrid courts have the added advantage of allowing developing states to pursue their own form of justice while developing a culture of legalism in line with global standards. This proliferation of international criminal courts to pursue international criminal justice began in 1993 when the UN Security Council created an international court to try those committing war crimes, genocide, and crimes against humanity.

CASE STUDY 10: THE INTERNATIONAL CRIMINAL TRIBUNAL FOR THE FORMER YUGOSLAVIA

The causes of the violent conflict in the former Yugoslavia were, and remain, complex and interdependent. When the multiethnic state of Yugoslavia broke apart, with several republics declaring independence, war ensued across the Balkans. The attempted forcible geographic dismemberment of Bosnia resulted in the Muslims becoming the victims of the worst violence. The disintegration of the former Yugoslavia gave rise to a virulent form of nationalism that led to gross violations of human rights committed by Serbs, Croats, and Bosniaks. The UN was challenged to again confront atrocities in Bosnia where the extreme and systematic violence was against Muslims residing in the heart of Europe. The Bosnian government asked for Security Council intervention; however, the members were unwilling to commit the armed forces necessary to stop the violence. The Bosnian government claimed that it was under attack from within and without. Croatia and Serbia were aiding Bosnian Croats and Bosnian Serbs; therefore, the crisis in Bosnia was not simply an internal affair. The governments of Croatia and Serbia were contributing to, if not actually causing, the ethnic cleansing in Bosnia.

The UN response, initially, was rather muted. The UN offered to send peacekeeping forces (UNPROFOR) with the consent of the parties involved. The UN also offered humanitarian assistance to those who were internally displaced. The UN created safe havens for Bosnian civilians and sought to mediate a negotiated settlement with the Serbs and the Croats. The UN also instituted an arms embargo on the region and placed economic sanctions against Serbia. To many, the UN's attempts to remain neutral played into the hands of Serbia, which continued its war in Croatia and Bosnia. The situation continued to deteriorate until 1995, when Serbian forces overran several UN safe-haven zones, committing mass murder of Muslim men and systematic rape of Muslim women.

The UN arms embargo did not completely stem the flow of weapons to Bosnia, as many Arab and Muslim states provided military assistance to the Bosnian government. In spite of UN declarations affirming Serb aggression, the UN maintained an embargo to the entire region and against all parties. Many European representatives argued that allowing arms for the Muslims would only add fuel to the nationalist fires. One does not put out a fire by adding gasoline. On the other hand, many developing states argued that the arms embargo only served to keep arms from the Muslims as Serbia and Croatia continued to receive outside assistance from Russia and former Eastern Bloc countries. The year 1995 marked a watershed in the Bosnian crisis because after four years of sustained and intense conflict, the UN, led by the United States, intervened decisively. NATO forces, with UN Security Council authorization, attacked Serb positions in Bosnia, particularly around the besieged city of Sarajevo. The G-7 also announced that it would support two war crimes tribunals: one for the former Yugoslavia and one for Rwanda. The Yugoslav tribunal, located in the Hague, the Netherlands, began hearing evidence of war crimes allegedly committed by Serb, Croat, and Muslim officials. By starting these judicial proceedings, the UN sought to apply as much political pressure as possible on the belligerents without rewarding the aggressors. Given that most of the war crimes were committed by Bosnian Serbs, the UN also wanted to divide the Serbian leadership by isolating the Bosnian Serb leader Radovan Karadijc and his lead general Ratko Mladic from Serbian president Slobodan Milosevic. Milosevic was later charged in 1999 for alleged crimes in Kosovo and was charged in 2001 with genocide.

After the UN issued indictments against Karadijc and Mladic, along with lower-ranking Croats and Serb officials, the United States and the UN invited the official Croat, Serb, and Bosnian leadership to meet in Dayton, Ohio, to work out a peace plan that would end the hostilities in Bosnia. The Dayton Accords called for an immediate cease-fire and an exchange of prisoners of war. All the parties agreed that indicted war criminals would be taken into custody and brought to trial at the Hague. Bosnian civilians would be allowed to return to their homes without fear of reprisals. The UN authorized the placement of 60,000 NATO troops (IFOR) in Bosnia to implement these provisions. Against this background, the international community turned to international criminal courts to enforce international human rights standards and punish those who commit war crimes and gross violations of human rights. Do these courts serve a useful purpose in international affairs? Whose interests do they serve? Who stands to win and who stands to lose? The theoretical approaches generate different interpretations regarding the efficacy of international criminal courts.

A Realist Cut

Realists, particularly those from powerful states, do not take international criminal courts seriously and if they do, it is a form of realpolitik to coerce others (Maogoto 2004). International criminal courts will only be effective against junior-level suspects offered up as sacrificial lambs, if at all. While human rights violations offend the human conscience, states also have pressing national interests relating to security and the balance of power. The Bosnian crisis is no exception. Most states were interested in international stability, and most would have preferred to maintain the status quo. Very few, save for Slovenia, Croatia, and Bosnia, wanted to see the disintegration of Yugoslavia. Most would have tolerated political repression as long as the former Yugoslavia remained intact; however, with its implosion, the best they could do was to manage the transition.

Transitionary periods in international politics tend to be characterized by violence. Conflicts on the scale and intensity of Bosnia are common as states break apart and new allegiances are formed. Most of today's states were formed in the fires of violent conflict. International criminal law is made by the victors to punish and control the losers. This kind of **"victors' justice"** is problematic because only the vanquished are brought before an international court to answer for their crimes, as German and Japanese officials discovered at the Nuremberg and Tokyo tribunals after World War II. During the Cold War, no one was ever prosecuted for "grave breaches" as identified in Article 147 of the Geneva Convention on the Protection of Civilian Persons in Time of War (1949). According to Article 147, grave breaches include

> [w]illful killing, torture or inhumane treatment, including biological experiments, willfully causing great suffering or serious injury to body or health, unlawful deportation or transfer or unlawful confinement of a protected person, compelling a protected person to serve in forces of a hostile Power, or willfully depriving a protected person of the rights of fair and regular trial prescribed in the present Convention, taking of hostages and extensive destruction and appropriation of property, not justified by military necessity and carried out unlawfully and wantonly.

The tens of millions of victims of the Cold War proxy wars realize these words are quite vague and subject to political interpretations. States must have compelling national interests to enforce this law because charging heads of state and other high-ranking government officials with war crimes is tricky business. In the first place, the Court must have a reasonable chance of taking the person into custody, which is not likely if the state in question retains its territorial integrity. Second, violent conflict usually requires a negotiated settlement, and mediators need somebody to talk to—someone who is not under indictment. Hence, those who wish to punish state officials accused of committing war crimes and grave offenses must have not only the capability but also the political will to do so.

The Bosnian crisis illustrates why human rights and justice take a backseat to other political considerations. Even though Serbian leader Slobodan Milosevic was eventually indicted by the Yugoslav war crimes tribunal (1999) and brought to trial (2000), his indictment went through only when the West allowed it. How could the man who, presumably, gave the orders—the man who provided military assistance to Bosnian Serbs—not be charged with war crimes until 1999? The simple and short answer is that Milosevic was a formal head of state and, as such, he was necessary to restore peace and stability in the Balkans. Although a prima facie case could easily have been made for indicting the president of the Republic of Serbia for war crimes, it was not prudent to indict the very individual who was crucial to negotiating a peace settlement. Only when NATO launched a massive air campaign against Serbia over Kosovo did they decide he was, in fact, a war criminal. The timing of indictment shows how easily the West manipulated the ICTY. At best, the war crime tribunals pay lip service to the rule of law, but they do little to punish aggressors or deter future gross violations of human rights.

Applying the rule of law includes more than being able to get a hold of perpetrators. It also involves the resolve of states, particularly those that are members of the UN Security Council. Both France and Russia expressed sympathy for the Serbian position. Russia has historically been allied with fellow Slavs, and France remembers Serb resistance against Nazi aggression during World War II. Germany made no secret of its support for Croatia.

Croatia has ethnic German ties and Croatians collaborated with the Nazis during World War II. The UK and the United States sympathized with the plight of Bosnian Muslims, largely because of their Muslim allies, particularly Saudi Arabia. Russia and China both have domestic human rights situations (Chechnya and Tibet, respectively) that they would rather keep from outside scrutiny. Given these political divisions on the Security Council, solutions to the Balkans crisis were elusive.

When the G-7 announced its financial support for the Yugoslav war crimes tribunal in 1995, it met with considerable skepticism. The ICTY was actually created in 1993 by the Security Council, but no state tangibly supported it. According to the UK's *Independent*, "The UN appears to be creating a tactical nightmare for itself. On the one hand it is trying to deliver peace in the former Yugoslavia, on the other it is threatening those with whom it has to negotiate that peace with long jail sentences" (U.S. Information Agency 1995a, 5). According to Germany's *Die Welt*, "[T]he increasingly absurd situation in Bosnia seems to support the view that the UN's plan to hold war crimes trials in The Hague . . . is about as likely to succeed as the League of Nations would have been if it had demanded the extradition of Hitler, Himmler, Goering, and Goebbels from Germany in 1943. The UN—and individual nations like Germany—are running the risk of losing even more credibility. . . . Nobody is talking about the main culprit Milosevic" (U.S. Information Agency 1995a, 5). Saudi Arabia's *Al Riyadh* reflects on the difference between war criminals and historic national heroes:

> Such a condemnation was previously leveled at many of the Zionist leaders: Begin, Shamir, Sharon, and others. However, they became, after the creation of Israel and the 1967 war victories, heroes in the view of those who earlier condemned their actions in the name of human rights. This is exactly what will happen to persons such as Saddam Hussein, the leaders of the Serbs and Rwanda and others. (U.S. Information Agency 1995a, 6)

The pessimism regarding the efficacy of the Yugoslav tribunal has proven to be justified. Years after Karadijc and Mladic were indicted, Mladic remains at large and Karadijc was only apprehended in 2008. NATO forces have made no effort to arrest the suspects in spite of having several clear opportunities. Political expediency again trumps the enforcement of human rights and the pursuit of justice. The existence of the Yugoslav tribunal did not deter Serb aggression. The brutal assault on Kosovo suggested that Milosevic was not particularly concerned with the threat of indictment.

Serbia sees the ICTY as being biased against Serbs. Serbs have been disproportionately charged and convicted, while Muslim and Croats have largely escaped indictment and those indicted have been acquitted (Simmons 2008). Prosecutorial discretion regarding indictments and appeals translates into victor's justice as fighters supported by the West escape effective prosecution. Powerful states can undermine the effectiveness of the tribunal by refusing to apprehend suspects (Barria and Roper 2005). Charges of "victor's justice" are still leveled against the ICTY in part because it has not held the victor's of the conflict (Croats, Muslims, and NATO forces) responsible for their atrocities during the conflict (Peskin 2005, 213–231).

For realists, what is more important is that the United States did not become a party to the ICC. The United States wanted prosecutions in the ICC to be approved by the Security Council, subject to permanent member veto. Opponents of the U.S. position held that all states needed be held to the same standard, including the great powers. According to Italy's *La Repubblica* (July 16, 1998),

> In reality, what is really at stake here is the balance of power which emerged out of the second World War. As a matter of fact, the "no" alignment group is led by four of the five permanent UNSC members. More than a concern about the exploitation of the court, they seem concerned about a projected "revision" of the entity: no longer an autonomous tribunal, but a new tool in the hands of the powerful of the earth, to use according to their political needs both as stick and carrot.   (U.S. Information Agency 1998c, 7)

The United States was unsuccessful at pushing through its demand of Security Council control and found itself in strange company, isolated from its allies. As Belgium's conservative *La Libre Belgique* opined, "It is most paradoxical that the great Western nation whose obstinacy made the Nuremberg trials possible, found itself in Rome on the same line as Iraq, Algeria and Libya, where human rights are still anathematized" (U.S. Information Agency 1998c, 9). For realists, this is not really a paradox. It exemplifies a state maximizing its power and national interest at Nuremberg and Rome. The company the United States keeps, be it Iraq or France, is determined by its national interests, not by shared values regarding human rights.

A Liberal Cut

The creation of criminal courts to prosecute gross violations of human rights is one way to promote and protect human rights. These courts can isolate those accused of violating human rights and function as a deterrent for those that might take the same path in order to achieve their aims. The ICTY seeks to ensure that the perpetrators of the Bosnian genocide and war crimes do not go unpunished. Liberals realize that these courts are far from perfect and are constrained by other political considerations. This does not mean, however, that human rights are marginalized. Human rights are obviously of concern to states and other international actors, or else the UN and/or NATO would not have become involved in Rwanda, Burundi, Bosnia, and Kosovo.

The former Yugoslavia was a crisis because of the loss of human life and dignity. It was not a crisis because of any dramatic shift in the balance of power or Serbian dominance in Central Europe. Even realists recognize that none of the great powers had any compelling interest, yet the UN and NATO committed significant resources and human capital toward managing the conflict. This was not misguided altruism. It represented a fundamental change in the nature and dynamics of international politics. Those accused of genocide and war crimes in Bosnia and Rwanda can never be accepted back into the international community until they have answered those charges in court. They cannot travel freely to other countries nor can they amass personal fortunes. They are virtual prisoners in their own countries. Human rights are not marginalized. Rather, those who engage in gross human rights violations are the ones marginalized in international politics.

Liberals argue that a true revolution has occurred as it relates state sovereignty and human rights. The human suffering caused by gross violations creates instability by displacing huge populations internally. Millions are also forced across borders, creating crises in neighboring countries. Whether or not the crisis in Bosnia is an internal or international affair is a question of semantics rather than a tangible distinction. According to former UN secretary-general Javier Perez de Cuéllar,

> It is now increasingly felt that the principle of non-interference within the essential domestic jurisdiction of states cannot be regarded as a protective barrier behind which human rights could be massively or systematically violated with impunity. The fact that diverse situations in the United Nations have not been able to prevent atrocities cannot be accepted as an argument, legal or moral, against the necessary corrective action, especially when peace is threatened. (UN Doc. A/461, 1991)

The creation of the Yugoslav and Rwandan tribunals demonstrated the international community's resolve to confront those who commit genocide and war crimes, even if the community cannot make the parties comply with their international commitments. As Saudi Arabia's internationally circulated *Al-Sharq Al-Aswat* claimed,

> [T]he decision of the Hague international war crimes tribunal . . . comes as an unexpected and pleasant surprise. Although the chances of arresting and bringing to trial the leader of the Serbs and the commander of their armed forces are slight, still the initiative remains an important political announcement during the coming round of the war. . . . Even if the court failed to achieve any progress on the ground, it has at least provided a verdict in the dirty war of Bosnia. (U.S. Information Agency 1995a, 6)

Liberals point out that human rights are among the principal values challenging the primacy of sovereignty and affecting the national interests of states. However, they recognize that sovereignty and political exigencies hamper the promotion, protection, and enforcement of human rights. A central factor determining whether international criminal court will become important, institutionalized features of the international political landscape depends on hegemonic leadership. Unfortunately, the United States has shown that it is not willing, for a variety of reasons, to assume that leadership role. According to Italy's *La Repubblica*, "By refusing to sign the treaty on the birth of the International Criminal Court, following its previous refusal regarding a ban against land mines, the United States has given up its role of moral leader of the world. . . . In both cases, Clinton's America has privileged domestic policy concerns and its national interest over those of the international community" (U.S. Information Agency 1998c, 5). Liberal institutionalists acknowledge that hegemonic leadership is a requisite for the creation of international organizations, but the hegemon is not going to support every institution-building effort.

A Marxist Cut

Marxists stress the hypocrisy of Western concerns with war crimes and human rights violations in the former Yugoslavia. Millions of people die every day because they lack adequate nutrition or access to clean water. What about their human rights? Why do civil and political rights warrant criminal prosecution and socioeconomic deprivations barely raise the eyebrows of the West? The Marxist lens, like the realist's, is focused on the pessimistic. The West's creation of the Yugoslav war crimes tribunal has, according to Slovenia's *Dnevnik,* only "quieted its conscience" (U.S. Information Agency 1995a, 4). They question the West's seriousness about prosecuting alleged war criminals. According to the Netherlands' *Algemeen Dagblad,* "Fearing revenge, the United States decided to back down. . . . The hunt is over. Karadijc and Mladic, responsible for the ethnic cleansing in Srebrenica, are going free. This is too cynical to be true. The two war criminals have made a fool of the entire world community and the world's strongest superpower. Justice can no longer be done" (U.S. Information Agency 1998a, 9).

Marxists also wonder if ethnic and religious biases affect the West's resolve to effective human rights enforcement. The West's historic suspicions of Muslims make the Muslims less sympathetic as victims of Serb aggression. According to Pakistan's *Muslim,*

> The United States bears a historic responsibility for these acts against the Kosovar Muslims especially since it voted against the International Criminal Court [ICC]: Ironically more than 100 countries voted in favor of ICC with the full blessing of the United Nations. . . . In the ultimate analysis, the United States is encouraging people like Milosevic to continue to act as criminals of wars and to crimes against humanity. . . . If no action is taken to save the Kosovar Muslims, the Muslims are doomed. (U.S. Information Agency 1998a, 12)

The U.S. insistence that the ICC be subject to Security Council review indicates its penchant for exempting itself from the same rules that it imposes on everyone else. According to Germany's *Berliner Zeitung,* "An ICC that depends on the blessing of the permanent members of the UNSC is, in reality, not an independent court. . . . It would mean open discrimination of all other states and would strengthen the antiquated special rights of the veto powers, thus undermining necessary reform of the UN constitution" (U.S. Information Agency 1998c, 3). International criminal courts serve to reinforce, rather than challenge, the status quo. Human rights enforcement centers on civil and political rights and ignores economic, social, and cultural rights. Like the realists, Marxists argue that only the weak and vanquished are likely to be prosecuted, while crimes committed by the capitalist states and their allies will be overlooked.

A Feminist Cut

Feminists identify several positive and negative aspects of human rights enforcement in the former Yugoslavia. On a positive note, many feminists applaud the role of the then U.S. ambassador to the UN, Madeleine Albright. Ambassador Albright was a leading advocate of creating the Yugoslav tribunal. Albright argued that in spite of the pessimism expressed by many in the international community, the Yugoslav war crimes tribunal was necessary for peace in the Balkans and for strengthening international law (Albright 1994, 209). Feminists, particularly liberal feminists, place special emphasis on women operating outside their traditional gender roles. Albright's leadership was instrumental in the tribunal's creation and should receive recognition for challenging the status quo.

Feminists also stress the importance of the ICTY in formalizing rape as a war crime. Rape had tended to be overlooked because it was just one of the unfortunate things that happen during war. Rape used to be considered as one of the "spoils" of war whereby women were plundered by occupying armies. The systematic rape of women in Bosnia demonstrated how rape could be a form of genocide and ethnic cleansing. Rape was used to terrorize and demoralize Bosnian Muslims and Bosnian Croat civilians. In other words, rape is often used as a weapon of war against the most vulnerable. In 2000, the ICTY brought violence against women to the forefront with the first convictions of several Serbs for their participation in rape camps. While prosecutions of rape crimes are an important step forward, the adversarial nature of the prosecution reinforces the idea of "woman as victim" and may affect the ability of women to find closure (Mertus 2004). The inclusion of women at the ICTY as judges, staffers, counselors, and lawyers has had an effect on prosecutions and sentencing. When women are among the jurists during sentencing, convicted rapists are more severely sanctioned than if the jurists were all male (King and Greening 2007, 1049–1071).

Feminists were quite critical of the inability of NATO to stand up and arrest those most responsible for the atrocities in the former Yugoslavia. The tens of thousands of women who were raped and/or killed may never have justice. It seems that justice is not worth the costs to the men who make the decisions. It is ironic that men who are armed "to the teeth" with the most sophisticated weapons are afraid of the consequences of arresting rapists and murderers. According to Denmark's *Politiken,* "The [U.S.] military was responsible for making the decision, despite the fact that leading American diplomats—Holbrooke included—have long called for the arrests to be made. Clinton is not a president who is able to go against the wishes of the military. They do not think that the 'purely moral nature' of the action is worth risking the life of a single military soldier" (U.S. Information Agency 1998a, 9). The so-called realist priorities are really masculinist priorities that put the interests of men over justice for women.

A Constructivist Cut

The ICTY is an example of how a variety of actors who have a largely Western identity are seeking to create a more just world order (Birdsall 2007, 397–418). This is a dynamic, intersubjective process by which norms are created and institutionalized. The ICTY is an important precedent, promoting multilateralism and respect for the rule of law. It paved the way for the creation of the ICC. While many states and individuals still value the norms of nonintervention and state sovereignty above all other values, many others have come to embrace the primacy of respect for human rights and international law. Eastern European states wishing to join the EU are required to cooperate with the ICTY. The values promoted by the ICTY still have not been internalized by Serbia, so there are limits to the extent to which international organizations can contribute to liberal norm diffusion (McMahon and Forsythe 2008, 412–435). While the other theories posit that states comply or do not comply with international law because of their material interests, constructivists argue that states comply because of their subjective interests (Goldsmith and Posner 2005). Compliance with ICTY orders and indictments is determined by the way states perceive their interests in relation to other actors and the international normative structure.

The ICTY is also important for establishing legal precedence and the development of international law. International criminal tribunal law is something that needs to be built (constructed) in order for alleged war criminals to be tried in the future. This law can be used by other tribunals or the ICC. The ICTY has taken domestic legal norms, like joint criminal enterprise and superior responsibility, and applied them at the international level (Meernik 2004, 356). The extent to which these norms and principles are embraced by others in the international community remains to be seen; however, the ICTY is an important first step in constructing an international system of criminal justice. Governments and other actors within civil society desired to do something in response to gross violations of human rights, so they created the ad hoc tribunals for Yugoslavia and Rwanda. Because of the experience of the ICTY, the international community learned from the challenges and arrived at the consensus upon which the ICC is based (Schiff 2008). While states may still seek to undermine the ICC because they value sovereignty more than multilateralism and normative curbs on their behavior, a great deal of consensus exists regarding the necessity and the efficacy of the ICC.

Postscript

Perhaps the most important person indicted and tried by the ICTY was Slobodan Milosevic, the head of state of the former Yugoslav and after its disintegration, Serbia. His 2002 trial represented a milestone in that he was the first head of state to be charged and tried for war crimes, genocide, and crimes against humanity by an international judicial body. His trial was fraught with procedural delays and legal disputes surrounding who qualifies as a war criminal. Milosevic's initial defense was not to respond to the charges but to question the court's jurisdiction and its right to charge him. After a series of delays, the ICTY determined that it did have the right to exercise jurisdiction in crimes relating to the former Yugoslavia and proceeded with the trial. Then came a series of personnel changes which delayed the trial, including the resignation of the chief judge and the decision by Milosevic to fire his lawyers and to serve as his own legal counsel. Milosevic was also beset with health concerns relating to his high blood pressure and heart disease. The trial was delayed again, and then in 2005, Milosevic requested to travel to Russia to receive medical treatment. Amidst allegations that Milosevic was either faking it or taking drugs to induce health symptoms to avoid further prosecution, the court determined that the health care system in the Netherlands was sufficient to meet Milosevic's medical needs. In March 2006, Milosevic was found dead in his jail cell in the Hague, apparently from a heart attack. His death meant a disappointing end to his trial—without any definitive statement on his guilt or innocence. Also, despite rumors in March 2006 that Ratko Mladic might be arrested, he remains at large. Radovon Karadic was finally arrested and turned over to the tribunal in 2008 and is currently on trial in the Netherlands.

The Responsibility to Protect (R2P)

The humanitarian crises in the 1990s led the UN to attempt to institutionalize the norm that sovereignty also involves the responsibility of states to protect their citizens from genocide, war crimes, ethnic cleansing, crimes against humanity, and other gross violations of human rights. The humanitarian crises discussed in this chapter were exacerbated by the unresolved tension between state sovereignty and the international community's concern for human rights. States are reluctant to concede any ground on their sovereign prerogatives for a variety of reasons, some legitimate—some to shield themselves from international criticism or from reaction to their bad behavior. At the same time, the UN often lacks the political will and the institutional capability to enforce and protect human rights. In 2001, the International Commission on Intervention and State Sovereignty (ICISS) issued a report, *The Responsibility to Protect,* which established the idea that sovereignty involved the responsibility to protect citizens, and if states are unable or unwilling to do so, that responsibility falls to the international community.

Both the High Level Panel and the secretary-general recommended in their respective reports that the responsibility to protect be further institutionalized as part of the UN reform effort in 2005. However, at the 2005 World Summit, the usual divisions remained. The best that member states could do was to acknowledge the principle of R2P and recognize the UN's obligation to use appropriate diplomatic, humanitarian, and other peaceful means to protect populations. Member states were willing to take collective action through the Security Council "on a case-by-case basis and in cooperation with the relevant regional organization as appropriate, should peaceful means be inadequate and national authorities manifestly fail to protect their populations from genocide, war crimes, ethnic cleansing and crimes against humanity" (General Assembly, A/68/L.1, 31). In other words, that status quo was reaffirmed as the Security Council has always had the authority to link gross violations of human rights to international peace and security. All that is required is permanent member agreement—something that has been in very short supply throughout UN history.

In September 2004, Secretary of State Colin Powell went before the UN Security Council and stated that the situation in the Darfur region of Sudan amounted to genocide. The crisis in Darfur centers on attacks by government-backed Arab militias, known as the janjaweed, on rebel tribes in the region. Over 300,000 people have been killed and over 2 million displaced. At present it is one of the worst humanitarian crises facing the international community. Seven-thousand African Union (AU) peacekeepers were deployed in the region; however, their mandate was to protect the monitors of a non-existent cease-fire, not civilians. In 2006, the Security Council reinforced the African Union force with a UN presence (UNAMID). UNAMID is a hybrid force of 20,000 peacekeepers with a mandate to protect civilians. Sudan lukewarm support UNAMID stalled its initial deployment. According to Jan Pronk, the special UN representative to Sudan, "They speak about recolonization, imperialism, they speak about Iraq and Afghanistan, they speak about the conspiracy against the Arab and Islamic world. It's easy to get heated opposition to the U.N. even among people who don't like the government" (cited in Hoge 2006a, A10). Once again one person's humanitarian action is another's imperialism. In the meantime, thousands continue to die and the lives of millions of people remain at risk in Darfur. In 2009, the ICC issued indictments against Sudan's president Omar Al-Bashir for war crimes and in 2010, for genocide. Bashir continues to travel frequently to other African countries, albeit awkwardly. The African Union in 2009 issued a decision calling upon its member states not to cooperate with the ICC investigations, reinforcing the perceived view that the ICC is biased against Africans.

CONCLUSION

International efforts to promote, protect, and enforce human rights have met with varying degrees of success. Human rights both challenge and reinforce the status quo. This statement is not contradictory if it is analyzed using the different theoretical frameworks. Human rights violations have been identified by the Security Council as a threat to international peace and security. Human rights violations have led to domestic instability and civil war. The nature of international conflict in the twenty-first century suggests that human rights will remain controversial in international relations. Disagreements regarding definition, implementation, and enforcement are inevitable. What is certain is that human rights will remain a permanent and important feature in twenty-first-century world politics.

KEY TERMS

United Nations High
Commissioner for
Refugees
(UNHCR)   264
1951 Convention
Relating to the Status
of Refugees and the
1967 Protocol   264
nonrefoulement
de jure refugee   264
voluntary repatriation,
resettlement, or
assimilation   264
internally displaced
persons (IDPs)   265
de facto refugees
World Food Program
(WFP)   265
World Health
Organization
(WHO)   266
Universal Declaration
of Human
Rights   267
political and civil
rights   267
economic and social
rights   267
collective rights   267

International Covenant on
Economic, Social and
Cultural Rights   268
International Covenant
on Civil and Political
Rights   268
Human Rights
Council   269
Commission on Human
Rights   271
United Nations High
Commissioner for
Human Rights
(UNHCHR)   271
the Cairo
Declaration   271
UN Conference on
Women in
Beijing   271 (1996)
International Labor
Organization
(ILO)   272
International Committee
for the Red Cross
(ICRC)   273
quiet diplomacy   273
"name and shame"   274
Amnesty
International   274

Human Rights
Watch   274
Doctors Without Borders
(Médecins Sans
Frontieres)   274
Responsibility to Protect
(R2P)   279
international human
rights law
(IHRL)   288
international
humanitarian law
(IHL)   288
international criminal
law (ICL)   289
The International
Criminal Tribunal for
the former Yugoslavia
(ICTY)   289
International Criminal
Court (ICC)   289
Special Court for Sierra
Leone   289
Special Tribunal for
Lebanon   289
Extraordinary Chambers
in the Courts of
Cambodia   289
victors' justice   291

SUGGESTED READINGS

Barnett, Michael N. 2003. *Eyewitness to Genocide: The United Nations and Rwanda.* Ithaca, NY: Cornell University Press.
Forsythe, David P. 1991b. *The Internationalization of Human Rights.* Lexington, MA: D. C. Heath.
Maogoto, Jackson. 2004. *War Crimes and Realpolitik: International Justice from World War I to the 21st Century.* Boulder, CO: Lynne Rienner.
Scott, Shirley V. 2010. *International Law and World Politics.* Boulder, CO: Lynne Reinner.

Global Governance in 2025

Prediction in politics is always hazardous, and international politics is no exception. What role will international organizations play in the governance of twenty-first-century international affairs? Will new international organizations be created or will existing organizations be significantly transformed? What are the prospects for international peace and cooperation? How will international organizations respond to pressing global problems? International relations have multiple futures with multiple interpretations.

A REALIST CUT

Realists predict continuity, both in international relations and in the nature of global governance. States remain the principal actors in international relations, and international organizations will serve the interests of the great powers of the day. Who those great powers will be depends on the outcomes of several wars and whether there is a global economic recovery. In 1998, observers were predicting a "new world order" and the costs and benefits of America's *hyperpuissance* (the military, economic, ideological, and cultural power). In 2010, some were predicting that the world was on the verge of a new dark age as U.S. power has waned. The international system will still be defined as anarchy characterized by some kind of balance of power. International organizations will continue to play secondary roles in the management of international affairs. War, violence, and conflict will remain at the forefront of the international stage. What will change, according to realists, is the distribution of capabilities among states. There is nothing inevitable about the liberal world order created under U.S. hegemony. The values, norms, and rules regarding state behavior in the year 2025 will be decided by the powerful. The behavior and interests of IGOs will reflect that underlying balance of power.

If the UN remains a viable organization, collective security will happen rarely, and if it does it will be a politically motivated and power-driven endeavor. Collective security will be triggered only when the geostrategic, military, and economic interests of all the great powers are engaged and those interests are congruent. A congruence of great-power interests will be just as difficult to achieve, if not more so, in 2025 as it was during the twentieth century. Liberal principles of justice and international law will not prompt UN action, rather only great-power interests. Whether or not the UN will continue to exist will be determined in large part by the answers to two questions.

1. *Can war between the great powers be avoided?* The historical record suggests that war is an inevitable part of international relations. States that want peace must always be prepared for war. Nuclear weapons may create a particular kind of balance of power that renders war between the great powers obsolete, but that is no guarantee against devastating terrorist attacks. War remains a likely possibility, particularly if the current international order experiences a crisis or some kind of breakdown. A global depression or a regional conflict that spins out of control could erode U.S. leadership capabilities to the extent that a revisionist challenger will seek to change the system. The United States could fight or abandon its leadership role. A new world leader, possibly China, may create international organizations that institutionalize its dominant role and legitimize its leadership position. The UN may meet the same fate as the League of Nations, finding itself on the trash heap of failed experiments. Even if global war can be averted, the United States or some other state (or a group of states) must be willing to commit the resources necessary to keep the UN operating. Chances are that great-power indecision and neglect will marginalize the UN.

2. *Can the UN adapt to the changing power distributions among states?* If nuclear weapons generate an effective stalemate among the great powers, then the UN must change to reflect the shifting distributions of conventional military and economic capabilities. The original composition of the Security Council reflected the balance of power after World War II. However, after the Cold War, the permanent members of the Security Council have resisted reforms that would give rising states more decision-making authority on the Council. The permanent members have rejected any change in the veto provision or other substantive decision-making procedures. The legitimacy of Security Council will be in question because if it is to be effective, it needs to function like a great-power concert. Otherwise, it will be bypassed by the great powers in favor of other arrangements that favor their interests. The great-power cooperation that occurred during the 1990s was more an aberration than the birth of true collective security.

The Security Council will be just as paralyzed as it always has been. The optimism of the 1990s quickly eroded as its collective security initiatives in Somalia and the former Yugoslavia proved disastrous. The sobering conflicts of interest and power realities have prevented effective collective security. As an institutional framework, collective security does little to curb unilateral uses of force by the permanent members. These states will continue to use violence to secure their national interests, which include forcibly changing the governments of other states and carrying out military reprisals. The proliferation of nuclear weapons will create multiple "cold wars" as adversaries stand off. The Security Council will likely remain paralyzed, unable to act to curb the proliferation of WMD.

The nature of conflict in 2025 does not lend itself to traditional collective security of the kind envisioned by the UN architects. Collective security in the twentieth century was designed to guard against the traditional landgrab and the territorial expansion of states through force. International conflict in the twenty-first century has internal sources and is low in intensity but prolonged. Terrorism is also a persistent threat. International conflict occurs in the marginalized areas of the world, where the permanent members have few interests. Marginalized states have disintegrated along ethnic and religious lines. Only strong states continue to survive internal and external challenges. International security between strong states will be achieved through a balance of power, just as it has been achieved for the last 500 years. The problem they collectively face is the proliferation of WMD to nihilist state and nonstate actors. Still they will find it impossible to cooperate unless their immediate interests are threatened. Existing organizations need to be transformed to reflect the material interests of the new dominant powers. Otherwise, they will fall by the wayside, discarded tools that are no longer useful. In short, they will become anachronistic institutions, relics of the past.

IGOs that relate to trade will meet the same fate as security IGOs. The WTO, which is based on free trade principles, will be effective only as long as the major powers stand to benefit from free trade. States will ignore any WTO decisions that go against their important national interests. And they will abandon free trade if they stand to lose significant national wealth. States will erect barriers to trade in order to arrest their decline or to maximize economic advantages. They simply will be more clever, paying lip service to the benefits of free trade, all the while managing to secure strategic advantages for government owned and national industries. States that engage in managed and strategic trade will take advantage of those that pursue free-trade policies. Their firms and state industries will have access to the markets of others while keeping their markets closed to international competition. Firms that have the full backing of their governments will have a competitive advantage because they do not have to worry about going out of business. They can sell the products or services below cost, driving competitors out of business and establishing a monopoly or oligopoly. These firms and their countries will control the leading sectors of the economy. Absent some kind of catastrophe, China is poised to overtake the United States as the largest economy by 2025.

Realists point out that globalization is neither inevitable nor new. States have the power to implement policies that control the forces of globalization. States can, and will, put controls on trade, currency, finance, and capital if it suits their national interests. "Globalization" and "a new world order" are hardly new ideas. U.S. presidents ranging from Wilson to Nixon to Bush to Clinton have all spoken of a new world order based on democracy and liberal economic principles. That vision has not been sustained by the historical record nor have international relations fundamentally changed. According to Nicholas D. Kristof,

> [G]lobalization . . . may not be quite as fresh as it sometimes seems. Since at least the 13th century, when Florentine merchants lent to the English to pay for King Edward's wars, international capital has roamed the world in search of highest returns. (The start was inauspicious: England defaulted causing the collapse of two Florentine banks.) What has changed . . . is the scale of capital flows and their ability to capsize small nations—even large ones. (1998, 6)

International organizations that deal with the substantive economic issues, such as trade and finance, are likely to experience serious crises. The WTO has already been under attack for undermining national interests, jobs, and national industries. In the twenty-first century, states will seek to regain control over their borders in order to curb job losses and to keep certain industries within their territorial boundaries. While the WTO will continue to promote free trade, states will subvert WTO rulings that compromise their national interest. A global economic recession may even cause the failure of the WTO, as states are forced to regroup and reassure their concerned citizenship that they can deliver economic prosperity. States must once again be responsible for ensuring a certain standard of living, which inevitably involves state intervention in the market and making the market subservient to the state. Realists argue that the logic of the market artificially puts individual and firm interests over national interests. Individuals and firms must recognize and promote the interests of the state because the state will ultimately protect and defend them. This recognition must be more than just patriotic lip service and the waving of national flags. States and industries must work together to improve and provide the best quality of life for citizens.

Economic growth in the developing world is likely to undergo a crisis. Developing countries realize that the nature of economic relations is, in many respects, a zero-sum game, and they are on the short end of the stick. Developing states need to take responsibility for their own national development and not rely on foreign capital and foreign assistance. Economic and human development has been arrested by ballooning external debt and currency crises, making developing states subservient to wealthier states. Free flows of capital have created speculative bubbles that can burst, taking entire economies with them. Again, according to Kristof,

> Most governments imposed capital controls early in this century and then lifted them in the 1970s and 1980s, and limitations on changing money came to be seen as quaint. Paradoxically, it is the holdouts on capital controls, like China and India, that have weathered the financial crisis much better than others, because they were not vulnerable to a sudden exodus of capital. (1998, 6)

In spite of stopgap measures implemented at the end of the twentieth century, the international monetary and financial order moved toward a global crisis in the twenty-first century as more and more currencies became vulnerable to speculators and multinational banks and financial institutions teetered on the edge of solvency. The dominant power of a hegemon is necessary in order to rebuild the institutions and rules of global finance. Unfortunately, U.S. leadership capabilities in the global economy has waned considerably in the twenty-first century, and its strategy has been to find "market" solutions to mask its inability to provide a stable international monetary and financial order. The system is an inherently political creature, and the creation of a global or regional currency will favor some at the expense of others, if at all. Realists point out that the international economy may not be based on liberal principles at all. Absent a liberal hegemon, the global economy could break apart into regional blocs that are intensely competitive, protectionist, and hostile.

The environment in 2025 will have degraded extensively. States have taken steps to renew their resources such as forests and fresh water; however, climate change and ozone depletion will have taken their toll. Whales are nearing extinction. Coastal and equatorial states have experienced the devastating effects of climate change. These states have lost territory due to the increase in sea levels, and they are subject to periodic and catastrophic floods. Historically, states have been both blessed and cursed by geography. Coastal and equatorial states will either have prepared for the effects of climate change or will have suffered the consequences. While it is not fair or just, states must respond and adjust to the changing environmental reality. Similarly, states will have to prepare and educate their citizens for the effects of ozone depletion. Humans will have to adjust their lifestyles, which will include spending more time indoors. While outside, humans will have to wear hats, sunglasses, sunscreen, long sleeves, and long pants.

On a positive note, the principal cause of climate change, the burning of fossil fuels, is no longer a major factor. The world's supplies of oil, natural gas, and coal are expensive, nearing depletion, and are being replaced with other forms of energy, including a supercell that harnesses electricity generated by solar, nuclear, or hydroelectric sources. Technology will solve some of the environmental problems of the twenty-first century, but states must actively develop and utilize that technology. Responsible states will have pursued alternative energy strategies, not so much because of climate change, but because world supplies are limited, expensive, and nonrenewable.

The protection, promotion, and enforcement of human rights remain in the realm of low politics in the twenty-first century. States will remain appalled by gross violations of human rights in other countries, but they are not likely to intervene unless significant national interests are at stake. Hence, international enforcement of human rights is a politically motivated endeavor—a noble mask for the not-so-noble interests of the intervening states. Given impending economic and energy crises, many states will use economic, social, and collective rights to reassert control over their borders and to manage these crises. Many states, particularly in Europe and the developing world, will use their responsibility to protect and promote human rights of their citizens to reassert their sovereignty over trade and monetary issues.

The International Criminal Court has fallen to the wayside, having failed in its attempts to indict, arrest, and prosecute state leaders responsible for war crimes and gross violations of human rights. The harsh reality is that the Court will not apply to the powerful, which means that other states will not ratify the Court's charter and those that supported its creation will ignore it in a case of buyer remorse. The Yugoslav and Rwandan war crimes tribunals demonstrated that only the vanquished will be prosecuted, and then only when it is politically expedient. In the twenty-first century, the promotion and protection of human rights will be largely voluntary and not a high priority of states. Definition and implementation of human rights will be determined by the powerful and will be used to manipulate and control the weak.

A LIBERAL CUT

International relations in the twenty-first century are fundamentally different from that of the past. International politics is conducted within the framework of a global society consisting of a variety of international actors tied together by computer and information technologies. This global society is founded on individual human rights and the global marketplace. The international system is characterized by a complex interdependence that significantly decreases the utility of military force to achieve goals. States have become transnationalized in that they are inextricably tied to the global economy and global civil society. Other actors such as MNCs, NGOs, and even individuals are part and parcel of global civil society. International law and organizations have helped states overcome collective action problems and UN framework will have been transformed into some loose form of federal world government, albeit a quasi-government, in which more international actors are allowed to participate.

The international system will not exactly be "perpetual peace" in the twenty-first century. International (global) peace and stability face several complex threats. These threats emanate from within states as certain segments of society resist change and globalization. Many societies will experience some form of "tribalism" as a reaction to global integrative forces. Some segments will revert to religious fundamentalism or virulent nationalism. This tribalism can threaten international stability, particularly if tribalist forces take over governments and disrupt markets. These tribalist governments can also represent a traditional territorial threat to transnationalized states and will require some kind of containment. This containment will be conducted through collective security provisions of the UN. The proliferation of WMD is still a problem, but the NPT and IAEA still pay pivotal roles in managing conflict relating to the peaceful use of nuclear technology with the security interests of states.

By the year 2025, China will have become more liberalized and more fully integrated into the global economy. The Security Council veto will be used sparingly, and more democratic procedures for membership and decision making will be instituted. The UN may even have a standing multinational military force that can be dispatched in emergencies. Military force will not be particularly useful, either because of a military stalemate or because the problems defy military solutions. Nonviolent means of leverage will become important and appropriate for responding to international security threats. The UN assists states in addressing internal violence, although the line between domestic and international has been erased for all intents and purposes. Government decisions may no longer reach all segments of society, and governments are unable to enforce their own laws. Criminal syndicates will also have transnational activities, requiring transnational approaches. The UN will help national governments by providing social and economic assistance. It will still engage in peacekeeping and peacemaking when appropriate and help provide social welfare and humanitarian assistance to global society's disadvantaged.

The international economy has become truly global. The production of goods and services takes place on a global scale. The concept of a national economy is obsolete; rather, the economy is divided between global and local. The local economy consists of local services such as taxi driving, hairstyling, child care, and lawn services. Most other goods and services will be produced and provided globally. The WTO functions as a laissez-faire entity enforcing trade rules, copyrights, and intellectual property rights. This is a crucial function of the WTO in the maturing stage of the technological revolution. Growth in the global economy is still in the areas of information, telecommunication, transportation, and aerospace technologies. The global economy has also been transformed by the costs and scarcity of fossil fuels and the switch to solar, hydroelectric, and nuclear energy. Adaptation is easier in the global economy because individuals and firms, not states and complicated bureaucracies, make private and public choices. Because the global market is allowed to operate, innovation is spontaneous and benefits are more easily diffused.

The international monetary and financial system experienced a systemic breakdown in the early part of the twenty-first century. The crisis affected all the national economies and caused a global economic recession. However, democratic states worked together, relying on negotiations and compromise, to stabilize the situation and to coordinate their national responses. They moved to create a single global currency controlled by a reformed and more robust IMF because this is necessary for financial stability in the global economy. Necessity is the mother of all invention. Even though no state possesses hegemony, states, MNCs, and NGOs can cooperate under existing international organizations to solve global financial problems.

The global market encompasses what was known as the "developing world" or the "South" during the twentieth century. Now practically indistinguishable from the "developed world" or the "North," these areas experienced significant economic growth and investment during their transition from traditional society into modern and postmodern consumer societies. The market has caused the diffusion of wealth, technology, values, investment, and capital. Liberals argue that this does not mean that the developing world has become Westernized. Rather, market forces work to sort out the best of all worlds, transforming both North and South, developed and underdeveloped.

Of course, not all liberals are this optimistic, despite their agreement that market forces are generally positive. They acknowledge that the gap between rich and poor will not disappear, as the market affords an uneven playing field. Nevertheless, they argue, individuals must have the opportunity to participate in the market. Gender, nationality, or race should not be allowed to interfere with the market nor should individuals be excluded from the market for these reasons. More people in the developing world will have access to the same amenities available to those living in the industrial and postindustrial societies. They will have access to health care, education, clean water, electricity, sanitation, computers, and some form of telecommunications. But access will not level the fundamental playing field. Thus, the UN, NGOs, and states of the twenty-first century will be needed to protect and assist those who fall between the cracks or fail to compete in the new global economy. However, the UN must emphasize individual initiatives, helping individuals help themselves. Given the scale of the global economy in the twenty-first century, the UN will only be able to provide for a minimum safety net. Individuals will have more control over their lives in the twenty-first century than they have ever had in human history.

Environmental threats continue to worsen in the early twenty-first century. International treaties and organizations are strengthened to address these problems and help bridge the gap between North and South. The expansion of global markets encourages more efficient industrial production, and new technology transforms dirty industries into cleaner industries. NGOs continue to play a crucial role in identifying and monitoring international environmental problems. They will continue to hold the feet of states, industries, and MNCs to the fire regarding environmental protection. NGOs will also offer plausible solutions to environmental problems. Since environmental problems affect all, without respect to geography or nationality, all states will be forced to cooperate and work together to solve these problems.

Like the international monetary system, the ecosystem permits no choice: Environmental issues must be addressed head-on. Collective international learning will help states overcome collective action problems. Most liberals argue that market forces should be allowed to prevail, but environmental costs should not be externalized. International organizations can help states and other actors ensure that environmental costs are included in the price of goods and services, thereby affecting demand via the price mechanism. Hence, a global cap and trade system is in place in 2025. The market remains the most efficient way to utilize and distribute resources. It is also the principal source of innovation. The twenty-first century has seen the rise of an entire eco-industry that provides environment-friendly technology, goods, and services. Environmental education has created consumer demands that protect the natural environment and place considerable value on biodiversity. The economic development of the South has allowed its governments and citizens to obtain the financial and human resources necessary to environmental protection.

Human rights now form the foundation of the legal system of global society. Local, provincial, national, and international law, recognize and implement the

Universal Declaration of Human Rights. Civil and political rights are specifically guaranteed by the UN. Individuals will be able to appeal to the UN or UN-sponsored agencies to seek redress for wrongs, particularly when national or regional petitions fail. Violators of human rights can be held civilly liable and criminally responsible for their acts. Those accused of committing gross violations of human rights or war crimes can be brought before the International Criminal Court for justice. Those found guilty of such crimes receive lengthy prison terms. The death penalty has been outlawed in most areas, and it is actionable as a human rights violation under international law.

Economic, social, and collective rights are not institutionalized on a par with civil and political rights because they do not form the foundation of global civil society. The UN is incapable of delivering such rights as the provision of health care and education to individuals. Rather, individuals working in their own communities must actualize for themselves their economic, social, and cultural rights. Collective rights remain elusive because it is hard to define the collective in the twenty-first century, outside of a generalized global citizenship. The rights to a clean environment and development are relative to the age. These rights mean quite different things in 2025 than they did in 2010.

International relations have fundamentally changed owing to the expansion of markets, human rights, and democratic forms of governments. The world in 2025 is far from perfect and serious inequities remain. Nevertheless, the quality of life for everyone on the planet is better than that in previous generations. International war is virtually obsolete, and violent conflict is seen as inappropriate for settling disputes. The rule of law is a norm that has been institutionalized. Law that is made by the people, for the people, through their elected representatives is the best way to promote justice and the peaceful settlement of disputes. International actors are expected to compromise, mediate, arbitrate, and adjudicate; but they will not use violence. After centuries of war, the international system is finally evolving into a stable and peaceful order. These conditions are not the result of a nuclear stalemate. They are the result of the evolution of human society and the natural collective learning process.

A MARXIST CUT

Dickens, that other nineteenth-century thinker (contemporary with Marx), said it all: "It was the best of times, it was the worst of times" (*Tale of Two Cities*). And in 2025, that much, at least, has not changed—the dialectic nature of change. Thus, the international system is still characterized by the persistence of class struggle; and if capitalism remains the dominant mode of production, it has become different from the late twentieth-century variety. Capitalism has transformed to the extent that many economic and environmental contradictions have been averted. However, human beings are no better off than they were in previous generations. While approximately 2.5 billion people enjoy an impressive standard of living, the quality of life for the remaining 12.5 billion people remains poor. This majority is still impoverished, even by the twentieth century's primitive standards. Most of the world's population has missed the technological revolution and benefits little from globalization.

Absent a catastrophic failure of capitalism, the global economy is still guided by retro-neoclassical economic principles. Capitalism underwent a series of mini-crises in the early twenty-first century. The social and environmental consequences of unrestricted, highly mobile capital were felt during the contagion currency crises and the resulting economic depression. States, once guided by Keynesian economic principles, were either unable to reimpose capital controls or were ideologically unwilling to do so. Transnational capital was able to solidify its dominant position in the new global economy by tying the fate of many workers to its own. Workers received part of their wages and most of their retirement payments in the form of stocks and bonds. States (principally core states) and the IMF had no choice but to bail out large banks and other businesses or face a full-scale depression. Of course, the bailout of investors and MNCs was paid for by national, as well as international, taxes. At the same time, transnational capital was able to use the relative immobility of labor and national rivalries to its own advantage. The relative wages and benefits of workers, save for a few high-tech industries, have declined globally.

International conflict is rooted in economic inequity and is exacerbated by ethnicity and nationalism in 2025. But in spite of the emergence of a "global society," international political and military institutions remain weak. The tribalism predicted by many liberals is far more than a sporadic, violent accident of globalism. Rather, tribalism is a systemic challenge, representing a pervasive contradiction to global market forces. International violence takes several forms. Unilateral uses of force by states continue in the twenty-first century, principally to protect key economic interests and ensure the safety of investments. Revisionist states or states that have adopted strong forms of socialism or corporatism are challenged, and their governments are removed by force if necessary. Terrorism remains a problem as religious fundamentalists and fringe groups challenge the status quo.

The globalization of production has provided opportunities as well as challenges to subordinate classes. The so-called tribes can be quite disruptive, particularly if they have access to or control of important resources. Strikes at a single plant can shut down global production. The technological revolution provides ample opportunity for serious failure and even sabotage. The twenty-first century started out with a technological glitch that cost billions of dollars. Hackers remain a threat to utilities, financial institutions and even the most advanced military. The speed, complexity, and volatility of the global market have caused many in the twenty-first century to question whether globalization should be valued by humankind, especially since it has a very dangerous malevolent side.

Weak political institutions help capitalism expand and evolve. But trade and monetary organizations have increased their power and authority. The WTO continues to be guided by neoclassical principles of free trade. It reviews local, provincial, national, and regional laws and regulations to determine whether or not they interfere with free trade. In the twenty-first century, almost every aspect of private and public life has become "commodified" and subjected to international competition. The Multilateral Agreement on Investment (MAI), which placed restrictions on how local and national governments could regulate multinational business, was ratified after the global economic recession in the early twenty-first century. The MAI was presented as the only way to stimulate the global economy and promote international investments after the recession.

The international financial system collapsed during the early twenty-first century, which prompted global recession. The IMF and the liberal capitalist economies then developed a single international currency, which is now issued and monitored by the IMF. The global currency signals the final subordination of national interest to the transnational interest in a stable monetary order. The initial value of the global currency vis-à-vis the national currency was difficult to set. The hard currencies, which were valued higher, were given preferential treatment by the IMF. The soft currencies lost most of their market value before the transition, which deepened the recession in the South. This situation gave the MNCs a great advantage because they could more easily afford the developing world's assets and resources.

Global economic development is a tale of two worlds. In the core, economic and technological developments race on at an impressive pace. However, the rest of the world is mired in grinding poverty. The gap between the richest and poorest continues to widen. Development in the twenty-first century is also distinguished by a dramatic increase of poverty among citizens of the "developed" world. More and more people in the North have been marginalized by technology and capital mobility. While poverty in the North is not as life-threatening as poverty in the South, it remains an important source of violent conflict. The average citizen struggles for adequate shelter, nutrition, and education. The technological revolution has left most people behind. They do not have the education or the skills to survive in the very competitive twenty-first century global labor force.

The status of the earth's natural resources is also grim. Biodiversity has been diminished drastically, as has the square acreage of tropical rain forest. The temperature of the atmosphere has risen by about four degrees, wreaking havoc on low-lying coastal regions. Countries like Haiti, Jamaica, Sri Lanka, India, Pakistan, Bangladesh, Malaysia, and Indonesia have suffered devastating losses in terms of property and territory. More important, millions of people have lost their lives, causing many in the developing world to claim that environmental genocide is being perpetrated against these countries.

Environmental conditions in the North have also deteriorated. Countries like Sweden, Canada, and Germany have been forced to lower their environmental standards in order to attract capital investments and to help their firms compete globally. The competition for capital has lowered environmental standards worldwide, causing the destruction of habitat and the depletion of resources. With oil reserves depleted, the new powerful MNCs are those that have harnessed solar energy effectively. The technological revolution, like the industrial revolution, has come with considerable environmental cost. While technology has made hard industries more efficient, the disposal of waste and technology by-products has proven problematic and expensive.

Marxists agree with liberals that human rights will be increasingly cast as civil and political rights. Economic rights, save for the right to own property, cannot be sustained by the markets or states. Firms cannot remain competitive if they have to pay a minimum wage, use unionized labor, or provide health insurance. The state is in no position to provide for these rights. Save for the tribal state, which is constantly being challenged from within and without, most governments have a laissez-faire approach to health, education, environmental regulations, and consumer safety, catering to the interests of business. The threat to human rights in the twenty-first century is not the government *per se*, but governmental neglect.

A FEMINIST CUT

Liberal feminists see improvements in the status of women in the twenty-first century. By 2025, more women are participating in national and international decision-making circles. Liberal states and international organizations now have heightened sensitivities to women's issues, and those sensitivities are reflected in their policies. The technological revolution has opened many doors for women in traditionally male-dominated positions, including combat roles in the military. The globalization of markets has released women from their traditional roles, empowering them economically and allowing them to control their lives (Bergman 1986). As a result, the poverty rates among women are declining, and women's human rights are respected.

Socialist feminists and essentialist neofeminists are not so confident that the lives of women will improve in the twenty-first century. Their picture is darker. War is still a permanent feature, and women still bear the brunt of international violence. The technological revolution allows men to press a button and rain death upon a society hundreds, if not thousands, of miles away. The military as an inherently masculine institution has not changed just because women have been allowed to join. Rather, women are expected to act like men and pursue the same strategies as men. International security continues to be conceptualized in masculine ways, and men continue to control decision making in states and most international organizations. IGOs, MNCs, and many NGOs still reflect patriarchy, subjugating women and trivializing the female experience.

The global economy threatens the gains made by women in the twentieth century. Entire sectors of the global economy are increasingly feminized. The Great Recession, also known as the man-cession, had a greater impact on men as housing, construction, and industrial manufacturing crashed, creating widespread male unemployment. Women, occupying low paying jobs in the education, healthcare, and service sectors, became the breadwinners struggling to make mortgage and credit card payments. In 2025, women, who must still work in the home, must also work in the global economy—and they are still making less than men. Women's wages are 78 percent of men's in the developed countries and the percentage is even less in the developing world. Global markets have made jobs far more competitive and driven wages down. Women also suffer more from environmental degradation. Worse, they are seen as the source of environmental problems. Women, many of whom remain disenfranchised, are part of forced population-control programs to curb population growth. In 2010, *The Economist* (March 6–12, 2010) asserted that technology, declining fertility, and prejudice were combining to create a "gender-cide" that has resulted in the disappearance of 100 million girls that would have otherwise been born. Without proper vigilance, the global population in 2025 can even become unnaturally skewed. The forced population-control policies can lead to an increase in infanticide among girls. Genetic engineering in 2025 allows couples to fix the sex of their child prior to conception. Unlike liberals, who assume a scientific tendency toward equilibrium, many feminists argue that patriarchy can have ill effects when coupled with the technological revolution.

The rights of women vis-à-vis those of men have far from equal status in 2025. Men's rights are still more respected and better recognized than women's, although women in the core have made great strides. Economic, social, and cultural rights of women are almost nonexistent, as state social welfare programs have been drastically cut back. In spite of the strides made by the women's movement in the twentieth century, women's rights have suffered some setbacks quantitatively and qualitatively in the twenty-first century. The weakening of the state has meant that no entity exists to enforce antidiscrimination laws or equality issues. The market determines wages, and women's wages are, for whatever reason, lower than men's. Ironically, just as women have gained the right to participate in government through voting and office holding, the state has waned in importance—it no longer serves as a vehicle for improving the lives of citizens. In 2025, women must now gain access to the IGOs responsible for global governance.

A CONSTRUCTIVIST CUT

Unlike the theories of international relations, the constructivist approach is not predictive. It focuses on how the world as we know it is socially constructed. Global governance in 2025 is what states, decision makers, and international organizations make of it. The ideas, beliefs, and identities of the individuals and states matter in understanding the nature of global governance. Leaders who seek to cooperate and act in a multilateral fashion will determine the extent to which international organizations will play an important role. The nature of that role will be determined by how international organizations create norms and values. Whether international security is understood as state security or human security, or women's rights as human rights, will depend on how international organizations promote the norms and the degree to which it is embraced by states and societies. The status of the norms is not fixed nor is there a natural progression from one norm to the other. It depends on the actor and their intersubjective identities.

The level of political intervention and management of global economic issues will be determined by the social relations of the major actors. The financial crisis which began in 2008 brought to the forefront competing values and norms about the extent to which markets should be allowed to operate unregulated and regarding which state policies are "appropriate." The "right" course of action is not based in some objective reality, but rather on what will restore confidence in the system and the institutions. Confidence comes from shared understanding and a bond of trust. These are social relations that result in our shared beliefs in particular political and economic models. The WTO and the IMF can be protectors of the environment and worker's rights if states want them to be. Conversely, WTO and IMF officials can also socialize states into considering the economic costs of not protecting the environment and worker's rights. However, if WTO and IMF economists are only interested in the sophistication of their mathematical models, then policies that result from those models will reflect that value—mathematical sophistication, not environmental protection and strengthened workers' rights.

The constructivist approach to international relations perhaps is better for bridging the divides between the major international relations theories because of its emphasis on the normative and social relations among actors. Constructivism allows us to explain change and how different concepts used to describe international relations have meant different things at different times. It also holds promise for scholars, especially those predicting a bleak future, who seek to understand how malevolent interests and values are constructed and disseminated. Such an approach may be useful to decision makers seeking to build a better world in the twenty-first century.

CONCLUSION

The theories and approaches to international relations allow us to improve our understanding of the nature of global governance and the behavior of international organizations. For many, governance is based on a great-power concert, or balance of power, which is facilitated by international organizations. For others, it is based on democratic cooperation and collective action, which is institutionalized and perpetuated by liberal international organizations. For still others, global governance is founded on capitalist exploitation, in which case international organizations are mechanisms of capitalist domination and exploitation. Most international organizations are dominated by men and, according to feminists, reflect masculine values. To others, global governance is what we make it, a reflection of the social relations of different kinds of actors. But if we ask which of these theories or approaches is right, we are asking the wrong question. There is a better question: What does each have to teach us about the nature of global governance and about the source of the policies emanating from international organizations?

Finding Employment in International Organizations

Finding employment is always tricky business as you have to balance your notion of the "ideal" position with the requirements of everyday life, that is, paying bills, repaying student loans, and successfully negotiating the always competitive job market. This section highlights a nuts and bolts strategy for finding employment in international organizations. Part I discusses the kinds of skills sought by international organizations and strategies for successfully presenting yourself for open positions. Part II details how you might find employment opportunities in the different international organizations discussed in this text.

PART I: SKILLS

No degree that you earn at any university anywhere in the world is going to guarantee you a job in an international organization, or in any field for that matter. International organizations hire different kinds of people, with different degrees and different majors and for different reasons. They hire accounting majors for accounting positions, human resource specialists for personnel departments, and international relations majors for human rights officers or political affairs specialists. Your first step is to ensure that you meet the minimal requirements for the position. A college degree is the credential that gets you in the door. The more advanced the degree, the more doors that are open.

After the baseline is met, it is up to you to present the "total package" that will separate you from all the other candidates for the position. What is the total package? That depends. If your degree and major are more quantitative, technical, and business oriented, you may want to show that while you provide specialized skills, you also understand the big picture and the politics and controversies surrounding your potential employer. If your degree is more grounded in the liberal arts, then you might want show that you possess special skills that might be useful like webpage design, grant writing, or social networking.

Almost all international organizations will be delighted if you have foreign language proficiency and many require it. French is the language of diplomacy, and Spanish is widely spoken. If you are proficient in one of the official languages of the UN, you will have an advantage. Proficiency and/or fluency in "in demand" languages such as Chinese, Arabic, or Pashtun is also a plus.

Not all skills are learned in a classroom. If you do not possess some of the skills just discussed, or are deficient in some of the skills desired for the position, you should demonstrate your willingness to acquire them as soon as possible. Skills are also learned through practice. Hence, you should avail yourself of internship opportunities while at university. Internship experience gives you "real-world" experience and helps you compete with others who have been working in the field for several years. It also provides you with a track record of work experience.

Woody Allen, a famous filmmaker and comedian, once said that 80 percent of life is just showing up. Expanding upon that idea, it follows that you will not be considered for a job unless you put yourself out there. The UN or Greenpeace is not going to come knocking on your door asking for you to come work for them. You have to find positions that you are qualified for and then present yourself in the best light that you can without being deceitful. The key is to stand out from the crowd in order to increase the probability of getting an interview. Of course, you do not want to stand out in a negative way, that is, applying for a position you are not qualified for or by submitting application materials that have grammatical mistakes. Another common mistake is by not providing the information required by the employer. Incomplete applications rarely get forwarded to the next level.

Finding employment in any organization takes common sense. Successfully landing the position often depends on things that are intangible. The short list of candidates almost always consists of people who are all very qualified for the position. The successful candidate may possess a sense of humor, seems to work well with others, or is able to quickly establish a rapport with the hiring committee. Sometimes, it may boil down to "who the candidate knows." Nepotism or patronage aside, often getting an interview or a position may turn on whether people have met you in a professional capacity. Networking is a well-established mechanism for enhancing employment prospects. Avail yourself of lectures or social opportunities that afford you the chance to meet others working in your desired field.

PART II: EMPLOYMENT OPPORTUNITIES

The Internet affords the best value for searching for positions in international organization; however, just posting your resume on www.monster.com is not likely to land you a job. Most reputable organizations post job openings as part of the personnel practices. So the first place to look is at their official Web sites. Intergovernmental organizations, such as the UN, the EU, and NATO, all post openings on their Web sites. NGOs such as the Gates

Foundations and Greenpeace do as well. MNCs post online but also use Internet employment lists. Below are a few Web sites to give you an idea of where to find employment opportunities.

https://jobs.un.org/
http://web.worldbank.org/WBSITE/EXTERNAL/EXTHRJOBS/
http://www.nato.int/structur/recruit/index-wide.asp
http://www.imf.org/external/np/adm/rec/recruit.htm
http://www.wto.org/english/thewto_e/vacan_e/vacan_e.htm
http://www.fpa.org/jobs_contact2423/jobs_contact.htm
http://www.gatesfoundation.org/jobs/Pages/overview.aspx
http://www.greenpeace.org/usa/about/jobs
http://www.amnesty.org/en/jobs
http://www.hrw.org/en/about/jobs
http://www.state.gov/p/io/empl/
http://www.intljobs.org/
http://www.idealist.org

The above sites are just a few of the places that list openings in international organizations. If you feel you are not qualified for the position, then explore internships that provide you with the requisite skills. Finally, you may want to think about starting your own international NGO and not-for-profit organization. Such organizations function very much like businesses. So if you have that entrepreneur spirit and see a need or niche, think about ways to start your NGO.

BIBLIOGRAPHY

Aboul-Enein, Sameh. 2010. The 2010 NPR Review and the Middle East: Challenges and Opportunities. *Palestine-Israel Journal* 16(3): 67–76.

Adelman, Irma, and J. Edward Taylor. 1989. Is Structural Adjustment with a Human Face Possible? The Case of Mexico. *Journal of Development Studies* 26 (April): 388–407.

Adler, Emmanuel. 1997. Seizing the Middle Ground: Constructivism in World Politics. *European Journal of International Relations* 3(3): 319–363.

Afrasiabi, Kaveh, and Mustafa Kibaroglu. 2005. Negotiating Iran's Nuclear Populism. *Brown Journal of World Affairs* XII (Summer/Fall): 255–268.

Agra Europe. 1999. EU Judge Rejects French GM Ban (November 26): 11.

———. 2000a. Public Ignorant of GM Issues (April 28): 5–7.

———. 2000b. Thailand Files First GMO Complaint at WTO (September 29): 9.

Ahmad, Feroz. 1991. Arab Nationalism, Radicalism, and the Specter of Neocolonialism. *Monthly Review* 42 (February): 30–35.

Ahmed, Leila. 1984. *Early Feminist Movements in the Middle East in Muslim Women*, ed. Freda Hussain. New York: St. Martin's Press.

Ahsan, Abdullah. 1988. *The Organization of Islamic Conference.* Herndon, VA: The International Institute of Islamic Thought.

Albright, Madeleine. 1994. Bosnia in Light of the Holocaust: War Crimes Tribunals. *U.S. Department of State Dispatch* 5 (April 18): 209(4).

Alger, Chadwick F. 1996. Thinking About the Future of the UN System. *Global Governance* 2 (December–January): 335–360.

Alleyne, Marc Da Costa. 2004. The Global Promotion to Gender Equality—A Propaganda Approach. *Human Rights Review* 5 (April–June): 103–116.

Allison, Graham. 1971. *The Essence of Decision.* Boston, MA: Little Brown.

Al-Radi, Selma. 1995. Iraqi Sanctions—A Postwar Crime. *The Nation* 260 (March 27): 416(2).

Alvarez, Jose. 1995. The Once and Future of the Security Council. *Washington Quarterly* 18 (Spring): 5–20.

———. 2005. *International Organizations as Law-Makers.* Oxford, UK: Oxford University Press.

Alvarez, Sonia E. 1997. Contradictions of a "Women's Space" in a Male-Dominant State: The Political Role of the Commission on the Status of Women in Postauthoritarian Brazil. pp. 59–100 in *Women, International Development, and Politics: The Bureaucratic Mire*, ed. Kathleen Staudt. Philadelphia, PA: Temple University Press.

Alwis, Malathi. 2004. The Purity of Displacement and the Reterritorialization of Longing: Muslim IDPs in Northwestern Sri Lanka. pp. 213–231 in *Sites of Violence: Gender and Conflict Zones*, ed. Wenona Giles and Jennifer Hyndman. Berkeley, CA: University of California Press.

Ambrose, Stephen E. 1988. *The Rise to Globalism: American Foreign Policy Since 1938.* New York: Penguin Books.

American Banker. 1990. Full Resumption of Lending to China Seen as Unlikely 155 (June 13): 18.

Amin, Samir. 1977. *Imperialism and Uneven Development.* New York: Monthly Review Press.

Anderson, Roy R., Robert F. Seibert, and Jon G. Wagner. 1998. *Politics and Change in the Middle East.* Upper Saddle River, NJ: Prentice Hall.

Aoi, Chiyuki., Cedric de Coning, and Ramesh Shakur. 2007. *The Unintended Consequences of Peacekeeping Operations.* Tokyo: United Nations University Press.

APS Diplomat Recorder. 2000. Arab Affairs: Cairo Summit Decisions 53 (October 28): NA.

——. 2001a. Arab Affairs: Leagues FMs Give PA $40m/Month. 54 (March 17): NA.

——. 2001b. Arab Affairs: PA Appeals to Arab League. 54 (May 26): NA.

Aron, oregonstate.edu/dept/iifet/2000/papers/aron.pdf William. 2000. The International Whaling Commission—A History of Malignant Neglect. *Microbehavior and Macroresults.*

Ascher, William. 1990. The World Bank and U.S. Control. pp. 115–140 in *The United States and Multilateral Institutions: Patterns of Changing Instrumentality and Influence,* ed. Margaret P. Karns and Karen A. Mingst. Boston, MA: Unwin Hyman.

Ascherio, Alberto, Robert Chase, Tim Cote, Godelieave Deharaes, Eric Hoskins, Jilali Laaouej, Megan Passey, et al. 1992. Effect of the Gulf War on Infant and Child Mortality in Iraq. *New England Journal of Medicine* 327 (September 24): 931(6).

Ashworth, Lucian M., and Larry A. Swatuk. 1998. Masculinity and the Fear of Emasculation in International Relations Theory. pp. 73–92 in *The "Man" Question in International Relations,* ed. Marysia Zalewski and Jane Parapart. Boulder, CO: Westview Press.

Ashworth, Lucian M., and David Long, eds. 1999. *New Perspectives on International Functionalism.* Houndmills, Basingstoke, Hampshire: Macmillan; New York: St. Martin's Press.

Associated Press. 2001. 165 Nations Agree to Rules for Pact Cutting Back Carbon Emissions. *The St. Louis Post Dispatch* (November 11): A15.

Aubrey, Lisa. 1997. *The Politics of Development Cooperation: NGOs, Gender, and Partnership in Kenya.* New York: Routledge.

Avdeeva, T. G. 2010. 2009 Copenhagen Summit: Failure, Success or Moment of Truth. *International Affairs: A Russian Journal of World Politics, Diplomacy and International Relations* 56(2): 130–145.

Axelrod, Robert, and Robert Keohane. 1986. Achieving Cooperation Under Anarchy: Strategies and Institutions. in *Cooperation Under Anarchy,* ed. Kenneth Oye. Princeton, NJ: Princeton University Press.

Barker, J. Craig. 2000. *International Law and International Relations.* London: Continuum.

Balaam, David N., and Michael Veseth. 1996. *Introduction to International Political Economy.* Upper Saddle River, NJ: Prentice Hall.

Baldwin, David, ed. 1993. *Neorealism and Neoliberalism.* New York: Columbia University Press.

Barnett, Jon. 2008. The Worst of Friends: OPEC and G-77 in the Climate Regime. *Global Environmental Politics* 8 (November): 1–8.

Barnett, Michael N. 2003. *Eyewitness to Genocide: The United Nations and Rwanda.* Ithaca, NY: Cornell University Press.

Barnett, Michael N., and Martha Finnemore. 1999. The Politics, Power and Pathologies of International Organizations. *International Organization* 53 (Autumn): 698–747.

——. 2004. *Rules for the World: International Organizations in Global Politics.* Ithaca, NY: Cornell University Press.

Barria, Lilian, and Steven Roper. 2005. How Effective are International Criminal Tribunals? An Analysis of the ICTY and ICTR. *International Journal of Human Rights* 9 (Autumn): 349–368.

Barringer, Felicity. 2003. Iran Is Urged to Sign Pact Giving Power to Inspectors. *The New York Times* (June 17): www.nytimes.com.

Bartlett, Bruce, James Glassman, Leon Hadar, and Lawrence B. Lindsey. 1998. Asia Unravels: Could This be the Sequel to Fall of the Berlin Wall? *The American Enterprise* 9 (May–June): 58–64.

Barton, John H., Judith L. Goldstein, Timothy E. Josling, and Richard H. Steinberg. 2008. *The Evolution of the Trade Regime: Politics, Law and Economics of the GATT to the WTO.* Princeton, NJ: Princeton University Press.

Bayne, Nicholas. 1997. What Governments Want from International Institutions and How They Get It. *Government and Opposition* 31 (Summer): 361–380.

BBC News. 1999. Indonesia and IMF Near Agreement (April 3).

——. 2000. Whaling Commission Struggles to Survive (July 4).

———. 2001. Rwanda Trial Opens Belgians' Eyes (June 7).

Bedjaoui, Mohammed. 1994. *The New World Order and the Security Council: Testing the Legality of Its Acts*. Dordrecht, NE: Nijhoff Publishers.

Beelman, Maude S. 1996. Fingerprints: Arms to Bosnia, The Real Story. *The New Republic* 215 (October 28): 26–29.

Bellamy, Alex. 2005. Responsibility to Protect or Trojan Horse: The Crisis in Darfur and Humanitarian Intervention after Iraq. *Ethics and International Affairs* 19(2): 31–53.

Bellamy, Alex, Paul Williams, and Stuart Griffin. 2004. *Understanding Peacekeeping*. Cambridge, UK: Polity Press.

Benedict, Richard E. 1991. *Ozone Diplomacy*. Cambridge, MA: Harvard University Press.

Bennett, A. LeRoy. 1991. *International Organizations: Principles and Issues*. 5th ed. Upper Saddle River, NJ: Prentice Hall.

———. 1995. *International Organizations: Principles and Issues*. 6th ed. Upper Saddle River, NJ: Prentice Hall.

Bennett, Andrew, and Joseph Lepgold. 1993. Reinventing Collective Security After the Cold War and Gulf Conflict. *Political Science Quarterly* 108 (Summer): 213–238.

Bennis, Phyllis. 1996. *Calling the Shots: How Washington Dominates Today's UN*. New York: Olive Branch Press.

Bentham, Jeremy. 1961. *An Introduction to the Principles of Morals and Legislation*. Garden City, NY: Double Day.

Berger, Peter L., and Thomas Luckmann. 1966. *The Social Construction of Reality: A Treatise in the Sociology of Knowledge*. New York: Doubleday.

Bergeron, Suzanne L. 1999. Imperialism. pp. 464–471 in *Elgar Companion to Feminist Economics*, ed. Meg Lewis and Janice Peterson. Brookfield, VT: Edward Elgar Publishing.

Bergman, Barbara. 1986. *The Economic Emergence of Women*. New York: Basic Books.

Bessis, Sophie. 2004. International Organizations and Gender: New Paradigms and Old Habits. *Signs* 29 (Winter): 633–649.

Betsill, Michelle M., and Elisabeth Corell, eds. 2008. *NGO Diplomacy: The Influence of Nongovernmental Organization in International Environmental Negotiations*. Cambridge, MA: MIT Press.

Bhagwati, Jagdish. 2004. Don't Cry For Cancun. *Foreign Affairs* 83 (January–February): 52–63.

Biersteker, Thomas J. 1978. *Distortion or Development? Contending Perspectives on the Multinational Corporation*. Cambridge, MA: MIT Press.

Binmore, Ken. 1992. *Fun and Games: A Text on Game Theory*. Lexington, MA: D. C. Heath.

Bird, Graham, and Dane Rowlands. 2007. The IMF and the Mobilisation of Foreign Aid. *Journal of Development Studies* 43 (July): 856–870.

Birdsall, Andrea. 2007. Creating a More "Just" Order. *Cooperation and Conflict* 42 (December): 397–418.

Blinder, Alan S. 1999. Eight Steps to a New Financial Order. *Foreign Affairs* 78 (September–October): 50–63.

Borlaug, N. 2003. Science vs. Hysteria. *Wall Street Journal* (January 22).

Bosch, Xavier. 2003. USA Fights Europe's Ban on Genetically Modified Food. *Lancet* 361 (May 24): 1798.

Bosco, David. 2005. The World According To Bolton. *Bulletin of the Atomic Scientists* (July–August): 24–32.

Boyer, Gabriela. 1994. GATTastrophe. *The Nation* 268 (June 13): 821(1).

Brecher, Jeremy, and Tim Costello. 1994. *Global Village or Global Pillage: Economic Reconstruction from the Bottom Up*. Boston, MA: South End Press.

Bresnan, John. 2000. Indonesia in Aftershock. *Great Decisions*. New York: Foreign Policy Association.

Broad, William J. 2009. Panel Sees No Need for A-Bomb Upgrade. *New York Times* (November 20): www.nytimes.com.

Broad, William J., and David E. Sanger. 2006. Restraints Fray and Risks Grow as Nuclear Club Gains Members. *New York Times* (October 15): www.nytimes.com.

Brookes, Peter. 2008. The Need for Missile Defense. *Policy Review* 151 (November–October): 31–43.

Brooks, Rosa E. 2002. Feminist Justice at Home and Abroad. *Yale Journal of Law and Feminism* 14: 345.

Brown, Bartram S. 1992. *The United States and the Politicization of the World Bank:*

Issues of International Law and Policy. London: Kegan Paul International.

Brown, Lester, and Hal Kane. 1994. *Full House, Reassessing the Earth's Population Carrying Capacity.* New York: W. W. Norton.

Brownlie, Ian. 1994. *Basic Documents on Human Rights.* Oxford, UK: Clarendon Press.

Brunne, Jutta, and Stephen J. Toope. 2009. International Law and Constructivism: Elements of an International Theory of International Law. *Columbia Journal of International Law* 39: http://ssrn.com/abstracts/1432539.

Buchmann, Claudia. 1996. The Debt Crisis, Structural Adjustment and Women's Education: Implications for Status and Social Development. *International Journal of Comparative Sociology* 37 (June): 5–31.

Buckley, William F. 1996. Has the WTO Threatened U.S.? *National Review* 48 (February 26): 70–71.

Budianta, Melani. 2000. Double Text: Representing American and Discussing Women's Issues in Indonesia. *American Studies International* 38 (October): 47–54.

Burns, John F. 1998. Nuclear Anxiety: The Subcontintent; India Glows with Pride as Outrage Rises Abroad. *New York Times* (May 13): www.nytimes.com.

Buss, Doris, and Manji Ambreena. 2005. *International Law: Modern Feminist Approaches.* London: Hart Publishers.

Butler, Richard. 1999. Bewitched, Bothered and Bewildered—Repairing the Security Council. *Foreign Affairs* 78 (September–October): 9–11.

Byers, Michael. 2004. Agreeing to Disagree: Security Council Resolution 1441 and Intentional Ambiguity. *Global Governance* 10 (April–June): 165(22).

Cahn, Steven M. 1997. *Classics of Modern Political Theory.* New York: Oxford University Press.

Caldicott, Susan. 1984. *Missile Envy: The Arms Race and Nuclear War.* New York: Morrow.

Callahan, Daniel. 2000. Food for Thought. *Commonwealth* 127 (April 7): 7–10.

Campbell, Horace, and Howard Stein, eds. 1992. *Tanzania and the IMF: The Dynamics of Liberalization.* Boulder, CO: Westview Press.

Caporaso, James A. 2002. *The European Union: The Dilemmas of Regional Integration.* Boulder, CO: Westview Press.

Cardoso, Fernando H., and Enzo Faletto. 1979. *Dependency and Development in Latin America.* Berkeley, CA: University of California Press.

Carpenter, Ted Galen. 1997. The Mirage of Global Collective Security. pp. 13–28 in *Delusions of Grandeur: The United Nations and Global Intervention*, ed. Ted Galen Carpenter. Washington, DC: Cato Institute.

Castleman, Barry, and Richard Lemen. 1998. Corporate Junk Science: Corporate Influence at International Science Organization. *Multinational Monitor* 19 (January–February): 28(3).

CBS News. 2001. Islamic Conference Condemns Terror (October 10).

Chadwick, Douglas H. 2001. Pursuing the Minke. *National Geographic* 199 (April): 58.

Chafetz, Glenn. 1993. The End of the Cold War and the Future of Nuclear Nonproliferation: An Alternative to the Neo-Realist Perspective. *Security Studies* (Spring/Summer): 128–146.

Charlesworth, Hilary, and Christine Chinkin. 2000. *The Boundaries of International Law: A Feminist Analysis.* Manchester, UK: Manchester University Press.

Checkel, Jeffery T. 1998. The Constructivist Turn in International Relations Theory. *World Politics* 50(2): 324–348.

———. 2000. Social Learning and European Identity Change. *International Organization* 55(3): 553–588.

———. 2005. International Institutions and Socialization in Europe: Introduction and Framework. *International Organization* 59(4): 801–826.

Chemical Week. 2001. Brussels Maintains GMO Ban 163 (January 24): 8.

Chomsky, Noam. 2004. *Hegemony or Survival? America's Quest of Global Dominance.* New York: Henry Holt.

Clark, Mark T. 1995. The Trouble with Collective Security. *Orbis* 39 (Spring): 237(22).

Claude, Inis. 1993. The Gulf War and Prospects for World Order by Collective Security. pp. 23–38 in *The Persian Gulf Crisis: Power in the Post–Cold War World*, ed. Robert F. Helms II and Robert H. Dorff. Westport, CT: Praeger.

Clausewitz, Carl Von. 1968. *On War*, trans. J. J. Graham. New York: Barnes & Noble.

Cockburn, Alexander, and Ken Silverstein. 1995. The Demands of Capital. *Harper's Magazine* 290 (May): 66–68.

Cohen, Benjamin J. 1986. *In Whose Interest? International Banking and American Foreign Policy.* New Haven, CT: Yale University Press.

Cohen, Roger. 1999. European Crisis Paves Way for More Accountability. *New York Times* (March 17).

Cohen, Susan. 1994. Consensus or Competition? Women, Population and the Planet. *Populi* (July/August): 7–9.

Cohn, Carol. 2006. The Relevance of Gender for Eliminating Weapons of Mass Destruction. *The Weapons of Mass Destruction Commission.* Background Paper #38. Stockholm, Sweden: Weapons of Mass Destruction Commission, www.wmdcommission.org.

Collier, Paul. 2007. *The Bottom Billion.* Oxford: Oxford University Press.

Commission on Sustainable Development. 1998. General Information (April 6).

Connors, Jane. 1996. NGOs and the Human Rights of Women at the United Nations. pp. 147–180 in *"The Conscience of the World": The Influence of Nongovernmental Organizations in the UN System*, ed. Peter Willetts. Washington, DC: Brookings Institution.

Cook, Alice, and Gwyn Kirk. 1983. *Greenham Women Everywhere.* Boston, MA: South End Press.

Cook, Helena. 1997. Amnesty International and the United Nations. pp. 181–213 in *"The Conscience of the World": The Influence of Nongovernmental Organizations in the UN System*, ed. Peter Willetts. Washington, DC: Brookings Institution.

Cooper, Richard N. 1998. Toward a Real Global Warming Treaty: Implications of the 1997 Kyoto Conference. *Foreign Affairs* 77 (March–April): 66–80.

Cooper, Scott, Darren Hawkins, Wade Jacoby, and Daniel Nielson. 2008. Yielding Sovereignty to International Institutions: Bringing System Structure Back In. *International Studies Review* 10(3): 501–524.

Cornwall, Rupert. 1995. A Global Money Crisis: The Sinking of the Greenback. *World Press Review* 42 (May): 8–10.

Cox, Robert W. 1987. *Production, Power, and World Order: Social Forces in the Making of History.* New York: Columbia University Press.

Crane, George T., and Alba Amawi. 1997. *The Theoretical Evolution of International Political Economy.* New York: Oxford University Press.

Crossette, Barbara. 1999. UN Details Its Failure to Stop '95 Bosnia Massacre. *New York Times* (November 16): A3.

Crow, Patrick. 1996. Defending the WTO. *Oil & Gas Journal* 94 (March 18): 37.

Crozier, Brian. 1991. Handling the United Nations: Bush's Triumph. *National Review* 43 (April 1): 40–42.

Cunningham, Shea, and Betsy Reed. 1995. Balancing the Budgets on Women's Backs: The World Bank and the 104th Congress. *Dollars and Sense* 202 (November–December): 22–26.

Cutler, A. Claire. 2008. Toward a Radical Political Economy Critique of Transnational Economic Law. pp. 199–219 in *International Law on the Left: Reexamining Marxist Legacies*, ed. Susan Marks Cambridge, UK: Cambridge University Press.

D'Amico, Francine. 1999. Women Workers in the United Nations: From Margin to Mainstream. pp. 19–40 in *Gender Politics in Global Governance*, ed. Elizabeth Prugl and Mary K. Meyer. Boston, MA: Rowman & Littlefield.

Damrosch, Lori Fisler. 1989. Politics across Borders: Nonintervention of Nonforcible Influence over Domestic Affairs. *American Journal of International Law* 83 (January): 1–50.

Danaher, Kevin, ed. 1994. *Third World: 50 Years Is Enough: The Case Against the World Bank and the International Monetary Fund.* Boston, MA: South End Press.

Davies, Frank. 1998. Florida Leads in Stripping of Voting Rights. *Miami Herald* 230 (October): 1A.

Davis, Christina L. 2003. *Food Fights over Free Trade: How International Institutions Promote Agricultural Trade Liberalization.* Princeton, NJ: Princeton University Press.

Diehl, Sarah J., and Moltz, James Clay. 2008. *Nuclear Weapons and Nonproliferation : A Reference Handbook.* Santa Barbara, CA: ABC-CLIO, http://www.loc.gov/catdir/toc/ecip0717/2007017651.html.

Dimitrov, Radoslav. 2010. Inside Copenhagen: The State of Climate Governance. *Global Environmental Politics* 10(2) (May): 18–24.

Department of Conservation. 2001a. Media Statement from the Office of the Prime Minister of New Zealand (July 19).

———. 2001b. South Pacific Whale Sanctuary Issue Sparks Renewed International Interest in the IWC (June 28).

Doctors Without Borders. 1998. General Information (September 24).

Doelle, Meinhard. 2010. The Legacy of the Climate Talks in Copenhagen: Hopenhagen or Brokenhagen? *Carbon and Climate Law Review* 4(1): 86–100.

Donini, Antonio. 1996. The Bureaucracy and the Free Spirits: Stagnations and Innovations in the Relationship Between the UN and NGOs. pp. 83–102 in *NGOs, the UN, and Global Governance*, ed. Thomas Weiss and Leon Gordenker. Boulder, CO: Lynne Rienner Press.

Donnelly, Jack. 1993. *International Human Rights*. Boulder, CO: Westview Press.

Duffield, John S. 1992. International Regimes and Alliance Behavior: Explaining NATO Conventional Force Levels. *International Organizations* 46 (Fall): 819–855.

———. 1994a. Explaining the Long Peace in Europe: The Contributions of Regional Security Regimes. *Review of International Studies* 20 (October): 369–388.

———. 1994b. NATO's Functions After the Cold War. *Political Science Quarterly* 109 (winter): 763(25).

———. 1998. NGO Relief in War Zones: Toward an Analysis of a New Aid Paradigm. pp. 139–159 in *Beyond UN Subcontracting: Task-Sharing with Regional Security Arrangements and Service-Providing NGOs*, ed. Thomas G. Weiss. New York: St. Martin's Press.

Earth Island Journal. 1992. Angry Activists Vandalize World Bank Booth 7 (Summer): 20.

———. 2001. UN Team Calls WTO a Nightmare 16 (Autumn): 17.

Easterly, William. 2006. *The White Man's Burden: Why the West's Efforts Have Done So Much Ill and So Little Good*. New York: Penguin Press.

Eaton, Sarah, and Richard Stubbs. 2006. Is ASEAN Powerful? Neo-realist Versus Constructivist Approaches to power in Southeast Asia. *The Pacific Review* 19 (June): 135–155.

The Economist. 1986. Voter Power: Japan and the World Bank 229 (April 19): 83.

———. 1991. Forgive Us Our Debt 321 (October 12): S23–S28.

———. 1995a. A Fork in the IMF's Road: The Fund Has a Credibility Problem That Cannot Be Dithered Away 334 (January 28): 14.

———. 1995b. Hazardous Morals: The Mexican Affair Has Left the IMF with Some Hard Thinking to Do 334 (February 11): 19–21.

———. 1998a. Back from the Brink. Mexico's Financial Crisis Was Different from Asia's but it Holds Valuable Lessons 346 (March 7): S8(3).

———. 1998b. Food Fights: Genetically Modified Plants are Already Commonplace in America. Europeans Would Be Better off if They Embraced Them with Equal Enthusiasm (June 13): 79–81.

———. 2000. Briefs in a Twist; WTO; The WTO Tries Too Hard (December 9): 6.

Edwards, Rob. 1998. Unfit to Eat. *New Scientist* (September 26): 13.

Eilperin, Juliet. 2009. In the Trenches on Climate Change, Hostility Among Foes: Stolen Email Reveal Venomous Feelings Toward Skeptics. *The Washington Post* (November 22).

Eldridge, Philip J. 1995. *Non-Government Organizations and Democratic Participation in Indonesia*. New York: Oxford University Press.

Enloe, Cynthia. 1990. *Bananas, Beaches, and Bases: Making Sense of International Politics*. Berkeley, CA: University of California Press.

———. 1993. *The Morning After: Sexual Politics at the End of the Cold War*. Berkeley, CA: University of California Press.

Epstein, Charlotte. 2006. The Making of Global Environmental Norms: Endangered Species Protection. *Global Environmental Politics* 6 (May): 32–54.

Esman, Milton J., and Shibley Telhami, eds. 1995. *International Organisations and Ethnic conflict*. Ithaca, NY: Cornell University Press.

Europa World Year Book. 1990. Brussels: European Publications.

European Report. 2000. EU/UN: France Hosts First Meeting Under the Biosafety Protocol (December 23): 504.

———. 2001. Eurobarometer Confirms Indifference of EU Citizens Towards the EU (July 21): 102.

Evans, Peter. 1979. *Dependent Development: The Alliance of Multinational, State and Local Capital in Brazil.* Princeton, NJ: Princeton University Press.

Fattah, Hassan M. 2006. At Mecca Meeting, Cartoon Outrage Crystallized. *New York Times* (February 9): A1.

Fehl, Caroline. 2004. Explaining the International Criminal Court: A "Practice Test" for Rationalist and Constructivist Approaches. *European Journal of International Relations.* 10: 357–394.

Feld, Werner J, Robert S. Jordan, and Leon Hurwitz. 1994. *International Organizations: A Comparative Approach.* Westport, CT: Praeger.

Fellmeth, Aaron Xavier. 2000. Feminism and International Law: Theory, Methodology and Substantive Reform. *Human Rights Quarterly* 22: 658–733.

Feminist Review. 1998. When the Earth Is Female and the Nation Is Mother 58 (Spring): 1–22.

Ferber, Marianne, and Julie A. Nelson. 1993. Introduction: The Social Construction of Economics and the Social Construction of Gender. pp. 1–22 in *Beyond Economic Man: Feminist Theory and Economics,* ed. Marianne Ferber and Julie A. Nelson. Chicago, IL: Chicago University Press.

Ferguson, Niall. 2004. *Colossus: The Price of America's Empire.* New York: Penguin Press.

Finance and Development. 1991. The Global Environmental Facility 28 (March): 24.

Finnemore, Martha. 2004. *Purpose of Intervention.* New York: Cornell University Press.

Fisher, Dana. 2010. COP-15 in Copenhagen: How the Merging of Movements Left Civil Society Out in the Cold. *Global Environmental Politics* 10 (May) 2: 11–17.

Flynn, Gregory, and David J. Scheffer. 1990. Limited Collective Security. *Foreign Policy* 80 (Fall): 77–102.

Foot, Rosemary, S. Neil MacFarlane, and Michael Mastanduno, eds. 2003. *U.S. Hegemony and International Organizations.* New York: Oxford University Press.

Force Comparison. 1987. Brussels: NATO Information Office.

Ford, Jane. 2003. A Social Theory of Trade Regime Change: GATT to WTO. *International Studies Perspectives* 4 (June): 115–138.

Foreign Policy. 2001. An NGO by Any Other Name (July): 18.

Forsythe, David P. 1990. *The Politics of International Law.* Boulder, CO: Lynne Rienner Press.

———. 1991a. Human Rights in the Post–Cold War World. *The Fletcher Forum* 15 (summer): 55–70.

———. 1991b. *The Internationalization of Human Rights.* Lexington, MA: D. C. Heath.

———. 1993. *Human Rights and Peace: International and National Dimensions.* Lincoln, NE: University of Nebraska Press.

———. 1998. The International Court of Justice at Fifty. pp. 385–405 in *The International Court of Justice.* The Hague: Kluwer Law International.

———. 2000. *Human Rights in International Relations.* Cambridge, UK: Cambridge University Press.

Foster, John Belamy. 1993. Let Them Eat Pollution: Capitalism and the World Environment. *Monthly Review* 44 (January): 10–21.

Fotopoulos, Takis. 2003. Iraq: The New Criminal War of the Transnational Elite. *Democracy and Nature* 9 (July): 167–209.

Fowler, Penny, and Simon Heap. 1998. Learning from the Marine Stewardship Council: A Business-NGO Partnership for Sustainable Marine Fisheries. *Greener Management International* (winter): 77–97.

Franck, Thomas M. 2003. What Happens Now? The United Nations After Iraq? *American Journal of International Law* (July): 607–620.

Frank, Andre Gunder. 1979. *Dependent Accumulation and Underdevelopment.* New York: Monthly Review Press.

Freese, Bill. 2008. Biotech Snake Oil. *Multinational Monitor* 29 (September/October): 10–14.

Friedman, Thomas L. 1999. Senseless in Seattle. *New York Times* (December 1): A31.

Friend, Theodore. 2000. South East Asia. *Asia Times Online* (February 19). www.atimes.com.

Frontline. 1999. The Triumph of Evil. *PBS,* aired (January 26).

Fukuyama, Francis. 2006. After Neoconservatism. *New York Times Magazine* (February 19): 62–67.

GA/9228 (Press Release). 1997. Assembly President Proposes Increase in Security Council. March 20.

Gardam, Judith Gail. 1993. Proportionality and Force in International Law. *American Journal of International Law* 87 (July): 391–413.

Gelb, Joyce. 2002. *Feminism, NGO's, and the Impact of the New Transnationalisms.* Berkley, CA: Global, Area, and International Archive. Retrieved from: http://escholarship.org/uc/item/3mr1z2kj.

Genest, Marc. 2003. *Conflict and Cooperation: Evolving Theories of International Relations.* 2nd ed. Belmont, CA: Wadsworth.

German Information Center. 1995. *German Support for the Reform Process in the Former Soviet Union and the Countries of Central, Southeastern, and Eastern Europe.* New York: German Information Center.

Gettleman, Jeffery, and Josh Kron. 2010. Rwanda Threatens to Pull Peacekeepers from Darfur. *New York Times* (August 31): www.nytimes.com.

Giddens, Anthony. 2010. Climate Change Meets Geopolitical Reality in Copenhagen. *New Perspectives Quarterly* 27 (Spring): 58–60

Gill, Stephen. 1991. *American Hegemony and the Trilateral Commission.* Cambridge, UK: Cambridge University Press.

Gilpin, Robert. 1981. *War and Change in World Politics.* Cambridge, UK: Cambridge University Press.

———. 1987. *The Political Economy of International Relations.* Princeton, NJ: Princeton University Press.

Glennon, Michael J. 2003. Why the Security Council Failed. *Foreign Policy* (May–June): 16–35.

Gluck, Sherna Berger. 1995. Palestinian Women: Gender Politics and Nationalism. *Journal of Palestine Studies* 24 (Spring): 5–16.

Goebel, Allison, and Marc Epprecht. 1995. Women and Employment in Sub-Saharan Africa: Testing the World Bank and the WID Models with a Lesotho Case Study. *African Studies Review* 38 (April): 1–22.

Goetz, Anne Maire. 1997. *Getting Institutions Right for Women in Development.* New York: Zed Books.

Goldgeiger, James. 1999. *Not Whether but When: The U.S. Decision to Enlarge NATO,* Washington, DC: Brookings Institute.

Goldsmith, Jack, and Eric Posner. 2005. *The Limits of International Law.* Oxford: Oxford University Press.

Goldstein, Joshua. 1996. *International Relations.* 2nd ed. New York: Harper Collins.

Goldstein, Joshua, and Jon C. Pevehouse. 2006. *International Relations.* 7th ed. New York: Pearson.

Goodby, James E., and Daniel B. O'Connor. 1993. *Collective Security: An Essay on Its Limits and Possibilities After the Cold War.* Washington, DC: United States Institute for Peace.

Gordenker, Leon. 1987. *Refugees in International Politics.* London: Croom Helm, Ltd.

Gourevitch, Philip. 1998. *We Wish to Inform You that Tomorrow We Will Be Killed With Our Families.* New York: Picador.

Gowa, Joanne. 1988. Rational Hegemons, Excludable Foods, and Small Groups: An Epitaph for Hegemonic Stability Theory. *World Politics* 41 (April): 307–324.

Graubart, Jonathan. 2008. *Legalizing Transnational Activism: The Struggle to Gain Social Change from NAFTA's Citizen Petitions.* University Park, PA: Pennsylvania State University Press.

Greene, Owen. 1998. *Environmental Issues: The Globalization of World Politics: An Introduction to International Relations.* Oxford, UK: Oxford University Press.

Greenhouse, Steven. 2001. Report Outlines the Abuse of Foreign Domestic Workers. *New York Times* (June 14): A16.

Greenpeace. 1999. The Food Industry's Secret Ingredient. *Greenpeace* (winter): 22–24.

Grogan, John, and Cheryl Long. 2000. The Problem with Genetic Engineering. *Organic Gardening* 47 (January): 42–55.

Grotius, Hugo. 1984. *The Law of War and Peace.* Birmingham, AL: Legal Classics Library, Division of Gryphon Editions.

———. 1995. *The Law of Prize and Booty.* Buffalo, NY: Hein.

Guzzini, Stephano. 2000. A Reconstruction of Constructivism in International

Relations. *European Journal of International Relations* 6(2): 147–182.

Haas, Ernst. 1958. *Uniting Europe.* Stanford, CA: Stanford University Press.

———. 1964. *Beyond the Nation-State.* Stanford, CA: Stanford University Press.

Hakke, Murat Metin. 2004. The Second Iraq War One Year On: Can George W. Bush and Tony Blair be Tried for War Crimes. *Human Rights Review* (January–March): 869–903.

Hale, Angela. 1997. Trade Liberalization and Women Workers. *The Ecologist* 27 (May–June): 87(2).

Halford, Nigel. 2001. Agricultural Biotechnology. *Chemistry and Industry* (August 20): 505–508.

Hamilton, Alexander. 1997. Report on Manufactures. pp. 37–47 in *The Theoretical Evolution of Economy: A Reader,* ed. George T. Crane and Abla Amawi. New York: Oxford University Press.

Hanke, Steve H. 2000. Abolish the IMF. *Forbes* (April 17): 84.

Hanley, Delinda. 2001. Women in Black Hold Solidarity Vigil. *Washington Report on Middle East Affairs* 20 (August): 96.

Hans, Asha. 2004. Escaping Conflict: Afghan Women in Transit. pp. 232–248 in *Sites of Violence: Gender and Conflict Zones,* ed. Wenona Giles and Jennifer Hyndman. Berkeley, CA: University of California Press.

Hardin, Garrett. 1968. The Tragedy of the Commons. *Science* 162 (December 16): 1243–1248.

Hawke, Steve H. 1995. Bob Rubin, Meet C. N. Parkinson. *Forbes* 155 (March 13): 110.

Haynes, Jeff. 2001. Transnational Religious Actors and International Politics. *Third World Quarterly* 22 (April): 143(16).

Hedges, Chris. 1996. Bosnia Reported to be Smuggling Heavy Arms. *New York Times* (November 8): A1.

Hegel, Georg Wilhelm Friedrich. 1967. *The Philosophy of Right.* Translated with notes by T. M. Knox. Oxford: Clarendon Press.

Heilbroner, Robert L. 1986. *The Worldly Philosophers.* 6th ed. New York: Simon and Schuster.

———. 1992. *The Worldly Philosophers: The Lives, Times, and Ideas of the Great Economic Thinkers.* New York: Simon and Schuster.

Held, David. 1999. *Global Transformation.* Stanford, CA: Stanford University Press.

Heins, Volker. 2008. Nongovernmental Organization in International Society: Struggles over Recognition. New York: Palgrave Macmillan.

Helm, Carsten. 1996. Transboundary Environmental Problems and New Trade Rules. *National Forum* 78 (summer): 29(17).

Henderson, Caspar. 1997. What Price Free Trade. *New Scientist* 154 (June 2): 14.

Herbener, Jeffrey. 1995. A Bail-Out of Third World Bureaucrats. *Insight on the News* 11 (July 31): 5–37.

Heredia, Carlos, and Mary Purcell. 1996. Structural Adjustment and the Polarization of Mexican Society. pp. 273–284 in *The Case Against the Global Economy and for a Turn Toward the Local,* ed. Jerry Mander and Edward Goldsmith. San Francisco, CA: Sierra Club.

Heyzer, Noeleen, Sushma Kapoor, and Joanne Sandler, eds. 1995. *A Commitment to the World's Women: Perspectives on Development for Beijing and Beyond.* New York: UNIFEM.

Hilderbrand, Robert C. 1990. *Dumbarton Oaks: The Origins of the United Nations and the Search for Postwar Security.* Chapel Hill, NC: University of North Carolina Press.

Hirata, Keiko. 2004. Beached Whales: Examining Japan's Rejection of an International Norm. *Social Science Japan Journal* 7 (August): 177–197.

Hoagland, Jim. 2004. Pakistan's Nuclear Ali Baba. *The Washington Post* (February 10): A23.

Hoare, Quentin, and Geoffrey N. Smit, eds. 1971. *Selections from the Prison Notebooks.* London: Lawren and Wishart.

Hobbes, Thomas. 1996. *Leviathan,* ed. Richard Tuck. Cambridge, UK: Cambridge University Press.

Hoffmann, Matthew. 2005. *Ozone Depletion and Climate Change.* Albany, NY: State University of New York Press.

Hoge, Warren. 2005. Report Finds U.N. Isn't Moving to End Sex Abuse by Peacekeepers. *The New York Times* (October 19): A5.

———. 2006a. Peacekeepers and Diplomats, Seeking to End Darfur's Violence, Hit Roadblock. *The New York Times* (March 1): A10.

———. 2006b. U.S. Won't Seek a Seat On the U.N. Rights Council. *The New York Times* (April 7): A6

———. 2007. Dismay over New U.N. Human Rights Council. *New York Times* (March 11): www.nytimes.com.

Hopf, Ted. 1998. The Promise of Constructivism in International Relations Theory. *International Security* 23 (Summer): 171–200.

Hovi, Jon, and Tora Skodvin. 2008. Which Way to U.S. Climate Cooperation? Issue Linkage versus U.S.-Based Agreement. *Review of Policy Research* 25 (March): 129–148.

Howard, Michael. 1990. The UN and International Security. pp. 31–46 in *United Nations, Divided World: The UN's Roles in International Relations*, ed. Adam Roberts and Benedict Kingsbury. Oxford, UK: Clarendon Press.

Hudnall, Shannon. 1996. Towards a Greener International Trade System: Multilateral Environmental Agreements and the World Trade Organization. *Columbia Journal of Law and Social Problems* 29 (winter): 175–215.

Hunt, Swanee, and Cristina Posa. 2001. Women Waging Peace. *Foreign Policy* (May): 38–42.

Hurd, Douglas. 1994. NATO's New Horizons. Policy Statement PS51/94. New York: British Information Services.

International Herald Tribune. 2000. UN Backs Women as Peacekeepers (November 1): 7.

Hyndman, Jennifer. 2004. Refugee Camps as Conflict Zones: The Politics of Gender. pp. 193–212 in *Sites of Violence: Gender and Conflict Zones*, ed. Wenona Giles and Jennifer Hyndman. Berkeley, CA: University of California Press.

Isaak, Robert A. 1995. *Managing World Economic Change*. 2nd ed. Upper Saddle River, NJ: Prentice Hall.

Jackson, Patrick, and Daniel Nexon. 2004. Constructivist Realism or Realist Constructivism. *American Journal of Politics* 47: 234–247.

Jacobsen, John Kurt, and Claus Hofhansel. 1984. Safeguards and Profits: Civilian Nuclear Exports, Neo-Marxism and the Statist Approach. *International Studies Quarterly* 28: 195–218.

Jacobson, Harold. 1984. *Networks of Interdependence: International Organization and the Global Political System*. 2nd ed. New York: Knopf.

James, Patrick. 2002. *International Relations and Scientific Progress: Structural Realism Reconsidered*. Columbus, OH: Ohio State University Press.

Jenkins, Tony. 2003. Exhuming a UN for "We the Peoples." *Peace Review* 15 (March): 479–482.

Jensen, Nathan M. 2008. *Nation-States and the Multinational Corporation: The Political Economy of Foreign Direct Investment*. Princeton, NJ: Princeton University Press.

Joachim, Jutta, Bob Reinalda, and Bertjan Verbeek. 2008. *International Organizations and Implementation: Enforcers, Managers, Authorities?* London: Routledge.

Joireman, Sandra F. 2003. *Nationalism and Political Identity*. New York: Continuum International Publishing Group.

Jolly, David. 2010. Under Pressure, Commission Discusses Lifting Whaling Ban. *New York Times* (June 21): www.nytimes.com.

Journal of Environmental Health. 2000. National Research Council Weighs in on Transgenic Plants 63 (July): 40–43.

Kabeer, Naila. 2005. Gender Equality and Women's Empowerment: A Critical Analysis of the Third Millennium Development Goals. *Gender and Development* 13 (March): 13–24.

Kahler, Miles. 1985. Politics and International Debt. Explaining the Debt Crisis. *International Organization* 39 (Fall): 357–382.

Kansas, Dave. 1998. Indoamnesia. *The New Republic* 218 (February 2): 12–14.

Kant, Immanuel. 1939. *Perpetual Peace*. New York: Columbia University Press.

Kapstein, Ethan B. 1996. Shockproof: The End of the Financial Crisis. *Foreign Affairs* 74 (January–February): 2–9.

Karl, Marilee. 1995. *Women and Empowerment: Participation and Decision-Making*. London: Zed Books.

Kay, Sean. 2005. What Went Wrong With NATO? *Cambridge Review of International Affairs* 18 (April): 69–83.

Kelly, Annie. 2008. Liberia Aims to Become an Inspiration to Others. *The Guardian*. http://www.guardian.co.uk/alloutonpoverty/liberia.

Kennedy, Paul. 2006. The Parliament of Man: The Past, Present and Future of the United Nations. New York: Random House.

Kennedy, Paul, and Bruce Russet. 1995. Reforming the United Nations. *Foreign Affairs* 74 (September–October): 56–71.

Kennedy, Elizabeth T., Thomas E. Lacker, Jr., and Diana M. Burton. 1998. The New Gemeinschaft: Individual Initiative and Business-NGO-University Partnership. *Greener Management International* (winter): 32–43.

Keohane, Robert O. 1984. *After Hegemony: Cooperation and Discord in the World Political Economy.* Princeton, NJ: Princeton University Press.

———. 1986. *Neorealism and its Critics.* New York: Columbia University Press.

———. 1989. International Relations Theory: Contributions of a Feminist Standpoint. *Millennium* 18 (summer): 245–253.

Keohane, Robert O., and Joseph M. Nye, Jr. 1977. *Power and Interdependence: World Politics in Transition.* Boston, MA: Little Brown.

Keohane, Robert O., and Lisa L. Martin. 1994/1995. The Promise of Institutionalist Theory. *Journal of International Security* 19 (winter): 39–52.

Khattak, Saba Gul. 2003. The U.S. Bombing of Afghanistan: A Women-Centered Perspective. pp. 367–370 in *Conflict and Cooperation: Evolving Theories of International Relations*, ed. Marc Genest. Belmont, CA: Wadsworth.

Khor, Martin. 1996. Colonialism Redux: Reconquering the World with Protocols instead of Gunboats. *The Nation* 263 (July 15): 18–21.

Khoury, Inge. 1994. The World Bank and the Feminization of Poverty. pp. 121–123 in *Fifty Years is Enough: The Case Against the World Bank and the International Monetary Fund*, ed. Kevin Danaher. Boston, MA: South End Press.

King, Kimi, and Megan Greening. 2007. Gender Justice or Just Gender? The Role of Gender in Sexual Assault Decisions at the International Criminal Tribunal for the Former Yugoslavia. *Social Science Quarterly* 88 (December): 1049–1071.

Kitfield, James. 2008. Nuclear Breakout. *National Journal* (July 12): 28.

Kivimaki, Timo. 2000. U.S.-Indonesian Relations during the Economic Crisis: Where Has Indonesia's Bargaining Power Gone? *Contemporary Southeast Asia* 22 (December): 527–550.

Klare, Michael T. 1996. The Guns of Bosnia. *The Nation* 262 (January 22): 23–25.

Klein, Edith. 2004. The Gendered Impact of Mulitlateralism in Post Yugoslav States. pp. 273–300 in *Sites of Violence: Gender and Conflict Zones*, ed. Wenona Giles and Jennifer Hyndman. Berkeley, CA: University of California Press.

Klotter, Jule. 2001. How Safe are Genetically-Engineered Crops? *Townsend Letter for Doctors and Patients* (October): 14.

Klotz, Audie, and Cecelia Lynch. 2007. *International Relations in a Constructed World.* New York: M.E. Sharpe.

Knickerbocker, Brad. 1992. The World from Rio de Janeiro. *Christian Science Monitor* (June 10): 3.

Koechlin, Tim. 1995. NAFTA's Footloose Plants Abandon Workers. *Multinational Monitor* 16 (April): 25–27.

Kole, William J., and Aida Cerkez-Robinson. 2001. UN Accused of Sex-Trade Cover-Up in Bosnia. *The Burlington Free Press* (June 14): 5A.

Kolko, Joyce, and Gabriel Kolko. 1972. *The Limits of Power: The World and United States Foreign Policy, 1945–1954.* New York: Harper & Row.

Kollman, Kelly. 2008. The Regulatory Power of Business Norms. *International Studies Review* 10(3): 397–410.

Korac, Maja. 2004. War, Flight and Exile: Gendered Violence among Refugee Women in Post-Yugoslav States. pp. 249–272 in *Sites of Violence: Gender and Conflict Zones*, ed. Wenona Giles and Jennifer Hyndman. Berkeley, CA: University of California Press.

Krasner, Stephen. 1983. *International Regimes.* Ithaca, NY: Cornell University Press.

———. 1985. *Structural Conflict: Third World Against Global Liberalism.* Berkeley, CA: University of California Press.

———. 1991. Global Communication and National Power: Life and the Pareto Frontier. *World Politics* 43 (April): 336–366.

Kratochwil, Friedreich, and John Gerald Ruggie. 1986. International Organization: A State of the Art or an Art of the State. *International Organization* 40 (Autumn): 753–775.

Kristof, Nicholas D. 1998. As Free-Flowing Capital Sinks Nations, Experts Prepare to "Rethink System." *New York Times* (September 20): 6.

Kuchment, Anna, and Malcolm Beith. 2000. Just Say No. *Newsweek International* (October 9): 5.

Kudlow, Lawrence A. 1994. Manana Is Another Day: Mexico Can No Longer Afford PRI Politics as Usual—Nor IMF Austerity as Usual. *National Review* 46 (June 27): 46–49.

Kumar, Krishna, ed. 2001. *Women and Civil War: Impact, Organizations, and Action.* Boulder, CO: Lynne Rienner Press.

Kurki, Milja, and Adriana Sinclair. 2010. Hidden in Plain Sight: Constructivist Treatment of Social Context and Its Limitations. *International Politics* 47: 1–25.

Laarman, Peter. 1996. Gattcha. *Dissent* 43 (Spring): 12(2).

Lal, Deekpak. 1996. The Misconceptions of "Development Economics." pp. 29–36 in *The Political Economy of Development and Underdevelopment.* 6th ed., ed. Kenneth P. Jameson and Charles K. Wilber. New York: McGraw-Hill.

Lambrecht, Bill. 2001. Europe's Concerns over Biotech Foods Don't Seem Likely to Be Assuaged Soon. *St. Louis Post-Dispatch* (November 4): A8.

Landell-Mills, Pierre, and Ismail Serageldin. 1991. Governance and the Development Process. *Finance and Development* 28 (September): 14–18.

Lane, Charles. 1995. The Fall of Srebrenica. *The New Republic* 213 (August 14): 14(4).

Lang, Andrew T. F. 2006. Reconstructing Embedded Liberalism: John Gerald Ruggie and Constructivist Approaches to the Study of the International Trade Regime. *Journal of International Economic Law* 9 (March): 81–116.

Langer, Gary. 2001. Behind the Label: Many Skeptical of Bio-Engineered Food (June 19). www.abcnews.go.com/sections/scitech/daily news/poll010619.html.

Leiteritz, Ralf J. 2005. Explaining Organizational Outcomes: International Monetary Fund and Capital Account Liberalization. *Journal of International Relations and Development* 8 (2005): 1–26.

Lewis, Neil A. 2001. Papers Show U.S. Knew of Genocide in Rwanda. *New York Times* (August 23): A5.

Li, Darryl. 2000. Anatomy of a Balkan Massacre. *Harvard International Review* 22 (Fall): 34–44.

Lincoln, Edward J. 1997. A U.S.-Japan Trade Agenda. *Brookings Review* 15 (Summer): 32–35.

Linner, Bjorn, and Merle Jacob. 2005. From Stockholm to Kyoto and Beyond: A Review of the Globalization of Global Warming Policy and the North-South Relations. *Globalizations* 3 (December): 403–415.

Locke, John. 1998. Second Treatise of Government. in *Philosophy of the Classics,* ed. Nigel Warburton. London; New York: Routledge.

Longman, Phillip J., and Shaheena Ahmad. 1998. The Bailout Backlash: How to Think about the IMF and Its Critics. *U.S. News and World Report* 124 (February): 37–39.

Lustig, Nora. 1995. The Outbreak of Pesophobia. *Brookings Review* 13 (Spring): 46.

Lynas, Mark. 2010. How China Made it and Unfair COP. *New Statesman* (January): 34.

Lyons, Gene M. 1995. International Organizations and National Interests. *International Social Science Journal* 47 (June): 261–277.

MacFarlane, S. Neil., and Yuen Foong Khong. 2006. *Human Security and the UN: A Critical History.* Bloomington, IN: Indiana University Press.

MacFarquhar, Neil. 2004. Summit's Collapse Leaves Arab Leaders in Disarray. *The New York Times* (March 21): 29A.

Machiavelli, Niccolo. 1952. *The Prince,* trans. Luigi Ricci. New York: Oxford University Press.

Mackinlay, John, and Jarat Chopra. 1997. Second Generation Multinational Operations. pp. 175–200 in *The Politics of Global Governance: International Organization in an Interdependent World,* ed. Paul Diehl. Boulder, CO: Lynne Rienner Press.

Makinda, Samuel M., and F. Wafula Okumu. 2008. *The African Union: Challenges of Globalization, Security and Governance.* London: Routledge.

Maksoud, Covis. 1995. Diminished Sovereignty, Enhanced Sovereignty: United Nations-Arab League at 50. *The Middle East Journal* 49 (Autumn): 582(13).

Mamdani, Mahmood. 2001. *When Victims Become Killers: Colonialism, Nativism, and the Genocide in Rwanda.* Princeton, NJ: Princeton University Press.

Mann, Jim, and Art Pine. 1990. U.S. to Oppose World Bank Loans to China. *Los Angeles Times* (January 10): A1.

Maogoto, Jackson. 2004. *War Crimes and Realpolitik: International Justice from World War I to the 21st Century.* Boulder, CO: Lynne Rienner.

March, James G., and Johan Olsen. 1998. The Institutional Dynamics of International Political Orders. *International Organization* 52 (Winter): 943–969.

Marfleet, B. Gregory, and Colleen Miller. 2005. Failure after 1441: Bush and Chirac in the UN Security Council. *Foreign Policy Analysis* (Spring): 333–360.

Martin, Andrew. 1952. *Collective Security.* Paris: UNESCO.

Marx, Karl, and Friedrich Engels. 1965. *The Communist Manifesto,* ed. Joseph Katz. New York: Washington Square Press.

Matlary, Janne Haaland. 2004. The Legitimacy of Military Intervention: How Important is a UN Mandate. *Journal of Military Ethics* 3 (June): 129–141.

Maynard, Cindy. 2000. Biotech at the Table. *Current Health* 2 (November): 22–25.

McFeely, Tom. 2000. The UN's Uncivil Society. *Alberta Report* (May 8): 14.

McIntyre, Richard. 2008. *Are Worker Rights Human Rights?* Ann Arbor, MI: University Michigan Press.

McMahon, Patrice, and David Forsythe. 2008. The ICTY's Impact on Serbia: Judicial Romanticism meets Network Politics. *Human Rights Quarterly* 20 (May): 412–435.

McWhinney, Edward. 2002. International Law-Based Responses to the September 11 International Terrorist Attacks. *Chinese Journal of International Law* (Spring): 280–287.

Mearsheimer, John J. 1990. Back to the Future: Instability in Europe After the Cold War. *International Security* 15 (summer): 5–56.

———. 1993. The Case for a Ukrainian Nuclear Deterrent. *Foreign Affairs* 72 (Summer): 50–66.

———. 1994/1995. The False Promise of International Institutions. *International Security* 19 (winter): 5–49.

———. 1995. A Realist Theory. *International Security* 20 (summer): 82–104.

MEED Middle Eastern Economic Digest. 2001. Arabs Opt for Token Action 45 (April 6): 3.

Meernik, James. 2004. Reaching Inside the State: International Law and Superior Liability. *International Studies Perspectives* (5): 356–377.

Meigs, A. James. 1997. Mexican Monetary Lessons. *The Cato Journal* 14 (Spring–Summer): 35–73.

Mertus, Julie. 2004. Shouting from the Bottom of the Well. *International Feminist Journal of Politics* 6 (March): 110–128.

Meyer, Mary K., and Elisabeth Prugl, eds. 1999. *Gender Politics in Global Governance.* Lanham, MD: Rowman and Littlefield.

Mieville, China. 2006. *Between Equal Rights: A Marxist Theory of International Law.* London: Haymarket Books.

Mikesell, Raymond. 1972. The Emergence of the World Bank as a Development Institution. pp. 70–84 in *Bretton Woods Revisited,* ed. A. L. Acheson, J. F. Chant, and Martin Prachowny. Toronto, ONT: Toronto University Press.

Milner, Helen. 1991. The Assumption of Anarchy in International Relations Theory. *Review of International Studies* 17 (January): 67–85.

Mingst, Karen A., and Margaret P. Karns. 2006. *The United Nations in the Twenty First Century.* Boulder, CO: Westview Press.

Mitrany, David. 1948. The Functional Approach to World Organization. *International Affairs* 24 (July): 350–363.

———. 1966. *A Working Peace System.* Chicago, IL: Quadrangle Books.

Modelski, George. 1978. The Long Cycle of Global Politics and the Nation-State. *Comparative Studies in Society and History* 20 (April): 214–235.

Moellendorf, Darrel. 2009. Treaty Norms and Climate Change Mitigation. *Ethics and International Affairs* 23(3): 247–265.

Moinuddin, Hasan. 1987. *The Carter of the Islamic Conference and the Legal Framework of Economic Cooperation among Its Member States.* Oxford, UK: Clarendon Press.

Moore, John A., and Jerry Pubantz. 2006. *The New United Nations: International*

Organization in the Twenty-First Century. Upper Saddle River, NJ: Prentice Hall.

Mor, Ben D. 2007. Power and Rhetorical Bargaining: The UN Security Council Debate on the Iraq War. *Global Society* 21 (April): 229–247.

Morengthau, Hans. 1967. *Politics Among Nations.* 4th ed. New York: Alfred Knopf.

Multinational Monitor. 1996. The WTO Strikes 17 (January–February): 5.

———. 1998. Lessons from the Asian Meltdown 19 (January–February): 5–7.

———. 2000. 20 Question on the IMF 21 (April): 22.

Murphy, Craig N. 1994. *International Organization and Industrial Change.* New York: Oxford University Press.

Mussa, Micheal, and Graham Hacche. 1998. The Asian Economic Crisis—Its Origin and the Way Out. *New Perspectives Quarterly* 15 (winter): 30–32.

Myers, Steven Lee, and Thom Shanker. 2008. NATO Expansion, and a Bush Legacy, Are in Doubt. *New York Times* (March 15): www.nytimes.com.

Myrttinen, Henri. 2003. Disarming Masculinities. *Disarmament Forum* (4): 37–46.

Naim, Moises. 2009. Minilateralism. *Foreign Policy* (July–August): 135–136.

Naito, Yosuke. 1997. Kyoto Could Have Achieved Much More, Expert Says. *Japan Times* (December 12): www.japantimes.co.jp/cop3.

Narine, Shaun. 2006. The English School and ASEAN. *The Pacific Review* 19 (June): 199–218.

Nelan, Bruce W. 1998. A Popular Bad Idea: Expanding NATO comes with Risks as Well as Costs. *Time* 151 (May 11).

Nelson, Julie A. 1996. *Feminism, Objectivity, and Economics.* New York: Routledge.

Nemeth, Mary. 1990. The Map-Makers' Legacy: Arabs Blame the Crisis on Colonial Powers. *Maclean's* 103 (August 27): 30.

Newell, Peter, and Jedrzej G. Frynas. 2007. Beyond CSR? Business Poverty and Social Justice: An Introduction. *Third World Quarterly* 28 (June): 669–681.

New Republic. 1999. The Whole and Awful Truth (December 13): 9.

New Scientist. 2001. Cruel to Be Kind 171 (August 4): 3.

New York Times. 1992. Excerpts from Speeches by Leaders of the Permanent Members of UN Council 141 (February 1): A5.

———. 1994. Islamic Group Offering UN a Force of 10,000 for Bosnia 143 (February 11): A6.

———. 1998. The Sea Turtle's Warning 147 (April 10): A18.

———. 2000. 50 Multinationals Sign UN Compact on Rights and Environment (July 27): A1.

Nielson, Daniel, Michael Tierney, and Catherine Weaver. 2006. Bridging the Rationalist-Constructivist Divide: Re-engineering the Culture of the World Bank. *Journal of International Relations and Development* 9 (June): 107–139.

Nincic, Miroslav. 1992. *Democracy and Foreign Policy: The Fallacy of Political Realism.* New York: Columbia University Press.

Nissen, Jill L. 1997. Achieving a Balance Between Trade and the Environment: The Need to Amend the WTO/GATT to Include Multilateral Environmental Agreements. *Law and Policy in International Business* 28 (Spring): 901–928.

Niva, Steve. 1998. Tough and Tender: New World Order Masculinity and the Gulf War. pp. 109–128 in *The "Man" Question in International Relations*, ed. Marysia Zalewski and Jane Parpart. Boulder, CO: Westview Press.

Noel, Emile. 1994. *Working Together—The Institutions of the European Community.* Luxembourg: Office for the Official Publications of the European Communities.

Nugent, Neill. 2003. *The Government and Politics of the European Union.* 5th ed. Durham, NC: Duke University Press.

Nye, Joseph. 1990. *Bound to Lead: The Changing Nature of American Power.* New York: Basic Books.

Oberleitner, Gerd. 2005. Human Security: A Challenge to International Law? *Global Governance* 11 (April–June): 185–203.

Off Our Backs. 1992. Occupation: Women Pay First 22 (February): 2–6.

Ogata, Sadako, and Johan Cels. 2003. Human Security—Protecting and Empowering the People. *Global Governance* 9 (July–September): 273–283.

O'Hanlon, Michael. 1996. Arms Control and Military Stability in the Balkans. *Arms Control Today* 26 (August): 3(6).

Ohanyan, Anna. 2009. Policy Wars for Peace: Network Model of NGO Behavior. *International Studies Review* 11: 475–501.

Oil & Gas Journal. 1996. The WTO's Gasoline Ruling 94 (July 8): 21.

Olsen, Elizabeth. 2000. Members Call for Change in WTO Dispute System. *International Herald Tribune* (October 23): 9.

Olsson, Louise. 2001. Gender Mainstreaming in Practice: The United Nations Transitional Assistance Group in Namibia. pp. 97–11 in *Women and International Peacekeeping*, ed. Louise Olsson and Torunn Tryggestad. London: Frank Cass.

Olsson, Louise, and Torunn Tryggestad, eds. 2001. *Women and International Peacekeeping.* London: Frank Cass.

Oneal, John R., and Bruce M. Russett. 1997. The Classical Liberals Were Right: Democracy, Interdependence and Conflict, 1950–1985. *International Studies Quarterly* 41 (June): 267–294.

Online Newshour. 1997. Airing It Out (December 8). http://www.pbs.org/newshour/bb/environment/july-dec97/eu_12-8.html.

Onuf, Nicholas G. 1989. *World of Our Making: Rules and Rule in Social Theory and International Relations.* Columbia, SC: University of South Carolina Press.

Paarlberg, Robert L. 2001. *The Politics of Precaution: Genetically Modified Crops in Developing Countries.* Baltimore, MD: Johns Hopkins Press.

Packenham, Robert A. 1992. *The Dependency Movement: Scholarship and Politics in Dependency Studies.* Cambridge, MA: Harvard University Press.

Page, Edward. 2007. Equity and Kyoto Protocol. *Politics* 27(1): 8–15.

Park, Susan. 2005. Norm Diffusion Within International Organizations. A Case Study of the World Bank. *Journal of International Relations and Development* 8 (June): 111–141.

Parks, Bradley, and J. Timmons. 2010. Climate Change, Social Theory and Justice. *Theory, Culture, and Society* 27 (March–May): 134–166.

Paris, Roland. 2001. Human Security: Paradigm Shift or Hot Air. *International Security* 26: 67–102.

———. 2003. Peacekeeping and the Constraints of Global Culture. *European Journal of International Relations* (9): 441–473.

Paul, T. V. 2003. Systemic Conditions and Security Cooperation: Explaining the Persistence of the Nuclear Non-Proliferation Regime. *Cambridge Review of International Affairs* 16 (April): 135–154.

———. 2009. *The Tradition of the Non-Use of Nuclear Weapons.* Sanford, CA: University of Stanford Press.

Paz, Reuven. 2001. From Tehran to Beirut to Jerusalem: Iran and Hizballah in the Palestinian Uprising. The Washington Institute for Near East Policy. *Peace Watch* 313 (March 26).

Pearlstein, Steven. 2000. In Prague, Capitalism with a Human Face. *International Herald Tribune* (October 2): 13.

Pease, Kelly-Kate S., and David P. Forsythe. 1993. Human Rights, Humanitarian Intervention, and World Politics. *Human Rights Quarterly* 15 (May): 290–314.

Peet, Richard. 2009. Unholy Trinity: *The IMF, World Bank and the WTO.* London: Zed Books.

Penrose, Angela, and John Seaman. 1996. The Save the Children Fund and Nutrition for Refugees. pp. 241–269 in *"The Conscience of the World": The Influence of Nongovernmental Organizations in the UN System*, ed. Peter Willetts. Washington, DC: Brookings Institution.

Peskin, Victor. 2005. Beyond Victor's Justice? The Challenge of Prosecuting the Winners at the International Tribunals for the Former Yugoslavia and Rwanda. *Journal of Human Rights* 4 (April–June): 213–231.

Peou, Sorpong. 2002. The UN, Peacekeeping and Collective Human Security: From an Agenda for Peace to the Brahimi Report. *International Peacekeeping* 9 (summer): 51–69.

Peteet, Julie M. 1991. *Gender in Crisis: Women and the Palestinian Resistance Movement.* New York: Columbia University Press.

Peterson, V. Spike, ed. 1992. *Gendered States: Feminist (Re)vision of International Relations Theory.* Boulder, CO: Lynne Rienner Press.

Peterson, V. Spike, and Anne Sisson Runyan. 1993. *Global Gender Issues.* Boulder, CO: Westview Press.

Pettenger, Mary. 2007. Constructing Themselves. pp. 51–74 in *The Social Construction of Climate Change*. Burlington, VT: Ashgate Publishing.

Pettman, Jan Lindy. 1998. Gender Issues. pp. 483–497 in *The Globalization of World Politics: An Introduction to International Relations*, ed. John Bayliss and Steve Smith. Oxford, UK: Oxford University Press.

Pettman, Ralph. 2005. Human Security as Global Security: Reconceptualizing Strategic Studies. *Cambridge Review of International Affairs* 18 (April): 137–150.

Phillips, Andrew. 1990. An Economy-in-Exile: Kuwaiti Exiles Keep Their Nation Alive. *Maclean's* 103 (October 1): 32–33.

Pires-O'Brien, Joaquina. 2000. GM Foods in Perspective. *Contemporary Review* 276 (January): 19–24.

Pishchikova, Kateryna. 2006. The Promise of Transnational NGO Dialogue: The Argument and the Challenges. *Cambridge Review of International Affairs* 19 (March): 49–61.

Pollack, Andrew. 2000. Montreal Talks Agree on Rules for Biosafety. *New York Times* (January 20): 1, 6.

Pollis, Adamantia, and Peter Schwab. 1979. Human Rights with Limited Applicability. pp. 1–26 in *Human Rights: Cultural and Ideological Perspectives*, ed. Adamantia Pollis and Peter Schwab. New York: Praeger.

Porter, Gareth, and Janet Welsh Brown. 1991. *Global Environmental Politics*. Boulder, CO: Westview Press.

Posner, Eric A. 2009. *The Perils of Global Legalism*. Chicago, IL: University of Chicago Press

Press, Robert M. 1992. Biodiversity Pact Ready for Ink at Earth Summit. *Christian Science Monitor* (May 26).

Pulse. 2000. Pulse Study: Americans Uncertain about Genetically Modified Foods (December 15).

Purvis, Nigel. 2004. The Perspective of the United States on Climate Change and the Kyoto Protocol. *International Review for Environmental Studies* 5(1): 169–178.

Quinn-Maguire, Tanya. 2003. Women and Trade: What Are International Organizations Doing? *International Trade Forum* 4 (October 16): 3.

Rabkin, Jeremy. 1994. Trading in Our Sovereignty. *National Review* 46 (June 13): 34(3).

Ralph, Philip Lee, Robert E. Lerner, Standish Meacham, and Edward McNall Burns. 1991. *World Civilizations* 8th ed. Vol. 2. New York: W. W. Norton.

Ramirez, Miguel D. 1996. The Latest IMF-Sponsored Stabilization Program: Does It Represent a Long-Term Solution of Mexico's Economy? *Journal of InterAmerican Studies and World Affairs* 38 (winter): 129–157.

Rauber, Paul. 1992. World Bankruptcy: The World Bank and the Environment. *Sierra* 77 (July–August): 34–35.

Reich, Robert B. 1991. *The Work of Nations: Preparing Ourselves for Twenty-First-Century Capitalism*. New York: Simon and Schuster.

Reuters. 2000. Report for UN Labels WTO a Nightmare. *International Herald Tribune* (August 12–13): 13.

Revkin, Andrew C. 2001. Deals Break Impasse on Global Warming Treaty. *New York Times* (November 11): A8.

———. 2004. Save the Whales! Then What? *New York Times* (August 17): D1, D4.

Ricardo, David. 1965. *The Principles of Political Economy and Taxation*. London: Dent; New York: Dutton.

Rich, Bruce M. 1993. The Greening of the Development Banks: Rhetoric and Reality. *The Ecologist* 19 (March–April): 44–53.

Riding, Alan. 1992. West Drops Malawi's Aid over Rights: World Bank and Leading Western Donor Nations Stop Economic Aid over Human Rights Records. *New York Times* (May 14): A6.

Riggs, Robert E., and Jack C. Plano. 1994. *The United Nations: International Organization and World Politics*. 2nd ed. Belmont, CA: Wadsworth.

Roach, Steven, ed. 2009. *Governance, Order and the International Criminal Court: Between Realpolitik and a Cosmopolitan Court*. Oxford, UK: Oxford University Press.

Rochester, J. Martin. 1986. The Rise and Fall of International Organization as a Field of Study. *International Organization* 40 (Autumn): 777–813.

Roett, Riordan, ed. 1997. *The Mexican Peso Crisis: International Perspectives*. Boulder, CO: Lynne Rienner Press.

Rohde, David. 1998. *Endgame: The Betrayal and the Fall of Srebrenica.* New York: Westview Press.

Rost-Rublee, Maria. 2009. *Nonproliferation Norms: Why States Choose Nuclear Restraint.* Athens, GA: University of Georgia Press.

———. 2008. Taking Stock of the Nuclear Proliferation Regime: Using Social Psychology to Understand Regime Effectiveness. *International Studies Review* 10: 420–450.

Rostow, Walt. 1971. *Stages of Economic Growth.* London: Cambridge University Press.

Roter, Petra, and Zlatko Sabic. 2004. New and Old Europe in the Context of the Iraq War and Its Implications of European Security. *Perspectives on European Politics and Society* 5: 3, 517–542.

Royte, Elizabeth. 1997. The Outcasts. *New York Times Magazine* (January 19): 37.

Ruggie, John Gerald. 1982. International Regimes, Transactions, and Change: Embedded Liberalism in the Post–Cold War Economic Order. *International Organization* 36 (Special Issue): 379–415.

Runyan, Anne Sisson, and V. Spike Peterson. 1990. The Radical Future of Realism: Feminist Subversions of IR Theory. *Alternatives* 16: 67–106.

Runyan, Curtis. 1999. Action on the Front Lines. *World Watch* 12: 12.

Rupp, Leila J. 1998. *Worlds of Women: The Making of an International Women's Movement.* Princeton, NJ: Princeton University Press.

Rupp, Richard E. 2006. *NATO after 9–11: An Alliance in Continuing Decline.* New York: Palgrave.

Russett, Bruce M. 1993. *Grasping the Democratic Peace: Principles for a Post–Cold War World.* Princeton, NJ: Princeton University Press.

Sachs, Jeffery. 2005. *The End of Poverty.* New York: Penguin Press.

Sagan, Scott D., and Kenneth W. Waltz. 1995. *The Spread of Nuclear Weapons.* New York: W. W. Norton.

Saikal, Amin. 2006. The Iran Nuclear Dispute. *The Australian Journal of International Affairs* 60 (June): 193–199.

Salinger, Pierre. 1995. The United States, the United Nations, and the Gulf War. *Middle Eastern Journal* 49 (Autumn): 595–614.

Sanford, Jonathan E. 1988. The World Bank and Poverty: The Plight of the World's Impoverished Is Still a Major Concern of the International Agency. *The American Journal of Economies and Sociology* 47 (July): 257–275.

Sanger, David E. 1998. Trade Arbiter Favors U.S. in Key Ruling. *New York Times* (February 6): C1.

Sanger, David E., and Mark Mazzetti. 2007. Israel Struck Syrian Nuclear Project, Analysts Say. *New York Times* (October 14): www.nytimes.com.

Sassoon, Anne Showstack. 1982. *Approaches to Gramsci.* London: Writers and Readers.

Sasvari, Adele. 2010. Changes in Climate Negotiations: Gender Equality Towards Copenhagen. *Global Social Policy* 10(1) (April): 15–18.

Satloff, Robert. 2001. The Arab League Summit. Opportunities Amid the Vitriol? The Washington Institute of Near East Policy. *Peace Watch* 314 (March 25).

Schiff, Benjamin. 2008. *Building the International Criminal Court.* Cambridge, UK: Cambridge University Press.

Schifferes, Steve. 2005. Final Round of Global Trade Deal. *BBC NEWS* (December 21). www.bbc.co.uk.

Schmemann, Serge. 2001. Annan Urges New Methods to Fight Terrorism. *New York Times* (September 25): B3.

Schmitt, Eric. 1999. Deal on U.N. Dues Breaks an Impasse and Draws Critics. *New York Times* (November 16): A3.

Schoenbaum, Thomas J. 1997. International Trade and Protection of the Environment: The Continuing Search for Reconciliation. *American Journal of International Law* 91 (April): 268–313.

Schrope, Mark. 2001. UN Backs Transgenic Crops for Poorer Nations. *Nature* 412 (July 12): 109–110.

Schweder, Tore. 2000. Distortion of Uncertainty in Science: Antarctic Fin Whales in the 1950s. *Journal of International Wildlife Law and Policy* 3 (Spring): 73–94.

Schweller, Randall L., and David Preiss. 1997. A Tale of Two Realisms: Expanding the Institutions Debate. *Mershon International Studies Review* 41 (May): 1–32.

Scott, Shirley V. 2010. *International Law and World Politics.* Boulder, CO: Lynn Reinner.

Seabrook, Jeremy. 1993. *Victims of Development: Resistance and Alternatives.* London: Verso.

Sell, Susan K., and Aseem Prakash. 2004. Using Ideas Strategically: The Contest Between Business and NGO Networks in Intellectual Property Rights. *International Studies Quarterly* 24 (143–175).

Sen, Amartya. 1996. Development. Which Way Now? pp. 1–28 in *The Political Economy of Development and Underdevelopment.* 6th ed., ed. Kenneth P. Jameson and Charles K. Wilber. New York: McGraw-Hill.

Setear, John K. 2005. Room for Law: Realism, Evolutionary Biology, and the Promise(s) of International Law. *Berkeley Journal of International Law* 23(1): 1–46.

Shahin, Mariam. 2001. Digging In or Bailing Out. *The Middle East* (September): 7.

Shanker, Thom. 2008. NATO Fails to Address Shortfalls in Kabul. *International Herald Tribune* (Saturday–Sunday, June 14–15): 3.

Shiller, Robert. 2008. *The Subprime Solution: How Today's Financial Crisis Happened and What to Do About It.* Princeton, NJ: Princeton University Press.

Shiva, Vandana. 1989. *Staying Alive.* London: Zed Books.

———. 1997. *Biopiracy: The Plunder of Nature and Knowledge.* Boston, MA: South End Press.

———. 1999. *Stolen Harvest: The Highjacking of the Global Food Supply.* Boston, MA: South End Press.

Simmons, Marlise. 2008. Former Leader in Kosovo Acquitted of War Crimes. *New York Times* (April 4): www.nytimes.com/.

Simmons, Pam. 1992. Women in Development: A Threat to Liberation. *The Ecologist* 22 (January–February): 16–21.

Simon, Roger. 1982. *Gramsci's Political Thought.* London: Lawrence Wishart.

Simpson, Gerry. 2005. The War with Iraq and International Law. *Melbourne Journal of International Law* 6 (May): 167–189.

Slaughter-Burley, Anne-Marie. 1993. International Law and International Relations Theory: A Dual Agenda. *American Society of International Law* 87: 205–239.

Slomanson, William R. 1990. *Fundamental Perspectives on International Law.* New York: West Publishing.

Smith, Adam. 1971. *The Wealth of Nations.* New York: Dutton.

Smith, Craig. 2004. For U.S. to Note, Europe Flexes Muscle in Afghanistan. *The New York Times* (September 22): A3.

Smith, Steve. 1998. Unacceptable Conclusions and the Man Question: Masculinity, Gender, and International Relations. pp. 54–72 in *The "Man" Question in International Relations,* ed. Marysia Zalewski and Jane Parpart. Boulder, CO: Westview Press.

Sneider, Daniel. 1992. The Soviet "Ecocidal" Legacy. *Christian Science Monitor* (January 11): 10–11.

Snow, Donald M. 1993. *Distant Thunder: Third World Conflict in the New World Order.* New York: St. Martin's Press.

Snyder, Fredrick, and Surakiart Sathirathai. 1987. *Third World Attitudes Toward International Law.* Dordrecht, Martinus Nijhoff.

Solidum, Estrella D. 2003. *The Politics of ASEAN: An Introduction to Southeast Asian Regionalism.* Singapore: Eastern University Press.

Stahn, Carsten. 2007. Responsibility to Protect: Political Rhetoric or Emerging Legal Norm? *American Journal of International Law* 101 (January): 99–120.

Standing, Guy. 1996. Global Feminization Through Flexible Labor. pp. 405–430 in *The Political Economy of Development and Underdevelopment.* 6th ed., ed. Kenneth P. Jameson and Charles K. Wilber. New York: McGraw-Hill.

Stanley Foundation. 1997. *The Pros and Cons of NATO Expansion: Defining U.S. Goals and Options.* Warrenton, VA: Stanley Foundation.

Staudt, Kathleen, ed. 1997. *Women, International Development, and Politics: The Bureaucratic Mire.* Philadelphia, PA: Temple University Press.

Steele, Brent. 2007. Liberalism-Idealism: A Constructivist Critique. *International Studies Review* 9 (March): 23–52.

Steinberg, Richard H. 1997. Trade-Environment Negotiations in the EU, NAFTA, and WTO: Regional Trajectories of Rule Development. *American Journal of International Law* 91 (April): 231–267.

Stevens, Scott, et al. 1992. Global Resources and System at Risk. *Christian Science Monitor* (June 2): 10–11.

Stienstra, Deborah. 1994. *Women's Movements and International Organizations*. New York: St. Martin's Press.

Stiglitz, Joseph. 2006. A New Agenda for Global Warming. *The Economists' Voice* 3(7). http://www.bepress.com/ev/vol3/iss7/art3.

Stoett, Peter J. 2005. Of Whales and People: Normative Theory, Symbolism, and the IWC. *Journal of International Wildlife Law and Policy* 8: 151–175.

Strange, Susan. 1983. Cave Hic Dragones. pp. 337–354 in *International Regimes*, ed. Stephen Krasner. Ithaca, NY: Cornell University Press.

Suleman, Arsalan M. 2008. Bargaining in the Shadow of Violence: The NPT, IAEA and Nuclear Non-Proliferation Negotiations. *Berkeley Journal of International Law* 26(1): 206–253.

Summerfield, Derek. 1996. Rwanda: When Women Become Killers. *The Lancet* 347 (June 29): 1816–1818.

Sunindyo, Saraswati. 1998. When the Earth Is Female and the Nation Is Mother: Gender, the Armed Forces, and Nationalism in Indonesia. *Feminist Review* 58 (Spring): 1–22.

Sun-Sentinel. 2005. Deal with Japan on Whaling Denied (June 21): A12.

Swedburg, Richard. 1986. The Doctrine of Economic Neutrality of the IMF and the World Bank. *Journal of Peace Research* 23 (December): 377–390.

Szasz, Paul. 1983. The Role of the United Nations in Internal Conflicts. *Georgia Journal of International Law* 13 (winter): 345–354.

Taft, William H. IV. 2005. International Law and the Use of Force. *Georgetown Journal of International Law* (Spring): 659–663.

Tannenwald, Nina. 2004. The UN and Debates over Weapons of Mass Destruction. pp. 3–20 in *The United Nations and Global Security*, ed. Richard M. Price and Mark W. Zacker. New York: Palgrave.

———. 2008. Nuclear Taboo: The United States and the Non-Use of Nuclear Weapons. Cambridge, UK: Cambridge University Press.

Tariq, Ali. 2003. Re-colonizing Iraq. *The New Left Review* 21 (May–June): 5–19.

Taylor, Paul. 1998. The United Nations and International Organization. pp. 264–283 in *The Globalization of World Politics: An Introduction to International Relations*, ed. John Bayliss and Steve Smith. Oxford, UK: Oxford University Press.

Taylor, Paul, and A. J. R. Groom. 1988. *International Institutions at Work*. New York: St. Martin's Press.

Taylor, Phillip. 1984. *Nonstate Actors in International Politics: From Transregional to Substate Organizations*. Boulder, CO: Westview Press.

Terriff, Terry. 2004. Fear and Loathing in NATO: The Atlantic Alliance after the Crisis over Iraq. *Perspectives on European Politics and Society* 5 (May): 419–446.

Terry, Fiona. 2002. *The Paradox of Humanitarian Action: Condemned to Repeat?* Cornell, NY: Cornell University Press.

Thomas, Caroline. 1998. Poverty, Development, and Hunger. pp. 449–467 in *The Globalization of World Politics: An Introduction to International Relations*, ed. John Bayliss and Steve Smith. New York: Oxford University Press.

Thucydides. 1963. *The Peloponnesian Wars*, trans. Benjamin Jowett. New York: Washington Square Press.

Tickner, J. Ann. 1988. Hans Morgenthau's Principles of Realism: A Feminist Reformulation. *Millennium* 17 (winter): 429–440.

Time International. 2001. Wailing Over Whales 158 (August 6): 26–28.

Timmerman, Kenneth R. 1996. Iran-Bosnia Green Light. *The American Spectator* 29 (August): L28–L33.

Timothy, Kristen. 2004. Human Security Discourse at the United Nations. *Peace Review* 16 (March): 19–24.

Totaro, Martin. 2008. Legal Positivism, Constructivism and International Human Rights Law: The Case of Participatory Development. *Virginia Journal of International Law* 48(4): 720–765.

Tribunal Watch. 1996. Rwanda Genocide Chronology. http://listserv.buffalo.edu/cgi-bin/wa?A0=JUSTWATCH-L

True, Jacqui. 2008. Global Accountability and Transnational Networks: The Women Leaders' Network and Asia Pacific Economic Cooperation. *Pacific Review* 21 (March): 1–26.

Tuchman, Barbara W. 1984. *The March of Folly.* New York: Knopf.

UN Chronicle. 1997. Flashback 4 (Spring): 31–32.

———. 2000. UNRWA Pioneer Microfinance Programme Benefitting Women and Men 37 (Winter): 56.

UN Commission on Sustainable Development. 1998. General Information (April 6).

UNESCO Courier. 1994. The Cairo Declaration (March): 44–46.

UN General Assembly. 1999. The Fall of Srebrenica (November 15): A/54/549.

UN Human Development Report. 2005. www.undp.org.

UNICEF. 1999. Results of the 1999 Iraq Child and Maternal Mortality Surveys (July 23). http://www.unicef.org/reseval/iraq.html.

United Press International. 2001. IMF-Indonesia Deal Sets Bank Sell-Off (August 27): p1008239u9086.

———. 2003. IMF: Indonesia Must Push Sell-Off (October 24): p1008277u3959.

UN Security Council. 2000. Press Release: Chairman of Independent Inquiry into United Nations Actions During 1994 Rwanda Genocide Presents Report to Security Council (April 14) (SC/6843).

UN Secretary General. 2001. Organization of Islamic Conference Has Central Role in Devising Effective Strategy to Combat Terrorism (October 9) (SG/SM/7989 AFG 154).

U.S. Chamber of Commerce. 1998. UN Climate Treaty?

U.S. Department of State, International Information Programs. 2001. Arab/Muslim Media Welcome Bush Gestures, Still Distrust Coalition (September 27).

U.S. Department of State Dispatch. 1995. U.S. Global Leadership Responsibilities: The G-7 and Beyond (President Bill Clinton, June 16, 1995) (July 6): 4–6.

Usher, Graham. 1993. Palestinian Women, the Intifada, and the State of Independence. *Race and Class* 34 (January–March): 31(13).

U.S. Information Agency, Office of Research and Media Reaction. 1995a. The Hague War Crimes Tribunal: A "Verdict," or an "Empty Gesture" (April 26).

———. 1995b. Mexico: Financial, Political Stress (March 17).

———. 1997a. Iraq: Regional Views Diverge—But Most Agree Crisis Is Not Over (November 26).

———. 1997b. Kyoto Conference on Global Warming: A Defective Accord Better Than None (December 11).

———. 1997c. NATO: Enlargement Debate Intensifies (March 12).

———. 1997d. WTO: A Miracle Year? (December 17).

———. 1998a. Former Yugoslavia: Criticism of International Role (July 29).

———. 1998b. Indonesia's Crisis Mounts: IMF's Prescription Evaluated (January 9).

———. 1998c. International Criminal Court: U.S. Opposition Criticized (July 21).

Valenius, Johanna. 2007. A Few Kind Women: Gender Essentialism and Nordic Peacekeeping Operations. *International Peacekeeping* 14 (October): 510–523.

Valenzuela, J. Samuel, and Arturo Valenzuela. 1978. Modernization and Dependency: Alternative Perspectives in the Study of Latin American Underdevelopment. *Comparative Politics* 10 (July): 535–537.

van der Pijl, Kees. 1984. *The Making of the Atlantic Ruling Class.* London: Verso Press.

Van Dyke, Vernon. 1970. *Human Rights, the United States, the World Community.* New York: Oxford University Press.

Van Glahn, Gerhard. 1992. Law among Nations. New York: MacMillan.

Vasquez, Ian. 1997. The IMF Through a Mexican Lens. *ORBIS* 41 (Spring): 259–277.

Vedder, Anton, ed. 2007. NGO Involvement in International Governance and Policy: Sources of Legitimacy. Leiden; Boston: Martinus Nijhoff Publishers.

Victor, Barbara. 2004. *The Army of Roses.* New York: Robinson Publishing.

Vincent, R. J. 1988. *Human Rights and International Relations.* Cambridge, UK: Cambridge University Press.

Viotti, Paul R., and Mark V. Kauppi. 1993. *International Relations Theory: Realism, Pluralism, and Globalism.* 2nd ed. New York: Macmillan Publishing Company.

Von Glahan, Glenn. 1992. *Law Among Nations.* New York: Macmillan.

Vuorela, Ulla. 1992. The Informal Sector, Social Reproduction and the Impact of the Economic Crisis on Women. pp. 125–146 in *Tanzania and the IMF: The Dynamics of Liberalization*, ed. Horace Campbell and Howard Stein. Boulder, CO: Westview Press.

Wadhams, Nick. 2006. U.S. will Pass on Rights Council, for Now. *The Houston Chronicle*. www.chron.com.

Wallerstein, Immanuel. 1980. *The Modern World System*. New York: Academic Press.

Walt, Stephen M. 1987. *The Origins of Alliances*. Ithaca, NY: Cornell University Press.

Waltz, Kenneth N. 1959. *The Man, State and War: A Theoretical Analysis*. New York: Columbia University Press.

Warwick, Hugh. 2000. Terminator Too. *The Ecologist* 30 (May): 50.

Washington Post. 1999. Indonesia Timeline (June).

Washington Report on Middle East Affairs. 2001a. OIC Condemns Raids on Iraq 20 (April): 38.

———. 2001b. Using a New Language 20 (October): 41.

Waters, Tony. 2001. *Bureaucratizing the Good Samarian: The Limitations of Humanitarian Relief Operations*. Boulder, CO: Westview Press.

Webb, Steven V., and Heidi Zia. 1990. Lower Birth Rate = Higher Saving in LDCs. *Finance and Development* 27 (June): 12(3).

Wedgewood, Ruth. 2002. Gallant Delusion. *Foreign Policy* 132 (September/October): 44–48.

Weidenbaum, Murray. 1992. A Different View of Global Warming. *Christian Science Monitor* (May 21): 3.

Weiss, Thomas. 2007. *Humanitarian Intervention: Ideas in Action*. Cambridge, UK: Polity Press.

Weiss, Thomas G, David P. Forsythe, and Roger A. Coate. 1994. *The United Nations and Changing World Politics*. Boulder, CO: Westview Press.

———. 2004. *The United Nations and Changing World Politics*. Boulder, CO: Westview Press.

Weiss, Thomas G., and Barbara Crossette. 2006. *The United Nations: The Post-Summit Outlook*. Great Decisions. Foreign Policy Association: 1–10.

Weiss, Thomas G, David P. Forsythe, Roger A. Coate, and Kelly-Kate Pease. 2007. *The United Nations and Changing*

World Politics. 5th ed. Boulder, CO: Westview Press.

Weiss, Thomas G., and Leon Gordenker, eds. 1996. *NGOs, the UN, and Global Governance*. Boulder, CO: Lynne Rienner Press.

Weissman, Robert. 1994. Secrets of the WTO. *Multinational Monitor* 15 (October): 9.

Welch, Susan, John Gruhl, John Comer, and Susan Rigdon Rigdon. 1997. *American Government*. 6th ed. Belmont, CA: Wadsworth.

Wendt, Alexander. 1999. *Social Theory and International Relations* (Cambridge, UK: Cambridge University Press.

Wendt, Alexander. 1992. Anarchy Is What States Make of It: The Social Construction of Power Politics. *International Organization* 46 (Spring): 291–424.

Weston, Burns H. 1991. Security Council Resolution 678 and Persian Gulf Decision Making: Precarious Legitimacy. *American Journal of International Law* 85 (July): 516–535.

Whitworth, Sandra. 1994. *Feminism and International Relations: Toward a Political Economy of Gender in Interstate and Nongovernmental Institutions*. Basingstoke, UK: Macmillan Press.

———. 2004. *Men, Militarism, and UN Peacekeeping: A Gendered Analysis*. Boulder, CO: Lynne Rienner Publishers.

Wiarda, Howard J. 1995. After Miami: The Summit, The Peso Crisis, and the Future of U.S.–Latin American Relations. *Journal of InterAmerican Studies and World Affairs* 37 (Spring): 43–69.

Wide. 1998. A Primer on the WTO (November). www.eurosur.org/IEPALA/wide/weng.

Willetts, Peter, ed. 1996. *"The Conscience of the World": The Influence of Nongovernmental Organizations in the UN System*. Washington, DC: Brookings Institution.

Willging, Jennifer. 2008. Of GMOs. McDommation and Foreign Fat: Contemporary Franco-American Food Fights. *French Cultural Studies* 19 (June): 199–226.

Williams, Mariama M. 1996. Trade Liberalization, Society, and the Environment. *Ecumenical Review* 48 (July): 345(9).

WIN News. 1995. World Bank Structural Adjustment and Gender Policies 21 (Spring): 31–33.

———. 1998. Violence in Rwanda: A Women's Perspective 24 (Summer): 34–35.

———. 1999. Indonesia 25 (Spring): 17–19.

Winslow, Anne, ed. 1995. *Women, Politics, and the United Nations*. Westport, CT: Greenwood Press.

Wolfe, Robert. 2005. See You In Geneva? Legal (Mis) Representation of the Trading System. *European Journal of International Relations* 11 (September): 339–365.

Wolff, Richard, and Stephen Resnick. 1987. *Economics: Marxian and Neoclassical*. Baltimore, MD: Johns Hopkins—Net Press.

Wolffe, Richard. 2003. Phoenix from the Ashes. *Newsweek* (October 6): 32–33.

Women's International Network News. 2003. Iraq: Rebuilding Process Must Include Women (Summer): 10–13.

World Bank News. 1997. Climate Change Debates Heats Up in Kyoto (December 4). www.worldbank.org/html/ extdr/extcs/w120497e.htm#kyoto.

World Commission on Environment and Development. 1987. *Our Common Future*. New York: Oxford University Press.

World Watch. 1999. NGO Friend or Foe (March–April): 2.

Wren, Christopher S. 1999. U.S. Told It Must Pay $550 Million or Risk Losing U.N. Vote. *New York Times*: A6.

Wright, Robert. 1995. Let Them Eat Hate. *New Republic* 212 (April 24): 4.

WTO. 1999. www.wto.org.

Xinhua News Agency. 2000. Indonesia, IMF Agree Not to Introduce Capital Control (June 5): 1008157h8953.

———. 2001. Jakarta Complains at Being Pushed Too Hard by the IMF (February 15): 1008046h8085.

Xue, Hanquin. 2007. Chinese Observations on International Law. *Chinese Journal of International Law* 6 (March): 83–93.

Yamamoto, Tadashi. 1996. *Emerging Civil Society in the Asia Pacific Community: Nongovernmental Underpinnings of the Emerging Asia Pacific Regional Community: A Twenty-Fifth Anniversary Project of JCIE*. Singapore: Institute of Southeast Asian Studies.

Yilmaz, Muzaffer Ercan. 2005. UN Peacekeeping in the Post-Cold War Era. *International Journal of World Peace* 22 (June): 13–29.

Ying, Ma. 2010. China's View of Climate Change. *Policy Review* 161 (June/July): 27–43.

Zacher, Mark. 1979. *International Conflicts and Collective Security, 1946–77*. New York: Praeger Publishers.

Zalewski, Marysia, and Jane Parpart, eds. 1998. *The "Man" Question in International Relations*. Boulder, CO: Westview Press.

Zarate, Robert. 2009. Cooperation Against Proliferation: How the United States and Russia Can Stem Future Nuclear Threats. *Brown Journal of World Affairs* XVI (Fall/Winter): 59–71.

Zengerle, Jason. 1998. Hagelianism. *The New Republic* 218 (February 9): 10–12.

Zweifel, Thomas. 2006. *International Organizations and Democracy: Accountability, Politics and Power*. Boulder, CO: Lynne Rienner.

INDEX